THE COMING
CATHOLIC
CHURCH

THE COMING CATHOLIC CHURCH

*How the Faithful
Are Shaping a
New American Catholicism*

DAVID GIBSON

HarperSanFrancisco
A Division of HarperCollins*Publishers*

FIRST EDITION

Designed by Joseph Rutt

Library of Congress Cataloging-in-Publication Data

Gibson, David

The coming Catholic Church : how the faithful are shaping a new
American Catholicism / David Gibson. — 1st ed.

p. cm.

ISBN 0–06–053070–7 (cloth)

1. Catholic Church—United States. 2. United States—Church history. I. Title.

BX1406.3.G53 2003

282'.73'09051—dc21   2003050811

03 04 05 06 07 RRD(H) 10 9 8 7 6 5 4 3 2 1

This book is dedicated to the children who survived sexual abuse, and to the memory of those who did not.

CONTENTS

ACKNOWLEDGMENTS

Thankfulness is a spiritual practice that ought never to end, and now that I have written a book, I realize that it never can.

As a first-time author I am greatly indebted to John Loudon of Harper San Francisco for giving me the opportunity to expand my writing range, and for showing the patience and tenacity to make sure I followed through.

Thanks also to my agent, the incomparable Jimmy Vines, who demonstrated as much trust in me as he does savvy in deal-making.

To begin at the beginning, I must thank Terry Golway, who seems to move effortlessly between the vocations of journalist and author, and who was kind enough to show me the way.

Much of this book grew out of my work as a journalist for the *Star-Ledger* of New Jersey, which has the great fortune to be owned by Donald Newhouse and edited by Jim Willse. They run the best regional daily in the country, hands down, and they provide the space for beat reporters to become better writers—and maybe even authors. This project would not have gotten off the ground without their support. Among the editing corps at the *Star-Ledger,* Fran Dauth and Suzanne Pavkovic provided encouragement, practical advice, and indispensible shelter from the clamor of daily deadlines, although no one is supposed to know that. And no one could ask for a finer collection of scribes and pals than my former colleagues in the *Star-Ledger*'s newsroom. Their moral support and sense of humor kept me from the twin perils of depression and hubris, mostly the latter.

In the larger journalistic cosmos, the sodality of religion writers is a special one whose members have carved out a unique, often overlooked niche in the newsroom. Their work illuminates the pages of newspapers and magazines and raises the level of journalism in America, and the solidarity of my mates in the Religion Newswriters Association has been invaluable.

I was told that book-writing is a solitary endeavor, but it seemed more like a team effort to me. As always, Clio and her *fusa* were my Muse. Pam Crabtree got me here, kept me (relatively) sane, and her generosity of spirit will keep me going forward. The prodigy Rocco Palmo dazzled me with his knowledge of the church, and I trust that one day the rest of the world will learn of his talents. At Seton Hall University the encyclopedic church historian, Father Robert Wister, pointed out my grievous slips and, being the fine teacher he is, left me to my own conclusions. Raymond Schroth, S.J., is the kind of Jesuit who first drew me to the Church, and the kind of priest who helps keep my faith strong. He is also the kind of teacher who nurtures the writer's vocation, and he was a great help in shaping the text.

Amid the clamor of scandal it was more important than ever to remember that there are so many wonderful priests who embody the holiness and humanity of the Catholic faith. Some of them are gracious enough to count me as a friend. They provided material and inspiration that inform almost every page, but such is the state of affairs in the church today that they are best recognized only *in pectore*.

Naturally, any heresies or errors of fact are inadvertent, but they are mine alone. Likewise any undue harshness in tone, or imbalance of criticism over praise.

There is simply no way this book would have been completed, or even started, had it not been for the eternal, fraternal correction and encouragement of Michael McKinley, and the cheerleading of his wife, the lovely Nancy Merritt Bell. As a reader, Nancy is as scrupulous as a Puritan and as generous as a Franciscan—lucky for me. Michael is my guardian angel. He provided writerly support and spiritual guidance every step of the way. He laid the foundations of this project, and many others to come, over many cocktails in many bars in many lands. This is only the beginning.

My family has contributed to my writing life in so many ways (not the least of which was providing blinds so that I might see). The love and faith of my mother and father is unfathomable, and has carried me safely through so much. Likewise I am immensely thankful for the prayers and support of my sister, Amy, my brother, Jeff, and of Beth and Abby.

Above all, I am grateful beyond words for Josephine Salvador. "Support" is not sufficient to describe her loving steadfastness. While this book grew, so did my love for her. The book is done, finally. Our life is just getting started.

INTRODUCTION
CATHOLIC SCANDAL, AMERICAN CATHOLIC

*There is nothing concealed that will not be revealed, nor secret that
will not be known. Therefore whatever you have said in the darkness
will be heard in the light, and what you have whispered behind closed
doors will be proclaimed on the housetops.*
—*Jesus, to his disciples, in the Gospel of Luke*

L ittle more than a year into the third millennium of Christianity, a milestone that Pope John Paul II heralded as the occasion for a rebirth of faith, the Catholic Church found itself plunged into a crisis over sexual abuse by priests that left historians reaching back centuries for comparisons. Many cited the French Revolution or the Protestant Reformation; others, the Inquisition and even the Holocaust.

So great was the tumult in the Catholic world in 2002 that none of those examples seemed like a stretch. But neither did any of them adequately explain how the scandal, and the reaction to it, had grown out of a larger, ongoing crisis in Catholicism that predated the revelations and continues to push the church in directions it has never gone before. In the decades before the scandal, most notably since the 1960s and the so-called Velvet Revolution of the Second Vatican Council, Catholicism was engaged in profound and unprecedented debates about the nature and future of the church. Occasionally those disputes made headlines, but generally they read like any political copy out of Washington, and disappeared from sight just as quickly.

For most of the world, and most of the Catholic Church, the dominant Catholic storyline of the last quarter of the twentieth century was the drama of Pope John Paul II, whose charisma and travels and *mano a mano* encounters with Communism drew most of the attention, while the great ferment beneath the surface of Catholicism often went unnoticed by the outside world (and unheeded by many Catholics themselves). In contrast to the galvanic presence of the globe-trotting pontiff, the arguments about the church he led were conducted in the lower registers of theological disputation, and eventually became the background noise of Catholic life—always present, but mostly ignored. People made do as they could and got used to things as they were.

But the crisis did not go away. Indeed, the sublimation of the tensions only worsened the problems, most notably by widening the disconnect among the laity, the clergy, and the bishops, and between all of those constituencies and the Roman papacy. The divisions were worsened by a growing ideological chasm within each camp, one that mirrors the worst aspects of the American scene and in the end could prove as debilitating as any scandal. In the feuds, neither side was wholly right or wholly wrong, but the fury with which the opposing forces prosecuted their agendas, to the exclusion of other views, inhibited the prospects for real change.

Now, with a year of scandal capping decades of crisis, the Catholic Church has suddenly awakened to find itself at a crossroads. Everyone agrees that the church must change—liberals and conservatives (I use those labels knowing they are loaded and inadequate, but finding them unfortunately indispensable), as well as the great majority of Catholics caught in between. If the church does not change, Catholicism will hardly disappear. But it will face the sadder fate of a slow-motion enervation. In that sense, the scandal may be a blessing, in that it concentrated the collective Catholic mind. The sexual abuse underlying the scandal was an unspeakable tragedy for the victims whose lives were shattered by emotional trauma or ended by suicide. But the shock of the revelations can also serve a broader purpose in alerting Catholics to the equally dangerous preexisting condition of the church, and pointing the way toward a solution.

To be sure, the scandal of 2002 on its own would have been enough to rock the church even in the halest of times, with a barrage of misdeeds that augured years of ugly headlines, investigations, subpoenas, protests, and comedy club ridicule.

The "Long Lent of 2002," as Father Richard John Neuhaus called it, started on Sunday, January 6, 2002, on the Feast of the Epiphany, which commemorates the Magi's visit to the infant Jesus. On that day the *Boston Globe* published its first story cataloging the sexual abuse that a local priest, John Geoghan, had inflicted on at least 130 children entrusted to his spiritual care over the course of a clerical career that spanned three decades. In his predations, Geoghan was not much different from the lineup of clerical monsters who had gone before him. He was an unregenerate pedophile, a serial predator who used his position of unquestioned trust to fondle and sodomize young boys. Geoghan favored the grammar school age; one of his targets was just four years old. A few weeks after the *Globe* stories began, Geoghan, then sixty-six years old and retired as a priest since 1996, was convicted in the first trial on one of the charges and sentenced to nine years in prison.

But the Geoghan case, for all its nightmarish details, was only the first in a tidal wave of revelations that would wash over Boston, and from there, inundate the rest of the country with tales of lurid behavior by abusive priests and repeated efforts to shield the culprits. Throughout the nation's 194 dioceses, inquiries by journalists and prosecutors, and finally many of the bishops themselves, churned up hundreds of cases. American Catholics were blindsided. This was the third wave of clergy abuse scandals since the first revelations of widespread molestation came to light in 1985, sparked by reports about a Louisiana priest, Gilbert Gauthé, who abused dozens of children while church leaders quietly settled with the victims to protect the priest. Subsequent accounts detailed cases against hundreds of priests nationwide and estimated that U.S. dioceses had quietly paid out $400 million, and perhaps as much as $1 billion, to abuse victims, largely in settlements aimed at keeping the problem under wraps.

In response to these accounts, the nation's bishops voiced the requisite concern and adopted policy guidelines in 1986—not binding rules, however—and the faithful rallied to their church. They remained loyal even when the 1992 abuse trial of a former Massachusetts priest, James Porter, spurred another round of revelations and another policy "tightening" by the hierarchy, whose most vocal members were still confident enough of their position to engage in a bit of ecclesiastical grandstanding. "The papers like to focus on the faults of a few," Boston Cardinal Bernard Law declared in May 1992. "We deplore that." Adding a rhetorical flourish that would come back to haunt him, Law then invoked the Almighty to touch the hard hearts of the media horde: "By all means we call down God's power on the media, particularly the *Globe*," Law declared.

In 2002, everything changed, and it was the media, and Law's own flock, who were taking the cardinal to catechism class.

This time, Catholics felt that they had been played for fools. Bernard Law was the most powerful churchman in what remains by far the largest and most visible denomination in the country, at 65 million Catholics and counting. He was the pope's man in America, a kingmaker whose word could make or break ecclesiastical careers. And from the bastion of Irish-Catholic America, Law spoke with the imposing voice of stern Catholic morality, reproving the faithful and excoriating the nation for its wayward behavior. In early 2002, when Law responded to early reports that higher-ups may have shielded Geoghan, his indignation was characteristic: "Never was there an effort on my part to shift the problem from one place to the next," he declared in his column for the archdiocesan paper.

The *Globe* stories showed otherwise. Law was at best Clintonesque in his evasions, and potentially criminal (though authorities eventually decided they couldn't charge him) in shuttling abusive priests from one parish to another. His own words of praise for abusive clerics, however, and his efforts to shame the victims and their families, were what really stuck with the faithful. When Law finally put Geoghan out to pasture in 1996—declaring him "permanently disabled" so that his pension would be paid out of a clergy medical fund—Law was still solicitous of his brother priest, with nary a word for those he had abused. "Yours has been an effective life of ministry, sadly impaired by illness," the cardinal wrote in a valedictory note. "On behalf of those you have served well, and in my own name, I would like to thank you. I understand yours is a painful situation. The passion we share can indeed seem unbearable and unrelenting. We are our best selves when we respond in honesty and trust."

By the end of January, more cases, nearly as bad, spilled onto the front pages of newspapers around the country. Plausible deniability was dead. Outraged Catholics demanded that Law resign, and as he sat tight, hiding behind a coterie of bodyguards and traveling on private jets, wild-cat protests at the cathedral settled into regular demonstrations, and do-nations dropped off precipitously. From Boston the wave of accusations then overwhelmed the Catholic Church in the United States and quickly sent shock waves around the world, sparking resignations from Australia to Europe and overshadowing the final years of the pontificate of John Paul II. The scandal even hit close to the Apostolic Palace: a longtime aide to the pope (and a fellow Pole), Archbishop Juliusz Paetz, whom John Paul had promoted to Rome from the Polish Archdiocese of Poz-nan, resigned in March after weeks of reports accusing him of sexually harassing young clerics. In America, four bishops were forced out be-cause of sexual misconduct, along with hundreds of priests who were pulled from their assignments. Overall, upwards of two thousand clerics, many of them dead or retired, were implicated in sexual wrongdoing with minors. One priest was shot and wounded by a victim, and two priests committed suicide after they were accused, bringing to sixteen the number of priests who killed themselves over actual or alleged miscon-duct after 1986.

While the misconduct itself was ghastly, the cover-ups by the bishops were enraging. Although Boston remained far and away the worst-case scenario, too many other bishops matched Law and his aides in the ease with which they put the interests of priests over victims. Brooklyn bishop Thomas V. Daily, who had reassigned many of the abusers while serving as an assistant bishop in Boston, was asked in a deposition why he had taken no action against a priest after a woman told him the cleric had abused her sons and nephews. Daily was matter-of-fact: "I am not a po-liceman; I am a shepherd." By mid-year, when a spokesman for the U.S. hierarchy sought to minimize the scandal by arguing that "this is not Watergate, it's Whitewater," his comparison was already a distinction without a difference. The crimes and sins of abusive priests were soon matched in the public's mind by the maneuverings of bishops who regu-larly shielded their brother clerics from exposure and thus placed thou-sands of children in harm's way.

At every step the bishops seemed to trip themselves up with public-relations miscues, hedging explanations, and halfway apologies that sounded more like political spin than the Beatitudes. An august body that had been revered for their combination of politesse and power now looked like little more than a stumbling bunch of vest-pocket aristos trying to stave off the Revolution. The fall from grace was a dizzying ride. In a flash, Catholic bishops were likened to the other great bogeymen of 2002, the venal chieftains of Enron, WorldCom, Tyco, Arthur Andersen, and other firms who had looted their companies, and their shareholders' life savings, for billions. In the legal world, the deference that had traditionally been accorded bishops vanished overnight. The hierarchy was being compared to the Mafia, and was regularly sued under racketeering statutes that were the prime weapon against organized crime. District attorneys who had reflexively bowed before church authorities began impaneling grand juries and issuing subpoenas, threatening to treat these Princes of the Church like common criminals if they did not turn over church records that were once off-limits to prying eyes.

On top of it all—the impact of this juxtaposition cannot be stressed too strongly—the sexual abuse scandal broke just four months after the shattering terrorist attack of 9/11, which had offered the world a truly "Catholic moment." As the Twin Towers of the World Trade Center burned toward an inevitable collapse, hundreds of firefighters, police officers, and emergency personnel, the vast majority of them Catholics, rushed in to help with a reflexive heroism that embodied the principles of Christian belief and Catholic social teaching. For months afterward, as rescuers pulled the remains of their comrades from the hellish pit, the Catholic funeral rite, broadcast from the working-class neighborhoods of the outer boroughs, became a national liturgy, and the mournful piping of "Danny Boy" became the hero's dirge. The terrorist attacks showed that if lay Catholics weren't obeying every codicil of the Catholic Catechism, as the bishops never ceased to remind them, they nonetheless had an innate understanding of Catholic teaching that plumb escaped their teachers.

Yet just a few months after 9/11, Catholicism was being compared to the Islamism that was behind the attacks, and the hierarchy was seen as the moral equivalent of the Taliban. "I clearly understand there is a difference between the theology of Islam and Catholicism and the men who run those religions. And God knows I am not abandoning my Catholic faith. But I cannot defend Pope John Paul and his minions in Rome," said Fox News's Bill O'Reilly, one of the legion of conservative commentators who had once provided cover from the bishops' right flank but who now scorned the prelates with the anger of the betrayed.

It was a stunning reversal. Politicians who once couldn't get enough photo ops with cardinals and bishops were suddenly canceling out on Catholic events. Columnists were withering in their scorn, and editorial cartoonists could ratchet up their normal irreverence without fear of rebuke. An Oliphant cartoon showed a herd of terrified children fleeing a church—"Saint Paedophilia's"—ahead of a pack of priapic priests in what was titled "The Annual Running of the Altar Boys." ("The bishop has first dibs," quipped the cartoon's peanut gallery.)

On the season finale of *Will & Grace*, Sean Hayes's *outré* gay character, Jack, exclaims, "Nobody's looked at me like that since I was an altar boy at St. Margaret's!" And an episode of the envelope-pushing cable television show *Sex and the City* chimed in by depicting the ease with which one of the women, a new and unmarried mother, was able to convince a priest to edit the traditional baptismal ceremony to her liking. "The truth is, in these troubled times, the Catholic Church is like a desperate thirty-six-year-old single woman—willing to settle for anything it can get," Sarah Jessica Parker said in the overdub. Identifying the Holy Mother Church with New York barflies barely occasioned a murmur of protest. In fact, it was sometimes hard to separate the comic from the serious.

A Texas wife-murderer, Michael Rodriguez, claimed at his trial that he should be spared the death penalty because a priest had initiated him into homosexual behavior, which in turn had led him to hire a hit man to kill his spouse. And in Michigan, administrators at Plymouth High School rejected the "Predator" mascot chosen by students because of concerns that it might conjure images of pedophiles.

Polls showed church attendance eroding and Catholics' faith in their own church plummeting. In 2002 clergy fell from the top of the "most trusted" professions list to the middle, and at the end of the year just 64 percent of Americans felt that they could rely on clergy to tell the truth, down from 90 percent a year earlier. In February 2002 less than 10 percent of Catholics said they held unfavorable views of the church; in December that figured had more than tripled, to 30 percent.

The headline in one newsweekly asked: "Can the Church Save Itself?" The question was not academic.

• • •

The answer, however, was far more complicated than anyone imagined.

A year after the Boston revelations hit the church, as the fog of rage subsided, it became clearer than ever that the sex scandal, like most sex scandals, was about much more than sex. For one thing, sexual abuse is about power and pathology rather than misdirected lust. For another, despite the steady stream of stories of priestly misdeeds, by year's end the harrowing of the priesthood had turned up numbers that showed Catholic clerics are apparently no more prone to sexually abusing children than members of the general population are, and may in fact be slightly less so. The fact is that predator priests claimed so many victims because so many bishops allowed them to operate unhindered for so long. The scandal seemed like an epidemic because the cases had been buried for decades and because they came to light all at once.

The sexual abuse scandal was principally about the abuse of authority—namely, the authority of the bishop. The sudden vulnerability of the hierarchy gave Catholics the indelible feeling, as exhilarating as it was disturbing, that something in the Catholic Church had suddenly changed, and changed irrevocably. Things would never be the same, they said, even if they weren't quite sure what that would mean. In a sense they were right. But it is important to realize that things have not been the same in the Catholic Church for a long time. The difference today is that the changes, and the questions they provoke, are out in the open, and the questions go well beyond matters of sex.

"Such hot-button issues as mandatory priestly celibacy and gay priests, while important, are but reflections of a deeper ecclesial crisis of identity. Who is the church? Where is the church? What is the church's purpose?" wrote Christopher Ruddy, a theology professor at Saint John's University and the College of Saint Benedict in Minnesota, in the Jesuit weekly *America*. While Ruddy's questions were offered in the hope of change, his examination of conscience—hardly unusual in this period—was remarkable in a church that prides itself on self-certainty, immutable dogma, and the confidence of the divine guarantee that "the gates of hell shall not prevail" against it.

This sudden swirl of doubt, this questioning of the very foundations and future of the Catholic Church, is where all the grand historical comparisons fall short. This is something different. The scandal of 2002 illuminated, like a flash of lightning, a kind of "perfect storm" of powerful forces that have been bearing down on Catholicism for decades, often right before our eyes, but with few of us taking much notice. The cumulative dynamics of these forces were building toward an inevitable clash, and the abuse scandals unleashed their pent-up energy like a force of nature and brought everything into the open, and into question.

The three systems in this "perfect storm" were the three "estates" of the church: the laity, the clergy, and the hierarchy. Each had its own internal tension, driven by forces that had been building long before they slammed into one another in the year of scandal.

First, there was a restive laity, the people who comprise 99 percent of the church but who had been growing frustrated by years of rising expectations and unfulfilled promises that they would have a greater voice in the church—that the days of "pay, pray, and obey" were really over.

Second, there was a priesthood that had been molded by the cultural upheavals of the 1960s and the collapse of vocations into a "graying and gaying" fraternity of overworked, sexually suspect men who felt trapped in a dying profession and caught between overbearing bishops and demanding parishioners.

Third, there was a hierarchy on the boil, with many bishops having grown tired of being a buffer between Rome and the pews, and privately wondering when change would come so that they could find a way to staff their pulpits and to stop the hypocrisy of defending Vatican dictates in public while ignoring them in their own conscience.

At the same time, in the back of everyone's mind was the growing realization that change was coming at the top of the Catholic heap—that the Polish pontiff who had redefined the Petrine office with his vibrancy and charisma was seriously ill and succumbing to age. During the year of scandal an infirm John Paul marked the twenty-fourth anniversary of his papacy and became the fourth-longest-serving pope—a remarkable achievement, considering that he had 263 predecessors over two thousand years. Whether John Paul might have handled the crisis more firmly in hardier days is an open question. But in 2002 the pope clearly was not able to exert his authority, either through church law, or by the suasions of a personality so magnetic that it had always united the factions that his own pronouncements were driving apart. The papal magic just didn't work so well anymore.

For Catholics in the United States, all of these developments, however, were manifestations of an even deeper tectonic force that had shaped—some say undermined—the landscape of American Catholicism for centuries, but which resurfaced during the scandal with greater urgency than ever before. The dilemma can be summed up in a single challenge that has become a fixation for Catholic leaders, academics, and intellectuals: How is a believer to be both American and Catholic?

This dual identity was difficult for Catholics at the dawn of American history, and the challenge of America remains a tough question with no easy answers. How much should Catholicism conform to modern life, and how much should it remain countercultural? How is a hierarchical church to exert its claims of absolute truth in a pluralistic, democratic society based on rationalism and pragmatism? And how much is a universal church of international scope, which exalts a conformity of belief among followers in all nations, to adapt to a national culture imbued with a Protestant religious sensibility that prizes individuality in belief, and exercises it through a local, congregational form of governance?

For most of their sojourn in America, Catholics have defined themselves by their differences with their host society, and other Americans have often reciprocated with an anti-Catholicism that Arthur Schlesinger Sr. famously called "the deepest-held bias in the history of the American people." But Catholics today are increasingly assimilated, having broken out of the parallel universe they created in reaction to the outright hostility they once faced. And assimilation means that Catholics have to engage more fully the dominant influences of American society; they have to decide how far they will go in adapting to a society that fosters cultural homogenization and that lives, and dies, by the absolutism of the bottom line.

America's 65 million Catholics are citizens of the world's lone superpower, yet the leader of their billion-member church resides in a foreign capital and often takes stands that are diametrically opposed to American positions on economic issues, human rights, refugees, and a host of other foreign policy matters. Catholics don't have to worry much about the "dual allegiance" accusation anymore, but their baptism in a universal church does force them to think hard about issues in a way that many other Americans do not.

The Catholic challenge is also one of assimilating culturally without disappearing religiously. America today is a noisy religious bazaar of competing religions all clamoring for attention and often doing most anything to market themselves. While mainline Protestantism continues to decline numerically, other faiths, including pseudo-faiths, do-it-yourself faiths, and immigrant faiths, are backfilling the cultural mold vacated by the old establishment religion. For Catholics the process of adaptation is especially fraught because Catholicism is so distinct from the Protestant model. In the midst of the scandal, many Americans wondered why Catholics didn't just switch denominations. And many Catholics, stung by the humiliation of their church, wondered if there wasn't something about Protestantism that really was better. The scandal and the subsequent demands for reform underscored the signal differences between Rome and other denominations—differences that have often been subsumed in the era of ecumenism and religious diplomacy. Centuries after the Reformation and the Enlightenment, Roman Catholicism remains hierarchical, not democratic, universal rather than congregational. It has unique beliefs and traditions of monasticism and mysticism, and its emphasis on tradition, liturgy, and ritual put it starkly at odds with the religious traditions that founded America and continue to dominate the New World.

That very contrariness sets Catholicism apart in a way that makes it both the paradigm of religiosity in America and a target when it falls short of that ideal. "Can you imagine this kind of coverage if the same scandal were in a Protestant denomination?" asked the Notre Dame church historian John McGreevy. "Catholicism matters in a way that maybe no other religious movement does in this country." As the late novelist Walker Percy once put it, the religious option in America is between Rome and California. Indeed, the Catholic Church in America is large, influential, compact, and different from most anything else, and all those things are alternately sources of pride and embarrassment for American Catholics.

After 2002 embarrassment seemed to predominate. But the threat was never so much that the Catholic Church would crumble. Reports of the church's death were understandable, though not terribly original. "People look upon [the church] and say, 'She is about to die. Soon her very name will disappear. There will be no more Christians; they have had their day.' While they are thus speaking, I see these very people die themselves, day by day, but the church lives on." That was St. Augustine writing sixteen centuries ago.

His words ring true today, and in fact on many levels Catholicism in America is as vibrant as it has ever been. In part that is because people still come to church for nourishment, for solace or celebration. Catholicism, like any religion worth its salt, is first about worship and comfort. Moreover, Catholicism, like politics, is local. Only later is it global. Many Catholics are quite happy with their parishes, and they won't let Cardinal Law or any other bishop ruin their experience. Others find the crisis in Catholicism a challenge; it engages them and draws them deeper into their faith exactly *because* the church is changing so much and so fast.

Given this context, the question at hand is not whether American Catholicism will exist in ten years, or twenty or thirty years, but what it will look like. How can the Catholic Church, under the fierce pressures of scandal and disillusionment and activism, change without conforming to the punch-stamp religious template that is making American Christianity about as differentiated as a string of Gap stores? How can Catholics resolve their identity crisis without compromising their identity?

Because of the scandal, these issues can no longer be ignored by Catholic leaders in the United States or in the Vatican. They are real and pressing questions. As Holy Cross professor David O'Brien said at the height of the scandal: "Our decisions about our Americanness will determine our church's future. The shape and form, the piety and practice of our community of faith will turn in part, in large part, on how we make up our minds about this land, and this people, our people."

Given the Catholic Church's enormous presence in U.S. society, especially in education and in health care, and its uniqueness on the religious spectrum, the answer to this question is also vital to America's future.

The one constant in the present equation is change. Change was already pressing in on the Catholic Church from all sides before the scandal, but the renewed demands are coming at a moment in church history in which change, rather than stability, is becoming the permanent mark of Catholicism. The scandal of 2002 was often compared to the first chapter in a Russian novel, with good reason. Much more drama is to come;

more plot twists are in store. In reality, Catholicism has always been changing. From the perspective of history the sacred immutability of the church, often invoked as a divine and unappealable defense against tinkering, becomes a swirl of scandals, reforms, counter-reforms, and, ultimately, transformation.

Still, the Second Vatican Council of 1962–1965 essentially consecrated the imperative to reform, a watershed decision whose impact cannot be overestimated. When Pope John XXIII stunned the world by convening the Council, an authoritative meeting of all the world's bishops that hadn't happened in 100 years, he said he wanted to "throw open the windows of the Church so that we can see out and the people can see in." It was, as he predicted, "a little holy madness," and the winds have been blowing through ever since.

"Vatican II was a revolution," Dominican father John Markey, a theology professor at Barry University in Miami, said in March 2003. "It was the most fundamental shift in self-understanding by the church in 1,500 years. It fundamentally altered the structures that no one could have foreseen or planned. It is a revolution because it is not over yet. We now realize we are in the middle—or early stage—of a transformation that takes years to complete and is beyond the power of anyone to control or stop."

The reforms of Vatican II were about much more than dropping Latin in favor of the vernacular, or turning the priest around to face the congregation. They expressed a whole new vision of the church, from raising up lay people as part of the "royal priesthood" to Rome's novel commitment to dialogue with other Christians and other faiths. The changes were a direct result of the decision by the Council Fathers (they were all men, of course) to reach out to the world—to be a leaven in the wider culture that the church once bitterly denounced from behind medieval ramparts. But the Catholic Church finally opened itself to the world just as the world, especially in America, was facing cultural and political upheavals that would permanently alter the terrain on which every institution had to operate. The tensions and polarization created in Catholicism by that nexus of events—societal and religious—were enormous. Ideological divides now afflict the laity, the priesthood, and the episcopate, and they may prove to be the greatest obstacle to a constructive resolution of the current crisis.

At their most benign, the tensions in Catholicism played out in contentious debates over what seemed like fairly minor issues, such as the legitimacy of altar girls, or when to kneel during Mass, or who gets to drink out of the chalice. But the sexual abuse scandal accentuated the splintered, Rashomon quality of church life as each faction diagnosed the "real" problem from its own vantage point. Depending on one's perspective, the culprit in 2002 was either old-time immorality, or repressive celibacy, or the swinging sixties, or conservative bishops, or homosexuals, or the pope.

In reality, all of these debates represent deeper questions, and they all boil down to arguments over centralization versus decentralization in the church, over what is essential to the faith and what is peripheral. What is the direction and means of change in the church? What is the "Catholic" way? Revolution? Evolution? Restoration? After the abuse scandal, Catholics want definitive answers. The question now is how change will happen.

Looking at the solutions that are possible today is the goal of this book. But to see where future roads might lead, we need first to understand where the church came from, where it is now, and what forks in the road it faces. The crisis in Catholicism has its roots in theology, and in the many ways that theology came to be employed in the politics of the church. Thus unpacking the crisis must start with the politics of the church, and only later deal with the theology. The crisis in Catholicism is a crisis of governance rather than a crisis of faith.

In that sense, I will look at what can happen "on the ground" in the Catholic Church as it exists. This is not intended as a sermon, however, nor as a wish-list (though both are popular temptations). This is a road map that hopefully can inspire as well as illuminate.

Pope John Paul has spoken of the scandal as a "time of trial [that] will bring a purification of the entire Catholic community" and lead to a holier church; and others, mainly conservatives, have used that exhortation as a cudgel to drive home the notion that personal immorality is at the heart of the scandal. The idea of the "fair fault" of original sin, which in turn offers the chance of greater glory through redemption, is a venerable one that has great value. In the words of Leonard Cohen: "Everything has a crack; that's how the light gets in." But emphasizing purification can also be dangerous, easily reduced to a purge of perceived sinners, or an exclusive focus on moral lapses, on being better Christians. Following a course of interior cleansing over visible reform sounds like the easy solution, but in fact it is harder. Christians are by definition sinners in need of salvation. They can always be better. Moreover, a centerpiece of the John Paul papacy has been personal moral rectitude, and yet the scandal happened on his watch, facilitated by some of the very men he appointed for their doctrinal purity. Forcing 65 million other Catholics to wear sackcloth and ashes for the sins of their prophets doesn't seem like a constructive recipe for renewal.

On the other side, some Catholics would like a return to the idealized, primitive church of the first century, where all was sweetness and light. That church never existed, of course, at least as they envision it, and ignoring the intervening two thousand years of tradition and history, both glorious and ignominious, is to give in to the illusion of a perfect church with perfect members. Others would like to convene a Third Vatican Council to magically resolve the current problems, or at least to implement what they see as the lost dream of the Second Vatican Council. But they would perhaps be surprised at who would show up at a prospective "Vatican III." Vatican II's reformist outcome was a close call, and in a Third Vatican Council conservatives might easily trump the liberalizing forces. The Catholic world has always pitched a big tent, but today it is more African, more Asian, and more Latino than ever. American Catholics understand too little that the church really is universal, that it encompasses not only the rich panoply of American Catholicism—a fractious and diverse family that grows bigger and more boisterous every year—but also the one billion *other* Catholics in the world who happen to call Rome home and who have other, much different priorities.

Catholics would do better to take Catholicism where they find it, warts and all, and go from there. The process is already underway, and while it will be a difficult road ahead, it promises also to be inspiring and invigorating. Crisis is not collapse, after all. It is, in the original meaning of the word, about choosing (like a critic) the better from the good, the good from the bad.

In examining the imposing edifice that is the Catholic Church, I will break it down into its three principal tiers: the laity, the priesthood, and the hierarchy (including the Vatican and the papacy). Each cohort has its own dynamic and its own responses to the crisis, and each will contribute to a resolution in a different, but complementary way.

My intent is to be informative rather than programmatic, to promote discussion about the issues at hand, which can in turn foster the *communio* that is the political coin of the church. Long before the scandal of clergy sexual abuse broke, there were bookshelves full of manifestos and apologias arguing one side or the other, taking offense or mounting a defense, agreeing only that the church is falling to ruin, the church has fallen to ruin, or the church will fall to ruin, and that ruin can be avoided only by following one prescription or another. Many similar proposals will follow the scandal.

No one plan will work, however. More important, no single agenda, most of which are presented with the asperity of the self-righteous (and often with patent self-interest), will be acceptable to the vast majority of Catholics to whom the pamphleteers too often condescend. The answers are manifold, the process organic. Despite the difficulties, my attitude is one of hope, if not optimism.

The Catholic Church today is aflame with passions and incendiary accusations that threaten to leave nothing but the charred remains of what William James called the "gloriously piled-up structure" of Catholicism—a *memento mori* for the wages of schism and deceit. A more uplifting image, however, and one that resonates with Christianity's roots in the Old Testament and with its New Testament message of Resurrection, is the church as the Burning Bush, speaking the voice of God, promising liberation and witness from the midst of that inferno without being consumed.

Now, more than at any other time since Vatican II, that promise has a chance to be fulfilled.

A final note: No one can write about faith in the "religion-mad" United States, as Harold Bloom has put it, and certainly not about the Catholic Church in the present era, without bringing a lifetime of experiences and a distinctive point of view to the page. That goes even for a work that is essentially journalistic. Thus it is eminently better to confess one's biases up front. They will leach onto the page anyway.

Given that I was raised as a Billy Graham–style evangelical in middle-class New Jersey, my acquaintance with *Roman* Catholicism (we always used the foreign identifier), apart from watching childhood friends in plaid uniforms head off to something alien called "catechism class," was destined to be roundabout.

When my own religious education came, however, it was something of a full immersion: I went to live in Italy, and to work at the Vatican.

It has been said that Catholics are fortunate that the Vatican is in Rome and the popes have been Italian, because the Mediterranean disdain for hyper-efficiency makes for a more humanistic religion. *Tutto e proibito; tutto e permesso,* as the Italians say. "Everything is prohibited; everything is permitted." It is no coincidence that Calvin thrived in Switzerland. But the real serendipity for Catholics is that Catholicism has been so closely associated with Italy itself, whose charms have been seducing pagans since the Visigoths arrived unbidden.

Even so, once I started on the right path, as Dante would have it, it was several years before I took the fateful step of becoming Catholic, in 1989, at the ripe age of thirty.

My formal conversion came shortly after I left the employ of the Holy See, where I had spent several years (by accident or Providence, take your pick) working at Vatican Radio—sort of an Armed Forces Radio for the pope, crossed with NPR. Whether my conversion came *because* I was working at the Vatican or *despite* it, I am still working out. But I do approach the Catholic Church from an oblique perspective, as a Protestant who worked for the pope and a Catholic convert who covers the church for the secular press. I like to think that provides some particular insights, or at the very least an interesting perch.

Another advantage of this wending pilgrimage is that it spared me the apparent childhood traumas of the Latin Mass and parochial school "Nunzillas," who provide so much entertainment (as well as income) to those lapsed Catholics who have astutely marketed their memories to finance the sweet revenge of living well. I have to agree with the observation that the Catholic Church most Catholics rail against is, for all its obvious failings, probably not the one they left. (Nor, conversely, did the church that the traditionalists want to restore ever exist.) But I also know that converts are a dangerous breed, always compensating for their delayed enlightenment by embracing their newfound faith more piously and rigidly than its most zealous adherents. I hope to avoid such a fate, but I keep the reminder before me always.

If mine was not exactly a clamorous conversion, I did have a "road to Damascus" moment of sorts in my spiritual quest, one that continues to shape my attitude toward Catholicism. It was not a blinding flash, but an illumination under the seductive sun of Umbria, where I first experienced Italy, during several weeks in the summer of 1983, in the limbo of post-college rumination, looking across the valley at golden Assisi sitting peacefully on the side of Mount Subasio.

At the time I was reading Graham Greene's *The End of the Affair*. My only previous experience of Greene had been the standard high school assignment to read his better-known *The Power and the Glory*. That novel's moving but standard drama of a sinner's path to redemption and martyrdom would seem to be more conducive to a religious awakening. But *The End of the Affair*, and Greene's literary treatment of such an unabashedly "Catholic" story, struck me in heart and mind, and caused me to wonder what kind of faith would attract someone like him, an irreligious Englishman. Only later did I learn that Greene had initially converted as a courtship stratagem. But such are the byways of the soul, and Greene remained a Catholic after that romance ended, up to his own death in 1991.

As much as Greene's novel, however, it was the oft-quoted epigram of that book that stayed with me, that kept percolating in the back of my head. It comes from Leon Bloy, a French mystic who is hardly a household name: "Man has places in his heart which do not yet exist, and into them enters suffering, in order that they may have existence." I can think of no better consolation for today's Catholics.

The suffering is there. The debate is over what to do with the sacred space that has resulted from that suffering. This book is an attempt to limn that unknown territory so that the Catholic Church will continue to be the kind of community that wants to attract, and hold, the likes of Graham Greene (or me, for that matter). Whether that makes me a liberal or a conservative, or something more recognizably Catholic, as I would hope, is up to the reader.

Part One

THE LAITY

All history shows clearly the hostility of the laity toward the clergy.
—*Pope Boniface VIII in the papal bull* Clericis Laicos *(1296)*

One

ANGER AND PROTEST

ROME TO DALLAS

The heat was on in downtown Dallas, and it had nothing to do with the scorching sun of a Texas June. Central air-conditioning in the luxury Fairmont Hotel took care of the weather. Other pressures were bearing down on the 250 Catholic bishops gathered in the hotel's grand ballroom, and as the morning wore on toward noon it became clear that the gathering storm was beyond their control.

For five months the churchmen had been blasted by a flock outraged not just at the endless reports of priests who had sexually abused minors, but at the revelations that so many bishops had covered up for the molesters, or had reassigned them to parishes where they had struck again and again and again. The hierarchy had only compounded their problems with ham-handed public-relations efforts to spin the scandal. First there were the outright denials, and then the claims of poor record-keeping (which was a tack Cardinal Law tried in Boston, to universal derision). And then, as more stories leaked more damning details, there were the hedging admissions that yes, something bad had happened, but the bishop wasn't at fault. He just got bad advice by psychiatric experts. Or the whole thing was being blown out of proportion by a Catholic-bashing media pandering to a secularized society that dislikes the church's teachings anyway.

A command performance with Pope John Paul in Rome a few months earlier had been expected to help, but that April 2002 meeting had only made matters worse. The Vatican had wanted to demonstrate that the Home Office was in charge and should be trusted to put things right, so they had called the dozen ranking American cardinals to Rome for a two-day summit that became a media circus and a public-relations disaster for the church. At every turn mediaphobic officials of the Roman Curia—the pope's civil service—sought to blunt the Americans' access to the press in public and to rein in the Americans' plans for reform in private. The summit ended in confusion and an embarrassing late-night press conference that was all but boycotted by Vatican officials and carefully avoided by most of the American cardinals, whose whereabouts were a mystery even to their brother bishops.

The joint communiqué released at the press conference was intended to be a road map for healing and reconciliation, but the Vatican couldn't have planned a worse detour. The document's stipulation that only a priest who is "notorious and is guilty of the serial, predatory sexual abuse of minors" could be subject to defrocking drew everyone's eye and considerable harsh criticism. That the cardinals included a special letter expressing the bishops' solidarity with their priests without a word about the victims didn't help matters. Nor was there any mention of the Catholic laity who make up 99.9 percent of the flock. No reference to their sorrow, their anger, or their possible role in ensuring that such a scandal would never happen again.

Washington's sure-footed Cardinal Theodore McCarrick was stuck selling the statement to the world press at 10:30 P.M., hours after the document had been promised. Why no mention of lay people? "I was looking for it because we had it in there last night," said a clearly exhausted McCarrick, scanning the pages they had spent hours trying to get right. "This document is a document that—words are in and words are out," he added gamely.

The cardinal was telling the truth. Over the previous twenty-four hours, during intense negotiations with Vatican officials, the Americans would agree on language with the curial staff, who would then send the draft to be copied at a shop outside the Vatican, explaining that the Holy See didn't have whatever amounts to the Italian version of Kinko's. When the drafts returned, however, the Americans would often discover that phrases had been deleted. The cardinals "certainly did want to tell the lay people of the United States that they must have a major role in this," McCarrick said, covering as best he could. But the damage was done.

"An awful mess," a senior papal aide admitted later.

Now, however, two months after Rome, the American bishops meeting in Dallas figured that they were back on track. The hierarchy meets as a group twice a year, in Washington in the fall and at different locations around the country for their spring conference. For this spring meeting they had cleared the agenda—normally filled with debates so soporific that the previous year just one wire service reporter had covered the event—so that they could take concerted action. This year, there were nearly eight hundred journalists from around the world checking to make sure they did.

Still, the bishops' timing, once again, couldn't have been worse. While Dallas had been chosen long before the scandal broke, this meeting fell a few days before the fifth anniversary of a $119.6 million judgment against the Diocese of Dallas for shuttling a former priest, Rudy Kos, around parishes even though church officials knew that he was abusing children.

The case reminded everyone that the bishops had been down this road before. Kos's trail of abuse, which started while he was a seminarian, ran from 1977 to 1992. He seduced dozens of boys as young as nine years old using candy, video games, alcohol, sedatives, and marijuana. Plaintiffs testified that they were often invited to spend the night in the rectory with Kos, who sometimes raped them after he drugged them. Many of the victims wound up with lives ruined by addictions. Kos was convicted on three counts of aggravated sexual assault and sentenced to life imprisonment on each count. But he continued to portray himself as the victim. He said he merely suffered from a "foot fetish" and was not a pedophile. "I think I have been through five years of hell already," Kos complained after his sentencing. "I have lost everything, everything. I have lost my friends. I have lost self-respect. I lost my dignity. I lost everything."

Dallas bishop Charles V. Grahmann was more upset at the size of the financial judgment in a subsequent civil suit—this one against the diocese rather than against Kos himself—the largest award ever against a church. Grahmann's lawyers got it reduced to $31 million because the diocese would have had to declare bankruptcy if forced to pay the original sum; the diocese still had to take out mortgages and sell property.

After the 1997 verdict, Grahmann did make a public apology, but he told the plaintiffs—ten victims and the parents of a victim who had committed suicide—that he would not meet with them in person to convey his regret. They would have to come to church to hear him say it from the pulpit. They declined. During Kos's predations Grahmann had been repeatedly warned that Kos was a "textbook pedophile," and in one report in 1990 a priest who worked with Kos told Grahmann that the priest would rub young boys "almost like they were a towel in which he was drying himself." Grahmann still refused to take action against Kos for another two years.

Now in 2002, a few days before Grahmann was to host the entire hierarchy for this momentous meeting, and five years after his diocese had been found "grossly negligent" in its oversight of Kos, Grahmann declared that he was ready to sit down with Kos's victims, but he stipulated that he would not initiate a meeting. The latter again declined. "Too little, too late," responded one of Kos's victims, Wade Slossstein.

By the time the bishops gathered a week later, after a year of unprecedented scandal and repeated missteps, the atmosphere was wired.

The man designated to deliver the bishops from this vise was Bishop Wilton Gregory, who had been elected president of the United States Conference of Catholic Bishops in November 2001, just two months before the crisis broke. At fifty-three, Gregory was a young man for such a high-profile post, and most remarkably, he was an African-American—the first black bishop to reach such a prominent role in a church that has had a hard time drawing and keeping black Catholics and black Catholic leaders. Gregory was one of just 11 black bishops out of 289 members of the hierarchy when he was elected, and from the start there were unspoken pressures on him to be the black Catholic role model. Before Gregory, the most prominent black churchman in the United States had been Eugene A. Marino, the first African-American to hold the rank of archbishop. But Marino was forced to resign in 1990, two years after being appointed in Atlanta, when it was revealed that he'd had an affair with a woman with whom he secretly exchanged wedding vows. Then Marino's successor, Archbishop James Lyke, died a year after he was installed.

But such was the breadth and depth of the sexual abuse scandal that within a few months of Gregory's heralded election, his race was an afterthought. The sense of personal integrity that he conveyed, combined with his political savvy in herding the bishops toward some sort of effective common policy, was all that counted now. Gregory was considered one of the "good" bishops. He had been appointed in 1994 to the small Diocese of Belleville, in downstate Illinois, to clean up the mess after a series of clergy molestation cases had tarnished the church there. Gregory purged the diocese of the abusers and was widely praised for his efforts. If the bishops were looking for a sign that divine Providence hadn't totally abandoned them, they could find it in the fact that Wilton Gregory was their leader during this year of scandal.

Still, as the bishop of a small midwestern diocese, and with no real power over his proudly autonomous fellow bishops, Gregory had to draw on all his talents. In Dallas, finally, he had the pieces in place to pass the tough policy that, together with a tough speech, he hoped would signal the beginning of the end of the bishops' crisis of credibility.

"This crisis is not about a lack of faith in God," Gregory told the prelates as he opened the meeting. "The crisis, in truth, is about a profound loss of confidence by the faithful in our leadership as shepherds, because of our failures in addressing the crime of the sexual abuse of children and young people by priests and church personnel. What we are facing is not a breakdown in belief, but a rupture in our relationship as bishops with the faithful."

The bishops had been pounded with the same criticism for months. Now they heard it from their own leader. All they could do was sit in silence and listen.

Gregory warned his brother bishops that they were facing the possibility of a schism—a frightening scenario for a church in which unity is a cardinal virtue—and then he recited an astonishing communal confession for "what we have done and what we have failed to do":

"We are the ones, whether through ignorance or lack of vigilance, or—God forbid—with knowledge, who allowed priest abusers to remain in ministry and reassigned them to communities where they continued to abuse," Gregory began his litany. "We are the ones who chose not to report the criminal actions of priests to the authorities, because the law did not require this. We are the ones who worried more about the possibility of scandal than in bringing about the kind of openness that helps prevent abuse. And we are the ones who, at times, responded to victims and their families as adversaries and not as suffering members of the Church."

For a full half-hour Gregory ran through his auto-indictment, repeatedly apologizing and asking forgiveness of the victims and the church, and lobbying the hierarchy to adopt the concrete solution before them: a policy, binding on all the bishops, that would permanently expel from ministry any priest, in the past or in the future, with just a single credible allegation of improper sexual contact with a minor.

The so-called zero-tolerance rule had been the subject of intense debate in the months since the Rome meeting, when the Vatican had appeared to put the kibosh on such an unforgiving plan. John Paul himself, raising the potent image of his long struggles against totalitarianism in Poland, told the American cardinals at a private lunch that he didn't want to recreate in his own church the "summary trials" of the Communism that he had spent his life trying to defeat.

Back home, however, after the debacle of the Vatican's statement and press briefing, the bishops continued to get hammered in the press and the public-opinion polls. Prelates who had just weeks earlier stood firm against expulsion for a single offense decades old realized that the anger would not be assuaged by anything but forceful action. Zero tolerance was the answer, they reasoned, and by the time they gathered in Dallas, the passage of an airtight policy was a lock.

Gregory knew, however, that the conference needed more than a good policy and a tongue-lashing from one of their own to put an end to their *annus horribilis*. Words from the bishops themselves cut no ice at that point. Which is why he invited two well-known Catholic intellectuals and several victims of clergy abuse to address the hierarchy after he finished his keynote dressing-down. This was truly stunning. Never before had lay people been allowed to speak to the bishops at their conference. Everybody soon found out why.

The first speaker, R. Scott Appleby, a widely respected church historian from Notre Dame, promptly informed the hierarchy that the Dallas meeting was only the middle of a long and difficult process that would require unheard-of concessions by the bishops to find a resolution. The root of the problem was not abusive priests, nor a bloodthirsty media, nor even greedy lawyers, Appleby said. It was the bishops themselves and a system gone wrong. "Whether the Catholic Church as currently governed and managed can proclaim the Gospel effectively in this milieu is an open question," Appleby warned them.

And sackcloth and ashes, he said, no matter how sincere, would not satisfy the faithful's hunger for real reform.

"I remind you that a remarkable, and to my mind encouraging, development in response to the danger we now face is the fact that Catholics on the right, and the left, and in the 'deep middle' all are in basic agreement as to the causes of this scandal: a betrayal of fidelity enabled by the arrogance that comes with unchecked power," he said. "I do not exaggerate by saying that the future of the church in this country depends upon your sharing authority with the laity."

With a few tough, sobering sentences, Appleby showed the world what was at stake and put the scandal into a perspective that told the bishops their troubles would not be over anytime soon: "The crisis confronting the church today cannot be understood, and thus not adequately addressed, apart from its setting in a wider range of problems that have been growing over the last thirty-four years. At the heart of these problems is the alienation of the hierarchy, and to a lesser degree many of the clergy, from ordinary laywomen and laymen. Some commentators say that the root of this scandal is betrayal of purity and fidelity; others say it is the aloofness of the bishops and the lack of transparency and accountability. They are both right: to be faithful to the church envisioned by the council fathers of Vatican II, bishops and priests must trust the laity, appropriately share authority with them, and open their financial, legal, administrative practices and decisions to full visibility."

Never before had a lay person—a non-ordained outsider—been given free rein to address the bishops, and no one would have ever thought that freedom could be used to such effect.

The break with tradition was especially pointed because bishops meetings have in recent years become echo chambers in which the only sound is the drone of prelates bouncing their own ideas off the walls. Moreover, as the hierarchy itself has become polarized, the bishops have been unable to forge strong initiatives of their own, and spend much of their time on matters of lesser import, or in responding to Rome's complaints about the few initiatives they have taken.

The bloodless atmosphere of these meetings only heightens the perception of the bishops as functionaries or perhaps corporate stockholders—well-fed, white-haired men in uniform dark suits who calmly crunch the numbers of religious observance to send back to HQ in Rome. When they break to recite the divine office at the prescribed hours, the sudden oasis of prayer seems almost incongruous.

At the Dallas meeting, even the office was loaded with import as the bishops stood as one and recited Psalm 80:

> Lord God of hosts, how long
> will you frown on your people's plea?
> You have fed them with tears for their bread,
> an abundance of tears for their drink.
> You have made us the taunt of our neighbors.
> Our enemies laugh us to scorn.

But even the ancient formulas could not dispel the sense of attending a corporate board meeting where each man thinks he is the chairman. Appleby cautioned the bishops that now was not the time to act like company executives. "An enormous mistake would be to adopt prudent, courageous, and enforceable policies regarding sexual abuse at this meeting, and then think that the work of reform has been accomplished." If the bishops fail to step outside their shells, he said, "the next scandal will come quickly on the heels of this one."

And still the bishops' public penance was not over—not by a long shot. The next speaker, Margaret O'Brien Steinfels, longtime editor of the prestigious Catholic periodical *Commonweal,* said that the scandal brought home to millions of non-ordained Catholics in the United States how truly helpless they are to affect anything of consequence in their church. "Whatever the causes of the scandal, the fact is that the dam has broken. A reservoir of trust among Catholics has run dry," Steinfels said. She then punctuated the bishops' failings in a devastating litany:

"Secrecy is one. Careerism another. Silent and passive acquiescence in Vatican edicts and understandings that you know to be contrary to your own pastoral experience. Another is a widespread sense of double standards. One standard for what is said publicly and officially, another standard for what is held and said privately. One standard for the baptized, another for the ordained. One standard for priests, another for bishops. One standard for men, another standard for women. One standard for the ordination of heterosexuals and what now threatens to become another standard for homosexuals. One standard for justice and dialogue outside the church, another for justice and dialogue within."

The immediate cost of the double standard was graphically demonstrated when several victims of clergy abuse followed Steinfels, telling their stories to the hundreds of bishops seated before them. In tearful, awful detail, they recounted the violations they had endured at the hands of priests, and the compounded trauma of being shunted aside, first by the institutional church and then by the church's lawyers. The victims told how they had been countersued by the bishops, how they had been hounded by private detectives hired by the church, and how church lawyers had dissected their private lives in open court and had routinely questioned their motives.

Every story of abuse is a story of anguish, and having interviewed dozens of victims, I know that each is unique even as the details of their molestation become numbingly familiar. Each of the victims who addressed the bishops in Dallas also had an unforgettable story. Craig Martin's talk was especially riveting. Now forty-six and married, with three daughters, Martin was eleven years old when he was sexually abused by his parish priest in Minnesota. In telling his story to the bishops and eight hundred journalists, he physically struggled to speak the words through tears and anguish. He referred to himself primarily in the third person, calling his alter ego John Doe.

"The most amazing part of when I allowed John to talk about his abuser was how this man offered kindness and love; how this man became John's best friend," Martin said in his indirect narrative. "John showed very little anger toward his abuser. I was amazed at who John directed his sorrow to. He directed his sorrow not at his abuser, but at his parents." At that point Martin broke down in sobs and lapsed into the first person, speaking once again as a child, but to parents who weren't there: "Mom and Dad, I am terribly sorry for how I have treated you. I now know that I only have love in my heart for both of you."

At the start of his talk, Martin said that the only words that conveyed his own experience, even to himself, were the lyrics to "The Sounds of Silence." He then stood before the prelates and haltingly spoke the words in a wrenching recitation that made a clichéd standard altogether new:

Hello darkness, my old friend,
I've come to talk with you again,
Because a vision softly creeping,
Left its seeds while I was sleeping,
And the vision that was planted in my brain, still remains,
Within the sound of silence.

This was Craig Martin's personal psalmody, a cry of utter isolation and rejection. But for all of the emotion on the dais, it was hard to gauge the bishops' reaction. Some may have been moved. Most sat quietly, or fidgeted, or looked down at the papers in front of them.

When David Clohessy, leader of the Survivors Network of those Abused by Priests, the main victims group, known as SNAP, got up to speak, he held up a photograph of Eric Patterson, who was repeatedly abused by his parish priest when he was a twelve-year-old boy. Eric grew up into a handsome young man who was fluent in Spanish and played bass in a rock band, but he struggled mightily with the emotional demons unleashed by the priest's abuse. Three years before the Dallas meeting, after years of agony, Eric killed himself at the age of twenty-nine. Four other young men whom the priest abused also killed themselves. (The priest, Robert K. Larson, pleaded guilty in 2001 to molesting four altar boys and was serving three to ten years in Lansing prison when the Dallas meeting convened.) Eric's parents, Janet and Horace Patterson of Conway, Kansas, were at the meeting. The couple remain salt-of-the-earth Catholics with a faith one can only envy. "My husband and I are not out to destroy the church," Mrs. Patterson, dressed in black with a picture of Eric hanging around her neck, told reporters. "We love the Catholic Church. But it's got to be purged."

Clohessy told the bishops that he was speaking there because Eric Patterson and too many others could not. He handed them Eric's picture and asked them to pass it around and to pray for Eric. The photo didn't make it very far. The impact of Clohessy's words was also unclear. Although Bishop Wilton Gregory had received a standing ovation and Appleby and Steinfels had been greeted with polite applause, the victims received a more constrained response, a courtesy carefully measured out.

The bishops broke for lunch after Clohessy's message, and as they gathered for the afternoon session they again joined in prayer, beseeching the Lord for help against the "foes who crush me all day long":

This I know, that God is on my side.
In God, whose word I praise,
in the Lord, whose word I praise,
in God I trust; I shall not fear:
what can mortal man do to me?

During the break, as we milled about the generic hotel hallways outside the generic hotel ballroom, the bishops gathered in kaffeeklatsches and looked for something appropriate to chat about. "Well, that was interesting," one bishop remarked to another. "Yes," the other responded mildly. "We probably needed to hear that."

The detachment was unnerving, though not unusual. The evening before, Cardinal Anthony Bevilacqua of Philadelphia had emerged from an intense private meeting between several abuse victims and a delegation of high-ranking bishops and declared that the victims' stories moved him because he had never met a victim before. He failed to mention that the victims had been seeking a meeting with the bishops for a decade but had always been rebuffed.

Cardinal Law, the designated villain of the piece and a media magnet wherever he was rumored to be, was not part of the group of bishops that met with victims, although he had been invited. He did not use the men's room everyone else did, and he generally steered clear of interactions with anyone except his fellow bishops. Law had flown into town secretly on the private jet of a wealthy friend (the normal cost of such a flight would be about $20,000), giving reporters the slip by making a reservation on an American Airlines flight.

But Dallas was not to be the end of the gauntlet for Cardinal Law or the rest of the hierarchy.

After he closed the three-day meeting, Bishop Gregory pulled one more surprise. At his final press briefing, Gregory introduced Oklahoma governor Frank Keating, a law-and-order Republican and a die-hard but "independent-minded" Catholic, announcing that Keating would head an all-lay review board that would be a watchdog to see that the bishops did what they had pledged to do. Tall and stern, Keating came off as the new sheriff in a lawless town, speaking in terms that would have been unimaginable from a layman just a few weeks earlier, or at most any time in recent centuries. He excoriated bishops and cardinals who had protected child molesters, and he said that if the law could not charge them, his panel would try to force their resignation (a power reserved solely to the pope). "Arguably they are obstructing justice, or arguably they are also accessories to the crime," Keating said. "To suggest that someone like that would not only get away with a criminal act but also get away with it in the eyes of the church is simply inconceivable to me."

As word of Keating's remarks filtered back to the bishops preparing to depart the hotel, many were not amused, an attitude that heralded tensions to come. "I'm very sad and disappointed to hear what the governor is saying," said Bishop Raphael Fliss of the Diocese of Superior, Wisconsin. "It's not what the lay people are called to do."

The laity, however, were in no mood to heed such reprimands from a hierarchy that covered for abusing priests but then conspicuously refused to sanction any of their own members. A zero-tolerance policy for priests had been passed in Dallas, but the bishops were slipping out of town scot-free. Within hours, the verdict of the faithful was in: Dallas was no more than a public-relations gambit. Once again, both camps in the church's bitter ideological war found a rare unity in their displeasure.

"There is little reason to believe that it is much more than a quick-fix pseudo-solution, a bone tossed to quiet the baying pack of journalists and lay activists," Rod Dreher wrote in the *National Review*, the conservative monthly founded by arch-Catholic William F. Buckley Jr. "Aside from not addressing the root causes of the scandal, the bishops refused to accept personal accountability for their paramount role in the scandal. Not one resigned. Not one was asked to resign, at least publicly. Words of apology ring hollow when not followed by action." Dreher concluded by quoting C. S. Lewis: "A long face is not a moral disinfectant."

On the liberal side, the *National Catholic Reporter* opined: "No matter how tough they get on priests who have been accused or convicted of sexually abusing children, the bishops continue to hold themselves beyond accountability, to the astonishment of everyone outside their exclusive club. . . . Such men apparently suffer from the delusion that they, alone, are still in charge, that somehow they still command respect and exercise authority."

Eugene Kennedy, a professor emeritus of psychology at Loyola University in Chicago and a former Maryknoll priest, labeled the meeting "The Latest Remake of Frankenstein," and said that Dallas signaled the end of the church's monarchical order.

The bishops pleased no one. Victims thought the policy wasn't tough enough on priests. Priests felt they had been sold out. The Vatican thought the bishops had caved to the dreaded beast of public opinion. And the laity thought the bishops had given themselves a free pass.

More than nine in ten Catholics wanted bishops who had covered up for molesters to be removed and subject to criminal charges, a consensus that would be hard to find on any issue in the church apart from the rejection of the church's teaching on birth control. A Gallup poll released right after Dallas showed that just 42 percent of U.S. Catholics said they had a "great deal" or "quite a lot" of confidence in the church, compared to nearly six in ten Protestants who said they had confidence in their church. A poll a decade earlier had showed no disparity in Catholic and Protestant ratings. The numbers were at an all-time low.

In Dallas, Wilton Gregory had told the bishops that they had to act because the crisis was "the gravest we have faced." After Dallas, as it turned out, the crisis was going to get worse.

The meeting had vividly demonstrated that the terrain in the Catholic Church had shifted, perhaps permanently. In the span of a few days the debate had moved beyond sex and abuse to the systemic weaknesses of a church that likes to present its every structure as divinely ordained. And the debate had moved beyond the realm of privatized dissent over church teachings or the long-running samizdat arguments among Catholic intellectuals about fine points of hierarchical politics. Now it was the laity who were taking the bishops to catechism class. For Catholics in America, the rule had always been, "Pay, pray, and obey." That was now over. As the liberal Marquette theologian Daniel Maguire wrote in *U.S. News & World Report:* "It is not often that we witness the death of a mystique."

The road ahead, however, seemed less certain after Dallas than before. As Rod Dreher put it in his postmortem on the Texas meeting: "The battle for the Catholic Church in America has only just begun." But how would that battle be fought? How would it end? And where would it lead?

It is a truism of church history that, as Notre Dame professor of theology Lawrence Cunningham put it, "Almost all significant change in the church happens from the bottom up and not the top down. It is really out of the matrix of the people within the church that you tend to see big changes." That may be true, but in earlier times the engine for renewal was always kick-started by the religious orders of monks and nuns—lay people who had taken special vows rather than ordination to the clergy ranks. In the Dark Ages and the Middle Ages and in the Counter-Reformation, these communities were powers the bishops had to contend with—great monastic orders such as the Benedictines, mendicant orders such as the Franciscans, Dominicans, and Carmelites, and religious communities led by extraordinary figures, women as well as men, such as Ignatius Loyola (the Jesuits) and Francis de Sales (the Institute of the Visitation). In their time, Catherine of Siena, Teresa of Avila, and Hildegard von Bingen were all potent forces for reform who would tell the pope where to get off, and expect he would heed them.

The contemporary era has witnessed a dramatic decline in those orders, with the numbers of nuns and brothers falling faster even than those of the priests. In 1965 there were 180,000 nuns in the United States and more than 12,000 brothers. In 2002 the numbers stood at 74,000 nuns and 5,600 brothers, falloffs that are only getting worse as the orders age. One result is that the institutional face of the church is more male and more clerical than ever before. The bishops run the show today, and the "rest" of the church is the laity.

If there is to be a "revolution from below" in the coming Catholic Church, it will be in this new context: it must originate primarily with "ordinary" lay people who lead busy lives in a world that is busier than ever, people who have little leverage in a voluntary organization that is proudly defined as a hierarchy and not a democracy. It will be a battle that will take place on uncharted territory and with uneven odds. Over the course of the last millennium the hierarchy has consolidated its grip on the reins of ecclesiastical power, from the sacraments to the finances. For centuries, theology and canon law have drawn a bright line between the clergy and the laity, and while there have been recent efforts to shift that boundary, religious authority still flows downward and controls every aspect of church life from on high.

Reversing the trend of centuries will be crucial to the renewal of Catholicism, and it will be a daunting task, as history has shown.

Two

PAY, PRAY, OBEY

OLD WORLD TO NEW

I t has been said that the Second Vatican Council of the 1960s was supposed to take Catholicism back to the days of Jesus but got stuck in the Middle Ages. Actually, the Council Fathers did a remarkable job of unpacking and revamping nearly two thousand years of doctrines, bulls, traditions, and anathemas. But that estimate is about right when it comes to the balance of power between the hierarchy and the laity. An organization that was born as a divine kingdom, grew up as the spiritual heir to imperial Rome, and flourished by donning the trappings of monarchy does not yield easily to retrofitting. The monarchical model of the church that took over around the turn of the second millennium of Christianity, about A.D. 1000, has been especially resistant to history's waves of reform, for the very reason that it was in this period that the struggles between hierarchy and laity that reverberate in today's conflicts were first joined in noisy clashes among larger-than-life characters.

The central political reality of that era of primeval Catholicism—and one that remains the source of so much tension today—was the porous frontier between secular and religious authority. The question was not only how much influence the church should have in the state and vice versa, but which one ran the show. Clerics claimed primacy over both worlds, while lay people—that is, powerful princes and rulers—had the muscle to do as they pleased, and they were often pleased to assert their own right to run the church and their temporal realm. As Eamon Duffy, a historian of the papacy, writes in *Saints and Sinners: A History of the Popes:* "No one in eleventh-century Europe thought of Church and state as separate or separable entities. There was only one Christendom, and the conflicts between Pope and Prince arose from conflicting claims to spiritual headship within that single entity."

The competition, however, edified neither camp. Emperors such as Henry III (1039–1056) paraded about in priestly robes with zodiacal symbols to show off their combined regal-sacerdotal role, and the secular ruler and his princelings, rather than the pope in Rome (as is the modern custom), made and unmade bishops, "investing" them, as the term had it, with the ring and staff of office.

Not surprisingly, this secular control of church affairs did not sit well with the popes, who felt theirs was the higher claim, not only because eternal matters of the spirit should by definition trump temporal concerns, but because the church was also pivotal in rescuing the very civilization that the princes were trying to commandeer. In the Western world the popes had been rulers rather than martyrs since the fourth century, when the emperor Constantine, and then Theodosius, granted the perks and privileges of a state religion to the fast-spreading Christian faith, largely ending the episodic persecutions that had plagued Christianity's early years.

But when Constantine moved the empire's capital to Byzantium (modern-day Istanbul) in A.D. 324, the globe's political center of gravity also shifted to the East. In the West, that left the Roman Catholic Church as the only bulwark against anarchy. In the face of that threat, great monasteries gathered up the threads of Western culture and wove them into a tapestry of civilization for future generations, while the church in Rome supplied grain to feed the citizens and paid wages to the army. The pope himself was often left to negotiate military treaties with the various foes who raided the peninsula with increasing frequency. In A.D. 452 it was Pope Leo the Great who convinced Attila to spare Rome from the Huns. A miracle, it was said, but one whose efficacy was apparently limited. When the barbarians returned three years later, Leo could only talk them out of razing the city. The Huns looted it instead. Leo then melted down the silver ornaments in St. Peter's to make chalices so that the city's priests could celebrate Mass.

As the church filled the vacuum left by the rapidly crumbling imperial power, it naturally took on the coloration of its surroundings, as it has in every time and every place, up to the present day. In the Dark Ages, the only model to follow was that of empire. Popes and bishops became like kings and princes, and clergy were viewed as feudal lords. From there it was a short step to establishing a papal kingdom on earth. That formally occurred on the Feast of the Epiphany in 754, when Pope Stephen II met the Frankish king Pepin and convinced him to extend papal rule over much of Italy. Pepin was happy to grant the request in exchange for spiritual legitimacy. A forgery of the so-called Donation of Constantine was circulated, in effect a backdated check (to the fourth century), to maintain the fiction that Pepin's actions were only in keeping with the wishes of the mighty Constantine, whose imperial mantle Pepin hoped to assume.

Despite the papacy's temporal base, the popes proved no match for divine-right kings. Empires and nation-states rose around the papal territories, and their leaders all challenged his authority, militarily, politically, and ecclesiastically. Princes appointed bishops and received tributes from the wealthy religious orders that had sprung up in monasteries across Europe. Those orders were themselves often a direct challenge to the popes, since their reason for being was to reform a papacy that by the turn of the millennium was increasingly corrupt spiritually and feckless politically.

Just as kings had taken to claiming divine rights to reinforce their temporal powers, the Roman pontiffs claimed regal rights to reinforce their spiritual supremacy. The strategy paid off for monarchs, at least until the eighteenth century or so. The popes' deal with the devil unraveled quickly, however, as the papacy soon became an unedifying spectacle in which claims to the keys of St. Peter were decided by political machinations and street-fights. The problem was, the pontiffs weren't very good at the rough stuff, and at the opening of Christianity's second millennium, popes were habitually humiliated, exiled, imprisoned, and forced to flee the holy city for their lives. At least one of them (Benedict VI) was not quick enough and was murdered.

A reform movement begun in the eleventh century under Pope Gregory VII restored much of the church's spiritual luster and by extension some of its temporal authority, but not for long.

Gregory focused first on reforming the clergy by ending the widespread practice of simony (that is, trafficking in ecclesiastical offices or spiritual goods) and the equally widespread and detrimental (to the church's finances) practice of clerics passing church property on to their offspring. That reform led to mandated priestly celibacy a century later, a discipline that would remain largely unaltered until the turn of the third millennium. His other chief aim was to assert the primacy of the pope, bishops, and priests over that of the non-ordained class of humanity. "Shall not an authority founded by laymen, even by those who do not know God, be subject to that authority which the providence of God Almighty for his own honor has established and in his mercy given to the world?" Gregory wrote in 1081 to the bishop of Metz. "Who can doubt that the priests of Christ are to be considered the fathers and the masters of kings and princes of the faithful?"

The Holy Roman Emperor at the time, Henry IV, would have none of it. He answered Gregory's question by claiming that he, not the Roman pontiff, could appoint, or "invest," bishops. Henry thought he was on solid ground; after all, his father had deposed three popes. But politics had changed in the intervening years, and the papacy's prestige had grown through its spiritual renewal. Gregory wielded the papacy's ultimate weapon and excommunicated Henry, and in one of the most famous scenes in European history, Henry was forced to kneel in the snow for three days outside the pope's mountain redoubt at Canossa, in northern Italy, in January 1077 until the Holy Father deigned to forgive the penitent emperor his sins.

Canossa became a metaphor for humiliating defeat, but it was the layman in this episode who had the last word. Henry recovered his political balance, dumped Gregory off his throne, and installed his own candidate as pope, driving the deposed pontiff into exile, where he died alone and bereft. Other popes would go on to fight other battles in the Investiture Controversy, as it was called, trying to guarantee the right of the church to govern its own affairs against the meddlings and machinations of kings and princes. But the papacy's efforts to rule both heaven and earth were doomed.

The rest of the millennium would largely be a hashing out of the terms of papal surrender—a steady retreat of the papacy's claims to power in the secular realm, culminating in the humiliation of 1870, when Italian troops, fighting to establish a unified secular Italian state for the first time, breached the walls of Rome at Porta Pia and left Pius IX a prisoner in the Vatican. Pius and his successors would remain there, glowering suspiciously at a world hostile to their historical claims of supremacy, until 1929, when Pius XI okayed a concordat with Mussolini. When the Papal States fell in the nineteenth century, the pope said, "All I want is a small corner of the earth where I am master." In the twentieth century, that's all his successors got—Vatican City State, 108 acres across the Tiber, all that remained of the once-sprawling Papal States and the even more grandiose claims of papal power.

To compensate for its steady losses on the political and military front, the church over the centuries increasingly asserted its sovereignty in the religious sphere, and increasingly made its claims within that sphere absolute and unassailable. The laity may be able to overpower the clergy in this world, but the ranks of the ordained would have the final say about the world to come.

In 1215, Pope Innocent III famously declared that no one outside the church could be saved *(Nulla salus extra ecclesiam)*, and about that same time the doctrine of transubstantiation—the signature Catholic belief that the bread and wine are transformed into the body and blood of Jesus during the Mass—was enshrined and codified as a miracle worked by the priest and the priest alone. Celibacy became the norm, and the clergy were professionalized and educated, greatly improving the quality of the priesthood but also increasing the distance and estrangement between them and the flock. "All history shows clearly the hostility of the laity toward the clergy," Pope Boniface VIII complained in 1296. His observation worked equally well in reverse. Dante Alighieri, one of Boniface's former emissaries, grew so disillusioned with the pontiff's ways that he stuck him in the *Inferno*. Boniface may have been the first, but not the last, pope to regret offending a writer.

After the twelfth century, popes were crowned and enthroned (a tradition that lasted until John Paul I, who chose to be "installed" in 1978, a practice John Paul II maintained), and their every vestment and title reflected a spiritual superiority to the lay person that the pontiffs could not assert in the secular sphere. The trend extended to church governance, as the papacy developed a heavily juridical style of authority, creating a bureaucracy in the Roman Curia, systematizing theology, and codifying church law (known as canon law), which regulated every aspect of religious life and was considered above civil law—a claim that would come back to haunt the church in the early twenty-first century.

To be sure, the church's claims to moral and legal exceptionalism were often critical in the turbulent centuries when temporal law was anything but civil. The church's standing apart from the temporal world offered an authority that no number of army divisions, as Stalin learned, could match. And the church's claims to a privileged position continue to provide vital protection to the millions of Catholics who live under persecution or harassment. In any discussion of Catholicism, it is crucial to view the American situation in the global context, as the Vatican must do.

Yet as the sexual abuse scandal unfolded, American Catholics witnessed the ways in which these medieval principles could also be used to undermine a modern system of justice for no other reason than to protect longstanding clerical privileges at the expense of children.

In 1990, for example, Bishop A. James Quinn, an auxiliary bishop in Cleveland and a civil as well as canon lawyer, told a seminar of church leaders and lawyers that they should consider destroying or hiding records of sexual abuse allegations to protect the church from lawsuits. "Personnel files should be carefully examined to determine their content. Unsigned letters alleging misconduct should be expunged," Quinn told the seminar, citing the church's canon law for justification. "If there is something you really don't want people to see, you might send it off to the apostolic delegate," meaning the Vatican's ambassador in Washington. "They have immunity. If it's dangerous, if it's something you consider dangerous you might send it off to them."

The tapes of Quinn's remarks emerged in April 2002, just as the scandal was reaching full force. But the shocked reaction to his statements had little effect on Vatican officials, who saw the claims of the ages as superseding any momentary controversy.

In May 2002 a leading Vatican canonist, Jesuit father Gianfranco Ghirlanda, wrote an article in *Civiltá Cattolica*—a journal that has the Vatican's stamp of approval—in which he said that informing the authorities or parishioners about sexual abuse allegations against a priest, or even subjecting a priest to psychological testing, would violate the cleric's rights under canon law. He also said flatly that bishops had no obligation to make legal settlements with victims: "From a canonical point of view, the bishop or religious superior is neither morally nor legally responsible for a criminal act committed by one of his clerics."

Then in October, after months of deliberations and mixed signals, the Vatican finally sent the vaunted zero-tolerance policy on abusive clerics—the policy that the bishops had drafted in Dallas—back for revisions, saying that it didn't pass muster under canon law. The Vatican saw two main problems. The first was that the bishops had effectively abolished the canonical statute of limitations for sexual abuse of a minor by a cleric. Currently, canon law says that a claim of abuse must be made within ten years after the victim reaches the age of majority, which is set at eighteen. In other words, if an abuse victim doesn't make an allegation by the time he or she is twenty-eight, the offending cleric cannot be defrocked (a process known in canon law as "laicizing"), even if he is guilty. That was actually a recent improvement over the previous statute, which set the age of majority at sixteen and allowed just five years—until a person reached twenty-one—to report an allegation.

Rome's other concern was that by mandating lay boards to review each diocese's policies, the bishops were giving lay people ecclesiastical power over ordained clerics, a small but unacceptable reversal in the church's polarity. "Theologically, lay people supervising bishops in exercising their hierarchical authority is entirely absent from church tradition," Father Robert A. Gahl Jr., who teaches at a pontifical university in Rome, told the *New York Times*. Added an unnamed Vatican official: "They [the bishops] are dealing with the matter as if they don't understand who they are. . . . The question becomes: What will they do next?"

The history of the rivalry between the clerically run Catholic Church and the secular world of the laity is the parable of the elephant and the whale—each unchallenged in its own domain, but powerless in the other's world. The difference is that while the lay world evolved over the centuries, the Catholic cosmos remained fixed. Christendom splintered, but the Vatican often acted as though the territory outside its walls were still run by the Holy Roman Emperor and populated by souls subject to its dictates. The Protestant Reformation led the Catholic Church to simply dismiss the dissidents as heretics and to ratchet up its control over the lay folk who remained within the Roman fold. The French Revolution and the violent rise of democracy almost took the Catholic Church down with the *ancien régime*. But the church survived that upheaval as well, its universal spiritual claims intact and, in fact, ever more insistent in the face of what it perceived as an implacable threat.

Indeed, with each successive jolt from a modernizing world the church became more like a paranoiac with real enemies. If the "laity" in centuries past meant divine-right monarchs who meddled in church affairs, then the Age of Democracy meant that every layman was king, and the peril was that much greater. "What is the province of the laity?" George Talbot, an English priest of the Victorian era, asked when the people in the pews were making noises about overweening bishops. Talbot's answer: "To hunt, to shoot, to entertain. These matters they understand, but to meddle with ecclesiastical matters they have no right at all."

Popes viewed representative democracy as tantamount to the chaos of mob rule—a populist dogma that had already infected Protestantism and now threatened to spill into Catholicism, compromising traditions and doctrines that had the sanction of divine mandate. And even when the Catholic Church belatedly embraced democracy—for society, not Catholicism itself—its leaders remained leery of its impact. "Democracy cannot be idolized to the point of making it a substitute for morality or a panacea for immorality," John Paul said in 1995, a point he has made repeatedly.

The battleground shifted, but the contestants remained the same: the clergy asserting their prerogatives and the laity claiming theirs, the power of the papal bull versus the authority of the people's ballot. Nowhere has that struggle manifested itself more keenly than in the United States, and that has caused both the Vatican, and American Catholics, no end of trouble.

On March 21, 2002, as tensions over the sexual abuse crisis in the United States church were building to epic proportions, the Vatican scheduled a rare press conference to release Pope John Paul's annual letter to the world's priests for Holy Thursday. That's the day when the church recalls the institution of the priesthood at the Last Supper, and reporters were watching to see if the pontiff would break his silence and address the scandal that had been battering the American church for three months. Lay people, priests, and bishops were looking for signs of leadership from Rome. In the letter, however, the pope made only a passing mention to "the sins of some of our brothers who have betrayed the grace of Ordination in succumbing even to the most grievous forms of the '*mysterium in-*

iquitatis'''—in lay terms, "the mystery of evil." No word for the victims, no nod to any larger problem than individual moral failings.

Reporters pounced, pressing Cardinal Darío Castrillón Hoyos, head of the Vatican department in charge of the world's clergy, for amplification. Castrillón is not known as a media-friendly churchman. A Colombian-born prelate who in his years in Rome has donned the mental armor of the Curia, Castrillón grew irritated and defensive at the inquiries over such a small matter. "The pope is worried over peace in the world," he said. "With all that is going on in the world, I'm just not sure it would be convenient for him to choose to speak on this." This piqued the journos even more. They pressed harder, and Castrillón couldn't resist singling out the Americans for criticism. "It's already an X ray of the problem that so many of the questions were in English," the cardinal said. "Concerning the problem of sexual abuse and cases of pedophilia, I have only one answer," he continued. "In today's culture of pansexualism and libertinism created in this world, several priests, being of this culture, have committed the most serious crime of sexual abuse."

In other words, this was a unique problem of "American" society that was being exploited for self-serving reasons by an "American" press. On the one hand, that was an understandable political effort to contain the crisis by limiting its scope to the United States, and to trace its underlying causes to the vices of a particular culture. But this view also reflected longstanding Vatican suspicions about America and, by extension, American Catholics. These suspicions go back to the very beginning of the American church, and the scandal of 2002 showed that they had survived the centuries almost unchanged, like mastodon meat recovered from a melting ice floe. Only now, with the abuse scandal raising questions about the viability of Catholicism in the United States, the stakes have been raised as never before. "We have here two points of view that really have to come to an understanding with each other," conceded Cardinal Francis Stafford, the former Denver archbishop who now heads the Curia's office on lay Catholics.

If past is prologue, however, the odds of a rapprochement are not good.

In the early years of Catholicism in America, the tensions between America and Rome were minimal since the Vatican had little reason to give colonial Catholics much thought. This was understandable. Out of the four million newly minted American citizens at the time of the Republic's founding in 1776, just 35,000 were Catholics. From the perspective of the twenty-first century, when America sits atop the heap as the world's lone superpower, it is important to remember that geopolitically speaking, the United States at one time barely crossed Europe's radar screen. The same was true for American Catholics in the eyes of the Vatican. In fact, it was only on June 29, 1908, when Pius X promulgated the apostolic constitution *Sapienti Consilio*, that America ceased to be considered mission territory requiring the direct control and tutelage of the Vatican's Congregation for the Propagation of the Faith, or *Propaganda Fide*.

In the late eighteenth and early nineteenth centuries, the papacy was worried only about surviving the French Revolution intact and with some shred of dignity. First the people's tumbrels, and then Napoleon's armies, concentrated the papacy's mind on the Old World. French revolutionaries kidnapped Pope Pius VI, who died in exile, while Napoleon imprisoned Pius VII in 1807, after forcing the feckless pope to crown him emperor in 1804. That left the papacy with little time to ponder the remarkable doings happening across the Atlantic.

In 1789, the same year that the French Revolution would turn the papacy's world upside down, George Washington was sworn in as the first duly elected president of the United States. The month after Washington's democratic inauguration, in May 1789, John Carroll was elected—albeit only by the clergy—as the first bishop for the United States. The Vatican agreed with Carroll's demand for "that Ecclesiastical liberty, which the temper of the age and of our people requires," and assented to this unusual exercise in church democracy. The approval was probably more a matter of benign neglect than a new policy, but either way Rome's inattention was a boon to American Catholics, who saw themselves as Americans as much as Roman Catholics, patriots who were part of the great experiment being undertaken in the New World. As Jay P. Dolan, the dean of American church historians, has described it: "In a very real sense all things were beginning anew; a new political and social order was being born; a new religious environment was taking shape as well. Onto this stage stepped John Carroll, and together with his colleagues among the clergy and the laity he began to articulate an understanding of Roman Catholicism that was unique in Western Christendom."

A central tenet of this new understanding was that American Catholics would be a "national" church free of "any dependence on foreign jurisdiction," as Carroll wrote to the Vatican in his successful plea to allow the clergy to elect one of their own as bishop rather than having Rome appoint someone. "This you may be assured of, that no authority derived from the Propaganda [the Vatican's mission arm] will ever be admitted here," Carroll wrote in a sharp note to Rome when he heard that the Curia was in the process of appointing an apostolic administrator for the new country. "The Catholick Clergy and Laity here know that the only connexion they ought to have with Rome is to acknowledge the pope as the Spiritual head of the Church."

American Catholics were proud heirs to an ancient spiritual legacy, but they were also steeped in the ideals of the Enlightenment and republicanism. They advocated the separation of church and state, which was still anathema to Rome, and their acceptance of religious pluralism in the larger society found an echo in their desire for a degree of populism within their own ranks. What is striking about today's hotly contested demands that bishops ease their absolute control of church affairs is that all of the proposals can find a recent precedent (two hundred years ago qualifying as "recent" under the Vatican's Sphinx-like gaze) in the early American church.

That goes for consultation in the choice of bishops and even more so in parish governance, where early American Catholicism functioned in ways that would be considered revolutionary, if not heretical, today. In the first century of the new United States, Catholic lay people routinely banded together to buy land and build churches, they set up lay boards to run their parishes, and in many cases they hired and fired their pastors. Catholics were a minority community who wanted to fit in with the larger culture, and not surprisingly the model of church governance they followed was that of congregational Protestantism. They were helped by the fact that most states, dominated by legislators who were no fans of Romish religion, passed laws mandating that lay people, not clerics, own church property.

These democratic models were also indirectly aided by the fact that there were so few priests in the United States, and almost as few churches. Necessity decreed that Catholics fill this vacuum any way they could. But even where there was a priest or bishop, this pattern of collaboration was

adapted as laymen (always men) worked as equals with their clerical counterparts.

In Boston, where there was a resident French *abbé*, lay people
founded the parish, they elected wardens, and they paid the priest's
salary. On the frontier in Kentucky and in emerging major cities such as
Philadelphia, the republican, lay-trustee system became the standard
model of parish governance. In 1785 in Manhattan, twenty-two Catholic
laymen set up the city's first Catholic parish and incorporated themselves
as "the Trustees of the Roman Catholic Church in the City of New York."
When Irish-born John England became bishop of Charleston in 1820, he
drew up a constitution for Catholics throughout Georgia and the Caroli-
nas that enshrined the lay-trustee system as a means of balancing American and Roman Catholic ideals so that "the laity are empowered to
cooperate but not to dominate."

In fact, clergy had more to fear from angry laity in this period than the
parishioners from the clergy. Italian immigrants, with resentment of the
Roman clerical imperiousness they grew up with still fresh in their minds,
were often quick to revolt against an unpopular priest, and independent-
minded German and French-Canadian immigrants did the same.

In New York, the trustees of old St. Patrick's Cathedral (the downtown precursor to the present church) were constantly at odds with the
city's third bishop, John Dubois, who was, perhaps tellingly, the only non-
Irishman to serve in that role. On one occasion the trustees of the cathedral threatened to withhold Dubois's salary. He replied: "I am an old
man, and do not need much. I can live in a basement or in a garret. But
whether I come up from the basement or down from the garret, I shall
still be your bishop." Maybe so, but Dubois's declaration didn't carry the
same weight in populist America that it did in Europe. Dubois asked that
he be buried under the threshold of the cathedral when he died. "Everyone walked over me in life," he said, "they may as well walk over me in
death." The lay trustees granted that request.

In reviewing this period to see what lessons it may hold for the present day, we must realize that trusteeism and related forms of participa-
tory governance were not solely an indigenous American experiment
fueled by the patriotic vision of 1776. Many Catholic immigrants, especially Germans, brought with them to the United States a template of
local sovereignty that was lifted directly from their home country.

The German tradition was not all that surprising, since German Catholics, like their new American brethren, were a minority in a pre-dominantly Protestant country where local self-government was the norm. In Cincinnati and Philadelphia, German Catholics replicated the Old Country ways by organizing "national" parishes where they could preserve the use of their mother tongue as well as the autonomy they had at home. By the middle of the nineteenth century, according to one survey, 62 percent of German parishes were run by lay trustees.

But the American experiment didn't last. Friction over clerical inde-pendence and lay power-sharing continued to spark disputes with the bishops, who began to reassert a traditional Roman view of the church—top-down, where the bishop, and in his stead, the pastor, ruled unchal-lenged. In their campaign the bishops were backed by the authorities in Rome, where the popes had emerged from the trauma of the Napoleonic era only to watch aghast as popular rebellions cropped up around Europe and further eroded the church's historical position. Angry and defensive, Rome reacted by becoming more monarchical and autocratic.

By that time Rome's attitude also suited the American bishops, who saw the benefits of centralizing their power as a useful foil to the bump-tious laity. Even an aged John Carroll, who had once warned Rome about trying to impose bishops on the Americans, wound up advocating direct papal appointments over consultation with local clergy. The trend toward centralization in America also reflected the metamorphosis of American Catholicism into a church dominated by Irish clergy and Irish lay people who came from a persecuted faith that had had to be unified to survive the English. From the mid–nineteenth century up through the 1960s, about 75 percent of the American bishops were Irish, a legacy that re-mains strong today. The Irishness of the church has been a source of untold strength in the American church, but at the level of church governance, the Irish who came to define American Catholicism also helped to propa-gate a reflex of deference to clerical authority where the parish was run like a fiefdom and the bishop was next to God.

The reassertion of episcopal control did not come about without sev-eral memorable clashes. A trustee election in Philadelphia in 1822 re-sulted in a riot that saw opposing factions of parishioners and priests fighting each other with clubs; and in Maine, Massachusetts, and Con-necticut, immigrant French-Canadians frequently and physically resisted the bishop to protect their interests. Congregants in Fall River, Massachusetts, stopped contributing to the parish and attending Mass over a dispute with the diocese, while in North Brookfield and other Massachusetts towns lay Catholics established their own parishes and were duly excommunicated. Eastern European Catholics were especially resistant to change. In Bridgeport, Connecticut, one hundred angry Slovaks marched into the rectory and barricaded the pastor—who had been appointed by the bishop without their consent—in the attic.

Throughout the upheavals over lay control, however, the gravitational pull of Rome proved strong, and the overwhelming majority of Catholics stayed put. They looked on as the hierarchy relentlessly curbed lay power by routinely ignoring state laws on lay ownership of church property and running their dioceses as the corporation sole. Even in dioceses with the model of a corporation aggregate, in which the diocese is legally defined as a collection of individual corporations—parishes, hospitals, universities—the bishop is the head of each corporate entity and thus controls everything that goes on. (The bishops may come to regret their power, since it leaves them legally liable for the actions of abusive priests.)

In a 1906 encyclical, Pius X said that the "one duty" of the laity "is to allow themselves to be led, and like a docile flock, to follow the Pastors." In 1907 the American hierarchy followed suit with a similar directive: "The Church is not a republic or a democracy, but a monarchy; . . . all her authority is from above and rests in her Hierarchy. . . . [W]hile the faithful of the laity have divinely given rights to receive all the blessed ministrations of the Church, they have absolutely no right whatever to rule and govern."

The experiment in parish self-government was over. But the tensions between Rome and U.S. Catholics were not.

While the American bishops were battling the laity for control of the parishes, successive popes in Rome watched the United States grow into an enormous and wealthy country with a political and cultural power to match. And they didn't like what they saw—a rough-and-tumble democracy where the free exchange of ideas and the exaltation of personal liberties created a society that would undoubtedly prove an irresistible temptation to corruption rather than holiness. In 1864, Pius IX pronounced on these developments by issuing a "syllabus of errors" condemning eighty "modern" ideas, among them notions such as freedom of religion and the press, and a host of other "heresies," all of which were, for Rome, embodied by the United States. Then in 1899 the pope's successor, Leo XIII, wrote to the American hierarchy condemning a tradition that had come to be called "Americanism," a vaguely defined school of thought that in Leo's mind urged Roman Catholics to compromise on church dogmas so that they could better assimilate as Americans. Leo attacked the American "passion for discussing and pouring contempt upon any possible subject, the assumed right to hold whatever opinions one pleases upon any subject and to set them forth in print to the world."

Finally in 1907, Pius X condemned all of these heresies under the label of "Modernism"—essentially a code word for "America." The Vatican was so resolute in its determination to stamp out Modernism that the campaign was dubbed a "White Terror." After 1910, priests were required to take a special anti-Modernist oath and bishops had to make sure that no one teaching in their seminaries held Modernist views.

The rise of world Communism and the role of the United States in preserving the Christian West led to a temporary truce in the Vatican's broadsides against American culture. Then John Paul II was elected in 1978, and following the fall of the Iron Curtain, a victory in which he played such a signal role, he began turning his focus to the moral failings of the West, especially the United States, warning that materialist capitalism could prove to be as dangerous to the soul as atheistic Communism.

As John Paul said during a 2002 visit to his Polish homeland, Western culture rejects "divine law and moral principles," and the blame, he said, rests in part with "the noisy propaganda of liberalism"—a direct echo of his predecessors' condemnations, and a harbinger of how the Vatican would try to deal with the sexual abuse scandal through a policy of containment: the scandal was an American problem caused by American society. As Hans Jakob Stehle, a German scholar of the Vatican has put it, "For this pope, in particular, America is the essence of secularization."

In past centuries the duel between the hierarchy and the laity centered on issues of the governance of Christendom. But at least the faith of the people was a given. More recently, though, the ascent of America—the triumph of American culture and the ideals of unfettered freedom in every sphere of human activity—has undermined the reflexive acceptance of age-old truths. Rome finally secured its hold on every aspect of church life, from the liturgy to the selection of bishops, only to find that the faithful are questioning the tenets of the faith itself. In Rome's eyes that poses an even greater threat, and the cultural antagonism born of the fear of the loss of faith is the background noise in every discussion of every aspect of the current crisis.

The gross irony of that perspective, however, is that American Catholics are the most religiously observant Catholics in modern-day Christendom, attending church and supporting the pope to a degree that has no parallel in the industrialized world, and certainly not in the bishop of Rome's own diocese. G. K. Chesterton's observation that the United States is a nation with the soul of a church persists. The Vatican's efforts to thwart reform thus became another example of the paradox that has been a hallmark of Rome's relations to its American flock: namely, that American Catholics have been the pope's greatest cheerleaders, welcoming him with open arms when he visits the United States, underwriting the bulk of Vatican operations, and maintaining an almost innocent faith in the church even as John Paul has repeatedly wagged his finger at them for their many perceived shortcomings.

The rage that American Catholics vented over the recent scandal is a direct result of their passion for their faith. American Catholics were mortified by the way their pastors had tarnished their church. They wanted the luster restored, whatever it took. While in Rome for the pope's scandal summit with the American cardinals in April, I stood in St. Peter's Basilica at the end of a papal Mass. Noticing my press pass, a Roman matron and her friends started talking to me of their surprise to find so many American journalists in town to cover the meeting, which began the next day. "You Americans take everything so seriously," said one of the women, affecting disdain for the Catholic trappings around her even as she kept a sharp eye on the Holy Father's halting progress down the nave. "Principle is so important to you in religion, in politics, in everything. For us, such a scandal wouldn't be quite so overwhelming."

She was right, of course. The crisis in Catholicism, in the United States, at least, is not a crisis of faith as much as it is a crisis about how that faith is practiced. In this battle for the soul of the church, the dedication of American Catholics has inadvertently contributed a new and volatile element, which is the burgeoning presence of the laity in liturgical roles that were once reserved exclusively to the clergy.

This development has taken place largely in the United States, and just in the past generation—the relative blink of an eye, in church terms. In centuries past, whatever threats the laity presented, priests and bishops could always feel secure in their standing because of the divine rights that accrued to them through their ordination. These berobed figures were the mediating presence for all things eternal, and the last word was always theirs. "When you grew up in that time in a strict Catholic atmosphere, it was pretty much known that anybody who wore a habit or a cloak represented Jesus on Earth. You were powerless," said Tom Paciorek, a former major-league baseball player whose courage in publicly recounting his childhood story of abuse by a priest encouraged untold other victims.

With the Second Vatican Council of the 1960s, all that changed, as did so much in that era. For the first time in more than 1,500 years, priests found themselves sharing space with lay people at the altar, the locus of Catholic worship and once the sole province of the clergy. Laymen and laywomen were now part of the machinery of holiness as they never had been before, and it happened just as the priesthood was undergoing a drastic loss of vocations that was transforming the clerical role in unprecedented ways.

The shift has been profound. But the scandal showed that many lay people think the change has not gone far enough, and that many priests and bishops think it has gone too far. Debates that were settled centuries ago, questions of the role of the laity and the power of the clergy, are suddenly new again. The focus of the debate is the altar, and the main arena is once again the United States.

Three

ALTAR EGOS

WHO RUNS THE SHOW?

At the time of the Second Vatican Council (1962–1965), the rites and formulations of the Roman Catholic Mass had remained largely unchanged from the rubrics that had been set forth by the Council of Trent (1545–1563) during the heyday of the Counter-Reformation. Latin was the ancient language of the Mass, which was presided over by the priest alone, and everyone involved in the celebration—including subdeacons, lectors, and acolytes (all of whom were technically members of minor orders)—was male and either ordained or on his way to ordination. Each had particular vestments to denote his rank in the hierarchy, and even the gender and surplices of altar boys were designed to reinforce the image of them as "junior priests." Indeed, many future clerics discovered their vocation by filling those roles.

The altar was sacred ground, and thoroughly male, and everything was geared to the exaltation of the priest's office. Lay people were spectators who processed to the altar rail, knelt in reverence, tipped their heads back, and received the holy wafer on the tongue, directly from the hands of the priest to whom the communicants would have previously confessed their sins in order to purify their souls to prepare for the reception of the Eucharist.

Fast-forward forty years, and the picture has changed dramatically.

Today, lay people read the scriptures at Mass and distribute the Host to congregants, who take the wafer in hand and feed themselves. Lay people work as pastoral associates, teach catechism classes to the next generation of American Catholics, and serve as chaplains in nursing homes and on college campuses—and more than eight in ten of these pastoral workers are women. In fact, girls are as likely to be altar servers (those priests-in-waiting of olden days) as boys, a fact of church life for years before the Vatican formally recognized it in 1994.

All of these changes can be traced directly to the new vistas opened by the Second Vatican Council's redefinition of what it means to be a lay Catholic. While Vatican II resulted in many extraordinary and visible transformations in the church, from the acceptance of the principle of religious liberty to the opening of dialogues with other religions, it was the Council's reformulation of the role of the laity that revolutionized the church internally.

For the first time, lay Catholics were presented in a positive rather than a negative light. The Council breathed new life into the Old Testament vision of the laity as "the people of God" rather than as second-class citizens in a church run by clerics. And the Council declared that lay Catholics were part of the "priesthood of all believers," a phrase that had been a governing principle of the sixteenth-century Reformation as Luther and his followers sought to throw off the shackles of clericalism.

The Council and its pronouncements galvanized ordinary Catholics with a newfound sense of empowerment, and that, combined with the sharp falloff in vocations, spurred lay people to assume an unprecedented amount of responsibility in parish life. Laymen and laywomen became ecclesial ministers, they helped the priest run the parish and oversee finances, and the reconstitution of the order of deacons after more than a millennia became a whole new avenue for laymen to join the ordained class without becoming priests. The numbers illustrate the remarkable growth in lay involvement.

A 1999 study by the National Pastoral Life Center estimated that nearly 30,000 lay ecclesial ministers worked in full- or part-time pastoral roles in more than two-thirds of the nation's 19,000 parishes, a 35 percent increase from 1992. Combined with the estimated 30,000 lay ministers currently undergoing training, lay people—mainly women—will soon outnumber the nation's 47,000 priests. Two inexorable trend lines are crossing, one going up, the other going down. Ministry is increasingly a function of the laity.

This ministerial role is different from the jobs held by lay people who make the parish machinery run, but the trend there is just as striking, and just as important to the changing equation of parish life.

In the area of parish staffing, the most dramatic change is in Catholic education, which was once the province of nuns, brothers, and priests at the high school level. According to the National Catholic Education Association, during the 1999–2000 school year, 93 percent (146,123) of the teachers and principals in Catholic elementary and secondary schools were laywomen and laymen. Just 7 percent (11,011) were religious sisters and brothers and priests—the exact reverse of the ratio when the association began to keep statistics in 1920.

Another major, and recent, change in parish governance has been the creation of a system of parish councils with lay members. The 1983 revision of the Code of Canon Law mandated that every parish have a finance council to review the congregation's budget, and it encouraged the creation of parish pastoral councils to help set ministerial priorities. Today, it is estimated that as many as three-quarters of all U.S. parishes have pastoral councils made up of a dozen or more lay people. Although the councils operate under the direction of the pastor, the very existence and scope of this system marks a striking change in the traditional understanding of the priest's role.

Nowhere is that change manifested more clearly than in the reinstitution of the order of deacons in 1968.

A distinct class of ordained ministers in the early church, the order of deacons (and deaconesses, an issue that will be dealt with in Chapter 4) effectively ceased to exist by the fourth century, except as a transitional office for seminarians about to become priests. The idea of reviving the practice was sparked by discussions among Catholics in the concentration camps in World War II. There, where the imminence of death and the democracy of dehumanization left everyone as equals before the prospect of God, lay people and priests discussed how Catholics could better live out their religion in the world, perhaps to avoid a repetition of the horror they saw around them.

This new class of ministers would not be able to perform the central Catholic sacrament of the Eucharist, but they could provide over the so-called life-cycle sacraments, such as weddings, funerals, and baptisms, as well as distributing communion that had been duly consecrated by the priest.

In the postwar years the movement to ordain lay people as deacons gained momentum in Europe, mainly in West Germany. But it never received the approval of the famously conservative Roman Curia until the Vatican II bishops, in their move to revitalize the church and redefine the role of lay people, deemed that this rank should be reinstituted after more than 1,600 years. Ironically, the impulse behind the decision was the desire to give Catholics in mission lands with few priests access to the sacramental life that is the glue of Catholicism. But it was in the West, especially in the United States, where lay people who did not feel called to the celibate priesthood enthusiastically welcomed the diaconate as the opportunity they had long been waiting for.

Since 1971, when the first class of seven deacons was ordained in the United States, the number of deacons has exploded. In 2002 there were more than 13,500 deacons in 67 percent of all parishes, with another 2,500 in various stages of training. That accounts for well over half of all deacons worldwide. Europe has about 7,500 deacons. In all of Asia there are just 142 deacons, and in Africa just 331.

But deacons exist in a new clerical gray area. While they are dismayed at being considered lay people, which happens frequently, they certainly *look* like laymen, not priests. Some 90 percent of deacons are married, with most of the rest widowed or divorced. Just 3 percent have never married. They have jobs and families, and they don't dress in black. Theirs is an office that's still being defined even as it's growing exponentially. "It's a new birth kind of thing," says Tom Welch, executive director of the National Association of Diaconate Directors. "It has been less than 35 years, and in church age, that is merely a blip. It is going to take time for the role of deacon to assert itself, and that is what we are seeing now."

The flowering of new forms of ministry becomes all the more dramatic when it is contrasted with the steep decline in vocations to the priesthood.

At the high-water mark of priestly vocations, during the Golden Age of American Catholicism in the 1950s, there was one priest for every 650 Catholics, studies show. By 1999, that ratio had nearly doubled, to one for every 1,200. According to one widely accepted survey, by 2005 the ratio could be one priest for every 2,200 Catholics, and the priests are getting older. In 1985 the median age of the American priesthood was fifty-four; in 1999 it was sixty-two, almost retirement age.

More than 3,000 (out of 19,000) U.S. parishes are without a resident pastor, and about 2,400 are forced to share a pastor. Some 13 percent of dioceses report closing parishes because there is no pastor to staff them. More than half—52 percent—say they use deacons in sacramental and liturgical ministries to compensate for the priest shortage, and nearly three-quarters say they use lay ecclesial ministers in these roles.

Bishops in many parts of the country have in recent years been warning that Catholics may have to prepare for Mass-less Sundays—an almost unthinkable development in a church where the Eucharist is the very lifeblood of faith.

Bishop Richard Hanifen of Colorado Springs, who headed the committee that produced the report, warned the 87,000 Catholics of his thirty-two-parish diocese to prepare for Sundays in which "Mass may not be possible." He called on parishes to develop guidelines for eucharistic services when no priest is available, and at the same time he asked his forty-five priests to avoid burnout by limiting themselves to fifty-hour work-weeks and to celebrating no more than three Masses on Sunday.

The upshot of these changes is that in a single generation the landscape of the Catholic liturgical and parish life has undergone a quiet revolution. But it has not been bloodless.

To be sure, the changes have created enormous new possibilities for engaging lay people in new ministries and as ordained deacons, and many priests have welcomed the changes, which have often enriched parish life and made it easier for the pastor by lifting many burdens from his shoulders.

But human nature being what it is—even more so in the village that is congregational life—many priests have been loath to yield control, while the rapid pace of change has raised expectations among Catholics that they would essentially be running the church. A retrenchment was inevitable.

On the level of daily parish life, the backlash came first through a concerted effort by church authorities to tame pastoral and finance councils. In the heady days after Vatican II, when the churches were filled with talk of grassroots reform, some councils tried to exercise power over the pastor in an echo of the trustee controversies that had afflicted the American church in earlier years. The Vatican Council had given no specific guidelines on how parish councils were to be set up, how they should operate, or who should sit on them, and as a result conflicts during what is called the "period of experimentation" were frequent and bitter.

One priest in the Mountain West told me that he had started a pastoral council after a twenty-five-year lapse. "I tried one at my first parish in 1978, and they gave me such grief I'd never done it again," he said.

Mark F. Fischer, an associate professor at St. John's Seminary in Camarillo, California, and a leading researcher of the effectiveness of parish councils, said that "when parish councils first came out there was a sense that they would be deliberative bodies where a priest would have a vote, not a veto. But there were enough horror stories about adversarial relationships that things didn't go very far."

The 1983 revision of the Code of Canon Law sought to put things aright, at least in Roman terms. In two brief canons of one paragraph each, the code dispensed with any uncertainty about parish councils' power, decreeing that they "possess a consultative vote only." And the new canons clearly downgraded the importance of such councils, declaring that a bishop can allow parishes to have lay councils only "if he judges it opportune" after consulting with his priests.

In 1997 the Vatican circumscribed the councils still further, issuing an "instruction" stating that parish councils "enjoy a consultative vote only and cannot in any way become deliberative structures." It said that the parish priest must preside at all meetings; otherwise any actions are "null and void." The instruction also clarified the threshold for membership, saying that any lay members must be "Christians of proven faith, good morals and outstanding prudence."

The heady visions of democratized parishes were over. While surveys have indicated that eight in ten parishes have pastoral councils, they often exist only on paper or to rubber-stamp the pastor's decisions. Sometimes they are simply ignored.

Parish finance councils are no better, and perhaps worse. There are no standard requirements for who should sit on these councils or how many members they should have, and church experts say that pastors often appoint two or three friends, along with perhaps a local businessperson, or even a relative. With so little oversight, cases of fiscal abuses, including outright fraud, have proliferated in recent years. "When we have problems with a priest, it is much more likely to be about money than sex," the vicar of one large diocese told me.

Given the extent of the sexual abuse scandal of 2002, that is not encouraging. But it may be true.

In July 2002, for example, while everyone's attention was focused on sexual misconduct by priests, several Brooklyn clerics came under scrutiny for financial misdeeds, including one who improperly spent $1.8 million before he was caught. In the ensuing uproar the Diocese of Brooklyn disclosed that one in five parishes had no finance councils at all, even though the councils are mandated under church law, and that ratio seems to be in line with the experience of many dioceses. Some dioceses said they do not even know whether their parishes have local financial oversight. "We have to make a real, significant effort to be transparent and accountable. It's the people's money, and we have to be very conscious of how we account for it," Msgr. John J. Bracken, who oversees finances for the Diocese of Brooklyn, told the *New York Times*.

Adding to the confusion, no one is yet clear about which council takes precedence, the finance council or the parish council. Oftentimes each group thinks its agenda—a balanced budget, say, versus a new initiative for the homeless—should be the priority. Not to mention the resentment that salaried parish staffs, the folks who run the day-to-day office operations, feel when volunteer parishioners start mapping parish strategies. The two sides can wind up being played off each other, and naturally it's the pastor, with his veto power, who is called in to referee.

In terms of liturgy, the campaign to reassert the priest's dominant role was also directed by Rome and took on the intensity of a holy war, which was not surprising in light of church history. Fiddling with the sacred identity of the priesthood gets to the core of authority in the Catholic Church. From early on in his reign, John Paul felt that it was imperative to remind lay people that their "priesthood" is of a different order from that of pastors. The laity is to spread Catholicism in the outside world, in this orthodox view, while the clergy takes care of everything inside the church.

After a 1987 Vatican Synod on the Laity that gathered bishops from around the world at the pope's behest to decide what lay people could and could not do, John Paul's conclusion was unambiguous: the church was sowing confusion by "equating the common priesthood and the ministerial priesthood" and was drifting dangerously toward a "clericalization" of the lay faithful that risked "an ecclesial structure of parallel service to that founded on the Sacrament of Orders." In other words, competition at the altar was out.

A decade later, however, the Vatican was still alarmed at the growing presence of lay people at the altar, and in 1997 Rome issued an instruction to the world's bishops that decried ongoing liturgical "abuses" and warned deacons and liturgical ministers against saying anything during Mass or wearing anything—stoles or chasubles, for example—that might be remotely construed as aping the office of the priest. The 1997 document also said it was "unlawful" for lay people to hold a position in the parish that was called "coordinator" or "moderator." The Vatican said that the rulings did not "stem from a concern to defend clerical privileges but from the need to be obedient to the will of Christ, and to respect the constitutive form which he indelibly impressed on his Church." That kind of revealed reasoning is tough to argue against.

As the fallout from the sexual abuse scandal continued throughout 2002, and the discontent with the clerical monopoly on the reins of power spread like wildfire, John Paul's warnings were repeated and sharp: no messing with a system that was divinely inspired. The church is not a political organization subject to amendment, he told a group of bishops visiting the Vatican in May 2002: "Some persons, we know, affirm that the decrease in the number of priests is the work of the Holy Spirit and that God Himself will lead the Church, making it so that the government of the lay faithful will take the place of the government of priests. Such a statement certainly does not take into account what the Council Fathers said when they sought to promote a greater involvement of the lay faithful in the Church. In their teachings, the Council Fathers simply underscored the deep complementarity between priests and the laity that the symphonic nature of the Church implies. A poor understanding of this complementarity has sometimes led to a crisis of identity and confidence among priests, and also to forms of commitment by the laity that are too clerical or too politicized."

He continued: "The commitment of lay persons is politicized when the laity is absorbed by the exercise of 'power' within the Church. That happens when the Church is not seen in terms of the 'mystery' of grace that marks her, but rather in sociological or even political terms. . . . It is the priest who, as an ordained minister and in the name of Christ, resides over the Christian community on liturgical and pastoral levels. The laity can assist him in this in many ways. But the premier place of the exercise of the lay vocation is in the world of economic, social, political and cultural realities."

No wiggle-room there. The lines were clearly drawn—or rather, reaffirmed. This hard definition of boundaries was (and had always been) critical to the church's sacred vision of itself and its model of governance. Priests were invested with holy power, the *potestas sacra;* the laity had to be content with everything else.

While Catholics may have grumbled about this imbalance of power, they were generally disinclined to do much about it. In reality, until the Boston earthquake struck, these Vatican fiats had little impact on the average churchgoer; indeed, they were probably little known beyond the relatively small circle of church functionaries and activists for whom such debates are the stuff of ecclesial cocktail chat.

Then came the crisis of 2002.

The tensions that had been rumbling, largely under the surface, burst into the open. It was one thing for the clergy to demand assent to a teaching (on birth control, for example) that lay people could ignore without feeling that their souls were in peril. It was another for the church's leadership to put their children at risk of sexual molestation by priests, and to use the laity's donations to fund agreements to keep that abuse quiet.

Catholics felt that they had been played for fools, and they were outraged. Catholics awoke to the fact that while Vatican II had produced beautiful words about the laity, the changes to the day-to-day life of the church were largely superficial, and determined as much by the institutional church's need for a new labor pool as by a commitment to a new way of being Catholic. The local church was staffed by lay people and funded by lay people, but the authority system was unchanged. The pastor—male and celibate and working alone—could still call the shots. During the year of scandal this enduring attitude manifested itself in everything from overt cases of clerical *lèse-majesté* to slips that revealed an almost subconscious disdain for the opinion of 99.9 percent of the church's members.

Catholic church leaders took to publicly chiding members of their dioceses for expressing views critical of the church. Relations grew especially testy between the hierarchy and Frank Keating, the Oklahoma governor hand-picked by the bishops to run the all-lay national board reviewing the bishops' record on dealing with sexual abuse cases. The relationship had been a rocky one from the start, but when Keating said that Catholics should avoid donating money or attending church in dioceses that weren't responding adequately to clergy abuse problems, church authorities grew irate at what they saw as a usurpation of their proper role.

"Governor Keating is not a spokesperson for the teachings and practices of our Catholic faith," Oklahoma City archbishop Eusebius Beltran said. "He happens to chair the review board. Faith practice and teachings are in no way subject to that review process." Cardinal Law's newspaper also weighed in, blasting Keating as a grandstander out of his depth in church affairs. "His well-known, no-nonsense attitude may play well in the secular media, but there are certain things that are not admissible in the Church," ran the editorial in *The Pilot*. "For a Church-appointed leader to publicly orchestrate a kind of protest that would call for the faithful to stop contributions or, worse, to boycott Sunday Mass—in effect calling all Catholics in a diocese to commit a mortal sin—is just surreal."

Keating was stunned. Whatever he had gone through in public life was nothing compared to the political shots he was taking in his new role as Catholicism's standard-bearer for the laity. "How could those who know the faith abuse those who love it, and humiliate those who are trying to save it?" he said later. "It was a real low point for me, because the issues themselves are so agonizing, and then you just hang your head in shame that you are being attacked by your own, fragged by your own troops."

Behind the immediacy and raw emotion of the confrontations were the echoes of an enduring rivalry that goes back more than a millennium, one in which the clergy has largely decided the battle terrain and the rules, and has, as a result, always emerged on the winning side. "Today, you're seeing almost the same battle over episcopal authority versus lay authority," said Thomas H. O'Connor, a historian and author of *Boston Catholics: A History of the Church and Its People*. "The laity simply feel that members of the hierarchy don't get it."

Flannery O'Connor's famous observation that Catholics are made to suffer more *from* the Church than *for* the Church seemed truer than ever.

But in America today, Catholics are the wealthiest, best-educated Catholic community that has ever existed, and they live in a veritable religious bazaar—churches and denominations of every species plus a host of non-Christian faiths and pseudo-faiths that are more than happy to welcome newcomers to their ranks. The reflexive loyalty that the clergy and hierarchy once relied upon was gone well before the 2002 sexual abuse scandal. But the scandal could not have come at a time of greater flux and vulnerability in the once compact Catholic community, widening a preexisting alienation between the laity and hierarchy and forcing the bishops to address the problem head on, or face the real prospect of churches without people in the pews.

Four

THE EXODUS

WHY THEY ARE LEAVING

T he enduring image of a dutiful Catholic flock that paid, prayed, and obeyed is outmoded today, but it was once a fairly accurate reflection of the church, as well as a source of pride to its members. During the 1950s, the ballyhooed Golden Age of churchgoing in the United States, no denomination could outdo the Catholics in levels of observance. Almost three-quarters of Catholics attended Mass once a week, about twice the rate of Protestants. A study of doctrinal adherence among Christians in the Detroit area in the fifties provided a window into the Catholic outlook: 62 percent of the Catholic respondents said that they took an orthodox view on matters of their faith, compared with 38 percent of black Protestants and 32 percent of white Protestants.

Catholics fasted on Ash Wednesday, ate fish on Fridays, confessed on Saturdays, and attended Mass on Sundays. They recited novenas at home and sent their sons to seminary in record numbers. They were born in Catholic hospitals, educated in Catholic schools, and buried in Catholic cemeteries. Catholics married each other (and in the Catholic Church), and they did not divorce or have abortions at anything close to the rate of non-Catholics. "Priests and sisters produced compliance by stressing the concept of sin, generating a great deal of guilt, and communicating the image of a stern God who punishes people for their sins," write the authors of *The Search for Common Ground: What Unites and Divides Catholic*

Americans (1997). "Not agreeing with basic Church teachings and not complying with its primary behavioral expectations were seen as mortal sins resulting in eternal damnation unless one confessed them to a priest."

Between the 1930s and the 1950s, they write, "Catholics certainly did not comply with all Church teachings, but the Church produced comparatively high levels of agreement with its doctrines and participation in most of its rituals. . . . With regard to faith and morals, unity prevailed over diversity."

That unity was transformed during the social upheaval of the 1960s. Catholic levels of churchgoing generally fell into line with those of other Americans, which dipped across the board. But because attendance had been so high, and the stakes for one's soul so dramatic—Catholics were warned that missing Mass was a mortal sin that would mean a quick trip to hell in the event of an untimely death—the drop-off was especially marked, to below 40 percent at times. The simultaneous reforms within the church also downplayed age-old traditions such as popular devotions, ecclesiastical titles, clerical garb, and ritual obligations, to the point that the priest and theologian Robert Barron, who was born in 1959, has lamented his upbringing in a "beige Catholicism" from which much of the richness had leached out. "Whether it was loved or despised, that Catholic world was, at the very least, colorful," Barron said of the era since past.

Individual confession suffered an even more precipitous decline than Mass attendance. In 1960 the three out of four Catholics who attended Mass weekly would have gone to confession at least monthly. By 1977 the number of Catholics saying they went to confession every month was down to 18 percent, and by 1995 that rate was down to just 8 percent. "Among Catholics there is an increasing tendency to think of one's faith as a direct connection between a person and God," without the intervention of a priest, said Purdue's James Davidson, a sociologist of Catholicism who conducted the research. Moreover, confession as "a heavy negative social control mechanism" has gone out of style. "They said if you are in mortal sin you could suffer eternal damnation. People were frightened into going. So the Vatican II generation stopped going as soon as they could, and they passed that on to the next generation."

The tenor of the times was a major factor in the change, and again, the reforms of Vatican II and the softening of the church's law-and-order approach to faith played a part in easing the demands of rigid compliance with the rites. So, too, did the steady increase in the education and wealth of American Catholics. But the event that really precipitated the changes and symbolized the revolution in Catholic culture came in 1968, three years after the Council ended, when Pope Paul VI, after much agonizing, released *Humanae Vitae,* the encyclical barring contraception. Overnight, untold numbers of Catholics "exited from the teaching," as the saying goes, if not from the church itself.

"Frankly, our reaction to that was a tragedy," said Mary Jo Bane, a prominent Catholic voice who moved to Harvard's Kennedy School of Government after a stint in the Clinton Administration. (She resigned from the latter in protest when Clinton signed the Welfare Reform Act of 1996.) "Those of us who were laity said, 'Well certainly this is silly and I'm not going to pay any attention to that.' And the clergy decided that 'Don't ask, don't tell' was the better part of valor. We didn't talk about it, we don't talk about it. We need to do it in our pulpits, we need to do it in our parishes, we need to bring those conversations in to the heart of our church."

Debates about the teaching itself will go on. The immediate challenge concerns the gulf that *Humanae Vitae* opened up between the institutional church and the flock. The central reality is that more than 90 percent of Catholics today say they use contraception—about the same as other groups—and apparently with little guilt. They also have abortions at the same rate as other Americans and divorce at the same rate. Yes, some people left the church altogether. But not as many as might have been expected, and nothing like the erosion that mainline Protestantism has suffered.

The real change was the fraying of the ties that bind Catholics to the church—a hollowing out of the Catholic community that left the grand structure of the 1950s church standing, but without the pillars of loyalty and adherence that had guaranteed its stability. Catholic identity used to be marked by what theorists call "identity from the outside"—an identification determined as much by their surroundings as by what they themselves were thinking. That is changing fast, and to the detriment of the unity of Catholicism.

A 1999 survey of American Catholics charting responses going back to 1987 details a steady erosion of institutional loyalty that appears to presage a further dissent from church teachings. For example, of the six elements that researchers listed as integral to Catholic identity, the "teaching authority claimed by the Vatican" was last on the list in 1999, with just 42 percent of Catholics agreeing it was "very important." Similarly, the number of Catholics who said you can be a good Catholic without going to church every Sunday rose from 70 percent in 1987 to 77 percent in 1999, and those who said you didn't need your marriage approved by the church jumped from 51 to 68 percent. But perhaps the most startling jump was the number of respondents who said you can be a good Catholic and ignore the church's teaching on abortion. That figure went from 39 percent in 1987 to 53 percent in 1999. The majority of Americans who support abortion rights might consider that a positive trend, but this detachment from church teaching has a flipside that they might not appreciate as much: in 1999 well over half of Catholics—56 percent—said you could be a good Catholic without donating time or money to help the poor. That was a sharp rise from 44 percent in 1987, and doesn't bode well for the rich tradition of Catholic social teaching.

The same trend toward detachment was reflected in a question on who has final moral authority, church leaders or the individual. Across the board, on issues ranging from homosexuality to sex outside of marriage to remarrying without an annulment, Catholics have steadily shifted away from giving that power to a cleric and are instead claiming it for themselves.

This phenomenon is often called "defecting in place," which means that Catholics stay Catholic but do not behave or believe the way the hierarchy, or church teachings (to whatever degree the two overlap), would like. A lot of conservative church leaders today would just as soon the dissenters defect for real. That is not a traditionally Catholic attitude, but the conservatives may get what they want. Polls are registering a steady decline in the number of those who say they "would never leave the church," from 64 percent in 1987 to 61 percent in 1993 and down to 57 percent in 1999. (And that last figure was recorded three years before the worst scandal in the church's history.)

Within the Catholic population three groups appear especially vulnerable to alienation: women, Latinos, and young people. They could be seen as the tripod on which the future of American Catholicism rests. Remove any of them, and the church will be in serious trouble.

• • •

While thousands of newly minted reformers debated the future of the Catholic Church inside a Boston convention hall, Siobhan Carroll stood in the corridor outside and quietly rocked that future in her arms. It was the summer of 2002, and Carroll had traveled from Rhode Island with her husband and three children to attend the national gathering of the nascent lay-led reform group Voice of the Faithful. Carroll's husband was still inside the hall discussing the details of reform and arguing about how that reform might be accomplished. Siobhan Carroll was taking a break from the debate, along with her kids. She was interested in the event, but her concerns were more familial. The couple have three children; at the time of the clergy scandals the oldest was seven, the middle child was five, and Siobhan Carroll was comforting their youngest, six-month-old Joe, who wasn't quite as keen on the esoterica of ecclesiology as his dad.

"My daughter just had her First Communion, and it got me thinking about it all," Carroll said, holding the infant in one arm and pushing a stroller with her free hand. "I figured if we are going to pass on the faith we'd better make sure it is a strong faith. I want to fix it before I pass it on."

A central paradox of Catholic life throughout history is that women have always been the church's greatest strength even as they have been pushed to the sidelines in matters of authority. Throughout the centuries an all-male hierarchy formulated the teachings, namely on sexuality, that governed Catholic women's most intimate life decisions, and those women continued to take their kids to church, led them in prayers at home, and encouraged their sons to go into the priesthood and their daughters to enter religious life. The nuns who entered those orders in droves also educated Catholic children in the basics of their faith, and in most other topics as well, and they cooked and cleaned for "Father" while serving the poor and nursing the sick.

While the religious orders suffered a steep decline in vocations in recent decades, Catholic laywomen remained deeply connected to the church through their families and social circles, and carried on their role as the chief transmitters of the Catholic faith from generation to generation. Across the board, women are much more likely than men to say religion is important to them (68 percent to 48 percent, according to a 2002 Gallup poll). They attend church with greater frequency, the surveys show, follow the rules more closely, read the Bible more regularly, and are more likely than men to be engaged at every level with their faith and in their local church. Women often have a good friend in their parish, whereas men rarely do, and women say they are more likely to *act* religiously because of their faith—to be forgiving and to offer words of kindness. Women are in effect the chief spiritual leader of what Catholic teaching likes to call "the domestic church"—the home. Indeed, it has often been argued that religion is "women's work," except that when it comes to the institutional authority, men still run the show.

But today, in the wake of scandal and in the midst of crisis, the logic of that paradox is beginning to wear thin, and the greatest strength of Catholicism—the dependable loyalty of Catholic women—may also be the church's weakest link. If the Catholic Church loses its female members, then the Catholic Church will lose the next generation, and who knows how many beyond that.

"I am doing this because I have teenage sons," Nan Alphen of Westford, Massachusetts, a church-going mother and CCD teacher told me during a break in the Voice of the Faithful meeting. "I want to show them that it's worth the fight. It may not be. But we've got to try. We have had many family discussions about why we're still here"—in the Catholic Church. "We can go anywhere. I don't know what we'll do next. I say let's stick with this fight and see what happens. None of us wants to leave the Catholic Church. But we are not afraid to leave the Catholic Church."

Even that hint of equivocation represents an enormous change in Catholic attitudes, especially among Catholic women who have always remained most steadfast in the faith. The trend lines are clear, and the data should give church leaders pause.

In 1987, for example, 59 percent of Catholic women said church was "among the most important parts of my life." In 1999 that figure was down to 48 percent for women, according to *American Catholics: Gender, Generation, and Commitment,* a book that reviewed surveys from 1987, 1993, and 1999 to chart the erosion of loyalties. Similarly, more than half of Catholic women in 1987 said they attended Mass once a week or more, a figure that dropped to 43 percent in 1999. (By way of contrast, the Mass attendance rate for men went from 35 percent to 31 percent.) More ominously, 68 percent of Catholic women said in 1987 that they would never leave the church. That dropped to 65 percent in 1993, and 56 percent in

1999. The church may be reaching a tipping point when it comes to the loyalty of its most reliable core membership.

"This flash point cannot be overlooked," write the book's authors. "Our data, along with data from other research, clearly indicate . . . that women's attachment to the Church is declining. This decline is the result of many forces in society as well as in the Church, including women's perception that their gifts are often overutilized but undervalued. . . . Unless leaders listen to women's concerns and address the conditions underlying them, the risk will be that women's alienation from the Church will turn to indifference and even lower levels of participation."

Nurturing the faith as mothers and worshipers is only one aspect of the Catholic woman's role, however. Active participation in the work of the church is another. That is a contemporary development and one that also holds both promise and peril for modern Catholicism.

On the promising side of the ledger, the explosion of lay ministries detailed earlier (in Chapter 3) has largely been the story of laywomen taking on roles that had once been reserved to nuns or even priests. Of the 35,000 lay ministers currently working in parishes, some 80 percent are women, and their numbers are booming. Also on the rise is an even more remarkable phenomenon, that of laywomen who serve as "pastoral leaders" of the growing numbers of priestless parishes.

In Kosciusko, Mississippi, for example, Barbara Sturbaum has led two priestless parishes in the Jackson diocese since the last priest in the area retired in 1987. Sturbaum visits the sick and prepares couples for marriage, and she balances the parishes' books and sees that the churches are ready when a circuit-riding priest can come along to celebrate the sacraments that she cannot. She is a laywoman with a doctorate in zoology and a master's in theology who earns a nun's salary of less than $20,000 a year.

And in January 2003, the Archdiocese of Baltimore named a former health-care executive and married laywomen, Anne Buening, to lead St. Clement I parish in Lansdowne. It was a first in the history of the nation's oldest diocese, and probably the first of many, as the archdiocese predicts its clergy shortage will worsen and the need for women like Buening will grow.

The numbers bear out the forecasts. In 1965 there were 549 parishes in the United States without a resident priest, and in 2002 the figure was more than 3,000. While most of those parishes are headed by a nonresident priest, lay people, among them many women, are running hundreds of parishes (the figure was 313 in 2001) that have no priest at all.

"Everyone knows that most Catholic parishes in this country would have to close up tomorrow if it weren't for women," said Luke Timothy Johnson, the Emory University New Testament historian and Catholic writer. "I mean this in the very specific sense that women are carrying out most of the work of ministry in many if not most parishes in this country."

Yet Johnson also noted that the growing numbers of Catholic women in ministerial roles has fueled the debate over perhaps the most contentious issue in the Catholic Church, namely the ban on ordaining women as priests. Women have gained "access to influence," as the authors of *Gender, Generation, and Commitment* write, but they have not achieved "access to authority," which remains vested in the ordained classes. The Vatican says the question is off-limits, even for discussion. But the clergy sex scandal served to spotlight the issue once again, as reform groups ratcheted up their lobbying efforts to allow women to serve at the altar.

Would the ordination of women resolve the crisis in Catholicism? Advocates of women's ordination argue that women would have been less inclined to be co-opted by the clerical culture that covered up for molesters, and they point to many instances of nuns who complained to their bishop about abusive priests, only to be rebuffed. Likewise, proponents of women priests point to female whistleblowers such as Colleen Rowley, the FBI agent who tried to pursue leads on the 9/11 terrorists before the attacks, and Sherron Watkins, the Enron executive who warned of the impending collapse, as further evidence that the church needs women in decision-making positions.

Such "pragmatic" arguments have their appeal, but also their limitations. The best of these arguments for women priests is that women simply do not sexually abuse children at anything like the rate men do. On the other hand, men do not have a monopoly on vice, and women in power can behave just as badly in other areas as charter members of the old boy's club can.

But the chief problem with putting the question of women's ordination front and center right now is that it would only divide the church further just when the fissures need to be bridged, not widened. The 1999 figures set forth in the *Gender, Generation, and Commitment* book show that while American Catholics are open to the idea of ordaining women, they are split on taking such a momentous step. Indeed, just over half of American Catholics—53 percent—said they would favor the ordination of married women, while the figure rose to 62 percent if the female priest vowed to be celibate. Surprisingly, the gender differential on this gender-loaded issue was minimal. About 55 percent of women said they favored ordaining married women, only slightly higher than the 52 percent of men who favored that move.

Clearly, the church is not ready to decide the issue, and again, American Catholics must take into account the universality of Catholicism when pondering such a historic change. While Catholics in America and Europe might be ready for a woman at the altar, Catholics in Latin America, Africa, and Asia are far less open to the idea. Not only are there huge cultural differences between the industrialized West and other nations, but church leaders in the developing world also argue that issues of female infanticide, female genital mutilation, wife-burning and many other pressing human rights questions tend to push aside debates over the theology of a unigendered priesthood. In this issue of women's ordination, a "local option" solution would be tantamount to schism, and that would vitiate the very goal of greater *communio* that Catholic women want to promote.

Moreover, the unparalleled import of the women's ordination is such that the church should be of one mind, or as close to an accord as possible, before making such a transformation. The ordination of women is an unprecedented step that would require a fundamental rethinking of the church's historic understanding of itself. It is a worthy debate, but it is also one that goes beyond mere questions of policy.

What is important at this point is that the issue be discussed openly. While American Catholics are not in agreement on having women at the altar, their opinions are clearly moving in the direction of accepting women as priests. In 1974, according to the Gallup Poll, just 29 percent of American Catholics favored ordaining women, a number that jumped to 40 percent in 1979 and then 50 percent in 1985. While the increase has leveled off somewhat, the rate is still trending upward, and the openness of younger Catholics to ordaining women as priests indicates the number will go higher in the future.

If the arguments against women's ordination are valid (and have the support of the Holy Spirit, who preserves the church from error), then the ban will hold. If, on the other hand, such a revolutionary step is in the offing, then the church must find a way forward *together* into that new era. For those who believe women's ordination is inevitable, the timelines for its acceptance range from the next generation to the next millennium—another indicator of how little anyone really knows about the church's collective mind on this issue. But the sequence of possible events is generally accepted: first the church will endorse a married *male* priesthood, and then it would proceed to open the ranks of the clergy to women.

For all of the official edicts and opinions against women's ordination, especially in recent years, that scenario is not entirely out of bounds. Along with the restoration of the diaconate for men in the wake of the Second Vatican Council came a debate over whether women could be allowed—*ordained*—into that order. While the doctrinally conservative papacy of John Paul II would have been expected to slam the door on such an argument, the Vatican in fact issued a statement in October 2002 indicating that aspects of the question were still up in the air. A commission of Vatican experts agreed that deaconesses existed in the early church (a historical certainty that it would have taken some moxie to argue away) but said they were not equivalent to male deacons of the day. That in itself was a significant concession to the possibility that the church will one day ordain deaconesses. But more important were the statements from some commission members emphasizing, in the words of one theologian, that the commission was allowing for a "future development" in thinking. The question is unsettled, and the ferment will keep alive the discussion over the role of women in the church.

Such discussions, along with honest dialogue on the whole range of questions affecting women, from contraception to paternalism, are vital to renewing the historical bond between women and the church and ensuring a vital future for Catholicism.

The issue underlying every aspect of the role of women in the church, be it the ordination of women priests or the attachment of Catholic mothers to their parish, is the problem of an alienation from the wider church polity. While Catholic women are more "religious" in their practice of religion than men, they are also significantly less likely to look to the institutional church's leaders as "the locus of moral authority." As the authors of *Gender, Generation, and Commitment* found, less than 25 percent of women said they would look principally to church leaders for guidance on moral questions regarding contraception, abortion, divorce, homosexuality, and premarital sex. For men the figure was 35 percent—not very good for the bishops, but significantly higher than the level for women.

Catholic women, in their great devotion to the church and their simultaneous alienation from it, represent the essence of the crisis in the Catholic laity. Surely, Catholic women have their particular burdens under church teaching and in dealing with an all-male hierarchy that has not done nearly enough in recognizing their talents or giving them a place at the table of church governance. But their alienation from the institutional church, even as they remain attached to the local parish, goes to the heart of the challenge facing the church today in regard to all lay people. If Catholic women—like other lay people—continue to drift away from the larger church, it will represent a grave erosion in the universal communion and unity that is the hallmark of Catholicism. Moreover, if they cannot connect with the larger Catholic community, it is unlikely they will remain connected much longer to the local Catholic community.

In this trend, Catholic women are, in a sense, just like other Catholics, only more so. And that should stand as a powerful warning to the church leadership.

Whatever the travails of the post–Vatican II years, whatever the increasingly vocal opposition to traditional Catholic teachings, the hierarchy has always been able to take comfort in the steadily rising numbers of Catholics in the United States. Since the end of the nineteenth century Catholics have been far and away the nation's largest denomination, and as fragmentation and decline struck mainline Protestantism after the 1960s, cutting their numbers in half in many cases, the Catholic Church continued to grow in absolute terms. In 1970 there were 48 million Catholics; in 1980 there were 50 million; in 1990 the figure was 59; and at the time of the scandal it was 65 million and counting, a spike that was the exact inverse of the decline in other denominations.

What those figures do not show, however, is that Hispanic immigration and high birthrates in the Latino community have been responsible for more than 70 percent of the church's growth over the past forty years, a trend that camouflages much of the domestic disaffection with the church. Solid estimates of what slice of the U.S. church is Hispanic are notoriously fungible, but educated guesses range from 17 percent to more than one-third, and all agree that the number is destined to rise. The American Catholic Church is rapidly becoming a Latin American church.

But there is another trend that reveals a serious weakness not shown in these numbers: namely, that a growing number of these Latinos, while nominally Catholic due to their baptismal certificate, are defecting to evangelical churches and other faiths—an exodus of as many as 600,000 per year. That is in addition to the fact that evangelical Christianity, bolstered by funding and preaching from North American Protestant missionaries, is making great inroads into traditionally Catholic countries in Latin America. Many Hispanics who arrive in the United States have already left the Catholic Church behind.

(In an ominous sign of the scandal's collateral damage, at their Dallas meeting the bishops had to table discussion of a program to stanch the loss of so many Hispanic Catholics so that they could focus exclusively on the abuse crisis.)

A major study released in 2002, "Hispanic Churches in American Public Life," produced the clearest picture yet of the situation. While the study showed that the percentage of Latinos who are Catholic has remained fairly steady—71 percent of the country's 35.4 million Hispanics were Catholic in 2002, about the same as in 1988—that stability was maintained by an influx of Latino Catholic immigrants. The worrying trend is that over the course of three generations, the survey found, the rate of Protestants in the American Hispanic population increased from 18 percent to 32 percent while the share of Catholics declined from 74 to 59 percent. In other words, while 74 percent of first generation Latinos are Catholic, that drops to 72 percent among their children, and 62 percent among their grandchildren, the third generation. The responses in the survey indicated that Hispanics remain very observant and find support in their church. But unlike previous generations of immigrants, that church doesn't have to be Catholic. "It's democracy in America. People have choices," said Olga Villa Parra, former executive director of the Midwest Hispanic Catholic Commission. "It runs all the way across, from the voting booth to the churches we select."

Equally worrisome for Catholic leaders is that many Latinos are not just defecting to non-Catholic churches. Many are simply dropping out of religious life altogether. Findings from the American Religious Identification Survey 2001 showed that the number of Hispanics who declared no religious affiliation more than doubled from 1990 to 2000, from 6 percent to 13 percent, from 926,000 to 2.9 million. That shift could also be a canary in the mine for the wider church as surveys indicate lay Catholics across the board are growing dissatisfied with their church but are finding few appealing alternatives.

Catholic efforts to attract and retain Hispanics face several obstacles.

One is that there are few Spanish-speaking priests among an already shrinking pool of priests, and the rising numbers of Hispanic Catholics are not translating into vocations. In 1999 there was just one Latino priest for every 10,000 Latino parishioners, according to one study; that compares to one priest per 1,200 American Catholics overall. The priest shortage is even worse in many Latin American countries, so borrowing priests from other nations is difficult for American bishops (many of whom have admirably learned good Spanish at a fairly late age). In addition, evangelical Protestantism and other denominations can set up small, storefront churches quickly and minister to immigrant needs rapidly without the long-term planning and top-down approval process the Catholic system requires.

Within the Catholic Church, moreover, Latinos often find themselves with no voice in the institutional structure, and isolated within the dominant white European Catholic community. A report by the bishops issued in 2000 found that Latinos worship in "separate and unequal settings" as compared to Anglo Catholics, and that non-Latinos often control central functions in parishes where Latinos make up the majority of the congregation.

The fallout from these attitudes is beginning to be felt. A 1999 survey showed that Latino Catholics are less likely to be members of a parish than Anglo Catholics, are more likely to support ordaining women as priests, and are even less likely than Anglo Catholics to give the church the final word on moral decisions. All of these factors are adding up to what Andrew Greeley has called "the worst defection in the history of the Catholic Church in the United States. . . . The loss is catastrophic. There is no reason to believe that it will not get worse."

The outlook is equally problematic when it comes to young Catholics of every ethnicity.

As he looked out over the muddy, rain-soaked airfield outside Toronto, the frail, hunched figure in brilliant vestments struggled against the ravages of Parkinson's disease and the weight of public opinion to find words that might convince the thousands of young Catholics arrayed before him to stay in the church. Pope John Paul had traveled from Rome to preside over one of his favorite events, World Youth Day, which is a kind of Catholic jamboree that is held every two years at a different venue around the world. Usually it is a grand party that the pontiff enjoys immensely. But this year World Youth Day could not have come at a worse time, after months of sordid stories about priests who sexually abused young people much like the young Catholics who normally come to this event. It showed in the turnout.

In Paris in 1998 close to one million young people came to the grand closing Mass, and in Rome in 2000 there were an astounding two million teens and young adults. In the year of the scandal, however, just 200,000 young people registered to come. Organizers chalked it up to a weakening economy and the hangover of fear after 9/11. But they also conceded, as one put it, that the sex scandals "did take the wind out of our sails." Not to mention their wallets—the Canadian church was left with a $30 million deficit after the poorly attended event.

The failing health of the once-vital pontiff did not bode well for his ability to reverse the harm done, and on top of it all, overnight downpours had left the young campers who did come drenched when they awoke for the morning celebration. In spite of the weather and his frailty—or perhaps because of it—John Paul eventually connected with the crowd, as he always seems to do, this time by personally identifying with their "deep sense of sadness and shame" over the scandal. The few words were enough to break the tension, and the young people interrupted the pope with rousing applause. "We needed to hear this from him," said Barb Legere, a forty-year-old youth ministry coordinator who led a group from Spencerport, New York. "To ignore it would be an awful thing. If you have something you're ashamed of in your family and the head of the family won't talk about it, it makes the shame bigger."

The pope's visit was considered a success, in the end, but it did not alter the hard truth that Catholicism's next generation is a question mark for the church. That was the case before the scandal, and it is even more so now. "For people over 40 the defining event of the Catholic Church was Vatican II. For people under 40 it is now the sex abuse crisis," said Notre Dame historian John T. McGreevy.

This is a generation for whom a ban on contraception is as antiquated as the Latin of *Humanae Vitae.* Tom Beaudoin, a theology professor at Boston College and a thirty-something Catholic who has chronicled the circuitous pilgrimage of his generation in books such as *Virtual Faith: The Irreverent Spiritual Quest of Generation X,* said the impact of the sex scandal is ominous. "Our Catholic Watergate," he called it, an event that will color the way an entire generation of Catholics will view the institutional church. To younger Catholics, Beaudoin said, "The post–Vatican II church is often a place of self-deception, abusive silence, and double-talk, especially about sexuality and about power. . . . We know now that our Church can cover up its spiritual deficits as well as World-Com or Enron can cover up their economic losses."

A mistrust of institutions is nothing new for young people, especially in the generation since Watergate. But it is especially perilous for a faith that is defined by its institutional face. "If you love Jesus, love the church," the pope told the worshipers in Toronto. Increasingly, young Catholics do not equate the two—certainly not like their parents, much less their grandparents, did. And this diffidence is not confined to young Catholics who are affecting the stylish slouch of Grunge-era rebellion. Rather, it is common among teens such as Andrew Griffin, a sturdy-looking guy with a brush-cut who was part of the Boston group that attended World Youth Day with Cardinal Law. "I think of my faith as something more independent of the church. I see them as two separate entities," Griffin told me. "The church is part of my faith, but it doesn't control what I think."

Griffin was saying that as an endorsement of Catholicism. But not his mother's Catholicism. Nor Cardinal Law's. Nor the Holy Father's. As Beaudoin has written: "This crisis is moving young Catholics closer to a more classically Protestant understanding of the church as deeply sinful, as ever in need of reform and, most important, as ultimately something to be set aside if it interrupts one's relationship to God."

How worried should the pope be?

In their 2001 book, *Young Adult Catholics: Religion in the Culture of Choice*, authors Dean Hoge, William Dinges, Mary Johnson, and Juan L. Gonzalez Jr. note that young adult Catholics, those aged twenty to thirty-nine, now constitute nearly 40 percent of the Catholic population of the United States, and they are a disproportionately large segment of the 20 million or so—about one-third—of Catholics who are effectively disconnected from the church. Some 30 to 40 percent of young Catholics have never been confirmed—the sacramental sealing of one's commitment to the church as an early teen—and that number rises to 60 to 70 percent among Latinos. Just 10 percent of the younger generation were defined as "core" Catholics who accepted almost all of the Vatican's pronouncements on the faith, with the others scattered across the vast spectrum of pick-and-choose "cafeteria" Catholicism. "The demise of religious traditions is about the loss of the young, not the death of the old," the authors say.

Among their other findings:

Just 39 percent of post–Vatican II Catholics (eighteen to thirty-eight years old) identify the church as "among the most important parts of life," as opposed to 66 percent of pre-Council Catholics; 27 percent attend Mass weekly as opposed to 42 percent of those who came of age during the Council period (thirty-nine to fifty-eight years old), or the pre-Council Catholics over fifty-nine, two-thirds of whom attend services weekly. Nearly half of young Catholics said they would never leave the church, but that number was 60 percent among their parents' generation and 76 percent among their grandparents'. They are less likely to consider obedience to church moral teachings as central to the faith, and they are even more likely than the older generation to accept homosexuals in the church and to support married and women priests.

They tend to disagree with the idea of Catholicism as "the one true church," and half of them agree that "all the great religions of the world are true and good."

Most intriguing, however, was a finding that came out of follow-up interviews: young Catholics have not learned to distinguish between "core" and "periphery" teachings. For example, they view the sacraments and commitment to the poor as important Catholic qualities, whereas teachings on abortion, the death penalty, and the right to unionize rank low. "The earlier generation found a way to dissent and stay. But the young today are not clear about how to think about essentials and nonessentials," the authors write.

These developments are key to understanding not just the membership of the church but its internal dynamic—the intangible qualities that will determine the church's future vitality and viability. As researchers John C. Cusick and Katherine F. DeVries have noted, the backbone of Catholic life, from parishes to the pulpit to fraternal organizations, has always been made up of people twenty-five to forty-five years old, the moms and dads with kids. "On most levels of the church today, the leadership is still held by that same group—not the same age group, but the same people now twenty to thirty years older."

In other words, younger Catholics are not involved in the structures of the church, and consequently they feel they have no voice and no stake. The Vatican II generation that was so motivated by the Council's reforms is still drawn by those visions. Not so for younger Catholics. The divide is comparable to the one in the African-American community over civil rights. Young blacks take the gains for granted and are not about to march in the streets for change, an attitude that leaves civil rights veterans aghast.

"Let's be honest and admit that most young Catholics, even into our 30s, are only semipracticing or nonpracticing," Beaudoin said. "That does not mean that they have abandoned God or been abandoned by God. How many of us know young adults who are waiting for a credible, believable church, a church that addresses real life issues, a church that treats us like adults, that takes our cultures seriously, a church that feeds us spiritually, that asks for our gifts."

The church can't afford to do otherwise. In America's postmodern world of hyper-stimulation, flavor-of-the-day faiths and Christianity as entertainment—"Jesus in Disneyland," it has been called—the allegiance of young people is a fickle thing. Young people may call themselves Catholic, but theirs is a "self-constructed" identity drawing more from the "blended faith" available in the American marketplace than from the ancient Catholic tradition. Beaudoin calls modern culture "a form of 'surrogate' clergy'"—where the likes of film director Kevin Smith, whose sensibility is both palpably Catholic and scathingly irreverent (as in, for example, *Dogma*), are religious touchstones as much as parish priests are.

There are caveats to the "lost generation" scenario. As sociologists have documented, young people are forever drifting away from the church, no matter what its current state. Getting up Sunday morning is hard, and even harder when it's something your parents make you do. Young adults often drift back, however, when faced with the prospect of marriage, or raising children, or facing a mortality they would never have considered a real threat when they were eternal twenty-somethings.

Timing can help. Sunday evening young adult Masses are gaining popularity. One Los Angeles parish has Mass at 10 P.M. on Sunday night, and it's packed. Popular Theology-on-Tap programs, in which Catholic young people gather in a pub to meet each other, have a beer, and listen to a church-approved speaker (Cardinal Theodore McCarrick is an SRO favorite at the program held at a Georgetown bar), are sprouting up around the country.

In addition, there is a small but significant trend toward what David E. Nantais, a thirty-one-year-old Jesuit (yes, they still come that young) calls "Retro-Catholicism"—a taste for bits of discarded Catholic culture that young people find comforting and even a bit cool, like vintage clothing and furniture. Others, such as the "New Faithful" of *St. Louis Post-Dispatch* reporter Colleen Carroll's 2002 book of the same title, are a small but potent cohort of young adults attracted to Christian orthodoxy of any stripe as a comforting port in a storm of uncertainty.

But there are not nearly enough such initiatives, and there is not enough creativity in carrying them out. As Nantais lamented in *America* magazine, "For the most part, Catholic catechesis has been sub-par since Vatican II. A friend of mine wryly commented that the religion classes for our generation, even in Catholic schools, consisted of, 'Jesus loves you; now draw a rainbow.'. . . How can 21-year-olds be expected to embrace their Catholicism as adults if they have no way of distinguishing themselves as part of a unique spiritual community? In that case, their only choice is between fundamentalism, which provides a unique identity with attractive black-and-white answers to their legitimate quandaries, and ditching the 'religion thing' altogether for their own individual brand of spirituality."

This is a gimlet-eyed generation of Catholic Holden Caulfields who won't be sold on pat answers to complex problems. "Young adults know a dysfunctional family when we see one," Beaudoin says. "We know that silence has helped cause this Catholic Watergate and only honesty, frank discussion, a truly adult church, and changing our Catholic family dynamics will get us out of it."

The most singular finding amid the flux, however, is that young Catholics do stay connected, however tenuously. No doubt, they cannot be taken for granted, and if Beaudoin's warning is not heeded, the hierarchy could wake up in a decade to find that it's too late to recapture the interest or loyalty of the young.

But as the authors of *Young Adult Catholics* note, nine in ten confirmed Catholics still identify themselves as Catholic by age thirty—a defection rate that other faiths would envy: "Catholics have a 'glue' that Protestants do not have. They see Catholicism as a basic part of their being. In spite of beliefs and practices that are sometimes divergent, they remain 'Catholic,'" the authors say. The respondents in the surveys said that they couldn't see being anything but Catholic, that "there is something very special about being Catholic that you can't find in other religions."

This dogged persistence of Catholic identity, in the face of centuries of tensions with priests and bishops, sharp disagreements with church teachings, and scandals culminating in this latest, greatest betrayal of the flock, is largely a mystery.

Why don't the faithful just leave? That question was asked again and again throughout 2002. But they don't. Catholic identity is a countervailing, centripetal force that is hard for Catholics themselves to quantify, and harder for non-Catholics to understand. It is the "dark matter" that makes up the bulk of the Catholic universe but cannot be measured or detected. Research is ambiguous about its source and contradictory about its impact. But appreciating its weight and gravity is crucial to understanding the future course of the post-scandal church.

If Catholics stay on their own terms, rather than the hierarchy's, it could mean trouble for the bishops. It could also mean a Catholic Church that looks different from anything that has gone before.

Five

THE MYSTERY OF CATHOLIC IDENTITY

WHY THEY WILL STAY

On a midsummer Sunday morning in Boston, in front of Holy Cross Cathedral, the usual preparations for Mass were unfolding. As parents wheeled strollers toward the massive doors of the great church, protesters bearing banners and bullhorns formed a noisy phalanx, as they had for months, ever since the scandal erupted from this cathedral and spilled outward, inundating every diocese and parish in the nation. Nowhere, however, had the villainy been as widespread, the anger as deep, and the protests as persistent—and all of it focused on the man that Massachusetts Catholics believed to bear the greatest responsibility for the abuses. "Cardinal Law of Boston is a liar and a coward!" Steve Lewis, a clergy abuse victim from Lynn, Massachusetts, shouted through a megaphone, in a word-for-word replay of the sloganeering he'd been doing every Sunday. "He's a reprobate, a charlatan, and a hypocrite. . . . As you go in there, hold on to your kids," he warned the Mass-goers. "Cardinal Law will screw your children!"

A few steps away, Cynthia Scott winced at the language, but her sentiments were on the same track. Scott is a mother of three, one of them a catechism teacher, and she is a grandmother of seven. "All baptized in the church," she said proudly. She was carrying a long banner with her husband that demanded Cardinal Law's resignation: "A disgrace to good Catholics," it read.

Cynthia Scott and her husband were regulars at these protests, and they had been active in other church reform groups, such as Call to Action, for nearly fifteen years before the latest crisis. The abuse scandal had not hit their own family members, but they had spoken to many victims, and they were outraged at the systematic abuse of power that they felt lay behind the priestly sins. But whenever Scott and her husband get angry at their church, they never get up and go. "Once you get over the initial fear that the church will say this, or the church will say that, or maybe I'm committing a mortal sin, then you see that the church is a good place to be. It just needs some reform. So you decide to stay and fight."

Inside the cathedral, the testimony to that stubbornness grew even more compelling. As lines formed for communion, several protesters left their placards outside and walked up the nave, waiting patiently to take the Host from the hands of the man that one of them, victim Arthur Austin, had called "a criminal, a murder of children, . . . an affront to Jesus Christ." Austin was wearing a "Reject Cardinal Law" button, and he was anticipating a rebuke from the cardinal. But when Law saw Austin, the cardinal recognized him and said, "Pray for me."

Austin later said, "It was a very healing moment because it was not the archbishop or the cardinal who spoke to me. It was my brother, Bernie, who responded to me. I touched him. I touched him literally and I touched him figuratively. And he was able to receive that. That's the radical grace of God in the world."

To many Americans, this scene would have been plainly confounding, as were the surveys throughout the year that consistently showed that the scandal had not sparked a massive exodus from the Catholic Church. Polls showed Mass attendance held fairly steady throughout the year, and with the exception of a few scandal-plagued dioceses, namely Boston, parishioners were not withholding their donations from the collection plate in anger. According to an April 2002 ABC News/BeliefNet poll, 11 percent of American Catholics said they may leave the church in the next few years, but a similar ABC poll in 1987 showed 6 percent of Catholics said there was a chance they could leave the church. Even at the height of the worst scandal in the church's history, the degree of flux was well within the range of dissatisfaction in any denomination, and better than most.

Explanations are required, not only for curiosity's sake, but because the answers are central to understanding the forces that are shaping contemporary Catholicism in this era of crisis. If the hierarchy can take the compliant membership for granted, they would seem to have little to compel them to change their ways. A flock of dissidents who refuse to leave, however, would pose a different set of problems.

So why do Catholics stay?

The question itself rankles Catholics, because it is posed so often, even in balmier times, and because of the implication that any well-educated, thinking person would leave as a matter of course. The feminist theologian Rosemary Radford Ruether, who is on the board of Catholics for a Free Choice (an abortion-rights group) and who famously once said that she had as much right to be a Catholic as the pope, recalled how taken aback she was when a Christian scholar assailed her during a break in an interfaith dialogue conference: "I don't see how any moral human being can be a Catholic!" the scholar declared. Helen Alvaré, a leading proponent of the church's teaching against abortion (and Ruether's polar opposite on the spectrum of Catholic politics), has endured the same experience—the attitude, she says, that "the Catholic part of you has disabled the thinking part of you."

It is an attitude that reflects the hoary view that Catholicism is incompatible with the basic American precepts of democracy, individualism, and freedom of conscience, and that the church demands such lockstep assent to its every canon that it would be impossible for any "thinking person" to stay. The question persists to the extent that after the success of his extended critique in *Papal Sin,* Garry Wills was moved to write a 390-page sequel, *Why I Am a Catholic,* to explain the apparent contradiction.

The late novelist Walker Percy had a pithier response when asked, as he often was, why he remained a Catholic: "What else is there?" Percy, writing in a 1998 collection of essays called *Why I Am Still a Catholic,* called that his "smart-mouthed answer."

Actually, there are plenty of options. America has always been a marketplace of faith, and never more so than at the turn of the third millennium. In her 1995 book, *Re-Discovering the Sacred,* author Phyllis Tickle counts some 2,500 distinct forms of Christianity in America, and mapping the theological genome has gotten only more complex since then. Every other religion under the sun seems to have taken root in the United States, and conversion is practically a cottage industry, with Jew-

Bu's (Jewish Buddhists) and celebrity Scientologists (Cruise and Travolta, to name just two) and Episcopalians-turned-evangelicals who get elected president. Religion is out, spirituality is in, and that has spelled disaster for the brand loyalty that was once the defining characteristic of the nation's religious landscape.

In 1958, for example, just four out of every hundred Americans had left the denomination in which they were raised. Today, more than one-third of American Christians identify with a church other than the one they were raised in, 60 percent have spouses from other denominations, and since 1991 the number of Americans expressing no religious preference has doubled from 7 to 14 percent. This trend has steadily eroded the bedrock denominations of the Protestant establishment, such as Lutherans, Methodists, Presbyterians, and Episcopalians, who have continued to see their rolls shrink.

"Religion has become a bit of a dirty word. It sounds dead, old-fashioned, archaic," said pollster George Gallup Jr. who has been tracking faith trends for decades. "Spirituality is a safer word. If you can say you are spiritual you don't have to make a commitment. For a lot of people it's a way out." Hence America's fascination with the panoply of New Age ideas and spiritualist accoutrements, such as crystals, angels, and channeling. Spirituality is experiential, individualized, psychologized, and focused on achieving peace of mind, washboard abs, or a fat bank account.

The appeal of a protean spirituality is especially strong among the aging Baby Boomers—the "generation of seekers," as the sociologist of religion Wade Clark Roof has called them—whose tastes drive the marketplace, and whose thoughts are increasingly turning toward a collective mortality that is bearing down on them fast. As Roof has found, eight in ten Boomers say you can be a good Christian without going to church, and three-quarters say people should explore other religions than the one they were raised in.

By any measure these trends should have left Roman Catholicism a teetering institution, with the sexual abuse scandal the *coup de grâce*. A few fundamentalist proselytizers tried to exploit the scandal for a bit of what is known in the trade as "sheep-stealing," but without much success.

What is surprising is that disaffected Catholics—and there are many in a community that is 65 million strong—have not fled the Catholic Church *en masse,* even to liturgically similar denominations, especially the

Episcopal Church. I know many alienated Catholics who have found happy homes in Episcopal congregations. But they must be the exception, since the ranks of Episcopalians continue to shrink, down to about 2.3 million from a peak of 3.6 million in 1965, a decline that, together with the bitter debates currently splitting that denomination, are threatening the future of what has been considered the closest thing the United States has to an established church.

The reality is that in spite of America's religious cornucopia, and in spite of the repeated failings of Catholic leaders and the relative powerlessness of lay people to directly affect church policies, Catholics do remain connected to the church, to one degree or another. The reasons are varied and complex, ranging from the religious to the psychological to the merely habitual.

While these bonds are largely unique to Catholicism, their cumulative effect probably finds its closest parallel in Judaism's mix of religious tradition, ethnicity, and tribal loyalty. (Even Freud, in distancing himself from belief, called himself a "godless Jew.") If Jews are the chosen people, Catholics have a corresponding sense of what Robert Bellah has characterized as the "givenness" of their faith. Even the commentators who inveighed against the church of their youth during the scandal of 2002, identifying themselves in my favorite coinage as "col-lapsed" Catholics, betrayed a deep and lingering attachment to Catholicism.

The parsimonious explanation for Catholic loyalty is the organizational pride that is common to most any group, but that has been honed to a sharp edge in the Catholic world thanks to the persistent strain of anti-Catholicism that runs through American history, an enmity that instilled in U.S. Catholics an equally persistent enclave mentality.

Since their earliest days in America's colonial past, Catholics have always been regarded as outsiders, a segregated—and sometimes self-segregating—religious minority that was viewed by the English settlers of the eastern seaboard as carrying the taint of Old World papism. In the frontier outskirts of North America, throughout the Spanish-dominated Southwest, and in French-speaking Quebec and Louisiana, Catholics literally represented the enemy. When the first Catholics arrived in the colonies, in 1634, they established the colony that would become Maryland (after Queen Henrietta Maria, wife of the next-to-last Catholic king of England, Charles I, who was executed by Roundhead Puritans), deliberately creating it as a haven of religious toleration for both Catholics and Protestants, but mainly so that Catholics could feel free to worship in relative peace.

Comity was hard to come by, however. Nine of the thirteen original colonies had established some form of Protestantism as the official religion, and as historian Chester Gillis writes, "The settlers left England behind but not their post-Reformation prejudice against 'Romanists.'" Catholics remained a minority in Maryland and were not able to prevent Anglicanism—the English mother church of Episcopalianism—from becoming the established church even there. During these early years of turmoil Catholics were regularly imprisoned or deported, and while the situation eventually improved as the fires of religious war in Europe were quenched, Catholics continued to face legal, social, and religious barriers to advancement in the burgeoning new nation.

That all began to change with the advent of the revolutionary period in the 1750s. Thanks to the patriotism of the Maryland Catholic leader Charles Carroll—a member of the landed gentry, as were most Catholics in that colony—Catholics were seen as allies in the struggle for a republic. Carroll signed the Declaration of Independence (the only Catholic signatory), and in the space of a few years past religious enmities were put aside in the face of a common enemy. (It also helped that the colonies were aided in their fight by Catholic France.) The ideal of liberty that had carried the American forces to victory over the English reverberated throughout the rest of society, and its impact was especially dramatic for Catholics.

"Though it could not root out bigotry, [the Revolution] did usher in freedom," writes the historian Jay Dolan. "For Catholics, a dream deferred had finally been realized. They stood on the threshold of a new age, ready to build a new church which would attempt to graft the spirit of the new nation onto their colonial tradition and create something new in the history of Roman Catholicism, an American Catholic Church."

But a century of European immigration, largely Catholic, began in 1820 and waylaid that development. These new immigrants brought with them an Old World sensibility of church that only inflamed the anti-immigrant prejudice of the larger New World society, still dominated by an Anglo-Protestant mentality. The wave of Catholic immigration was enormous, and a threat to the Protestant establishment.

At the start of the nineteenth century, there were fewer than 200,000 Catholics in the United States. By 1850, however, Catholicism was the largest single Christian denomination in the nation, with 1.5 million members. That figure doubled in the next decade alone, and quickly doubled again, fed by nearly 34 million immigrants from Europe who arrived during these years—Italians, Germans, Eastern Europeans of every stripe, and above all, the Irish, who would dominate the hierarchy up through the present day.

Anti-Catholic mobs regularly harassed and battered the new immigrants, while nativists and xenophobes of the Know-Nothing Party organized to exclude Catholics from social and political power. The cartoonist Thomas Nast is famous for creating our contemporary idea of Santa Claus, that jolly old elf. But in the late nineteenth century he was best known for his corrosive caricatures of goonish Irish Catholics, corrupt priests, and power-mad popes, all of them threatening to end the American way of life.

During the 1884 presidential campaign, the Reverend Samuel Burchard warmed up a crowd for the Republican candidate, James G. Blaine, by denouncing the forces of "rum, Romanism, and rebellion," a slap at Catholics, Southerners, and drinkers. The barb so angered local Catholics that they turned out in unprecedented numbers for the Democrat, Grover Cleveland, giving him a razor-thin 1,100-vote victory in New York, which also gave Cleveland the edge in the Electoral College. Blaine later rued: "I should have carried New York by 10,000 if the weather had been clear and Mr. Burchard had been doing missionary work in Asia Minor or Cochin China."

The victory energized Catholicism, which had transformed from a rural, agricultural, Southern-based church to one centered in the burgeoning big cities. Catholic leaders allied themselves with the Democratic Party and built urban political machines (which were often as corrupt as their enemies supposed) that reached the apex of their influence with the 1928 nomination of Al Smith, the popular governor of New York and the first Catholic nominated to a major party ticket. The landmark triumph, however, quickly turned to humiliation. Smith lost big for many reasons. He had a strong New Yawk accent and he was a "wet" during Prohibition. But he was also accused of "taking orders from the pope."

Throughout this period Catholics responded to the hostility by creating a parallel universe—an entire system of schools, universities and hospitals, fraternal organizations, youth groups, and newspapers, all linked by a network of parishes and regulated by a daily liturgical calendar. For decades afterward, American Catholics would live and die in the secure womb of an encompassing Catholic culture that was as much Old World as New, a "Catholic ministate," as author Charles Morris called it.

The retreat was as much psychic as physical, Morris noted in *American Catholic,* especially after Smith's defeat. After 1928, he wrote, "Catholics executed a remarkable emotional withdrawal from the rest of the country." Catholic defensiveness turned more than ever into a strain of anti-Protestantism, and Catholics were trained through the Baltimore Catechism that theirs was the "one, true Church" and that they should avoid even walking into a Protestant church, not to mention marrying into one. Uniformity and obedience—necessary weapons against a hostile world—were the watchwords.

Paradoxically, Morris notes, "the more the Church turned in upon itself, the more powerful it became. Its public image in the 1940s and 1950s was nothing short of spectacular." Movies burnished the image of every Catholic priest as either a wartime chaplain or a saintly pastor, and Bishop Fulton Sheen's *The Catholic Hour* beat out Milton Berle, far and away the nation's most popular television personality, in what remains one of the biggest ratings coups. "A team of alien anthropologists would have reported that 1950s America was a Catholic country," Morris writes.

The combination of this high public profile plus the fierce pride that Catholics took in their church enabled Kennedy to edge out Nixon in the 1960 presidential race, though by the slimmest of margins. (Kennedy won by 100,000 votes, but it is estimated that he lost 500,000 because of his religion.)

Ironically, just as Catholics were savoring this triumph, the old Catholic cradle-to-grave world was passing away. Catholics were becoming well-to-do and well educated (thanks to the GI Bill) and were moving out to the suburbs. Internally, the church itself was undergoing a rapid and remarkable modernization with the reforms of Vatican II. Externally, the cohesiveness of Catholics, along with some of the reflexive defensiveness, was going the way of the Latin Mass.

Whatever the changes in their demographics over the decades, however, Catholics today still continue to view themselves with a minority mindset that most other groups do not have, and they still define themselves in contraposition to an essentially Protestant nation that cannot understand why Catholics would be so sensitive to perceived slights—or why, for that matter, they would continue to root for Notre Dame football. This is more than reflexive tribalism.

Part of the explanation is the topography of Catholicism, which is lived as a local church while it tends to be perceived from the outside as a supranational corporation.

Despite its elaborate superstructure, Catholicism in its social expression has always been a religion of *communio,* the regularized gathering of the faithful in worship. This experience could not be further removed from the appeal of watching a televangelist's electronic pitch, or from the pull of nature felt by a growing bloc of "Blue Domers"—those spiritual descendants of Thoreau who prefer to worship under the canopy of God's sky rather than in the musty air of man-made cathedrals. One of the top sociologists of religion, Nancy Ammerman, calls this a trend toward "Golden Rule Christianity." Make nice, but make no commitments. Nothing could be further from the Catholic tradition.

"You cannot pray at home as at church, where there is a great multitude, where exclamations are cried out to God as from one great heart, and where there is something more: the union of minds, the accord of souls, the bond of charity, the prayers of the priest," St. John Chrysostom, a doctor of the church, preached in the fourth century.

In America that ideal was concretized in the network of ethnic national parishes that were the venue of first allegiance for many Catholics. For decades, Catholics identified themselves by their parish when asked where they were from. You couldn't join a church outside your parish boundaries, and the parish was the organizational unit of one's life. "Catholics used the parish to map out—both physically and culturally— space within all of the northern cities," Notre Dame historian John McGreevy has written. Today, Catholics must still marry in the church, in the physical, geographical sense. No weddings on the beach or in the family's backyard. The nuptials are a sacred event communally as well as for the couple.

This religious principle of church as the center of worship and community, fervently held by American Catholicism since its inception, inculcated an extraordinary social compactness that went beyond obedience to the hierarchy, and this glue held throughout the demographic upheavals that vastly altered institutional Catholicism.

For Protestants and Jews, on the other hand, houses of worship were portable commodities in the changing nation, and there were no geographical rules for membership. You went where you liked, and conversely, when the people moved, the temple or the church moved with them. This has been quantified in studies showing that as "white flight" hit urban centers, white Catholics tended to stay. In the 1999 book *Urban Exodus: Why the Jews Left Boston and the Catholics Stayed,* author Gerald Gamm showed how the proportion of white Catholics rose from 59 to 73 percent in the Boston neighborhoods of Dorchester and Upper Roxbury from the 1950s through the 1970s while the overall population of whites fell from 137,000 to 95,000. Much the same occurred in Brooklyn, where the proportion of white Catholics rose from 26 to 44 percent during the same period. (Gamm and others have also noted that this contributed to bitter racial tensions between white Catholics and minorities, especially African-Americans. Conversely, Protestants and Jews who moved away from inner-city neighborhoods to more homogeneously white areas showed higher levels of racial tolerance.)

Today, although the Catholic Church continues to be bolstered by Hispanic immigration, the glory days of immigrant faith are gone—the days when you would find Italians at San Rocco's, Irish at St. Patrick's, and Poles at St. Casimir's, all celebrating the sacred mysteries in their mother tongue. Fast disappearing, too, are the attendant festivals and parades and celebrations associated with a parish's patron saint and a community's country of origin.

The reforms of Vatican II and the demographic shifts since the 1960s effectively ended automatic membership in one's neighborhood parish. Now Catholics "vote with their feet," not by leaving Catholicism but by driving to a parish they like. But the "parochial" mindset, in its positive sense, remains, and it played an important role as the 2002 scandal unfolded by allowing Catholics to feel that they could remain in their local church without being complicit in the wider abuses. This emotional separation is not a cognitive dissonance (a term coined in the 1950s to describe the psychological outlook of believers who maintained their faith despite apocalyptic prophecies that went unfulfilled), but a description of the reality of Catholic practice as it is lived.

To paraphrase the late house speaker Tip O'Neill (Boston Irish Catholic, of course), "All religion is local." That is true for every faith, to a degree, but more so for Catholics.

The distance between the local and universal manifestations of Catholicism is often overlooked by those outside Catholicism because so many people (including many Catholics) tend to equate the church with its hieratic manifestation: the pope speaks and the bishops deliver his orders. The assumption is that the faithful obey. The view is understandable. Covering the Catholic Church is a journalist's dream, because it has such a clear table of organization. The Vatican issues a press statement, and that covers it for the world's one billion Catholics. The process works just as well in reverse: i.e., when an abortion law is passed or a priest is arrested, a statement from the bishop or from Rome is easier to get than curb-shopping for Catholic-in-the-street comments. The bulk of the headlines, then, are about what the hierarchy thinks, with the implicit assumption that the flock will follow.

A study by Andrew Greeley done at the height of the scandal, in March 2002, showed that nearly three-quarters of non-Catholic Americans (73 percent) believe that Catholics "do what the pope and the bishops tell them to do," and that more than half (52 percent) believe that Catholics "are not permitted to think for themselves."

Even after years of covering religion, and Catholicism in particular, I sometimes find myself lulled by this mythic view and am caught short when I talk to "ordinary" Catholics, often quite devout, and find that they haven't read or heard a word about the recent papal encyclical that we journalists were all convinced would rock the Catholic world. Such ignorance, willful or not, is not necessarily a good thing for Catholicism, which prides itself on global unity and fidelity to common teachings. But it works well as a necessary shock absorber in times like the present. As Purdue University sociologist James Davidson said: "I'm always impressed by the buoyancy of individual faith. People don't know who their individual bishops are. They don't know what's going on in the politics of the hierarchy. The institutional church at large is more remote than it is primary to them. So I think that buffer zone is probably helpful in sustaining whatever faith people have."

In fact, there is an argument to be made that the sexual abuse scandal was the first time in recent memory that the bishops had a real impact—albeit a negative one—in making Catholics reflect closely on their beliefs and their faith. For the most part, when Catholics speak of "the church" they mean their own parish, and "the clergy" is their parish priest. Given the news coverage, non-Catholics can be forgiven for thinking that the only things Catholics think about are condoms and sex. Yet try to find a Catholic who can recall the last time he or she heard a pastor preach on birth control or homosexuality. Catholics are nearsighted in their faith, and so the pope is a remote, gauzy figure in white, probably an Italian. Indeed, historians of the church say that up until the nineteenth century and the advent of what the Jesuit historian John O'Malley has called the "papalization" of Catholicism, most Catholics couldn't name the sitting pontiff. From such a distance flaws are imperceptible, and it is easy to see popes as infallible. Even local bishops, for the most part, were grandees (some still are) who showed up to confirm parish children and have their picture taken like a pol on the stump.

On the upside, this dynamic allows parish priests far more latitude to arrange liturgies to suit their flock's tastes, rather than their bishop's demands. "I don't care what the bishop says. We'll do what's good for the parish," pastors often say, and they are hardly rebels. The fact is that the Vatican does not run parish life.

On a day-to-day basis, the bishop generally intrudes into one's religious life only when the parish has to borrow money for a new roof, or when, as is increasingly likely today, the diocese decides to close a parish or a school. Catholic weeklies, even in major archdioceses, have press runs of 25 thousand or so, and it is questionable how many of those are read. Documents from the Vatican and the bishops conference, such as detailed pastoral letters on the economy, or nuanced statements on U.S. military campaigns or on abortion or capital punishment, are perceived in vague terms, at best.

The idea of local loyalty over a slavish identification with the hierarchy is also reinforced by the longstanding Catholic principle of "subsidiarity," which is the idea, expressed in the Catholic Catechism, that "a community of a higher order should not interfere in the internal life of a community of a lower order, depriving the latter of its functions, but rather should support it in case of need and help to coordinate its activity with the activities of the rest of society, always with a view to the common good."

Popes and councils have generally intended this principle for government and society rather than the church polity, but subsidiarity finds a strong echo in the idea of the family as "the domestic church," and the parish community as an extension of that family. This "local option" not only provides the first and strongest bond to the universal church, but it also allows for a latitude in practice that makes remaining in a church one disagrees with less of the compromise with one's integrity than it might appear.

The most salient and persistent feature of Catholic identity, however, is its distinctive aesthetic, what Andrew Greeley has called "the Catholic imagination"—the enchanted religious sensibility that is formed by Catholic rites and traditions and pervades every aspect of the Catholic's world. This is a sacramental vision that invests the created world with religious magic and in turn fleshes out the spiritual world with physical attributes: icons, statues, ashes, candles, incense, bells, stained-glass, frescoes, holy water, pilgrimages, processions, even the desiccated bits of long-dead holy people.

"The Catholic religious sensibility is often almost overwhelmed by the thickness of the metaphors in its dense forest of imagery and story. God and grace lurk everywhere," Greeley writes in *The Catholic Imagination,* a continuation of the arguments he started in *Religion as Poetry.* For Greeley, this peculiar vision is critical in maintaining a sense of Catholic identity in the modern world and a connection to the institutional church, however tenuous. The best evidence for the power of this "rainforest of metaphors" is the way it flourishes outside the boundaries of formal worship, in Catholic art and social justice movements, in Dante's *Divine Comedy* and in Springsteen's "Badlands." Catholics like this style of faith in part because it permeates an otherwise impenetrable barrier between this world and the world to come; it gives the divine a physical home in this world.

In the 1902 lectures that formed the basis of his seminal work, *The Varieties of Religious Experience,* William James captured the essence of this view, and, with his characteristically Brahmin New England style, its intractable difference from the Protestant psyche.

Protestants, James said, would never attract many Catholic converts because Catholicism "offers a so much richer pasturage and shade to the fancy, has so many cells with so many different kinds of honey, is so indulgent in its multiform appeals to human nature, that Protestantism will always show to Catholic eyes the alms-house physiognomy. . . . To intellectual Catholics many of the antiquated beliefs and practices to which the Church gives countenance are, if taken literally, as childish as they are to Protestants. But they are childish in the pleasing sense of 'childlike'— innocent and amiable, and worthy to be smiled on in consideration of the dear people's intellects. To the Protestant, on the contrary, they are childish in the sense of being idiotic falsehoods.

"The two will never understand each other," James concluded; "their centres of emotional energy are too different."

A century later theologian David Tracy, a colleague of Greeley's at the University of Chicago, elaborated on this idea in his book *Analogical Imagination,* in which he demonstrated how diametrically different—not superior—is the Catholic imagination from the Protestant imagination. It is an imagination that finds expression through metaphor, which Tracy contrasts with what he calls the "dialectical imagination" grounded in strict linear thinking.

God is explicit in the Catholic world, Tracy explains; he is largely absent from the world in the Protestant view. Protestants thus typically focus on reaching out to the Almighty to forge a bond. Catholics figure that God enjoys the world he created, and so should we. Physical sensuality goes hand in hand with the Catholic sensibility, as is obvious to anyone who has envied (or raised an eyebrow at) the transports of Bernini's *Saint Teresa in Ecstasy,* or the myriad other sexually charged images that mix freely in Catholic art and devotions. Where else could you find a chaste nun like the irrepressible Sister Wendy, complete with wimple and overbite, reveling in the sensuality of great art in a popular televised series for the BBC and unabashedly lauding the "lovely and fluffy pubic hair" of a Stanley Spencer nude?

For Catholics who have not taken vows of chastity, the joys of sex often stand in for art appreciation and put the lie to old stereotypes about guilt-stricken, sexually inhibited Catholics.

Studies such as the landmark 1994 investigation "The Social Organization of Sexuality" (and other surveys) show that Catholics enjoy sex more often than non-Catholics, with more than two-thirds of Catholics engaging in sex at least once a week, compared with 56 percent of non-Catholics. Furthermore, 64 percent of Catholic women rank high on a sexual playfulness scale, versus 42 percent of non-Catholic women. Catholics are more likely to shower or bathe with their spouse than non-Catholics—and not as a function of tenement life.

Catholics are more likely than Protestants to patronize the fine arts, more likely to socialize with friends, and more likely to stop off at a bar for a drink. If, as the old saw goes, no great industry ever came out of a Catholic country, Catholics certainly made up for it by inventing la dolce vita. Catholics drink, they dance, they smoke, they swear, and they tell off-color stories. And those are the priests. How strikingly different from Protestants, both of the clichéd sherry-sipping variety and their modern heirs, the bluenoses who speak for contemporary evangelical Christianity. (Q: Why don't Baptists have sex standing up? A: They don't want anyone to think they're dancing.)

Of course, the worst of these traits have led to untold domestic misery. And true to their creative nature, Catholics have transformed pain into art, from kitchen sink dramas to the memoirs of Mary McCarthy and Frank McCourt. Catholics are a people of the book, like Jews and Muslims, and they share a gift for narrative. But of all Christian denominations, Catholics are most inclined to incorporate story into faith practices. Just look at the fanciful elaborations of bare-bones Bible stories into full-blown narratives, or the colorful lives of saints whose very existence is doubted even by church authorities.

Or limbo. The place where good but unbaptized people go when they die is an idea that has persisted in the Catholic imagination although it has been dropped from official church teaching. Catholic theologians also constructed purgatory on the slimmest of scripture references, but with the greatest rewards for literature and spiritual contemplation, from Dante Alighieri to Paulie Walnuts, the hit man on the popular television series The Sopranos. Paulie's purgatorial calculations, in a moment of uncharacteristic reflection, made Catholic viewers cringe, chuckle, and wonder if he was right. "You see, you add up all your mortal sins, and multiply that number by fifty," Paulie figured in one episode. "Then you add up all your venial sins, and multiply that by twenty-five. You add 'em together, and that's your sentence. I figure I'm going to have to do about 6,000 years before I get accepted into heaven. And 6,000 years is nothing in eternity time. I could do that standing on my fuckin' head."

Mafiosi aside, purgatory is an eminently humanistic concept, a theological representation of the reflex to pity. Thus a sin-stained believer who has been saved by God's grace but hasn't fully atoned for her actions on earth (and is thus unworthy to enter immediately into the presence of the Almighty) can make things right by doing a few millennia first, on his head or otherwise.

More than just infusing its followers with the unique sights, smells, and sounds of the faith, Catholicism is also ingrained through what believers *do* as much as what they *feel*. In unison, Catholics recite the creed, confess their sins, ask God's mercy, and offer up prayers. Conversely, Baptists and evangelicals reject anything that hints at a binding creed and tend to regard Catholic devotions as rote exercises of indoctrination.

And while the emphasis on good works has gotten a bad rap—often with good reason—the idea that Catholics live their faith in concrete ways (no small obligation if one takes seriously Catholic social justice teachings), that they "co-operate" with God in the work of salvation, has always been central. Catholicism is not only about *sola fide* (being saved by faith alone); it is also about living out one's faith. (Of course, faith alone *can* be enough. As a priest I know likes to say, "There is no free lunch—except grace.")

Catholics must go to confession (at least once a year, and preferably once a week), eat fish on Friday in Lent (still), attend Mass every Sunday and on major feast days, and receive the Eucharist at least once a year, on Easter. Catholics may not wake up every day feeling like Jesus is their best friend, but they believe that by carrying out the requirements of Catholicism, they will return to belief. Or, if belief is not a problem, then they will become better Christians. In Catholicism the focus is on sanctification; in Protestantism, on justification. And thereby comes a whole bloody history. But in modern culture, the notion of *doing* one's faith remains as strong as it was for St. Teresa of Avila in the sixteenth century, who prayed:

Christ has no body on earth but yours;
no hands but yours; no feet but yours;
Yours are the eyes through which is to look out—
Christ's compassion to the world.
Yours are the feet with which he is to go about doing good.
Yours are the hands with which he is to bless others now.

Conservative Protestantism, especially in the contemporary American version, is about evangelizing and proselytizing and saving souls from an eternal damnation that is right around the corner, either from death or the Apocalypse, both of which are always imminent. It was St. Francis who summed up the Catholic approach when he said that believers must always preach the Gospel—using words if they have to.

Catholicism is about orthopraxy—right practice—as well as orthodoxy—right belief. In Bernard Lonergan's phrasing, Catholics are "constituted by meaning." In Catholicism, to a great extent, you are what you do, and that is a powerful idea that over the centuries has inculcated certain kinesthetic reflexes into the Catholic pysche that make Catholicism something of a self-propagating faith. In the fifth century the theologian and papal secretary Prosper of Aquitaine famously summed up the inextricable relationship between experience and faith in the dictum, *lex orandi lex credendi*, or, "the law of praying founds the law of believing." That is a far cry from the *sola fide*, or "faith alone," emphasis of Protestantism, especially in its modern incarnations.

In Catholicism, ritual shields the experience of faith from the vagaries of pure emotion, and tries to make belief habitual through the practice of sacraments that have a concrete reality.

In baptism, confirmation, communion, confession, marriage, last rites, and, for priests, ordination, the invisible is made human. These seven sacraments, largely fixed in number by the twelfth-century Scholastics, are all-encompassing, marking every stage of a Catholic's life, and they are imbued with awe through their unabashedly miraculous power. In its search for a purer, uncluttered faith, the Protestant Reformation reduced the number of sacraments to two—baptism and communion.

For Catholics, on the other hand, daily life itself remains sacramental. Catholic theologians, including the current pontiff, often speak of sex—

only when occurring in the context of marriage, of course—in terms of a sacrament that should be indulged to the fullest.

From the perspective of his wheelchair, the late novelist Andre Dubus even saw the sacramental in his preparation of school lunches for his daughters: "A sacrament is physical," Dubus wrote, "and within it is God's love; as a sandwich is physical, and nutritious and pleasurable, and within it is love, if someone makes it for you and gives it to you with love; even harried or tired or impatient love, but with love's direction and concern, love's again and again wavering and distorted focus on goodness; then God's love, too, is in the sandwich. A sacrament is an outward sign of God's love, they taught me when I was a boy, and in the Catholic Church there are seven. But, no, I say, for the Church is catholic, the world is catholic, and there are seven times seventy sacraments, to infinity."

The foundational sacrament of Catholicism is the Eucharist, and it remains the bright line dividing Catholicism from much of the rest of the Christian world. Catholics come up with all sorts of formulations to describe the Real Presence—Christ truly present in the bread and wine— and not always in ways that would please Rome. But then again, learned theologians have been writings thousands of treatises for thousands of years trying to explain it. What is important is the consistent and persistent belief that something magical happens: *hoc est enim corpus meum,* in the Latin formulation that the priest intones over the Host—"for this is my body." (The phrase was apparently the source of the magician's incantation "Hocus pocus," which may in turn have led to the word "hoax.")

Catholic memoirs abound with tales of Catholic children terrified at the awesome power of taking Jesus into their mouths for the first time; of fasting until fainting to properly prepare for the great event; of trying not to let Jesus' body touch their teeth; and, in McCourt's hilarious episode, of vomiting up Jesus after indulging in too much celebratory candy.

In many ways the legalistic view of the Eucharist still reigns. In 1994, responding to requests from Catholics who suffer from celiac disease (which causes a dangerous reaction to the gluten in wheat), the Vatican mandated rules for all bishops that non-gluten substitutes such as rice wafers "are invalid matter for the celebration of the Eucharist." Jesus used a wheat-based bread at the Last Supper, and so it shall be. In an incident that was quickly forgotten in light of later events, Cardinal Law in 2001 told the family of a five-year-old celiac sufferer, Jenny Richardson, that she would not be able to take a rice wafer for her First Communion. The cardinal said she could still take the wine, which would be just as efficacious. But the family decided to switch to a Methodist church. "It was hard. It's hard to make a decision to change," said the girl's mother, Janice Richardson. "She feels different wherever she goes but shouldn't be made to feel different in church."

Eucharistic literalists have even been debating whether to mandate a change in the color of the wine used at Mass, from white, which has been prevalent for several centuries, to red, which is seen as more evocative of Christ's blood. White wine came into fashion because it left fewer stains, a pragmatic reason that does not sit well with many who want to reinforce belief in the Real Presence.

Nothing, however, seems to have diluted Catholics' reverence for the miracle of the Eucharist, which they can find only in the Catholic Church. With Flannery O'Connor they seem to say, "Well, if it's only a symbol, to hell with it."

For example, the 1999 survey of American Catholics that found a growing disconnect with the institutional church also showed that Catholics retain a strong attachment to the church through their sacramental life. In a hierarchy of six beliefs, eight in ten respondents listed the sacraments as very important to them as Catholics, followed closely by "spirituality and personal growth," helping the poor, and traditional church teachings about Mary as the Mother of God. Last on the list, by a wide margin, was the centrality of the teaching authority claimed by the Vatican.

An earlier 1997 study also found that "core" Catholic beliefs such as the Trinity, the Resurrection, the Incarnation, and the Real Presence form "the single most important basis of Catholic unity [and] the reason why Catholics remain loyal to the church even when they disagree with it on other matters."

Even young Catholics, whose ties to the church are the weakest, seem held by the sacraments. The 2001 survey of Catholic young adults cited earlier listed nineteen elements of Catholic teaching and belief and asked which were most essential to their vision of the church. The top three were the belief that God is present in the sacraments, charitable efforts to help the poor, and devotion to Mary. Surprisingly, nearly half of these young adults said that the prohibition on non-Catholics partaking of the Eucharist "should never be changed."

Even Madonna (the pop star, not the Blessed Virgin Mary) had her daughter baptized in the Catholic Church, despite her profound differences with the pope. "I can disagree with doctrines and dogmas and still celebrate them," she said, an explanation that gives church conservatives the willies but contains a real insight into the Catholic mind.

All of this underscores the reality of an American Catholicism that retains a distinctive outline amid the haze of religious assimilation. It also demonstrates that amid the noisy tumult of America's religious emporium, with its drive-thru communion, rave liturgies, PowerPoint Bible stories, and poll-driven innovations aimed at attracting greater market share (especially among the young), a significant number of Americans of all ages and attitudes still crave that "tiny whispering sound" of God's voice that Elijah heard in the quiet of his cave. These days, more than ever, the Mass is a refuge from the vulgarization of religious culture, from the spiritual ephemera found in programs such as *Touched by an Angel* and from the snake-oil spiritualism of television talk shows such as *Crossing Over.*

Frank McCourt was not alone when, in an essay in *Time* magazine prompted by the abuse scandal, he rued the loss of the Latin Mass "because it was a universal language, and anywhere you'd go in the world, it was the same Mass." Historian Jay Dolan defined the "Catholic ethos" by the "four marks" of devotional Catholicism—authority, sin, ritual, and the miraculous. The power of the first two, authority and sin, may have eroded. But the ritualization of the miraculous somehow endures. That is what makes the Catholic culture, if not the institutional church, a comfortable place for Catholics to situate themselves, even in times of difficulty, or perhaps especially in those times.

Novelist Alice McDermott has said that she and her coreligionists are forever doomed to be Catholic. The saint of Catholic social activism, Dorothy Day, described her loyalty more bluntly, though just as lovingly: "She's a whore, but she's my mother."

Rebellion and nostalgia coexist in the Catholic mind, perhaps more noticeably and uneasily than ever before. The irony of the sexual abuse scandal is that it actually underscored the differences between Catholics and Protestants at a time when many Catholics may have been looking for a viable religious option.

To some it would seem hypocritical for Catholics to stay in the church at this point, or at best an indicator of unjustifiable passivity. Then again, maybe it's the sign of a first-rate intelligence.

A final element in the physics binding Catholicism is the premium that the church, and its culture, places on the principle of unity. In the past, as anyone with a passing familiarity with history knows, cohesion was often maintained through brute force as much as force of argument. In more recent times the church has sought to use what John XXIII called "the medicine of mercy" to advance its claims. That may appear counterintuitive, given that the church always seems to be remonstrating with its members. But the disputes, destructive as they are, tend to be conflicts over uniformity, which Rome also holds in high regard. Uniformity, however, is different from unity, and the Vatican has tried to keep Catholics in rather than drumming them out. A century ago Cardinal John Henry Newman said of the laity, "The church would look foolish without them." In recent decades, the church itself grew to appreciate Newman's wisdom and adopted a less hectoring tone.

Again, the 1960s and Vatican II provided the turning point. From the reforms of that period the ecumenical movement was born, centuries-old anathemas were lifted, the Index of Prohibited Books was abolished, and even Galileo was rehabilitated. The Vatican's opening to the world was matched, perhaps to a lesser degree, by a less adversarial tone toward its own flock. Certainly, Vatican revanchists have in recent years been trying to restore some of the old methods of persuasion with efforts that would have been comical if they had not been so misguided and harmful to the church. Can anyone doubt that censures and condemnations by Cardinal Joseph Ratzinger's Congregation for the Doctrine of the Faith (the successor to the Holy Office and the Inquisition) have brought great notoriety to "subversive" theological works that would otherwise have remained known only to other theologians?

But the truth is that the Vatican's huffing and puffing rarely reaches the churches where Catholic life is lived, and the more clement vision of the faith propagated by the Council has taken hold in parish life. Today Catholics can marry non-Catholics without fear of divine retribution, and their children can be baptized in the church, as can those of unmarried women or men. Divorced and remarried Catholics, openly gay people, and cohabiting couples can usually find a parish sanctuary. (And Catholics get to enjoy membership in a form of monarchy without being subject to its whims, a pleasant indulgence akin to that allowed to citizens of the British Commonwealth.)

In reality, there has always been a great deal more attitudinal, if not institutional, flexibility in the Vatican than earnest-minded Catholics outside Italy would believe. The Vatican is a bureaucracy, with all the foibles of any civil service, and not a particularly efficient one at that. And despite the "internationalization" of the Roman Curia in the past fifty years, it remains an Italian institution, with all the vices and virtues that that conveys. As Jesuit Alan Figueroa Deck of the Loyola Institute for Spirituality in Orange, California, has put it: "Mediterranean peoples separate the ideal from the reality—there's always a gap between the two, and they can live with that ambiguity. Northern Europeans have a harder time with gray."

Graham Greene's story of his meeting with Paul VI in Rome in the 1960s neatly illustrates the difference between Rome's reputation and the reality. When the pontiff told the novelist that he had very much enjoyed *The Power and the Glory,* Greene's story of a dissolute whiskey priest who eventually seeks martyrdom, Greene was surprised and pointed out to Paul that his own Holy Office had condemned the book. The pope brushed Greene's concerns aside: "Parts of all your books will always offend some Catholics and you shouldn't pay any attention to that."

As Greeley writes in his contribution to the book *I Like Being Catholic,* "Those rigid people who try to draw the boundaries tightly (so as to exclude the ones with whom they disagree) misunderstand what Catholicism is about. We are not a religion for only the saved, much less for those who think that they are saved. We are a religion for everyone. Even those who have been excommunicated are still Catholics. The only way you can get out is by formally and explicitly announcing that you have renounced the faith or by joining another denomination. Even then neither the church nor your own imagination gives up on you. Never!"

This preference for inclusion over exclusion is borne out in the wider Catholic polity, where members decide to "opt in" whether they agree with the church's disciplines or not. Alan Wolfe, the sociologist of religion whose books include *One Nation, After All* and *Moral Freedom: The Search for Virtue in a World of Choice,* put it this way: "I think Catholicism makes judgments. I don't think Catholics do."

A good share of this, of course, can be chalked up to the entropy that affects a large number of the members of most organizations, and especially religious organizations. There is also the fact that Catholics are like other Americans in that they have been more religiously observant over a longer period of time than the population of any other industrialized country. Gallup surveys show that close to 40 percent of Americans go to church regularly, and more than 90 percent consistently express a faith in a God of one sort or another. In Canada, for example, the weekly church-going rate is 31 percent, down from 58 percent in 1955; in England, just 12 percent attend weekly services. Catholic Americans, on the other hand, want to worship someplace, so why not in a Catholic church?

The lure of orthodoxy, particularly in a tumultuous world that seems more uncertain all the time for Americans in the post-9/11 era, also comes into play for Catholics. The draw of tradition was first explicated by Dean Kelley in his 1977 book, *Why Conservative Churches Are Growing,* which argued that denominations that embrace high standards, preach a clear and focused message, and seek to make religion meaningful for their members gain adherents, while those that become fuzzy and undemanding engender little allegiance. Subsequent research has bolstered Kelley's findings.

That the Catholic Church remains traditional seems indisputable, except to those on the right-wing fringe who think that John Paul has sold out to the liberals. Indeed, the real threat to Rome's unity is, oddly enough, from its right flank, where traditionalists periodically threaten to set up a parallel hierarchy that they claim, as all schismatics do, would be "the one, true church." They actually did produce a schism in 1987, the first in Catholicism in more than a century, when the maverick French archbishop Marcel Lefebvre ordained several bishops in Switzerland in defiance of papal warnings, thereby incurring automatic excommunication. After years of strenuous efforts, Rome has finally healed much of the rift. But it had to offer a number of concessions, including allowing the old Latin Mass to be celebrated again (proving that Catholicism never really gets rid of anything forever).

For the most part, however, the tradition and stability of Catholicism is a decided plus for Catholics and for a growing number of Catholic converts, especially conservative Protestants attracted by the clarity of Catholicism's teachings, among other things. But the draw of stability and certainty also works for those who would not necessarily define themselves as conservatives. More than 160 thousand American adults convert to Catholicism each year through the Rite of Christian Initiation of Adults program, a steadily increasing number that includes Ann Turner, a one-time Congregationalist and author of a book of her experience of child sexual abuse. On March 30, 2002, in a Massachusetts parish, Turner was formally confirmed as a Catholic. A few months later she was leading a chapter of the reform group Voice of The Faithful, and she has no intention of leaving. "I wanted something with more ritual, more tradition, more mystery, more drama and more meaning," Turner said.

Catholicism's genius is that for all its doctrinal certitude, one of its main tenets is that all should come under its Catholic embrace. Thus one finds an astounding variety of types who proudly wear their Catholicism like a badge—peaceniks such as the Berrigans, charismatics who pray like Pentecostals, traditionalists who chant in Latin, feminists who celebrate underground women's liturgies, and even those annoying "holy idiots" who sometimes turn out to be saints. It also encompasses miscreants who have abused children—even if they are defrocked, ex-priests remain Catholics—as well as an astonishing number of their victims.

Barbara Blaine, for example, is the founder of SNAP, Survivors Network of those Abused by Priests. She was repeatedly sexually abused by a priest as a girl, an experience that scarred her psyche and led to years of anguish. Today, married to a Jewish divorcé with two sons, Barbara Blaine is a dogged crusader who works as a legal advocate for the poor. Her Catholic sense of social justice lives on, as does her faith, which surprised me as we talked in Boston during the summer of scandal. "I go to church, not every Sunday, but more than my brothers and sisters," she said, as if she would be surprised there was any question. "I figure they took everything else away from me, they're not going to take my faith." Blaine said friends have often wondered why she doesn't become Jewish, or her husband Catholic, or something else altogether. But they both laugh at the idea. "I'm Catholic. I mean, 'Blaine,' the whole Irish thing. There's something about being Catholic."

Reformers, dissidents, and zealots may not receive the Vatican's stamp of approval, and will always face complaints, even persecution, from the official church. But these days they usually shrug it off and soldier on.

"As a layperson teaching in a non-Catholic theological seminary, the hierarchy has little power over me and I don't hear from them personally. So I am not 'oppressed' by them on a day-to-day basis," says Rosemary Radford Ruether. "I know the evil ways of much of this institution perfectly well. That is why I avoid getting under its power. But I am also committed to contributing something to the well-being of this particular historical community." Besides, she adds, why leave the Catholic Church "to the Cardinals and their supporters"?

As Michelle Dillon explains in her book *Catholic Identity: Balancing Reason, Faith, and Power,* this is a very Catholic reaction: "By contrast with Protestantism, the Catholic Church's institutional self-understanding is one of historical continuity with the early pre-Reformation church. Its attendant accent on unity and catholicity rather than factionalism seems to make staying rather than leaving the 'natural' or more 'meaningful' option for Catholics who disagree with official church teachings. The historical motif of continuity appears to confer upon Catholics ownership rights that motivate them to deal with interpretive difference by reconstructing the church from within rather than leaving it."

Dillon says that Catholics who advocate change in the church have developed an "achieved identity" that undergirds their stake in the church. Protestantism was born of schism, she says, and that template has persisted as Protestants continue to fracture their institutions, up through the present day, with successive theological, doctrinal, and political disputes. This history has in turn produced both a comfort level with division among Protestants, and an infinite variety of distinct yet related denominations for dissenters to choose from. In fact, given Protestantism's orientation toward local autonomy over hierarchy, a disgruntled Protestant can find another congregation within the same denomination that has a decidedly different take on the Gospel. The upshot is that Protestant worshipers can easily shift among churches in order to find a creed and a practice that conform precisely to their beliefs, allowing them to remain true to the supreme Protestant ideal of personal religious integrity. "Here I stand; I cannot do otherwise," as Martin Luther told the Diet of Worms.

Disagree strongly enough with one's church, in other words, and there are options.

Of course, there are plenty of die-hard Methodists, Presbyterians, and Episcopalians who are giving their denominational leaders schismatic fits for the very reason that they won't leave. But the phenomenon of "the loyal opposition"—Garry Wills's label for himself—is especially widespread in Catholicism, left, right, and center. Everyone wants the church to reflect their vision, and they won't leave till they see it happen.

Perhaps an oppositional stance is an inevitable result of the Roman church's jot-and-tittle approach to every aspect of the faith, ensuring that everyone will step out of line once in a while, if not more frequently. Wills's explanation in *Why I Am a Catholic* is not unusual. Yes, he dissects the papacy, but he prays the Rosary every day, goes to Mass, and studies the Gospels: "I have never even considered leaving the church. I would lose my faith in God before losing my faith in it." He has "never felt closer" to the church, he says. "We flawed believers live with our flawed fellow believers, even with flawed brothers like the pope."

The Catholic Church is a church of sinners. It always has been. That is a comfort.

There is a lot of loyal opposition in the Catholic Church these days. Four decades after the Second Vatican Council, an entire generation has grown up with the idea that they are the people of God, that they constitute "the church" as much as does the ordained caste. Catholics can live with the notion of papal infallibility (widely misunderstood anyway) because there is an instinctive appreciation of their own role as contributors to the *sensus fidelium*—the prophetic "sense of the faithful"—and the equally revered principle of "indefectibility," which holds that the Holy Spirit remains with the church for all time and will not allow it to deviate from the truth of the Gospel. In plainer terms, the laity is saying that the church isn't going anywhere without them.

But stubbornness is not a vote of confidence for future change. Catholic identity is one thing; Catholic practice is another. Identity allows for all levels of involvement, and increasingly that has meant noninvolvement. Considering the virtual powerlessness of the laity in terms of church governance, the forceful engagement of lay Catholics is going to be critical to any meaningful change in the church. Cultural captives who equate their Catholicism with rooting for Notre Dame but do little else are not enough, not these days.

The questions then become: Will the laity do anything? And, just as important, What can they do?

Six

REVOLUTION
FROM BELOW

"WE, THE PEOPLE OF GOD . . ."

O n October 31, 1517, Martin Luther nailed his ninety-five theses to the door of the Wittenberg cathedral and sparked the Protestant Reformation. On April 19, 1775, colonial militia fired at British regulars on the Lexington Green, the "shot heard 'round the world" that heralded the American Revolution.

And on July 20, 2002, in a convention hall in Back Bay Boston, some four thousand middle-aged, middle-class Catholics ("rebels in Rockports," as they were dubbed) gathered to channel the spirits of both those historic events while at the same time pledging to remain loyal to hierarchical Catholicism. That kind of "revolution from below" is tricky in any organization, and in none more so than the Catholic Church, as history has shown.

This meeting was the inaugural convention of the newly formed lay organization called Voice of the Faithful, and whether future historians will remember their gathering in the same breath as those other watershed events, or whether it will wind up as a mere footnote to the sexual abuse scandal, may not be known for years. There was no doubt, however, about the spiritual zeal that the participants brought to their mission, or the fact that after decades of false starts and false hopes, the American laity were finally getting the hang of harnessing their faith to the cause of church politics. The laity still have a long way to go. But every bishop in the nation took note of Voice of the Faithful. They had to.

The convention took place in the Hynes Center, just a mile from Cardinal Bernard Law's own cathedral, and it finished with a public Mass celebrated by one of Law's own priests, to a spillover crowd the likes of which Law could only dream of on his best day. And these were not Law's best days. Indeed, that the most powerful churchman in the United States was powerless to stop any of this from happening showed how far the cardinal's star had fallen, and how quickly an angry and focused laity could overtake a slow-footed hierarchy.

While Voice of the Faithful seemed to spring from nowhere, it was not a miraculous conception. There were reasons that this organization—this *movement,* its founders insisted—began. And even if Voice of the Faithful falters in coming years, the story of its rapid gestation and sudden birth will remain a cautionary tale for the bishops long into the future.

Voice of the Faithful started in January, within weeks after the first reports surfaced about the abuses by John Geoghan and the efforts to cover up for him, when parishioners at St. John the Evangelist Church in Wellesley, Massachusetts, decided to organize weekly "listening sessions" in the basement of the parish school to address the growing concerns. At the first Monday night meeting, six hundred people showed up. And each week more came. Chapters were organized in other parishes, and soon this spontaneous eruption of controlled anger was shooting toward 25 thousand members nationwide. It had a prophetic-sounding name, an acronym—VOTF, which rhymes with "votive"—a Web site, a motto ("Keep the Faith, Change the Church"), and a core of dedicated volunteers who were wearing themselves out keeping abreast of the galloping developments.

What VOTF did not have was a plan—a concrete idea about how to effect the changes they wanted, or even exactly what those changes could be, or should be, in a hierarchical church that makes little provision for populist activism. That is why, a month after the bishops' June debacle in Dallas, VOTF called together some 4,200 members from nearly forty states and several foreign countries for a day of speeches and workshops and lay preaching. "There is a spirit in this auditorium today," announced VOTF cofounder and keynote speaker Jim Post (a devoted Catholic, a grandfather of three, a professor at Boston University's School of Management, and a veteran of the Nestlé boycott movement). "It is moving across the land . . . and across the oceans. It is the spirit of hope. It is the spirit of renewal. Some would say it is the *Holy* Spirit. Who am I to disagree?" he said to wild applause.

But the convention was as much politics as Pentecost. There was a "Declaration of the Faithful" announcing that "We the faithful, in order to form a more perfect Church . . ." There was a manifesto, signed by sixty theologians, that outlined the moral underpinnings for their movement. And there were speeches that had the crowd stamping their feet. "The core of the problem is centralized power, with no voice of the faithful. The people of Boston know what to do about absolute power—they showed the world two hundred years ago," VOTF leader Jim Muller told the crowd to whoops of approval. "No more donation without representation," Muller said. "We have to gain financial power in this church. They say the laity are weak, but we are 99.9 percent of the church and 100 percent of the money, and we now have a structure where we can exert that power."

A mild-looking fellow with an intimidating résumé, Muller is exactly the kind of guy the hierarchy should be afraid of. He is a faithful Catholic. He is smart—a world-class cardiologist from Harvard Medical School who did his graduate degree in Russian studies. And he knows how to organize a grassroots movement for change, which is demonstrated by the Nobel Peace Prize that he won in 1980 along with two other Americans for founding International Physicians for the Prevention of Nuclear War, a peace group that was a constant spur—or thorn—to the superpowers in the final decade of the Cold War. The movement grew to 150 thousand members in more than forty countries within five years, and it is the model Muller wants to follow for VOTF.

"I've never seen anything like it, it's absolutely from the bottom-up," SNAP's leader, David Clohessy, told me during a break in the workshops. For more than a decade Clohessy and his fellow victim advocates had been ducking the spitballs of the lay faithful who were furious at them whenever they revealed a priest's misconduct. In an instant, that had all changed. "A few years ago the best we could hope for from the laity was silence, not to actively oppose us," Clohessy said. "Ten years ago lay people were on the sidelines. Now they're in the game. They're making errors, they're throwing to the wrong base. But they're learning."

Voice of the Faithful represented, as *Boston Herald* columnist Margery Eagan put it, "the radicalizing of the gray-haired and sensibly shod, of middle-aged and older white, suburban, bred-in-the-bone Catholics from well-heeled parishes."

That was obvious from the moment the convention opened. "Let me be clear about the terms of this dialogue," Post told the crowd. "We will not negotiate our right to exist. We will not negotiate our right to be heard. We will not negotiate our right to free speech as American Catholics. And we will not give the bishops a free pass on telling the truth." He drew parallels to the Exodus of the Jews from Egypt, echoed the cry of Holocaust survivors ("Never again!"), and referred to the Reaganesque slogan of the Cold War ("Trust . . . but verify"). Yes, the Catholic hierarchy was now the Evil Empire.

On this day of sweeping historical comparisons, Father Thomas Doyle, the heroic Cassandra of the scandal saga, was the star orator.

In 1985 Doyle was a canon lawyer working at the Vatican's embassy in Washington and a priest who had a bishop's miter in his future. With the first wave of scandals breaking over the bishops, Doyle, along with another priest and a lay civil lawyer, was commissioned by the hierarchy to write a secret report on the scope and nature of the abuse among the clergy. The report ran ninety-two pages and warned the bishops to take concerted action, and to take it quickly. Pedophiles were virtually untreatable and should never be returned to ministry, it said, and if the bishops did not move decisively, the cost to the church could exceed $1 billion.

Needless to say, everything that Doyle and his coauthors warned about came true. And Tom Doyle, his career stalled because of his dogged efforts to cajole the bishops into acting, left the Vatican's diplomatic corps and became an Air Force chaplain. He is stationed at Ramstein Air Force Base in Germany but spends much of his time counseling abuse victims and badgering the bishops, now as an outsider, to change their ways.

"I'm still a loose cannon and I'm still a time bomb," Doyle told the appreciative Boston crowd without preface or apology. "What we have experienced in our lifetime is a disaster the horror of which is perhaps equaled by the bloodshed of the Inquisition but which certainly makes the indulgence scam of the Reformation pale by comparison." Dressed in a blue blazer, tie, and khakis, Doyle proceeded to indict the institution that had trained him as a canon lawyer. "What we see before us are the beginning death throes of the medieval monarchical model that was based on the belief that a small select minority of the educated, privileged and power-invested was called forth by God to manage the temporal and spiritual lives of the faceless masses on the presumption that their unlettered states equaled ignorance. This is 2002, not 1302. We have grown up, we are not ignorant, we are educated and demand a voice," he said, as one listener yelled out, "Doyle for bishop!"

"Today," Doyle responded, "we're taking back what's been hijacked from us."

But as the applause died down, and as the rally wound up with the solemnity of the Eucharist, a central question remained: How to translate VOTF's enthusiasm into concrete actions and policies? Muller's opening presentation had alternated roundhouse rhetoric with an entertaining PowerPoint presentation showing the current church as the Leaning Tower of Pisa, and a remade church standing upright thanks to the flying buttresses of lay faithful. It was good for laughs but short on details. As Post said, "People still ask, 'What are you really about?' Or, repeating our motto, 'Keep the Faith, Change the Church,' they ask, 'What does that mean?' Those are important questions." By the end of the one-day convention, they still had no answers.

There was a sense that the leaders of VOTF, along with millions of other Catholics, were still fumbling toward an agenda for action. The hesitation was understandable. Lay people aren't used to telling the hierarchy what to do. "I love the Catholic Church, but our fatal flaw has been the passivity of the laity," said Stephen J. Pope, chairman of the theology department at Boston College and a VOTF backer. "Many Catholics have to get over the idea that the mission of the laity is to clean up the deck chairs after the parish picnic."

Moreover, grassroots politicking is tough in an organization that has no election cycles. Lay Catholics don't know how to lobby the bishops, and as the scandal showed, most bishops don't know how to deal with them when they try, except by resorting to suppression. Bishops can do that. In the Catholic Church, the bishop calls the shots in every diocese, from doctrine to budget. Not only is the bishop entrusted with the unchallenged duty to protect and promote Catholic teaching, but he has legal control of every Catholic parish, hospital, university, and school in his ecclesiastical jurisdiction. He decides who can, or cannot, meet there. His authority is spelled out clearly in Canon 212: "The Christian faithful, conscious of their own responsibility, are bound by Christian obedience to follow what the sacred pastors, as representatives of Christ, declare as teachers of the faith or determine as leaders of the Church."

But that power is not as absolute as it might seem. The next two paragraphs of the very same canon clearly stipulate that lay people should speak their minds to church leaders.

"The Christian faithful," the canon reads, "have the right and even at times a duty to manifest to the sacred pastors their opinion on matters which pertain to the good of the Church, and they have a right to make their opinion known to the other Christian faithful, with due regard for the integrity of faith and morals and reverence towards their pastors, and with consideration for the common good and the dignity of persons."

So what are Catholics to make of this? Resolving the crisis in Catholicism will depend in large part on defining the unmapped space between those two statements. The question is whether the laity can do that in time to make a difference. "The move beyond these precipitating events has got to happen in the next year or the window will be closed," said Leonard Swidler, a professor of Catholic thought at Temple University who has been pushing reforms, including a "Catholic Bill of Rights," for more than twenty-five years. Writing in the *Boston Globe* just two weeks after he addressed the VOTF conference, Holy Cross professor David J. O'Brien was already asking if the gathering was "a baptism or a wake."

Change is, of course, possible. We know that, because the Catholic Church has changed over the centuries, often quite dramatically. And Catholicism being first a faith and next an institution, the rationale for change has an entire branch of theology—ecclesiology—to explain the process. In the midst of the crisis, ecclesiology can seem abstract and remote from the practical steps that would seem to be so urgently needed. But it provides both crucial theological underpinnings for change and insights into how the nuts and bolts of reform can occur. Ecclesiology is the ground of the church's being, one might say, and it is the starting point for any successful reform movement.

The classic text on ecclesiology remains Avery Dulles's *Models of the Church*, first published in 1974 and in print ever since. Dulles is himself an interesting model of theological evolution. A scion of the WASP establishment clan that includes his father, John Foster Dulles (Eisenhower's secretary of state), and his uncle, Allen Dulles (head of the CIA), Avery Dulles converted from the Presbyterian Church to Catholicism (by way of agnosticism) as a young man, causing much consternation to his family. He was subsequently ordained a Jesuit priest and became a renowned theologian at Fordham. In 2001, when Dulles was eighty-two, John Paul conferred upon him the dignity of cardinal, the first U.S. theologian ever so honored. Because of his age Dulles could not vote in a conclave to elect the next pope—eighty is the cutoff point—and he declined to be made a bishop because he felt that a bishop should be in charge of a diocese. The "red hat," as it is known, was essentially an honor for a lifetime of distinguished work by the tall, craggy Dulles. *Models of the Church* is a pillar of that reputation.

In his book, Dulles identifies five principal models for conceiving the church: as institution, as mystical communion, as sacrament, as herald, and as servant. Dulles is certainly no reformist, and he has grown more tradition-minded over the years. But the centerpiece of his ecclesiological argument remains, namely, that no single model is sufficient unto itself and (just as important) that when a single model predominates, it is often to the detriment of the faith. In that regard he cites the "juridical model" of the church that developed in the Middle Ages. Using the legalisms of that model, medieval church leaders exploited the theology of penance and created the spiritual abuses that led to the Reformation. "Financially, the theory succeeded: The empty coffers of the Holy See were replenished. But was this success a confirmation of the theory?" Dulles asks. "A model that leads to practical abuses is, even from a theoretical standpoint, a bad model."

That statement is just as true in the twenty-first century as it was in the sixteenth century, and it is the best argument we have for structural change in addition to spiritual renewal within the Catholic Church.

"To a great extent . . . changes have been accepted because they help the Church to find its identity in a changing world, or because they motivate men to the kind of loyalty, commitment, and generosity that the Church seeks to elicit. The People of God image, for example, was adopted in part because it harmonized with the general trend toward democratization in Western society since the eighteenth century. Since Vatican II the Servant Model has become popular because it satisfies a certain hunger for involvement in the making of a better world—a hunger that, although specifically Christian in motivation, establishes solidarity between the Church and the whole human family."

This relatively quick evolution bodes well for those who hope for meaningful change in the wake of the scandal of 2002. There is no shortage of templates. Dulles cites one study that finds some ninety-six images of the church in the New Testament, and Paul VI, he notes, variously referred to the church as God's temple, his people, his vine, his field, and his city, among others. Take your pick.

As important as finding a *new* model, however, is the current debate over how much to deemphasize the regnant model of the church as institution, a model that Dulles agrees is fundamentally different from the others. This model has been the default mode of Catholicism since Robert Bellarmine, a Counter-Reformation Jesuit, argued that a monarchical Catholicism would be best equipped to combat rampant Protestant heresy. The Catholic imagination feasted on this grand image, as did the church's foes, for their own reasons, and the idea of church as primarily an institution became set in stone. That this would be the commonly accepted image of the Catholic Church is natural to a degree, because the institution is the "container" for all the other models, and because it presents the most appealing images—purple-clad grandees overseen by a revered figure in white whose throne is in the greatest of all churches in the Eternal City.

Who wouldn't equate the two? Who wouldn't want to? The church is supposed to be beautiful—the "Bride of Christ," as she is called—and Catholics have spent untold treasure making sure she appears worthy of the ideal. This ornate institution, however, is also a strictly vertical model that can often work at cross-purposes with the more horizontal idea of communion, where laymen and laywomen have an equal voice.

The intersection of these two models—the hierarchical and the communal—is the flashpoint of the current conflict.

Even engaging the debate is not easy. It provokes knee-jerk opposition among many Catholics, not just the hard right. Catholics tend to see a certain crudeness in quibbling over what the Bride of Christ should actually look like. The church, after all, is elegance and ineffability, not a runway model. She is, as Dulles says, a mystery. And, he says, "Mysteries are realities of which we cannot speak directly. If we wish to talk about them at all we must draw on analogies afforded by our experience of the world."

That allusiveness can be frustrating for non-theologians—that is, the vast majority of us lay folks—who find that as soon as we think we've laid hands on the church so as to refashion her, she slips behind the veil of a different ideal. Moreover, the popular image of an ageless church is considered so integral to her majesty that any reworking must be done by sleight of hand so as not to disillusion the faithful. Thus the politics of the church are often cloaked in divine language, and the political change that is constantly taking place is perceived only long after the fact. The church herself must remain free of the messiness of the historical process, the thinking goes. The apologies that John Paul has offered in recent years for terrible chapters in the church's past—most notably, for Catholic silence during the Holocaust—illustrate this problem. Rather than apologizing for what the Catholic Church per se has done, the pontiff invariably apologizes for the sins of the "sons and daughters" of the church who went astray. John Paul's tradition of apologizing is widely welcomed, but this distancing language can appear so couched and diplomatic that it fuels the very resentments it was designed to assuage.

The furor over the sexual abuse scandal, however, has opened a new, public debate about rethinking the exalted notions of the church.

In the most detailed proposal along these lines, Father J. Michael Byron, an assistant professor of theology at the University of St. Thomas in St. Paul, Minnesota, offered a list of "correctives" for a "chastened theology of church" that would respond to the problems raised by the sexual abuse scandal. In an eight-point agenda that he presented in *America* magazine, Byron started with a call to teach that "the church is not Jesus Christ."

Byron noted that "this apparently obvious axiom in ecclesiology has received scant acknowledgment in pastoral praxis, in the documents that emanate from teaching authorities and in sermons preached on Sunday mornings. Several implications flow from this simple principle. One is that nothing is self-evidently God's will simply because some cleric, council or Roman dicastery has said so. While Jesus Christ can be afforded that kind of respect, the church is a more ambiguous reality. However intimately and beautifully interrelated are Jesus and church, they are not coterminous. A related implication is that the reverence owed to the church, while real, is not the same as the deference due to Jesus Christ. That is because the quality of 'holiness' attributable to each is not the same. The holiness of Jesus is such as to push aside all sin and darkness. The holiness of the church still allows for the possibility of harboring pedophiles. One who points out this fact in public is not thereby unfaithful, notwithstanding some recent episcopal comments to the contrary."

Byron's second point, that "the church is the people of God," reiterates the mantra of those who want to see a more open and collaborative church emerge from the crisis.

"That this, one of the most fundamental images of Vatican II ecclesiology, labors so mightily in practice after two generations is a scandal of its own," Byron says. "All the charisms bestowed by Christ upon his community of disciples are enjoyed by virtue of baptism, albeit not in identical ways. The council was clear on this concept. This means that it is never the case that some of the baptized have great moral standing and others have none, even in deliberations over ecclesial identity and practice. When concerned relatives and friends point out to church leaders the possibility of serious sin in the clergy, it is not merely good organizational and communication strategy; it is good ecclesiology. It is taking co-responsibility seriously. The Christian response to such complaints is neither 'You are mistaken' nor 'Trust me to handle it.'"

For lay Catholics this is the battleground: a Vatican II model of church as the people of God versus the institutional, hierarchical model that reigned for centuries and is struggling to reassert itself. The priority for lay Catholics, as Thomas Groome, a theologian at Boston College, says, is "to reclaim our vocation as a priestly people" in keeping with the spirit and documents of Vatican II. "The theology is in place; now we must implement it 'on the ground.'"

Alas, that is where it gets messy. The process of implementation has in recent decades been characterized by "party politics" that have left the church so polarized that reform is impossible and gridlock reigns. After Vatican II, buoyed by the flurry of unprecedented changes, the first side to organize its forces in the struggle was what has come to be known as the Catholic left.

• • •

If the Catholic Church were most any other organization, reconfiguring it for popular approval would be relatively simple. The poll numbers are clear, and by the lights of majority rule the Catholic Church—in the United States, at least—would have married priests and women priests, and lay people would have a say in choosing their parish pastor as well as in deciding how the parish's money is spent. In fact, about two-thirds of Catholics say they want a democratic decision-making process that reaches through the diocesan level and all the way to the Vatican. Reform-by-the-numbers is enticingly easy, and many progressive Catholic groups, aptly labeled "breezy rebels," have yielded to the temptation of simplicity only to run smack into a double-edged truth: one, the hierarchy has the power and won't give it up; and two, their fellow lay people may like majority rule in theory better than they do in practice.

The temptation to invest heavily in a populist agenda was understandable, given that Catholic activism was born in the 1970s, in the heyday of America's era of protest and change, and in the wake of Vatican II.

During those years many Catholics were active in civil rights causes, peace groups, and the women's movement, and it was only natural that these protesters would try to translate their experience of grassroots organizing to the church that gave birth to their ideals. *Humanae Vitae* and the tumult over contraception had flung open the door to debate, and all the complex issues of authority and tradition were dumped into the single topic of gender and sexuality, where they have unfortunately remained to the present day. That trend was reinforced by the 1973 *Roe v. Wade* decision. The ruling left the hierarchy aghast, and many Catholics remained uncomfortable with abortion even as they supported abortion rights in general. Other Catholics, however, saw the decision as a moment to recast the history of church teaching on abortion, and the abortion-rights group Catholics for a Free Choice (CFFC) was formed. Its signature event came when CFFC founder Patricia Fogarty McQuillan crowned herself pope on the steps of St. Patrick's Cathedral in New York City on the first anniversary of the *Roe* decision. McQuillan's act was in keeping with the spirit of the times, but it didn't endear her to mainstream Catholics, much less the Vatican.

Dozens of other reform groups followed the CFFC lead.

In 1977, the Women's Ordination Conference was incorporated after an inaugural conference drew 1,900 people to a Detroit hall on

Thanksgiving weekend; Dignity/USA, a group advocating for the rights of gay, lesbian, bisexual, and transgendered Catholics, was founded in 1973; CORPUS, an association of priests who have married and been forced to leave active ministry, started in Chicago in 1974; and in 1976, the Quixote Center, a self-described band of "impossible dreamers," was organized to promote "dialogue between the laity and hierarchy on issues of sexuality, sexual orientation and reproduction." Their motto was a conscious recognition of their idealistic vision: "A gathering of people who work and pray with laughter, to reach for stars that seem too distant to be touched, or too dim to be worth the effort." In 1990 a group called FutureChurch formed in Cleveland under the banner of ordaining women and married men and promoting inclusive language "and Church decision-making that involves all the faithful, as called for by Vatican II."

Until the 2002 scandal spawned Voice of the Faithful, the largest and most prominent reform group promoting a more collaborative church was Call to Action. CTA, as it is known, is rooted in orthodox soil, in a 1971 exhortation by Paul VI that it is the laity who have received the primary "call to action" to effect change in the world. A Rome synod later that year underscored that charge, and the United States bishops came home full of an infectious enthusiasm to spread the good news. They launched a three-year process of consultation, hearing testimony from more than 800,000 Catholics about the state of the church and the world and what to do about it.

On October 21, 1976, in a celebration echoing America's bicentennial of independence, more than a hundred bishops took part in a historic assembly of 2,500 priests, nuns, monks, and lay people who crowded Detroit's Cobo Hall for a three-day meeting that was unique in the history of American Catholicism. The city's cardinal, John Dearden, captured the moment by declaring in his keynote address that they were "beginning a new way of doing the work of the church in America." For three days American Catholics prayed, worshiped, and debated, cardinals and bishops side by side with laymen and laywomen. At the end, the assembly approved thirty resolutions containing more than 180 recommendations for the hierarchy, most notably calls to reevaluate church positions on priestly celibacy, a male-only clergy, homosexuality, and birth control, and demanding collaboration at every level of the church. The Detroit conference recommended that each diocese take the resolutions home and act upon them.

It was an unprecedented moment that held an extraordinary sense of promise. And it was all over before the closing gavel came down. Many bishops had been suspicious of the event before it started, and others who had once supported the conference grew dismayed by the extreme disorganization and rank politicking that went on during it. Before returning home, Archbishop Joseph Bernardin, who would later go on to become the cardinal-archbishop of Chicago and the patron saint of middle-road reformers, told reporters that "too much was attempted at the meeting," and that "special interest groups advocating particular causes [had] dominated the conference as a whole."

Andrew Greeley, who is regularly castigated as a "liberal," dismissed the various lay-led lobbies at the conference as a "ragtag assembly of kooks, crazies, flakes, militants, lesbians, homosexuals, ex-priests, incompetents, castrating witches, would-be messiahs, sickies, and other assorted malcontents." Conservatives were even less enthusiastic. The bishops quickly put an end to any notion of implementing the conference's resolutions (even though many of them were admirable and widely praised initiatives about peace and social justice), and the momentum died before it got going.

The conference that was to revitalize the Catholic Church left it more divided than ever.

Out of the detritus, however, some lay people drew strength. They founded a group, dubbed it Call to Action, and based it in Chicago, where Catholics have historically been unabashed about speaking their minds. And they continued to push for change. CTA developed a small but sturdy national following, drawing about six hundred people to their annual conferences. On Ash Wednesday in 1990, CTA published a "pastoral letter" in the *New York Times* that remains the organization's manifesto. It featured what had by then become the basic catechism of "progressive" groups: reforming church structures, revamping church teachings on sexuality, discarding "the medieval discipline of mandatory priestly celibacy" and opening the priesthood to women, allowing "committed" lay people and clergy a say in electing bishops, and achieving financial glasnost. The statement was published with 4,500 signers and an invitation for more. Within a few months it had 25,000 signatories, and the annual conferences began to draw more people—up to five thousand for the twentieth anniversary in 1996.

The Vatican and its like-minded bishops certainly did everything they could to publicize CTA and other reform groups by employing ham-handed tactics of suppression that seemed like an atavistic reflex from another era. The 1980s and 1990s were years of high tension throughout the Catholic Church as the Vatican reaction against progressive trends, an integral part of John Paul's agenda, started to take hold. Liberation theology proponents such as the Franciscan Leonardo Boff were being silenced in other countries, and in the United States liberal theologians such as Charles Curran were being suspended or fired. Priests and lay leaders with any links to suspect groups were regularly barred from parishes, and Catholic theologians were called on the carpet in Rome to explain their views; if the explanations did not satisfy the Vatican, the Vatican pressured them into silence, or they left. The conflicts drew intense news coverage and equally intense reactions from many lay people.

In March 1996 a CTA chapter was formed in Lincoln, Nebraska, where a hard-core conservative, Fabian Bruskewitz, had recently been named bishop. (Bruskewitz had been working in the Roman Curia for several years but was none too popular among his colleagues there, which hints at how archconservative he is; the Vatican then followed a common habit by dumping him on an American diocese.) Upon hearing of the CTA invasion, Bruskewitz informed his flock that any Catholics who joined CTA faced excommunication. Some 75 people showed up at CTA's first meeting; 200 came to the next one.

But this sort of popular reform always remained local, never managing to grow beyond the bounds of a single diocese to catch the imagination of the wider Catholic community. That was graphically demonstrated in the late 1990s when American Catholic reformers tried to imitate the success of a European reform group called We Are Church. We Are Church had launched a petition drive that garnered 2.3 million signatures in Germany and Austria, countries that have far fewer Catholics than the United States. On Pentecost 1996, with great fanfare, the U.S. version of We Are Church launched a similar effort with the goal of collecting one million signatures by the next Pentecost. There were some 61 million American Catholics at the time, most of them sympathetic to many of the petition's goals, such as the ordination of women and a married priesthood, so the threshold seemed like a cinch.

A year later the drive had netted 37,000 adherents and the organizers were chastened, though not humbled.

In a biting verdict, Loretto Sister Maureen Fiedler, the principal force behind the U.S. petition, attributed the failure to fear, apathy, homophobia, and an absence of "felt pain" among U.S. Catholics. "We overestimated the theological maturity and underestimated the pietism of the Catholic laity," she said.

This is how bad it got: in a sermon on January 17, 1998, during a liturgy for a meeting of the National Center for the Laity, Chicago's Cardinal Francis George, an orthodox-minded prelate whose lectures have earned him the moniker "Francis the Corrector," preached a sermon in which he declared that "liberal Catholicism is an exhausted project." For good measure he called it "parasitical." George later regretted the parasite analogy but stood by the "exhausted" part. What was most telling, however, was that for all the consternation over George's remarks, there was also extensive agreement among liberals that something had gone seriously wrong in the reform movement.

The year of scandal in 2002 further highlighted the problems in changing the Catholic Church along the lines of a secular government, and served to underscore the growing differences among reform-minded Catholics about what they should do next.

Old-time activists such as Leonard Swidler, who has managed a long-running campaign to call a "constitutional convention" of the Catholic Church, went to the 2002 VOTF conference hoping to relaunch his thirty-year-old idea. At the convention, Swidler again played the endearing rabble-rouser, his enthusiasm for change animated by his love for the church. "We come here by the thousands—and in spirit by the millions around the world—to proclaim loud and clear: That we, the laity, have rights!!!" (Swidler included the exclamation points in his written text, and in his fiery delivery.)

But such direct comparisons between the church and the secular political system did not sit well with those Catholics who are considered just inside the liberal fringe. A campaign like Swidler's "to extend those kinds of rights to the Catholic Church has always seemed misconceived," the editors of Commonweal magazine wrote in August 2002. "This is so, not only because of historical, cultural, and structural differences between the church and the United States, but because 'rights talk' in this country is usually short on talk about responsibility and obligation, which is part and parcel of any understanding of the Christian life. If we want to talk about rights in the Catholic Church, we need to conceive a new form, a challenge now more important than ever."

Commonweal was right. Not only is the Catholic Church *not* a democracy, but most Catholics, including many outspoken reformists, do not want it to be one. They want to have a voice, they want to be heard, but they do not necessarily want to elect their pastor or hold quadrennial conventions to nominate their bishop. "Electing bishops is something I've never thought about," said Joseph Abatemarco, a newly energized VOTF reformer who works with divorced and separated Catholics in his New Jersey parish. "I'm no radical," he told me. "It's just balancing out that's needed."

There are good reasons why Catholics are not comfortable with absolute majority rule. Democracy is a winner-take-all game, whereas church—the arena of faith—is about eternal matters that are supposed to be inclusive of everyone; religion is about finding salvation in the next world and expanding virtue in this one. Reductive strategies that reward the few, or even the majority, at the expense of others is not what Jesus would do.

Progressives have to find a better way.

For the Catholic right, on the other hand, church politics have never been of much interest except as a means to blunt the Catholic left, or to trumpet their view of Catholic morality for an audience who never doubted their positions.

To these conservatives, church reform, as such, has always been considered the domain of liberals, which is no surprise since the church is by definition about conserving rather than changing. In a basic sense, all Christians are conservatives, demonstrated by the tendency in any denomination to conflate, over time, every finial in the church's infrastructure with the *depositum fidei*, the deposit of faith that is the vital core of Christian belief. Hence the old joke—Q: How many Christians does it take to change a lightbulb? A: Change? What do you mean change? My grandmother gave the church that lightbulb!

Furthermore, conservatives have had little reason to mobilize at the grass roots, since they have enjoyed a quarter-century run as the house favorites of the man at the top of the Catholic heap, Pope John Paul II. But if conservatives did not have a grassroots movement, they did have an agenda: namely, a two-front war—against liberals, whom they see as pillaging the church's spiritual treasury from within, and against a secular culture that they consider the church's principal external threat.

The problem for conservatives is that this strategy stretches their resources to the breaking point, because there are actually precious few "right"-thinking Catholics. The most optimistic polls (from the conservative point of view) show perhaps 10 percent of American Catholics identifying with "core" Catholic teachings, and even that core seems to be in flux.

Another difficulty is that conservatives themselves cannot agree on who qualifies as a "true" conservative, and so they often spend as much time tearing each other apart as they do fighting the liberal menace. Conservative Catholics regularly, and loudly, disagree with statements from the bishops and the Vatican on a range of issues, from military action by the United States (the former often supporting it, the latter denouncing it) to John Paul's denunciations of the evils of rampant capitalism.

Like liberal dissent, the modern history of conservative dissent parallels the changes of the Vatican II era. It began with William F. Buckley Jr.'s famous *"Mater Si, Magistra No!,"* a 1960 essay that rejected John XXIII's *Mater et Magistra* ("Mother and Teacher") encyclical and it runs up through the pronouncements of today's ur-Catholic, Patrick J. Buchanan, who flat-out rejects the church's stands on immigration and refugees and much else.

The current pontiff's firm opposition to capital punishment has prompted another crisis for conservatives, widening their rift with Rome. Governor Frank Keating, for example, who was appointed after Dallas to head the lay board overseeing the bishops' compliance (as noted earlier), was lauded for his law-and-order credentials. But those same epaulets, earned by his frequent resort to the death penalty, have also led to public conflicts with Oklahoma City archbishop Eusebius J. Beltran. In 1999 Beltran grew so agitated with Keating that he sent a letter to all priests to be read from the pulpit stating that "Governor Keating does not speak on behalf of the Church nor does he reflect her authentic teaching."

The threat of a bishop's wrath has not stopped Supreme Court justice Antonin Scalia, another poster boy for Catholic loyalists, from repeatedly taking John Paul to task. Scalia has frequently argued that John Paul was simply wrong on capital punishment and that in fact the infallible pontiff had contravened infallible church teaching. "Either the moral principles taught by the Church are unchanging . . . or the Church is a fraud," Scalia wrote in *First Things* in October 2002. That is strong stuff.

Catholicism, in short, is as much a burden for the right wing as it is for the left. Conservatives don't see it that way, of course. They cast themselves as the true defenders of the faith, and that has been a source of as much *agita* for the church as any vast left-wing conspiracy. Through a network of periodicals, television programs, and fellow travelers among the punditocracy, conservative Catholics regularly blast church leaders—even those considered conservative by everyone else—for selling out the faith.

The dispute among conservatives, and especially between conservatives and the bishops, is a steady, low-grade guerrilla war that continues every day in dioceses around the United States but rarely gets as much notice as the hierarchy's difficulties with liberals. Newspapers such as *The Wanderer* regularly decry the perceived abuses of the nation's bishops, along with outlets like *National Catholic Register, Catholic World Report,* and *Crisis* magazine. Advocacy groups such as Catholics United for the Faith, Adoremus, and Roman Catholic Faithful (whose motto is *Qui parcit nocentibus innocentes punit,* or "He who spares the guilty punishes the innocent") publish pieces with titles like "A Few Blunt Words to the Hierarchy."

The most visible proponent of Catholic orthodoxy has been EWTN, the Evangelical Word Television Network, a cable channel founded by Mother Angelica, an elderly, sweet-voiced nun with a spine of steel. Mother Angelica fears no one. In 1997 she took on Los Angeles cardinal Roger Mahony for a pastoral letter he had issued on the Eucharist—a letter that she said fostered a heretical view of the Real Presence—and she called on Catholics in the nation's largest diocese to practice "zero obedience" toward the cardinal. That call, tantamount to fomenting schism, sparked a rancorous series of exchanges that left Mahony appealing to Rome to rein in Mother Angelica, whose electronic pulpit gives her a much larger audience than any bishop, even if he is a cardinal.

As Mahony said: "Some of the voices claiming to be Catholic and which give the impression of speaking for the church are, in fact, not so. Who decides?"

Mahony, who is considered one of the more liberal cardinals, though orthodox in belief, is not alone in his frustration with conservatives. Overlooked in Cardinal George's blast at liberal Catholicism's "exhausted" project was his follow-up critique of right-wingers who look to solve the church's woes through "a type of conservative Catholicism obsessed with particular practices and so sectarian in its outlook that it cannot serve as a sign of unity of all peoples in Christ." He also criticized conservatives' "excessive preoccupation with the church's visible government."

In other words, for Catholic conservatives, as opposed to liberals, the system is fine, even divine. Their strategy for improvement is based purely on moral exhortation. If the Catholic left is preoccupied with agendas and "rights talk," the so-called right is focused on wrongs—the wrongs of the countercultural sixties and the creeping moral relativism that is invading even the Holy Roman Church. The late Malachi Martin, a cranky former Jesuit who specialized in novels portraying the church's decline, was the master of this apocalyptic view. His final novel, *Windswept House,* was his most baroque and bizarre, featuring ritual sex and animal sacrifices in the Vatican, and the ascent of Lucifer to the throne of St. Peter, thanks to a "Slavic pope" who had compromised his values and secularized the church. It was a paranoid fantasy barely disguised as a *roman à clef,* and it showed how far the right wing had strayed.

Their gloom is understandable.

Despite the conservative Golden Age since John Paul's ascendance in 1978, Catholic opinion keeps shifting away from the conservatives' views, and changes in church practices continue to follow suit, almost inexorably. While John Paul's policies have held the line on many issues, such as scripture translations and some liturgical practices, those actions come off as desperate rearguard actions after a Pyrrhic victory.

For conservatives, the scandal of 2002 was the *coup de grâce.* With the sins of their bishops on public display, there was no disguising the truth that John Paul had appointed most of the leaders whose misdeeds created the scandal. And if the pontiff had a genetic replicant in the U.S. hierarchy, it was Bernard Law, the man whose chilling protection of pedophile priests at the expense of innocent children had precipitated the disaster.

After some initial, and uncharacteristically weak, attempts to blame the media and defend Law and his fellow bishops, the conservatives rediscovered their voice and wound up turning on the bishops with a venom that outdid their counterparts on the Catholic left.

The rage of the right, however, was the anguish of a child betrayed, and right-wing complaints oddly echoed the sort of victimization that conservatives had scorned among the liberal set: "There is a striking psychological parallel (though far from parity) between the sexually abused child and the spiritually abused orthodox lay person in the post-conciliar American Church," Bruce Walters wrote in *Latin Mass* magazine.

Conservatives as sodomized altar boys. Now there was a leap.

For a brief interlude at the height of the scandal, left, right, and center were in accord—a veritable transfiguration. "It's true that some of the old alignments of right and left are shifting," Father Richard John Neuhaus, editor of the conservative journal *First Things,* said in July. "There are some interesting new ways in which questions are being framed." Some conservatives even credited the Catholic left and the secular media for bringing the scandal to light. But the comity didn't last long. Both sides soon reverted to form, the right wing with a vengeance. In order to appear consistent with their previous stands—again, the illusion of immutability is crucial to the obsessively orthodox—conservatives did not blame the church structures they have long exalted. Rather, they personalized the scandal and argued that it was due solely to moral failings by some bishops. Their litany of sins included an acceptance of homosexuals in the priesthood and a weak-kneed acquiescence to the wider secular culture— in short, a failure to be the kind of Catholics that conservatives were saying they should be. "The failure of the bishops of America is irreparable," one letter-writer wrote to *Inside the Vatican,* a tradition-minded monthly magazine. "The bishops have been so totally, thoroughly discredited as to be meaningless in the fight for the Church and the faith."

With no visible defenses for the failure of their own pope and their own bishops, the Catholic right fell back on their old ways and pinned the entire fiasco on a too-cozy relationship between Catholicism and America's decadent culture.

Catholic World Report, edited by Philip Lawler, the former editor of Law's archdiocesan newspaper, responded to the clerical crisis by calling on the bishops to get tough with the lay people. "The resolution of this crisis will begin, we respectfully suggest, when you, our bishops, firmly insist that the teachings of the Church must be upheld, and the discipline of the Church must be enforced, in the seminaries, parishes, and schools under your authority." An editorial in *Our Sunday Visitor* took a similar tack: "The lack of 'correct moral teaching,' an over-reliance on psychology and the mainstreaming of theological dissent have left the Church with an uncertain message and unconfident messengers, for which we have paid a high price," it said. Other commentaries took it a step further. They argued that the recourse to abortion by Catholics was a far worse scandal than pedophilia, and that abortion had directly contributed to the scandal because it had drained the pool of available Catholic men for the bishops to choose from. That left the seminaries with the dregs. Others laid the blame for the scandal of the sexual abuse of children by priests on the laity's disregard for the church's teaching on contraception.

The conservatives' logic had large gaps, but their argument had the comfort of familiarity. And there wasn't much else they could do. "Reform" is not part of their vocabulary, except when it comes to individual moral behavior.

So rather than join the calls for change, Catholic conservatives attacked the reform groups, claiming that they were Trojan horses for a democratized, congregationalist, Protestantized Catholic Church in which lay people would meddle in matters beyond their ken and make things worse than they already were. "Minds that have not been steeped in theology are almost certain to foul things up when they touch upon theological issues," *Our Sunday Visitor* columnist David Carlin wrote (an interesting echo of Sister Maureen Fiedler's aspersions after the failure of the 1997 petition drive): "The person who deals with Catholic doctrinal questions has to have a theological habit of mind formed along very traditional Catholic lines."

The primary manifestos of the outraged orthodox were Father Benedict J. Groeschel's book *From Scandal to Hope* and George Weigel's *The Courage to be Catholic: Crisis, Reform, and the Future of the Church.* Groeschel is a Franciscan from New York who is a favorite among tradition-minded Catholics and a regular on Mother Angelica's show. Groeschel pinned the scandal on the "viciousness" of the media and a "moral relativism" that has seeped into Catholic teaching, and he said that Catholics need to reform themselves before they can call for reform in the church. Weigel, who is a longtime conservative political commentator and the author of a well-regarded authorized biography of John Paul, *Witness to Hope,* was equally blunt in pointing the finger of blame at the liberal Catholic establishment—"Catholic Lite," he calls it—which "still holds the commanding heights" of the church: "The results of its promotion of 'faithful dissent' are now on display, in clerical sexual scandals and irresponsible episcopal leadership. The game is over." Apparently, lay Catholics have had a lot more influence on their bishops than they ever realized, albeit a corrupting influence.

For Weigel the tonic is simple: "The answer to the current crisis will not be found in Catholic Lite. It will only be found in a classic Catholicism—a Catholicism with the courage to be countercultural, a Catholicism that has reclaimed the wisdom of the past in order to face the corruptions of the present and create a renewed future, a Catholicism that risks the high adventure of fidelity."

Groeschel and Weigel, whose tone Margaret O'Brien Steinfels aptly termed "condescending," were at the high end of the debate. One conservative Catholic writer described those who have been advocating reform as "liturgical terrorists," an especially unhappy reference coming just a month before the first anniversary of 9/11.

In 2002 the polarization that has been a besetting sin of American Catholicism since the 1960s had reappeared, stronger than ever. Both sides had lost their paladins among the hierarchy to the scandal; for the right, it had been Bernard Law since 1984, and for the left, Rembert Weakland since 1977. The opposing troops were now left to wage the battle by themselves.

Back in 1967, the Jesuit Bernard Lonergan saw the problem coming with typical perceptiveness: "There is bound to be formed a solid right that is determined to live in a world that no longer exists," Lonergan wrote. "There is bound to be formed a scattered left, captivated by now this, now that new development, exploring now this and now that new possibility. But what will count is a perhaps not numerous center, big enough to be at home in both the old and the new, painstaking enough to work out one by one the transitions to be made, strong enough to refuse half-measures and insist on complete solutions even though it has to wait."

What Lonergan sketched was, in essence, an avenue to reform that depends on a politically mature laity and a large dose of patience. With no formal mechanisms in place by which lay people can affect church policy, diplomacy and politesse are indispensable, like it or not. And while history is moving faster than ever before, the institutional church still thinks, and often acts, in terms of centuries. In order for lay people to jump-start reform, the "deep middle," as Scott Appleby called that heretofore silent majority of lay Catholics, will have to find a voice that goes beyond deafening moral hortatory and calls for a constitutional convention in St. Peter's Basilica.

During the heady days of the Call to Action conference in 1976, as bishops and lay people hashed out groundbreaking resolutions in small-group meetings, Philadelphia's legendary Cardinal John Krol smiled at his fellow delegates as they steamrolled toward one especially radical proposal. "You can vote for it, but you're not going to get it," the man known as Old King Krol told them. He was good-natured about it, and dead right.

More than twenty-five years after Krol made that observation, the polarization had only grown worse, and efforts to bind up the wounds had not brought healing.

So what is the answer? Can lay Catholics find a way through the minefields of canon law, church tradition, and their own divisions to change the course of the Catholic Church?

After three decades of hard lessons, the reformers know what *not* to do. As Boston College theologian Lisa Sowle Cahill told the Voice of the Faithful crowd: "Even though we are beginning new reforms in our own lives, in our own communities, and in our own parishes, and right here at this convention, we also need not to become too directly oppositional to the official structure. The pope and the bishops are also part of historic Catholicism, and if we are too confrontational . . . we might become labeled as fringe type and outsiders.

"This is a very tricky business," Cahill warned. "It's going to be hard to figure where the balance is, but that will be important."

A promising strategy has emerged, however, and it is contingent on a two-track approach to reform that disengages issues of church teaching from issues of church governance. To be sure, both teaching and governance are matters of authority, and both are changing in response to the times. But governance can be negotiated and addressed more directly than teaching, and without threatening the core of the faith or the province of the bishops in guarding doctrines that a lot of lay Catholics don't want to put up to a vote.

In her writings and speeches in 2002, Harvard's Mary Jo Bane sketched out how this might work. Changes on issues of sexuality and a celibate priesthood, Bane argued, should wait for change at the Vatican. That's how it should be, she says, because "the Church is both a sacrament of our faith and a human institution. The church doesn't in fact exist to meet our needs as we express them. In that sense, it's not, in fact, a democracy. The church exists to proclaim God's kingdom and to carry out the mission of Jesus—the mission of Jesus to bring the good news to the poor, to set the prisoners free, to open the eyes of the blind, to bring justice to the oppressed. That's the mission of the church. That's the mission we want to share. We don't want to vote on whether that's the mission. We know that's the mission."

But she also noted that there is plenty that lay Catholics can do to exert some measure of influence in church operations. They can join their parish council (or lobby to create one), press their diocese for greater financial transparency, or form clergy-lay boards to have input on the personnel process. "To these, what I would call secular aspects of the church, we can in fact legitimately and sensibly bring our demands for openness, for accountability, and for shared decision-making. We can also bring our expertise." This, she says, can lead to "new models" of governance suited to the church's "sacred character."

What Bane and other sober-minded advocates of reform wisely avoid is the red herring that the Catholics should chuck it all and try to recover some primeval church of the first century, when it was all democracy and, probably, women priests. In the first place, that never existed. The early church was a rough-and-tumble affair of competing agendas and egos, all of them *male* egos. Much of the Catholic Church as we know it is here to stay, and just as important, much is worth keeping. Garry Wills was surprised when readers of his blistering dissection of the papacy, *Papal Sin*, thought he was endorsing an elimination of the papal office. On the contrary, he said, the papacy is an important symbol of unity. Likewise, Paul Wilkes, one of the most thoughtful Catholic writers today, also warned his fellow lay people against worshiping the "false god" of innovation. "Don't change for change's sake," he wrote in the *National Catholic Reporter*. "Sometimes the tried and true ways really are the best."

Such Catholics—"liberal" in temperament and "conservative" in faith—are the majority, at least in America, and the seeming contradiction of their positions is a source of endless confusion to a non-Catholic culture that prefers the comfort of preexisting categories.

The promise of the two-track approach was, to my mind, given its most eloquent endorsement by Frank DeAlderete, a technical writer and computer products trainer from Bedford, Massachusetts, who is a self-described "ordinary parishioner dealing with extraordinary times." DeAlderete is a father of three who was invited to speak at the VOTF conference and offered a presentation that belied the bomb-throwing image that conservative critics like to stick on the group. DeAlderete, burly and bearded, is the image of a Catholic mensch. Catholicism, as he told the reformers, is as integral to his being as his DNA. He is Catholic "from the Rosary in my pocket, to the wedding band on my hand, to the medal of the Blessed Mother on my chest."

In that context, DeAlderete said, proposals to "change" the church naturally elicit a visceral response. "I feel as if I am lying on an operating table and there are a lot of learned men and women standing over me, and they're discussing what to do, and they don't agree. So I say with all due respect, put the scalpels down and let's talk about this.

"For starters," he continued, "let's agree that we're going to stay Catholic. And that means that dogma, theology, and to a great degree, tradition, is off the table for now. The scandal that prompted this is not a failure of dogma. It is a failure of morality. It is a failure to enforce canon law."

The first step, DeAlderete told the gathering, echoing Bane's approach, is to get everyone familiar with the avenues already available. "We have to renew wherever possible and replace as a last resort. When we replace infrastructures it requires resources, and those resources have to come from somewhere. Don't rob Peter to pay Paul. If you think your parish council should be an elective body, don't create a new one. Fix the old one. We must work for gradual, incremental, and reasonable change. What do you think we have a better chance of getting in the next six months? The vote for a bishop? Or the right to review a priest's résumé and public ministry? Remember that it takes a mile of water to stop a battleship. We have to accept our sphere of influence, which means that we do what we can where we can. We have to build from our parish out-wards. We can discuss, as all families do, what we would do if we were in charge. But we have to be practical in where we invest our energies.

"Picketing for the ordination of women in front of the cathedral is like asking a crossing guard to renew the FBI," DeAlderete concluded. "We simply—and even the archdiocese—do not have the authority to change Vatican policy. We have to take the long view, the millennial view, and not react to the temporal things in ways that our descendants are going to regret."

DeAlderete didn't get the most enthusiastic reception, but his ap-proach is the closest thing American Catholicism has to a consensus in this turbulent era. It is something a lot of Catholics can live with.

The first step in the strategy of pragmatic reform could come in the arena of church finances.

If there is one thing that both bishops and laity can agree on, it is that money is the lifeblood of the church's daily operations, and that all of it comes from the pews.

As the revelations of abuse kept coming in 2002, Catholics grew just as angry over the number and size of secret settlements that had facili-tated the cover-ups as they did over the abuse itself. The flock may have struggled to understand the psychology of the abuser, but they were ab-solutely clear on the venality—and fungibility—of money. And in few places is money more fungible than in the Catholic Church, to the degree that the bishops themselves often don't have any idea how much parishes or their pastors have, or how it is spent. It is even more likely that the parishes are in the dark about how the bishop is spending money, or even how much he makes (actually, it's not much—but the perks are great).

In 2002, for example, it was revealed that Milwaukee archbishop Rembert Weakland sold a building donated by a Catholic philanthropy so he could pay $450,000 to a man with whom he had apparently had a rela-tionship that he had cut off. When the accuser came forward despite the payment, Weakland resigned and donors were shocked, both at what he did, and that diocesan bishops can spend up to $1 million without consult-ing their financial committees. "Some of us are beginning to feel disap-pointed and even alienated from the church," said Erica John, a Miller brewing heiress whose foundation had donated the building that Weakland sold.

We have seen repeated examples of how the lack of internal controls leads to fiscal shenanigans, only a fraction of which ever become public; papering over financial irregularities is even easier than covering up for molesters. In 2000, for example, a Brooklyn priest, Msgr. Thomas J. Gradilone, was finally caught after years of hoarding money from parish collections, some $1.8 million of which he had funneled to three ex-convicts in what he claimed were charitable donations. The bishop called it fraud and dismissed Gradilone. But pastors have so much legal leeway on finances that the priest was never charged by the civil authorities with any wrongdoing.

Lay Catholics aren't immune to temptation, either, of course, which should serve as a warning to those who think that lay participation in the church will be an automatic panacea. Four years before the Gradilone episode, the Brooklyn diocese's longtime and trusted pension manager, a quiet Italian-American woman named Vincenza Bologna, was nabbed after embezzling more than $1 million from the diocese, which she used on gambling trips to Atlantic City and Las Vegas, college tuition for her two sons, a nineteen-foot boat, two plots of waterfront land in Florida, and three cars. And in August 2002, a layman who was the business manager at an Arkansas parish pleaded guilty to embezzling $499,063 from his church.

Despite such financial problems, American dioceses have no nationally accepted auditing or disclosure agreements, and while many dioceses release annual financial statements, you'd have to be a CPA (Arthur Andersen excepted) to understand them. Transparency of that sort can be deceptive. Concerned over the lack of internal controls, the United States Conference of Catholic Bishops in 1995 published tough new guidelines for parishes and dioceses. But there is little evidence that those guidelines are being followed.

When New York cardinal John O'Connor died in 2000, he left an annual operating deficit that was estimated to be upwards of $20 million. It was born not of profligacy but of generosity; O'Connor couldn't say no to the range of well-meaning folks out there with wonderful projects to fund, and he disliked the kind of fundraising that turns off the faithful but is so necessary to doing's God's work. O'Connor's style of stewardship forced his successor, Cardinal Edward Egan, who was already less than beloved, to clean up the mess by making a lot of tough decisions.

The sexual abuse scandal underscored how little financial accountability there is in the Catholic Church. Not only did the national bishops conference have no idea exactly how many priests had been accused over the years, they also had no idea how much of the faithful's money had been paid out to victims over the years. They disputed the claims that put the figure at more than $1 billion but had no response beyond a guesstimate of $300 to $400 million. To lay people, a hundred million dollars here or there is real money.

"I am convinced that it is of paramount importance for every diocese in the nation to prepare and widely circulate—at the soonest possible moment—a comprehensive, clear, lucid, understandable, transparent and brutally honest financial accounting to the people—Catholic and non-Catholic alike—of their region," Fred L. Hofheinz, program director for religion at the Lilly Endowment, Inc., told diocesan financial directors at a September 2002 conference. Hofheinz said he was speaking "not so much as a thirty-year program director at the Lilly Endowment but as a sixty-four-year-old, lifelong, faithful, and believing Catholic." He warned: "If the current scandal is followed in the next months or years by even the suspicion of financial misdealings on the part of church officials, I do not believe the Catholic people will tolerate it."

Lay Catholics want to know where the money is going; they don't, contrary to a widespread notion, want to stop giving.

In fact, even as the scandal rocked the church and as the economy went south, Catholics dug deeper into their pockets. In Baltimore, the annual cardinal's appeal was up 22 percent, to $5 million in 2002, and parishioners in Chicago contributed $317 million all told to the church, up 6 percent over the pre-scandal year—and that despite a boycott organized by a group of prominent Catholic businessmen. So it went, across the board, with the notable exception of Boston and a few similarly scandalized dioceses.

The problem for Catholics is that by withholding money they are either penalizing their own parish—the destination for the bulk of their donations—or the poor and needy who benefit from diocesan programs. A Catholic community is so intertwined that a shot aimed at one faction will inevitably hurt someone else.

Lay Catholics can certainly demand greater financial accountability from the bishops, and there are indications that those demands are being heeded by some dioceses. Canon law says little about financial statements, and lay people should press hard for greater openess. What canon law does stipulate is that every diocese and every parish must have a finance council; it is up to lay people to join them and to use them as a springboard for transparency. This is grunt work, and it is crucial. Following the money leads to greater collaboration and responsibility in any organization.

But as lay Catholics raise their voices on this issue, they may also want to consider their own track record of financial support for the church. For years before the scandal, Catholics were donating money at about half the rate Protestants were, about 1.1 percent to 2.2 percent, even though Catholics today have a higher per capita income on average. Researchers have cited numerous factors in the disparity, many of which contribute to, or derive from, the growing gap between the laity and clergy.

One major factor is size. A study in the 1980s found that the average Catholic parish had 2,300 members, about eight times the size of the average Protestant congregation. (This ratio may be growing as the priest shortage worsens.) The smaller the church, the greater the sense of involvement and the higher the rate of giving. And vice versa. Large churches mean greater distance, a decreased sense of ownership, and hence a lessened sense of financial responsibility. In addition, Catholics like the hierarchical nature of the church when it comes to finances, because the bishop, like a Sugar Daddy, can always step in to bail out a parish.

With an estimated $7.5 billion going into Catholic collection plates each year, simply doubling donations would not only be a powerful display of lay ownership and authority in the church, but it would provide some real leverage, as well as an enormous boost in the good works that the church could do.

Money isn't the laity's only avenue to change, of course. In fact, writing a check is perhaps the most passive form of activism. Concrete reform in the governance of the church, a true revolution from below, will be predicated on lay people becoming more involved in the daily life of the church. If the Catholic hierarchy has spent the last thousand years walling off the sanctuary from the laity, it is also true that lay Catholics have been, in the contemporary term, enablers of that clerical culture through their own disinterest. Yes, sinful priests abused children and morally blind bishops covered up for the molesters. But honest advocates of change also recognize that Catholic lay people have for too long been happy to let Father run the show, and thus they bear some of the responsibility for the consequences.

As David O'Brien told the VOTF conference: "If we had built shared responsibility in parish and diocesan pastoral councils, if we had formed self-confident associations of diocesan priests, religious, and lay people, if Catholic academic, medical, social service, and ministerial professionals had acted responsibly, these scandals of clerical sexual abuse would have ended between 1984 and 1993. . . . Catholic church reform has its deep and mysterious dimensions, to be sure, but the basics are not rocket science: we know how to ensure transparency, accountability, and shared responsibility in ways which support the mission of the church, strengthen, not weaken, the authority of pastors, and insure the integrity of the community of faith. We knew how to do it, but it didn't happen. What was lacking among us was not knowledge or imagination but will and skill, commitment, organization, strategy, and tactics.

"Our failure," O'Brien concluded, "was not theological or spiritual but political."

Similar assessments came from Catholics across the board. One of the more incisive and remarkable analyses of the scandal—and one that again demonstrates the untapped talents of lay Catholics—came during a "listening session" held at a New Jersey church near my home. During the session at Corpus Christi in Chatham Township, one parishioner dissected the faults of clergy and hierarchy with laserlike precision and an anger born out of deep disappointment. But she did not spare herself or her fellow Catholics:

"We all bear a portion of the guilt for what has happened to these children and for any similarly hidden evil behavior that may yet be revealed," she said. "We share the guilt because we have allowed ourselves to be turned into unquestioning sheep who have been banished from any positions of real leadership within the church. For far too long, we the laity have silently accepted a medieval system where every decision of any real importance has been made by an insular group of men."

While no one wants to return to the brass-knuckle politics of the old trustee controversies of the early American church, lay Catholics do have to change their docile ways before they can change the church. As Tom Beaudoin put it: "Are you and I willing to resist the cheap grace of non-involvement, and to pursue the costly grace of reform? What are we willing to commit ourselves to?"

Before the scandal, the answer to that question would not have been encouraging. In survey after survey American Catholics have registered higher levels of satisfaction with their pastors and their parishes, and reported far fewer conflicts, than their Protestant counterparts. In most every category, Catholics are more likely than other churchgoers to say they are happy about the direction of their parish, the mission of their church, and the state of their church's finances. If things are as bad in the church as everyone now says they are, lay people certainly haven't been too keen on doing anything about it.

The problem, according to Father Thomas J. Reese, a Jesuit whose books on church politics are essential texts, is simple: "Lay people don't really want to put everything up to a vote in the parish. They talk democracy. But the trouble with democracy is it takes up too many evenings. Do you want to spend every evening down at your parish church running it? No!"

Indeed, Catholics may want to be careful what they pray for; a chat with any Protestant who has sat on pastor search committees or endured vestry meetings and budget battles might temper the fires for reform. Moreover, democracy without involvement winds up, as the world of secular politics too often attests, in a beauty contest, especially in Catholic parishes that are on average so much larger than Protestant churches. "I've seen parish council elections and they put the pictures of the candidates in the parish bulletins and the prettiest women get elected or the people with the best photographs get elected," Reese said. "People in the parish don't know the other people there."

The late Jesuit sociologist Joseph Fichter did a survey early in his career, before the Second Vatican Council, which showed that about 25 percent of the members of any given parish were involved in some way in parish life, beyond showing up for Mass. Decades later, following the galvanizing innovations of Vatican II, Fichter repeated his survey. He got the exact same result.

The opportunities were there. In the wake of Vatican II, for example, many dioceses set up priest personnel boards to help the bishop match the right priest to the right parish in a collaborative process. But the "town hall" experiment went nowhere and largely ended in the 1980s. One problem was that parishioners had so many conflicting visions of what they wanted in a pastor. Another was that many parishioners wanted a man for all seasons—a priest who had a gift for reaching both young people and the elderly, who had a great singing voice and preached wonderful sermons, who could enforce orthodoxy but be flexible with them, who could bring fiscal discipline to the parish but generously fund every program, all without pain. "Basically what people want is Jesus Christ with an MBA from Harvard," Reese said. "Or a cross between St. Francis and Lee Iacocca. It was totally unrealistic."

One bishop told me how he grew exasperated with a particularly ornery parish that kept complaining about the priests they were offered. Finally, the bishop told them the truth—the parish's three top choices had been offered the job but they all declined because they knew the parishioners would eat them alive. That is not what parishioners like to hear.

When he gathered a group of reporters for dinner to announce his retirement toward the end of 2002, Bishop Frank J. Rodimer of the Diocese of Paterson,. in New Jersey, spoke of how the scandals that had dogged his own diocese had also reinforced his conviction that lay people must be incorporated into the administrative structures of the church. He said that greater lay participation would prevent a repeat of the abuses and also reinvigorate the life of the church. "In the priest crisis it's very obvious that the decisions made without a broader consultation haven't worked, and actually worked to our detriment."

But Rodimer also noted that direct democracy doesn't always translate easily to the church, even with the best of intentions. Recalling his own years as a parish priest, in the heady days after Vatican II, Rodimer said that he did everything he could to build a collaborative parish, to the point of letting the congregants vote each year on whether to pay to cool the church, which grew stifling in the summer. "Every year I tried to get air-conditioning, and every year they voted it down," Rodimer said. "We never got it until the last year I was there. Two people passed out one day and one of them died. I said, That's it. I put in the air-conditioning. It cost $1,000, but I was wrong not to just do it before."

Another dilemma of majority rule in the church is that a straight congregational approach goes against the grain, not to mention the structure, of the communitarian nature of Catholic life. Parishes are part of a diocese, dioceses are part of a national church, and each national church is part of the universal church, and so on—a skein of interconnections that is mediated by the bishops. Bishops assess an annual tax on parishes that is redistributed to poorer parishes and schools and social services, as well as causes far removed from a parish's borders, including the Holy See. Dioceses are wealth-levelers par excellence. Marx called it socialism. Catholics call it Christianity.

This balance between the local and the global, the individual and the community, is a delicate matter that runs through every rung of the reform debate—in the relationship between the individual and his or her congregation, between well-to-do Catholics and marginalized, voiceless Catholics, between the congregation and the bishop, and between the American church, in its privileged but still numerically minor role (6 percent worldwide), and the worldwide church, where parish elections are often of minimal concern.

Lay people who take seriously the call for renewed activism should not presume that when they join a parish everyone will be waiting to storm the barricades of the chancery. Throughout the post–Vatican II period millions of lay Catholics have become deeply involved in their church, in highly organized and committed associations. However, these movements are often highly traditional in orientation, or embrace a spirituality that is not inclined to rock the boat. They include the Neocatechumenate Way, Communion and Liberation, Opus Dei, the Legion of Christ, the Focolare, and others. These orthodox groups are in addition to longstanding associations such as the Knights of Columbus, parish Rosary societies, and pro-life groups, none of which is aimed at rocking the Catholic boat. Likewise, the Ancient Order of Hibernians, which organizes New York's annual St. Patrick's Day parade, is made up of devoted Catholics, and they haven't budged on their policy of excluding gays from marching, despite the tolerant attitude of the larger Catholic community.

The natural conservatism of the most devout Catholics holds true across the board, from members of tightly run lay movements to Catholics who faithfully attend Mass each week. Polls show that members of liberal Catholic groups, on the other hand, tend to be much less involved in church life. If these streams of Catholic life start to mix at the parish level, they will have to learn to get along there.

The activism has to start now. At this point Catholics cannot, and should not, remain passive and simply hope to pray their way to a healthier church. Remember, Catholicism is about doing as well as believing. Lay people have to join parish councils, or start them. Greater collaboration is needed, true, but the structures of collaboration are already there, if Catholics care enough to use them.

Even the smallest changes will not come without a struggle. Bishops and priests will protest the erosion of their total authority, and the Vatican will fight (as it has repeatedly signaled) changes that give lay people any sway over priests. The Dallas policy's call for lay review boards, like Keating's panel, was one reason Rome sent the charter back for revisions. And in June 2002, the same month that the bishops were calling for those lay review boards, the Vatican quietly rejected the election of a religious brother to be president of a U.S. province of Capuchin Franciscan priests and monks. Members of the order had duly elected Brother Robert Smith to a three-year term, and the province's Rome-based leader had approved it. But the Vatican would not allow a monk, who is technically a member of the lay order, to hold a position "with authority over priests."

In the Curia's eyes, this rule applies even in gray areas, and Rome doesn't care who it offends. In 2000, leaders of the U.S. bishops conference sought to have a longtime associate general secretary of their organization, Sister Sharon Euart, moved up to the post of general secretary, essentially the executive responsible for day-to-day affairs. The Vatican said no, the job had to go to a priest. Several bishops and church officials voiced their consternation, but the decision stood. "Nothing you do in the job requires you be ordained," said Msgr. Daniel Hoye, a past general secretary.

Morever, conservative lay-Catholics can defend clerical privileges just as vociferously as any cleric. Mary Ann Glendon, a law professor at Harvard and a strongly orthodox Catholic who sits on the Vatican's Council for the Laity, wrote in a November 2002 essay that reform-minded Catholics should not complain when bishops freeze them out. "No good shepherd will invite wolves to look after his flock," Glendon wrote. Given that those same "good"—i.e., conservative and clerical—shepherds allowed priest molesters to prey on children, Glendon's statement not only subverts logic but puts pedophiles on a par with well-meaning lay Catholics. Yet it is a classic enunciation of the conservative mindset to maintain a close identification between matters of governance and the core of Christian teaching, so as to preserve the status quo from top to bottom. Theirs is the classic "slippery slope" nightmare. Or, as Mary Jo Bane put it: "Let 'em monitor the finances and pretty soon they're gonna want to vote on the nature of the Trinity."

That deep-seated fear was evidenced by the harsh reactions against Voice of the Faithful, which spent the months after its summer convention battling with bishops who wanted to quash them before they took root. In New Jersey, Archbishop John J. Myers launched a preemptive strike in October, barring VOTF from church property even before the group tried to set up a chapter. Voice of the Faithful, Myers said, was "anti-Church and, ultimately, anti-Catholic." He argued that the true purpose of the group is "to act as cover for dissent with the faith; to cause division within the Church; and to openly attack the Church hierarchy."

In a Haverhill parish near Boston one pastor barred VOTF, saying, "They have a right to their opinion, but when they interfere with my work they can go to hell." And Father Robert Carr, a top aide to Cardinal Law, gave VOTF sympathizers a love-it-or-leave-it ultimatum: "If you're working for Coke," he said, "you don't drink Pepsi." VOTF's Web site was hacked repeatedly, and inflammatory and derogatory postings from right-wingers forced the group to suspend its bulletin board.

Many liberals were also upset with VOTF, criticizing the group for trying to play it safe through a policy of appeasement. Frances Kissling, head of Catholics for a Free Choice, frowned at VOTF's rush "to occupy the center," while Marquette's Daniel Maguire tweaked VOTF as "much too timid and fearful to do the job they've set out for themselves."

Meanwhile, other progressives tried to exploit the organization's ready-made platform to pursue their own agenda, and left VOTF's leaders struggling to stay the middle course, maintain their momentum, and at the same time put some flesh on their vague pledge to keep the faith and change the church. "In January we were a young organization when we adopted those broad principles," said Luise Dittrich, one of VOTF's founding members. "I'm not sure we knew what we meant then. Little by little we are coming to see that we need to be clearer. This is our organization learning and growing."

They may not have much time. But they also may not have much choice. Giving voice to a heretofore mute Catholic middle will be a long slog of discernment and action. The Catholic left and the Catholic right have a big head start, and they both have the advantage of rock-solid certainty, and of simple ideas that can be shouted through megaphones. Yet a broader and more sophisticated lay reform movement can also accomplish the unprecedented changes that neither end of the ideological divide has been able to achieve, and in the end, that will be a victory for everyone, not the triumph of a few.

Given the horrors uncovered by the sexual abuse scandal, calling for reform through a tempered balance of activism and consensus might seem like a fainthearted response. But the year of trauma and outrage did not alter the fact that the wider body of believers still has no vote, and is not likely to get one anytime soon. That is the reality, as frustrating as it may be. In addition, most Catholics do not want to chuck their Catholic tradition because of the misdeeds and misconduct of the bishops and priests entrusted with teaching that faith. It is the faith of the laity as much as of anybody else in the church. As long as children are protected by a tough sexual abuse policy, the legitimate fury of the laity must turn to the underlying crisis in the church, and to changing the structures and dynamics that made the scandal possible.

In the Catholic Church, revolution is evolution. The great virtue of that style is that it works to keep everyone in the community. Yet like any deliberate process, this kind of change is often imperceptible to the naked eye of daily journalism; only the telescoping lens of history can appreciate its progress. The changes are coming, though. The activism spurred by the scandal—the parish meetings, the conferences, the Web sites, the op-ed pieces, the protests and boycotts—has not been for naught. It reflects legitimate, necessary demands for justice, for charity, and for change. And those demands are being heard.

True, the institutional church resists change while staring down the barrel of an opinion poll. Responding to the *vox populi* in such a "political" way is considered beneath the dignity of the church's caretakers. So the church has become adept at changing by co-opting its opponents. Long before Hegel proposed his dialectic, Catholicism was synthesizing contradictory ideas into coherent philosophies. From paganism to Pentecostalism, from the Scientific Revolution to the American Revolution, the church has often stood in public opposition, on the one hand, while on the other using doctrinal legerdemain to incorporate elements from its foes and adjust its traditions to the truths they revealed.

One doesn't have to reach back to the Middle Ages to see the process at work. In 1950, Pope Pius XII released an encyclical, *Humani Generis,* which soundly rejected what he called the "new theology" that was emerging from the ferment of the postwar world. Pius's words would be used as the basis of the harsh condemnations and suppressions imposed against popular theologians such as Henri de Lubac, Jean Danielou, Yves Congar, and Karl Rahner. Their books were banned, and Congar was forbidden to teach. Eight years later Pius was dead, and four years after that these same theologians were being hailed as the architects of the Second Vatican Council. Eventually, Danielou and de Lubac were made cardinals.

In the wake of the current crisis, as well, "change is going to come from the exigencies of what is actually going on," said Lawrence Cunningham, head of Notre Dame's department of theology. The theology is there; it was endorsed by Vatican II. Now it needs to catch up with the reality "on the ground." When it does, Cunningham said, "it will get ratified, or encouraged, or guided by the Magisterium of the Church and by the pope and the bishops. And that, ideally, is the way things ought to happen. Then we theologians will come along and show how that was always consistent with the teaching," he added. He was only half joking.

When revolution from below comes, it will be in this classically Catholic way, a peculiar dialectic of percolation that eventually heeds the demands of the faithful. It may start with nuts-and-bolts discussions about greater collaboration in the governance of the church in fiscal transparency, in the assignment of pastors, and in the reinvigoration of parish and diocesan councils by a newly committed laity. But the theology will evolve as well, as it must. That will happen on a parallel track, through the symbiosis of ecclesiology. Tradition and church teaching are as integral to reform as issues of governance, and should not be ignored by the laity. But there, too, the evolution is well underway.

Nowhere is that more obvious than in the changing role of the priesthood.

Part Two

THE PRIESTHOOD

I remember a song . . . "It's a long way to Tipperary."
—Pope John Paul II on prospects for reforming the priesthood (1987)

Seven

THE MEN IN THE MIDDLE

On September 10, 2002, the papers and airwaves were full of little news other than the impending anniversary of the 9/11 terrorist attacks. Rumors of war and the future of America and the unstilled grief of thousands were the understandable motifs of the day, especially at places such as St. Teresa of Avila in New Jersey, which lost several parishioners when suicidal Islamists destroyed the Twin Towers a few miles distant. In the St. Teresa rectory, where he had moved on retiring as a full-time pastor a few years earlier, Frank McNulty was also preparing to mark the anniversary. Now in his mid-seventies, but looking a decade younger, McNulty helps out with Masses and other functions at the vibrant congregation, while also maintaining a busy schedule of travel around the country to lead parish renewal programs, priest retreats, and workshops with titles such as "The 'Going My Way' Priest Is No More."

The priesthood has been Frank McNulty's life, and on this day, when I visited him at the rectory at St. Teresa of Avila, he was also remembering another anniversary, one that would go unnoticed this year, but that had intense personal meaning for him and for his confreres among the thinning ranks of the 47,000 men in the ordained Catholic priesthood in America. Fifteen years earlier, on September 10, 1987, McNulty had delivered a remarkable speech to Pope John Paul II in a public forum in

Miami, where the pontiff had just arrived for the first leg of what was to be an intensely scrutinized ten-day coast-to-coast tour of his restive flock in the United States. Frank McNulty is too modest to make such a claim, but there is good reason to believe that if the pope had heeded the priest's words back then, much of the church's current anguish might have been avoided.

The 1980s were a time of extraordinary upheaval in the Catholic Church in America, but the turmoil was largely an internal struggle of almost academic interest to the outside world, rather than the public humiliation that floored Catholicism in 2002. The first round of sexual abuse scandals had erupted in 1985, triggered by the case of a Louisiana priest, Gilbert Gauthé, whose trail of molestation was tracked by the crusading journalist Jason Berry and the *National Catholic Reporter*. Those stories in turn churned up other cases. This was the first time such crimes had come to the public's attention. Catholics were repulsed, but they rallied around their church, and the bishops professed to being shocked at the priests' misconduct, à la *Casablanca's* Captain Louis Renault. The bishops followed up with a pledge to stamp out sexual misconduct in the priesthood, and they passed new guidelines (not, however, binding rules) to ensure that the scandal would never be repeated.

So many other issues were roiling Catholicism in these years, that the sex scandal was almost a sideshow in a larger struggle as John Paul sought to enforce the conservative policies he had been implementing since his election in 1978. During this time the pope was regularly calling theologians on the carpet and chastising bishops privately, and sometimes embarrassing the latter publicly, as in the case of Seattle archbishop Raymond Hunthausen, whom the pope saddled with a Vatican-appointed assistant bishop to make sure that Hunthausen did not stray from Vatican-directed orthodoxy.

Rome feared that its American flock was itching to exploit any opening for reform, and this clash between an Old World "autocracy" and the democratic yearnings of a New World church was the "sexy" religion story of the decade, with reason. Despite John Paul's inherent conservatism, there was a sense in those days that much was in flux, in ways it hadn't been before. It is hard to recall now how up for grabs everything seemed then, just a few years ago. Pope John Paul II was the 263rd successor to Peter, yet he was something wholly new. The first non-Italian pontiff in more than 450 years, John Paul was a magnetic figure whose globe-trotting pilgrimages and unblinking showdowns with Communist authorities in his native Poland were changing the geopolitical landscape before the world's eyes and transforming the Roman pontiff into a media celebrity. In 1987 John Paul was less than a decade into his pontificate, and he was already legendary. He had survived a shocking assassination attempt in St. Peter's Square, at the site of the martyrdom of Peter, the first pope, and yet he returned to his mission with as much enthusiasm and purpose as before. John Paul hiked and skied, and even allowed himself to be photographed doing so. He spoke dozens of languages and brought such avuncular warmth and Reaganesque optimism to his mission that even those who disagreed with him were captivated by his charisma and popularity, by the humanity he wore on his sleeve. Catholics of all persuasions were convinced that here, finally, was a pope who would listen, whose heart could be touched, and perhaps changed. They felt that if they could just have a minute with him, to explain how things really were, he would understand. More important, as an all-powerful pope, he would actually be able to do something to fix the situation.

Thus it was a natural, if highly unusual, development when the U.S. bishops decided to build the pope's 1987 U.S. tour around a series of "structured dialogues" in which representatives of different constituencies in the church—priests, nuns, laity, and so on—would be selected to tell the Holy Father of their concerns, to speak their minds, and thereby (it was hoped) to let a little steam out of the pressure-cooker that was the American church. Years of frustration were focused on this moment, and the man chosen to speak to John Paul on behalf of the nation's Catholic clergy was Frank McNulty.

The choice made sense. McNulty was a well-known speaker who was considered a top-notch vicar for priests in the Archdiocese of Newark in New Jersey, the seventh-largest U.S. diocese. (A vicar for priests looks after the well-being of the other priests in his diocese and is someone besides the bishop to whom those priests can go in confidence.) Speaking for the clergy before the pope was an awesome responsibility; nothing like it had happened before (or has happened since, for that matter). There was no one better equipped to do it than McNulty. He called his talk "If Priests Could Open Up Their Hearts." The conditional note of the title suggested how much priests felt bottled up—besieged by changes around them, yet unable to catch a break, either from the flock, whose demands were growing more insistent, or from the Vatican, which was cracking down.

In front of 750 fellow priests gathered at a North Miami church (two from every diocese in the nation), McNulty spoke with great respect, but he signaled right off that he would be forthright as well: "These recent years have not been easy for priests," McNulty told the pope.

"If priests could open up their hearts and tell you of their priesthood, they would speak of worries. There is a real and dramatic shortage of priests, a situation critical enough to make us worry about the future. In some areas, each passing day finds the priest less able to meet needs and fulfill expectations. Age and ministerial fatigue are harsh realities. Morale suffers when we see so few young men follow in our footsteps. . . . We worry that we might become only a Church of the word and lose our sacramental tradition. The suffering intensifies when we realize that in ten years we could have half the present number of priests."

McNulty then ventured into more perilous terrain, asking the pontiff to reconsider mandatory priestly celibacy, to allow theologians a "free sense of inquiry," to give priests a say in the selection of bishops, and to provide greater roles for women in the church. McNulty knew that he was courting headlines, but he also knew that the issues could not be avoided any longer. "If priests could open up their hearts and tell you of their priesthood," he told John Paul, "they could not do so without some controversial questions surfacing. In our country there is an attitude toward questions; it comes from our heritage, those historical events which help make us the way we are. We treasure freedom—freedom of conscience, freedom of religion, freedom of expression. Questions brought our nation into being. In such settings people do not run from questions about what they believe and how they live out those beliefs. Priests know well that there are no easy answers but want to face the questions with honesty.

"Your Holiness," he concluded, "our prayer is that today's words will be the deepening of an honest, ongoing, heart-to-heart dialogue."

McNulty's address was extraordinary, it was courageous, and it was interrupted thirteen times by thunderous applause from his fellow priests. McNulty said later that he had been struck by "how much humanness the pope showed," how he maintained eye contact with him, smiled at him, and even joked with the priest when McNulty cited a poem that John Paul, a heralded and prolific poet in his pre-pontifical days, had written years before. As McNulty ended, the pope put out his arms and hugged the priest, then gave him a Rosary. "At that point, I really felt as though he was not merely embracing me, but all the priests in the country, especially the unsung priest-heroes out there who will never get that kind of opportunity."

The encounter was the dramatic highlight of a day full of theater, yet there was no lasting catharsis.

In his formal response, John Paul did not address any of the specific issues McNulty had raised, even though McNulty's text had been given to the Vatican beforehand. The pope instead stressed the need for holiness by priests, calling them to consistent prayer and unity with Rome.

John Paul's most memorable—and telling—line was an ad-libbed comment to McNulty after the priest had finished laying out his call for change. "I remember a song," John Paul said with a smile. "'It's a long way to Tipperary.'"

The remark seemed winningly enigmatic at the time, and drew laughs. In retrospect, however, it looks sadly prophetic.

"Not much happened," McNulty said quietly as we sat in the rectory, late-summer sunlight glancing through the venetian blinds. "Not much happened."

McNulty has thick white hair and is the kind of pastor any Catholic would love to see in the pulpit. He has a soft-spoken demeanor that both conveys his seriousness of purpose and plays to his wry sense of humor. McNulty loves his life as a priest. He loves the parishioners and his brothers in the clergy. "Looking back, the real good I did with that talk was for the priests. I still meet priests who will tell me they got teary-eyed hearing it, it was such a tribute to them. That somebody was honest enough to not only speak for them, but to be honest in facing the issues. My mail reaction was about 98 percent positive, priests and people. . . . And that was good. That's what I felt I was called on to do.

"But," he added again, "it didn't change much."

In fact, the issues that Frank McNulty raised only grew worse over the years, and other, darker problems festered unbeknownst even to priests such as McNulty, who spent years dealing with clergy problems. Until 2002. "As much as I knew about priests I was genuinely shocked that so much happened. I know it's a small percentage, but for it even to happen once, it's sad. . . . And I was surprised and shocked at some of the stuff that happened, especially some of the more terrible cases in Boston, those guys like Geoghan. That they would almost have a lifestyle of doing that. That just rocked me."

And it rocked the church. Just as the scandals of 2002 bared trends and tensions that have been convulsing Catholicism for years, from the pews to the See of Peter, they also forced the church to confront profound changes and problems transforming the priesthood—some obvious (such as the unrelenting priest shortage), others subtle (such as the growing polarization and isolation of priests), and a few willfully ignored (such as the burgeoning gay subculture in the priesthood). "Change has to come," McNulty said. "Monumental change." The process was already underway by the mid-eighties; the sexual abuse scandal only accelerated it.

An inescapable sign that the priesthood has been changing is the ongoing, steep decline in vocations and in the number of active priests. This has been public knowledge for three decades, and the shortage is the backdrop to almost every other force now transforming the priesthood. While some wishful thinkers see a leveling off in the decline, the figures are still not nearly enough to halt the erosion; even before the scandal hit, experts warned that the situation was destined to worsen.

The numbers bear repeating. Priestly ordinations have been dropping at a rate of 7 percent per decade, from 771 men ordained to the priesthood in 1975 to 442 in 2000. In 2000 there were 30,607 diocesan priests and 15,092 religious priests (that is, members of religious orders such as the Franciscans and Benedictines). That total of 45,699 compares with the 57,317 priests in 1985. In 1999, for the first time, more priests died than were ordained.

At the same time, the number of Catholics continues to rise, passing 60 million, and leaving the priest-to-laity ratio at one to 1,257, which is twice what it was in 1950, when there was one priest for every 652 Catholics. The rate of resignations from the priesthood, which spiked during the upheavals of the late 1960s and early 1970s, has increased in recent years as well; it is now estimated to be about 12 to 15 percent annually. The priesthood is graying by the year, and some religious communities resemble geriatric wards, with each active member supporting three or four aged and infirm retired members.

Catholic University researcher Dean Hoge, whose most recent study of the data came out in late 2002 in *The First Five Years of Priesthood,* says the numbers are irrefutable: "New ordinations are not nearly numerous enough to keep the priesthood at a stable size. Our best estimate is that ordinations in the past few years stand at approximately 35 percent of replacement level, that is, for every 1,000 priests dying, retiring, or resigning from the active priesthood, only about 350 new ones are being ordained. Clearly, the parish as we have known it cannot continue to be maintained."

The shortage contributes to the dynamic of the contemporary priesthood in several ways, all of them challenging, some of them catastrophic.

Bishops, for example, have been so eager to find young men to ordain—to fill the pulpits primarily, but also to keep the Vatican happy— that they have been willing to overlook the potential problems that in many cases have come back to haunt them. The shortage has also led bishops to take in foreign-born priests from countries where vocations are more plentiful, or where the church is too poor to educate its aspiring priests. So an American prelate will often educate the priest and use him either to minister to immigrant communities or simply to fill a post in a parish. Even Catholic Ireland, which once exported thousands of priests to mission fields across the globe and to the United States, was forced to consider importing clerics from Africa in 1998 when, for the first time ever, a parish was told that there was no Irish priest to replace its recently retired pastor.

Foreign-born and missionary priests, however, often have little oversight from either their home diocese or their host diocese, and they often come from countries where scant background information is available to judge the man's credibility. As many cases in 2002 showed, foreign-born priests who commit crimes of abuse can easily and quietly return home, beyond the reach of U.S. law or a victim's lawyers.

The shortage may also have contributed to one of the most sensitive and controversial phenomena of the contemporary priesthood—namely, the growing number of homosexual priests, a figure that many believe will soon top 50 percent of all priests. Bishops turned a blind eye to the trend, knowing that to confront the issue would be a no-win scenario: barring homosexuals from the priesthood simply for their orientation was not considered fair, or even licit under church teaching. If gay men could live a celibate life as well as heterosexuals, why not ordain them? And who wanted to cut the number of priests by half in one fell swoop? Yet the bishops also knew that too many gay men were coming to the priesthood without a healthy understanding of their sexuality, and many were coming to escape or suppress their yearnings, a psychosexual time bomb that was destined to go off eventually.

For priests already in ministry, the shortage exacerbated problems of overwork and "over-responsibility," which in turn led to diminished opportunities for priests to develop spiritually and intellectually and to an epidemic of priestly burnout and the attendant psychological problems of excessive stress (such as substance abuse).

Running through all of the surveys about the priesthood is the constant refrain of an abiding loneliness that hits clergy morale on the personal and cosmic level. Loneliness has always been part of the celibate's experience, of course. But parish priests today are much more likely than their predecessors to be on their own in the rectory, or saddled with another priest whom they do not like but are stuck with because the bishop has no options.

Priests have started comparing themselves to the Shakers, the nearly extinct band of chaste ascetics whom everyone admires, but mainly for their simple furniture. More than ever, priests today are the men in the middle—the "lower clergy," as they are known—stuck between a querulous flock and an overweening hierarchy. They live in a culture that is more likely than ever to regard them as oddities and less likely than ever to view them as fonts of authority. Yet they are called to task by their bishop if they do not adequately implement the unprecedented flow of Vatican dictates that the diocese passes along, while congregants generally ignore such statements and besiege their priest with their own concerns, many of them impossible to fulfill.

Father Donald B. Cozzens, who has spent years counseling and studying clergy as vicar for priests in the Cleveland diocese and as president-rector of the seminary there, grapples with these issues with unstinting candor in a landmark book called *The Changing Face of the Priesthood*, which has become a definitive guide to the problems, challenges, and hopes of the contemporary clergy. While Cozzens has drawn some criticism, the wide acceptance of his reading of the priest's dilemma—acceptance that for political reasons is conveyed privately more than publicly—attests to his keen eye.

Cozzens's credentials are bolstered by the fact that he published the following words, which were years in incubation, in 2000, two years *before* the sexual abuse scandal confirmed the scope of priestly problems for the rest of the world:

"The post-conciliar years have tested the mettle of priests—crisis after crisis 'shaking their foundations' and turning their lives inside out and upside down. They have looked inward in search of their core identity; wrestled with their conscience to maintain their integrity; haltingly acknowledged a need, linked to the very soul of their spirituality, for authentic human intimacy. During these years they watched as almost half of their peers left active ministry, some clearly the best and the brightest. Deep wounds rent the fabric of the clerical image. . . . When bishops did speak with their priests, they seemed to listen as wise teachers seeking only to answer the questions of their less experienced students and to communicate papal and curial directives. . . . After a while priests became accustomed to the lack of real dialogue. The hope and energy left most of their eyes. Many priests simply settled into making their lives 'work' by pastoring to the best of their ability, by shrinking their world to the borders of their parishes. Large numbers resigned to pursue less conflicted life in the sacrament of marriage. Some priests simply went through the motions, husbanding their energies for comforts and pursuits that dulled their profound disappointment. A few became cynical and bitter. The rest, I believe, held to the conviction that eventually the confusion and angst would be soothed by the liberating breath of the Spirit."

And then came the scandal.

Overnight every intimate aspect of priestly life was subject to public scrutiny, a harsh spotlight that exacerbated the issues as well as bringing them to light. Every priest was considered a potential child molester, or an out-of-control homosexual, or at best a closet Lothario. Many Catholics—generally angry conservatives who had been the clergy's greatest champions—now derided priests as members of a "lavender Mafia" educated in seminaries that were referred to as "pink palaces." Priests who had once been tenderly compared to "rumors of angels" were now the source of endless gossip. Their holy vocation became fodder for watercooler humor to the point that serious efforts to address the situation—such as designing new confessionals with windows—sounded like a bad joke.

The guilty priests didn't help matters. Compounding the emotional damage that they had inflicted on their victims and their church, many resorted to behaviors that ranged from revolting to bizarre. The rest of the priesthood suffered for such episodes. One priest I know recounted coming upon a longtime acquaintance he hadn't seen in months. Without preamble, the man looked at him, his eyes resting for a second on his clerical collar, and said with incredulity, "Are you still a priest?" before walking on. Father Ed Dura of San Francisco described his state of mind as "an emotional hemorrhage." Priests began fending off the hugs of children whom they used to embrace after Mass, and "defensive ministry" became the watchword of rectory chat.

To a degree, Catholic priests had become habituated to both the blatant and the unspoken suspicions of an American culture that had never been amenable to the notion of a priestly caste. In the early years of the Republic, priests had been beaten, caricatured, and slandered as corrupt, mind-warping Svengalis who led Catholics astray spiritually, psychologically, and certainly sexually. Worse still, priests could never be good Americans.

In the twentieth century, American culture developed a dualistic view of Catholic priests. On the one hand, the priest was a visual short-hand for a man of God. Not just cardboard clergy like Bing Crosby or Barry Fitzgerald, but priests with spine and spirit, like Karl Malden's Father Pete Barry (based on the real-life Jesuit John Corridan) in *On the Waterfront* and Robert DeNiro's Rodrigo Mendoca and Jeremy Irons's Father Gabriel in *The Mission*. The generic Protestant minister no longer resonated, and the evangelical pastor was still suffering from the associated guilt of television preachers who had done yeoman's work in resurrecting the nefarious Elmer Gantry. Catholic priests, however, with their formal promises to forswear lucre and intercourse, were also excellent stand-ins for hypocrisy, the favorite foil for dramatists exploring vice and virtue.

Some of it was rank bias; but much of it was the effort of writers and filmmakers to address an unspoken reality that no one in the church was willing to address honestly. The 1994 movie *Priest*, for all the criticism it drew, dug up discomfiting truths with its central character, a closeted but sexually active gay priest. Many priests I know praised the film, though never publicly.

The scandal was the tipping point. Overnight, the genial Father Dowling was out. If a priest appeared on television it was to play a criminal deviant, and there was little reason to seek any dramatic balance. "We say our shows are ripped from the headlines, so should we ignore this?" Dick Wolf, the creator of NBC's *Law & Order* shows, told the *New York Times*. Wolf, who was an altar boy for Cardinal Francis Spellman at St. Patrick's Cathedral in the 1950s, had as the season finale for his *Law & Order: Special Victims Unit* a plot about a murder linked to a pedophilia cover-up. "What can we say that would be any worse than what has been in the newspapers?"

In November 2002 the ABC legal drama *The Practice* featured a hard-hitting episode about a respected priest who abused a child. One of the show's main characters left the church in disgust over the case and argued that the whole institution should be torn down. "There is no balance, it's just an atrocity," the Emmy-winning screenwriter David E. Kelley told the *New York Times*. The newspaper headlined its interview with Kelley "A Catholic Writer Brings His Anger to 'The Practice.'" Almost three weeks later the *Times* corrected itself: Kelley was raised Protestant, not Catholic. At that point, it mattered little. Everyone felt free to take a shot.

Within the church, too, the events of 2002 put an end to the strong standing that priests had always maintained in spite of past controversies.

In their own parishes, many priests felt like fellow travelers during a Red Scare, where a quiet word could end what for them was not just a career but an existence, a sacralized way of being. Catholics with petty grudges began whisper-campaigns about the supposed proclivities of priests or bishops whose politics they didn't like. Some of the contrived allegations made the newspapers; many, fortunately, did not. At least two priests who faced credible allegations—and the vast majority of the reports that surfaced *were* credible—committed suicide. Another priest attempted suicide, and the victim of another Baltimore abuser knocked on the priest's door and shot him. Some priests guilty of molestations were denied public funerals.

"There is a tremendous anxiety that any of us could be accused," Father Robert Silva, head of the National Federation of Priests' Councils, told me halfway through the year. "We are extremely vulnerable. It's pretty raw out there." The sense of abandonment only grew worse with time. At the Vatican, Pope John Paul started making pointed comments about how priests must be holier and humbler: you "must be perfect," he told a group of newly ordained priests in April. Meanwhile, Vatican officials, while on the one hand invoking various church legalisms to protect priests from civil and criminal laws, also announced measures to keep homosexuals and anyone deemed insufficiently doctrinaire out of the priesthood.

The year 2002 was a serial drama with no apparent happy ending, and priests were the villains of the piece. Hundreds had been caught out for horrible crimes, but many of their blameless brother priests grew defensive, and more than a few lashed out with an asperity that confirmed suspicions that priests were as nasty and waspish as any clique. "I don't have much sympathy for people who somehow couldn't stop whatever happened. I'll take all of these people who were abused, and I'll abuse them with a baseball bat," Father Dick Ross of Joliet, Illinois, told the *Chicago Tribune.* (He later apologized, saying that he'd thought his comments were off the record.)

Such incidents obscured the actions of the vast majority of priests, who showed genuine concern for the victims. Untold numbers of them were courageous pastors who won back the hearts of any doubters by encouraging dialogue, starting with their own public examination of conscience. But for innocent priests the primary emotion was one of shame and deepening solitude and introspection. They felt that they had been betrayed by members of their own fraternity and scapegoated by many of the very same bishops whose actions in covering up for abusive priests had precipitated the crisis. Almost to a man they felt that in Dallas the bishops had hung the priests out to dry while exempting themselves from any sanctions apart from a collective expression of regret.

Nearly all of the priests I spoke to during the year said that at one time or another they had traded in their clerical garb to go about in mufti. The Roman collar was suddenly akin to the mark stuck on the depraved Peter Lorre in *M,* and every priest was considered "a monster waiting for the sun to go down," as one cleric put it. The whispers of passers-by, and even the outright insults from strangers on the street, had left them unnerved in a way they had never experienced. When a popular Massachusetts priest, Father Bob Bowers, showed up at the Voice of the Faithful meeting in July, he confessed that he was scared to wear his "dog collar" and black clerics. "I am a nervous wreck," Bowers said. "People look at me as the enemy. They wonder if I am one of them."

Father J. Ronald Knott, vocations director for the Louisville archdiocese, gave a compelling description of the impact of the scandal, which had left him "with a sick feeling in my gut." He wrote in *America* magazine, "I am at the lowest point I have reached in 32 years. In response, I have done predictable things, like 'isolating' myself. A few weeks ago, however, I did something that I have never done before. I was driving somewhere wearing my Roman collar. When I pulled up to a light, I put my hand over the collar so that the people on each side would not see it. In the latest of three nightmares, I dreamed I was back in the seminary when the police came and took everything I owned: my books, my homily collection, my spiritual journals, my clothes, my family photos, my money, everything! My heart is obviously bleeding from many holes."

Knott's first concern, he said, was for the victims. But his portrayal of an irrevocably altered clergy life was poignant and personal: "Now we priests are sitting around rectories, homes and apartments combing through our lives for every thought, word or deed, for every youthful indiscretion, every joke, every hug, every touch, that could come home to haunt us. . . . We know that if we are falsely charged we might as well be guilty, because once accused, we would never fully recover our reputations. I am sad to say that I don't know any priest who is now completely at ease around children."

This "dark night of the priest's soul," as Cozzens called it, now seems to promise many more years of painful—and public—purification before the *via negativa* emerges into spiritual enlightenment. Whenever that happens, the Catholic priesthood at the end of that path will surely look drastically different than it has in centuries because this journey of transformation did not begin in 2002. At the heart of the crisis is a longstanding and unprecedented questioning of the priest's identity, not only by lay people but by priests themselves, who are in "a whirlpool of self-doubt," as Knott put it.

Again, Cozzens is unparalleled in framing the depths of the identity crisis: "Behind and beyond issues of integrity and intimacy that shape the quality of [a priest's] soul lies the lingering question of his true self as one ordained into the priesthood of the one High Priest. So fundamental is this question that it colors every aspect of his life—his very carriage and demeanor, the way he communicates and relates, the manner in which he speaks to parishioners, friends, and brother priests. . . . While some priests deny concern about their priestly identity, most concede that the issue hangs over their heads like a storm cloud, robbing them of the confidence they once knew, rendering them awkward and self-conscious in certain parish and social situations."

This is an extraordinary and unsettling situation for the entire church. Priests are indelibly stamped by ordination; they are not supposed to harbor doubts, but rather to be steady guides who shore up the shaky faith of others. This unique role has been a source of strength for both the priest and the flock over the centuries. Recasting it will have a profound impact on the priesthood and on Catholicism. After the scandal, that process of recasting, already well underway, was accelerated enormously. Everything is now on the table, and the priest himself will not necessarily have much say in the outcome, which will be affected by forces outside and inside the church.

The most immediate engine of change, of course, is sex, along with sexual abuse. The two issues are different, but both follow intertwining trails through the thicket of the psyche, and both are fraught with controversial implications regarding the behavior and role of homosexuals and the pathology of pedophiles.

The problems of the contemporary priesthood surely go well beyond sex. But sex is what started the scandal, and sex is the place where any discussion of the changing face of the Catholic priesthood must begin.

Eight

SEXUAL ABUSE, SEXUALITY, AND THE MODERN PRIEST

L ong before the latest wave of scandalous revelations, the aura of sexual mystery surrounding the celibate priesthood had made Catholic clerics an irresistible target for ribald comics and a favorite source of elbow-in-the-ribs glances among their own parishioners. Priests have always elicited an odd reaction: on the one hand, people want to believe in priests' asceticism, while at the same time people project onto the blank screen of impossible priestly virtue every possible sexual sin, even if they know the suspicions to be outlandish. But the events of 2002, by their sheer volume and meticulous depravity, swept away any uncertainty or hesitancy in the public's mind. Whatever the reality, the culture at large now saw priests as synonymous with pedophiles—compulsive and pathological men who lived in some inexplicable, alternate moral universe. The disgust was heightened by the gap between the priest as ideal Christian and the priest as sexual predator, a chasm that widened with every sordid tale, one worse than the other.

If none of the stories churned up by the scandal approached the scope of the Boston cases, the litany of misdeeds brought to light day after day were numbing in their variety and repetition:

In New Hampshire, a beloved priest who died of a heart attack at his home was found with a black leather strap around his genitals and a Viagra prescription in his name in a rectory littered with pornography and sexual devices. In Arizona, a priest was found to have kept a detailed video log and card files tracking nearly two thousand sex acts he had performed with youths and other men. A California cleric paid for a sixteen-year-old's abortion after he got her pregnant, and an Illinois priest was convicted for making and distributing the date-rape drug GHB. One Massachusetts priest confessed that he and other priests attended drag-queen revues while under treatment for pedophilia, while another Bay State cleric was charged with giving a ten-year-old boy an enema, telling him that he was "cleansing [him] with holy water." In Las Vegas, a priest confessed to a judge that he had made five southern Nevada boys at his parish strip and spread their arms in a mock crucifixion before he sexually abused them.

The seemingly endless list left Catholics struggling to maintain perspective and fighting to quell the unspoken fear that someone they knew, and liked, was destined to be next. My own sense of balance was nearly undone in July 2002 when the phone rang at home late at night. My newspaper was following a breaking story about the arrest in Montreal, in a sting operation in the city's red-light district, of two New Jersey priests. Canadian police said that one of the priests, a seventy-year-old former headmaster of a prestigious Catholic prep school, had been taped negotiating the terms of a deal with an adolescent male prostitute on behalf of his companion, a sixty-year-old priest. The kicker was that the news broke just as Pope John Paul arrived in Toronto for the Catholic World Youth Day event to rally young people to the church.

The next day's story ran the basic facts. All I could focus on was the unanswered question: What could possibly have compelled these men, after six months of scandalous headlines, to continue with such brazen behavior—and right under the pope's nose, too? Not that laying low with their behavior would have been a virtue, but still. When author Thomas Cahill complained that there is "a psychological sickness at the heart of the priesthood," it was hard to dispute him.

When one stepped back from the immediate welter of events, however, it became clear that despite the serialized stories of priestly misdeeds, Catholic clerics are still apparently no more prone to sexually abusing children than the rest of the population, and may in fact be slightly less so.

First and foremost, congregants rightly expect priests (and pastors of all denominations) to be better than the average worshiper when it comes to the balance sheet of virtues and vices, and they certainly don't expect them to fall within the "average" range of sexual deviation. Thus when men who are supposedly paragons of the morality they preach are found to be sinners the anger is redoubled. When they are found to be child-molesting criminals, the natural reaction is pure outrage.

The fact that so many bishops allowed abusive priests to range freely through parishes for so long also compounded the perception that all priests were molesters. Moreover, there are simply far more Catholic priests than there are clerics of other denominations. In addition, the institutional construct of the Catholic Church leaves a paper trail to track them, and a big legal target for civil suits when the criminal avenue closes down, as it often does in these cases because of the expiration of the statute of limitations. Many of the worst recorded cases of clerical child abuse have been in independent fundamentalist or evangelical churches, but since each congregation in that type of polity is free-standing and has little in the way of bureaucracy, there was no entity to sue, and often no personnel files to subpoena. Experts say many of those cases simply never came to light because by the time a child was old enough to file a complaint, the pastor was long gone, and perhaps the church, too. The cases that were reported rarely made headlines, and since those churches have no overarching denominational organization, there was no way to quantify the number of cases, as there is in the Catholic Church.

Naturally, trying to put the *rate* of Catholic priestly abuse in context is disconcerting after the litany of scandalous misconduct, and this perspective is not to diminish by one iota the awful trauma endured by the thousands of victims who suffered at the hands of these men. Obviously, there is no such thing as an "acceptable" level of abusers in the ranks of the clergy. All abuse is immoral, criminal, and devastating, but abuse by a cleric can be especially destructive. Catholic priests hold a sacramental role as arbiters of the miraculous and shepherds to their flock's spiritual lives, and their position of trust as the vicarious "Father" means that sexual abuse by a priest can devastate the psyche in almost unfathomable ways—"soul murder," as it has been rightly called. Contextualizing the cases should also not play into the argument, wielded by reflexive church apologists, that the scandals were a case of "moral panic"—a problem blown out of all proportion by intensive media coverage. The problem is real. It is horrifying. It is unacceptable. It can, and it must, be reduced if not eliminated altogether.

Above all, there is no doubt that if not for the courage of the victims of abuse, the revelations that are now reshaping the Catholic Church would have remained little more than gossip whispered in the darkness of church rectories or concealed in confidential court papers. The cover-up was the Catholic Church's unique crime, and the victims deserve enormous credit for their role in unmasking this perfidy.

During the year of scandal I spoke with dozens of victims, or *survivors*, as they prefer to be called. Some of them had been publicly lobbying for more than a decade to draw attention to their cause, with little success. Others were coming forward for the first time. Their stories were the most wrenching I have ever heard. Their quiet, almost matter-of-fact recounting of past traumas belied the years of pain and healing it had taken to reach the point where they could discuss the events—and with a journalist, no less, who wanted to print the details of their humiliation in a newspaper for the world to read. While some victims came in for harsh criticism as the scandal wore on, accused of exploiting their experience or fabricating it outright, the overwhelming majority of abuse victims were people emboldened by a newly receptive climate for their stories and united by individual trauma in a desire to see justice done and to ensure that no one else would suffer their fate. As one young man who had been repeatedly abused by a monk while in grammar school told me, "Someone should be held accountable. . . . I just hope it's not too little too late."

Accountability and justice are ongoing struggles. The prevention and punishment policies being implemented by the church, despite the controversy surrounding them, are tougher than those of any other denomination and those of many professions that deal with children, and there is good reason to believe they will be effective.

But that should not stop Catholics from asking legitimate questions about the nature of the sexual abuse crisis among the clergy. Even if the rate of abuse is not higher than average, why is it present at all among men who are called to be saints? Is there something about Catholic priests themselves, or something in the priesthood, that either draws abusers or helps to create them? And can something in the priesthood be changed so that the natural, constructive relationship between a priest and young people does not erode to the point that parish interactions re-

semble prison on visiting day? The investigation must start with a difficult, and controversial, parsing of the data on abuse and its various manifestations. That will inevitably lead to even more difficult questions
regarding pedophilia, homosexuality, and the psychosexual problems of
the modern priest.

First, before we tackle the numbers on child sexual abuse, a caveat. If
there could be one beneficial result of the awful revelations of 2002, it
would be to spur greater research into this area to determine just how
prevalent child molestation is, and who molests children and why. The
larger parameters of the pathology are familiar, but much else, especially
regarding the perpetrators, is unknown. In part that is because child molesters are by nature extremely secretive, and thus their crime is rarely
found out and prosecuted. This means that *convicted* abusers do not provide a representative sample of the pathology.

As far as victims go, it is generally accepted that about one in four
girls and one in six boys is likely to be sexually molested, in some setting,
before turning eighteen. But few of those cases come to light, much less
to court. It is widely believed that the sexual abuse of children is one of
the most underreported crimes; the U.S. Department of Justice estimates
that only 30 percent of abuse is reported. That is because the victims are
so young, and because memories of abuse are often repressed until long
after the statute of limitations has expired. (This is another issue that the
nation needs to reconsider in the wake of the clergy scandal. Most states
have a statute of limitations that expires five years after a person reaches
the age of majority, which is generally eighteen. That makes canon law's
ten-year limit look positively generous.) Experts say the victim's enduring
guilt and shame also inhibit many of them from speaking up, a phenomenon that may be especially true of boys who have been abused by
men, which is the predominant category of clerical abuse; the constricted
emotional tenor of the male psyche, combined with the enduring stigma
of a homosexual liaison, especially if the abused boy grows into a heterosexual man, makes it especially difficult for many men to volunteer information on their trauma.

Precise information on the molesters themselves is even harder to
come by. It is estimated that in 90 percent of the cases the perpetrator is

male, and the victimizers tend to be relatives with absolute control over the children. The Sexuality Information and Education Council of the United States (SIECUS) reports that 77 percent of reported abusers are parents and 16 percent are other relatives. Anywhere from 2 to 6 percent of adults have abused minors. Thomas Plante, chairman of the psychology department at Santa Clara University, says that 8 percent of the population is sexually attracted to children and that 5 percent of priests harbor a similar predilection. Critics of the priesthood maintain that up to 6 percent of priests abuse children. Results from the few dioceses that have fully disclosed their past histories of child sexual abuse by priests, either voluntarily, as in the case of the Baltimore archdiocese, or at the behest of the courts, as in Boston and Manchester, New Hampshire, show the rates to be in line with those estimates. Baltimore records show that during the last fifty years, some 6 percent of the archdiocese's priests were credibly accused of misconduct. The figure was about 5 percent in Boston, and nearly 8 percent in Manchester. (Tellingly, that rate is two to four times higher than the rate reported by dioceses that did not make their records public.) A *New York Times* survey in January 2003 of all publicly known cases showed that about 1.8 percent of priests ordained from 1950 to 2001 had been accused of abuse. If that represents a third of the cases, as the reporting trends would indicate, then the rate again approaches the 5 to 6 percent level.

If over the decades some two thousand priests have been credibly accused of child sexual abuse, as victim advocates contend, that would still put their incidence of abusive behavior at the lower end of the 2 to 6 percent range. There are currently 47,000 priests in the United States, and over the course of the decades covered by the scandal, that number would go up by tens of thousands, to well over 100,000, according to church statisticians.

To better understand the nature of the problem in the priesthood, however, it is also important to make a critical and controversial distinction between clinical pedophilia and sexual abuse of a postpubescent teenage minor.

Reviews of the abuse cases by priests show that a minority of the acts reported, perhaps 10 percent, qualify under the strict definition of pedophilia. As set forth by the American Psychiatric Association's *Diagnostic and Statistical Manual of Mental Disorders,* fourth edition (DSM-IV), pe-

dophilia involves sexual activity by an adult with a prepubescent child—
that is, a child thirteen or younger. The criteria for diagnosing pedophilia
stipulate that the offender be at least sixteen years old and that the victim
be at least five years younger. By and large, the age differential between
all abusers and their victims is much greater, as in the case of adult men
abusing an eight- or ten-year-old.

True pedophiles can be sexually attracted to girls or to boys or to
both. They are almost exclusively interested in prepubescent minors and
generally have no sexual attraction to or involvement with adults or ado-
lescents. There are two crucial facts about pedophiles that relate to the
priest situation. One is that pedophilia often develops later in life, and
even if it is present in early adulthood, pedophiles are by nature so deceptive about their activities—or their fantasies—that picking them out from
the rest of the population is all but impossible. That poses problems for
those who suggest that seminaries should simply weed out potential pedophiles through psychological testing.

Second, pedophilia resists treatment, much less a "cure." According
to the American Psychiatric Association, "Unlike the successful treatment
outcomes for other mental illnesses, the outlook for successful treatment
and rehabilitation of individuals with pedophilia is guarded. Even after intensive treatment, the course of the disorder usually is chronic and lifelong in most patients."

The accounts by pedophilic priests and experts who have dealt with
them are chilling in the clinical approach that the abusers take toward
their victims, and their lack of remorse (even decades later) when confronted with the enormity of the destruction they caused.

"We just got carried away," one former Detroit priest, eighty-two-
year-old Robert Burkholder, told a local paper after he was brought
back from retirement in Honolulu and charged with two counts of criminal sexual conduct for a 1986 incident with a thirteen-year-old boy.
Burkholder said he had had sexual encounters with "maybe a dozen or
two boys" during his career, but they were always consensual. "The boy
likes the priest because he's friendly and kind," Burkholder said. "You
don't communicate with anybody else about it. [But] it takes two to
tango. It was always a two-way thing." By way of explanation he offered,
"[The boys] might have been lonely. And priests are lonely persons, too.
We need friendships and kids love priests. I weakened. I was looking for

affection." He continued: "The boys work in the rectory with the priest and you just get friendly. You sit down in the rectory and have a Coke. It's a mutual deal . . . an affectionate thing and a friendly thing. . . . It's a friendship between two people that has been made into something horrible, rotten. People are trying by hook or by crook to make me look bad. Some of the accusations are true, but so what? I was a priest—a good priest—who had a weakness."

Burkholder eventually pleaded no contest to two second-degree criminal sexual conduct charges and served only thirty days in the Wayne County jail. He was released just after Thanksgiving 2002 and remains on probation for five years.

In his book *The Changing Face of the Priesthood,* Father Donald Cozzens recalls how disturbing it was for him to deal with abusive priests who had "something amiss at the core of their personalities." Cozzens said that the molesters implicated in the scandal may have been effective priests—the polished charms of the seducer (or "groomer," as such people are called) can be the same as those of the good pastor—and they were often popular with parishioners. But they had shockingly little guilt over their crimes with children, he says, their only regret being getting caught. Cozzens considers them sociopaths. "I don't remember one priest acknowledging any kind of moral torment for the behaviors that got him into trouble. The absence of remorse and concern for their victim continues to trouble me."

This is troubling for everyone. Sadly, the priesthood may simply be one of those professions—like teaching, coaching, or scouting (or the other denominations, which attract a similar rate of child molesters)—that will always draw unregenerate pedophiles because that is where the targets are. The key is to implement as many defensive strategies as possible, to educate children and adults to the warning signs, and to respond aggressively to allegations—the latter being the Catholic Church's great sin of omission up to this point.

More problematic than strict pedophilia, however, is the issue of priests who molest teenagers, and more specifically, teenage boys. Priests abusing adolescent boys accounts for the vast majority of church cases— perhaps 80 percent or more. That gender ratio is the reverse of the pattern in the wider society, where most teenage victims are girls. There are indications that many female victims of priests have not come forward, but they would still constitute a minority of the cases of clergy abuse. Thus the peculiar, central reality of sexual misconduct by priests is improper homosexual activity. On the one hand, this kind of abuse may yield to more comprehensive explanations and possible solutions. But this topic, as much as any other aspect of the scandal, is freighted with controversy, because it is so closely connected to the growing homosexual subculture in the priesthood, and it plays into the temptation to scapegoating that is the easy out for many angry Catholics today.

Some commentators try to finesse the issue of improper homosexual behavior with teenagers by resorting to a linguistic dodge and using the term *ephebophilia,* a word derived from the Greek for *youth,* to categorize the preference of an adult for a postpubescent minor, male or female.

But ephebophilia is not a classified disorder like pedophilia. At best, the term might have certain helpful clinical uses, were it not wielded so explosively in the current atmosphere. Apologists who want to diminish the scope of priestly misconduct often use the term *ephebophilia* as if tampering with teenagers were somehow less repulsive than the sexual abuse of small children. That view does have the weight of cultural history on its side. The adult attraction to youths had a storied past in classical times, and it was once common, even in Puritan America, to marry off older men to girls barely past the age of menarche. Selling the sexuality of teens is also a surefire money-maker in today's culture. Apart from the multi-billion-dollar pornography industry, mainstream fashion retailers such as Abercrombie & Fitch and Calvin Klein have scored big by presenting youths as louche seducers. Meanwhile, young pop divas such as Cristina Aguilera and Britney Spears have careers predicated on the social acceptability of a man's "natural" lust for teenage girls, especially virgins, which is how Spears explicitly presented herself initially. Indeed, Spears faced a career crisis in 2002 because she was growing too old (at twenty) to play the sexy teen naïf, so she undertook the risky transformation to a more "adult" presentation. As *Newsweek*'s religion commentator Kenneth Woodward put it, "The problem [with ephebophiles] is that they're too hard to tell from everybody else" in this sexually charged culture.

But whatever ephebophilia may be, it is not the main issue in the priest abuse scandal. The abuse was largely the result of the actions of emotionally immature homosexual men who preyed on teenage boys. This is dangerous terrain, because it plays into homosexual stereotypes and into the homophobia that lurks just under the surface of American society and traditional religions. True to form, many Catholics, particularly conservatives, have attacked the presence of homosexuals in the priesthood as the source of the scandal, and by extension, the root of the crisis in Catholicism. By putting the blame on "homosexual" activity, these critics can also play a shell game that "reduces" the number of strictly pedophile priests to less than 1 percent; most of the "abuse," they say, is just homosexual behavior, and so—*voilà*—they can reassure everyone that priests are actually *less* guilty of pedophilia than everyone else.

In truth, gay priests did not cause the scandal, nor is the "gaying" of the priesthood over recent decades—a trend that had been widely ignored until the scandal—a cause of the Catholic crisis. Rather, it is a symptom of many other changes in the priesthood. And yet it is a transformation that cannot be brushed aside as irrelevant. The scandal brought the issue of homosexual priests front and center. How the church deals with their presence in the clergy may determine the very future of the priesthood itself, and the daily practice of Catholicism as it has been understood for centuries. The truth is that if homosexuals are banished from the priesthood, that will do nothing to stop sexual abuse and it will do everything to undermine the Catholic Church's understanding of itself as a place where saints are made.

For nearly a decade, Father Mychal Judge was the best-known Catholic chaplain in what has been called the "profoundly Catholic institution" of the fire department of New York, so it was natural that when the brass wanted to rededicate a refurbished firehouse in the Bronx, they would do it with a Catholic Mass, and they would have Mike Judge preside at the liturgy.

Never one to miss a chance to spend time with the firefighters he loved, or to take center stage, which he also loved, the irrepressible Franciscan was, as always, up to the task. With his silver hair and perpetual smile, Judge was a natural in the limelight. He was a Brooklyn-born Irishman with a Gaelic knack for storytelling, a New York accent to tell those stories, and a Catholic spirituality that he communicated with every word and deed.

"This truly is a chapel," Judge said as he began the Mass on a late-summer morning at a makeshift altar for the firefighters and city officials in the classic, century-old fire station that housed Engine Company 73 and Ladder Company 42. The ersatz congregation included Mayor Rudolph Giuliani and Fire Commissioner Thomas Von Essen. Vested in white robes adorned with a green Celtic cross, the priest spoke in his homily of the uncertainties that are part of every life, but especially the life of the firefighter, and of the blessed assurance of faith that they could all turn to for comfort.

"You do what God has called you to do," Judge said. "You show up, you put one foot in front of another, you get on the rig and you do the job, which is a mystery and a surprise. You have no idea when you get on that rig, no matter how big the call, no matter how small, you have no idea what God's calling you to do. . . . You love this job. We all do. What a blessing that is. A difficult, difficult job, and God calls you to it, and he gives you a love for it, so that a difficult job will be well done. Isn't he a wonderful God? Isn't he good to you, to each one of you? And to me. Turn to him each day, put your faith and trust and your life in his hands, and he'll take care of you, and you'll have a good life."

Mychal Judge gave his homily on the morning of September 10, 2001. Just twenty-four hours later, the Franciscan priest was at the World Trade Center, along with his comrades from the department, a stricken look replacing his trademark smile, standing in the lobby of Tower One as the colossal skyscraper next door collapsed in a maelstrom of debris and shattering noise and corpses. In the hagiography that immediately grew up around Judge's memory, Father Mike had removed his helmet to listen to a dying firefighter's last words and a chunk of debris struck him in the head. Some witnesses said he was giving a dead firefighter from Company 216 last rites. Others said he may simply have had a heart attack. Either way, Mike Judge died at that precious moment of vulnerability and grace.

Amid the carnage, Judge's stunned brothers-in-arms took time to carry the corpse of their beloved chaplain out of the billowing dust cloud and into a nearby church, where they laid him on the altar. Of the many sacred images of that day, few had more power than the picture of Mychal Judge's lifeless body being carried away, a modern-day Descent from the Cross that perfectly reproduced the spirit and iconography of an Old Master painting.

A police office named José Alphonso Rodriguez began searching desperately for a priest to give Judge last rites. Unsure of what to do, Rodriguez asked a woman in the church who was tearing up the liturgical linen into bandages if he could do the ritual himself, and she said Rodriguez could, since it was an emergency situation. Rodriguez knelt beside Judge's body, took the dead priest's hand, and recited a quick Our Father and a Glory Be together with another officer, Billy Cosgrove, also a Catholic, who placed his hand on Judge's head. "I felt like an altar boy again," Rodriguez said. Although he described himself as a lapsed Catholic, Rodriguez was wearing a crucifix around his neck that day, and a medallion of Saint Michael, the patron saint of New York police officers. It was inscribed with the words, "Protect Us." Rodriguez later asked a bishop and friend of Judge's if what he and Cosgrove had done was proper. The prelate said that technically laymen couldn't give last rites but added that it was "the greatest thing [the officers] could have done."

"I am just a lowly cop. Why me? Why was I there? How did I cross paths with this man?" Rodriguez told Judge's biographer, Michael Ford. "Was it my Catholic calling?"

Mychal Judge was listed as the first official victim of 9/11, death certificate number 00001. He was just the first of many Catholic martyrs of that day, but the best known.

The fact that Mychal Judge was also gay did not get in the way of his instant hagiography. There was little reason it should. The pathos of Judge's struggles as a celibate only added to the story of how wonderfully human he was.

It was a story known by most any reporter who ever covered a fire in the New York area during the ten years Judge was fire chaplain. Whenever the alarm bells rang, the Franciscan priest was always there with a sound-bite or a camera-ready smile. Judge had, as a *New York Times* account put it, "a keen sense of the limelight and a touch of vanity," and his confreres would tease him about it. "The first priest I met who used hair spray," his fellow Franciscan, Father Brian Jordan, recalled with a smile. At Judge's funeral Father Michael Duffy brought the house down when he reminded the mourners that before Mike Judge rushed off to the Twin Towers disaster he paused to check his appearance in the friary mirror.

But Mike Judge knew suffering even as he conveyed joy. He was a recovering alcoholic for twenty-three years before his death at sixty-eight, and he endured illness in his later years. He was a homosexual who never broadcast his sexuality. He lived as a celibate but struggled with his orientation, and he felt insecure about his intellectual prowess. Whatever his private struggles, Judge seemed to channel them all into loyalty and charity. He was one of the first priests to minister to AIDS victims in the early 1980s, and he marched in the alternative St. Patrick's Day parade for homosexuals who were frozen out of the main celebration. He worked with the poor and handed out dollar bills to the homeless. He was beloved, and he returned the affection in kind, never failing to respond to a request for help. Judge often had as many as forty messages a day on his answering machine, which he had to replace regularly because it broke down from overuse. He swore like a sailor among his buddies and comforted the grieving with the words of Christ.

"His prayers were like a hot line to God," said Vina Drennan, who met Judge after her husband, a firefighter, died in 1994. "When he prayed it was the most blessed thing. In the midst of despair and fear and sorrow and great, great grief you felt like he was a presence that would get you through things." Thousands of others could offer similar testimonials. "He was a saint, a wonderful man," said Rudy Giuliani. "Above all, he was a living example of Jesus Christ," said former NYPD officer Steven McDonald, whom Judge befriended after McDonald was shot in the neck and left a quadriplegic.

Judge's fellow Franciscans established a relief fund in his name, a commuter ferry line christened a new boat after him, and the French awarded him the Legion of Honor. A television producer set up a Web site, saintmychal.com, to lobby for Judge's official canonization. Catholics prayed to Mychal Judge for aid, and miracles were attributed to his intervention.

Whether Judge was gay or straight, saint or sinner, his comrades in the city's firehouses didn't care. After Judge died, the firefighters wouldn't let his body be taken to the morgue. Instead, they took him to a firehouse across from the friary on West Thirty-first Street and laid him out in a back room. All of the friars came over and lit candles, and together they waked Mike Judge. A month later, eight FDNY firefighters gave Judge's white chaplain's helmet, a valuable "second-class relic" (a first-class relic would be a bit of a saint's corpse) to Pope John Paul II during a service in St. Peter's Basilica in Rome.

Then, in one of the more stunning reversals in a year of tumult, Mychal Judge became a martyr all over again, along with the thousands of other gay priests who were blamed for causing the sexual abuse scandal. In this atmosphere of anger and recrimination, sober discussions about a homosexual subculture in the priesthood and the preponderance of gay priests among the abusers quickly slipped past logic and into polemics, as critics trotted out stereotypes that equated homosexuals with pederasty, hypersexuality, and deviousness.

Just a few months after Judge was honored at the Vatican, the favored solution in Rome to the scandal of sexual abuse was a blanket ban on ordaining gay men as priests. In March, the pope's personal spokesman, Joaquin Navarro-Valls, went so far as to suggest that the ordinations of homosexuals already in the priesthood were invalid.

"People with these inclinations just cannot be ordained," Navarro-Valls told the *New York Times*. "That does not imply a final judgment on people with homosexuality. But you cannot be in this field." Navarro-Valls said that ordaining a homosexual would be comparable to a gay man marrying a woman, a situation that would annul the marriage sacrament as having never been valid. If that logic were followed through, church experts say, it could wreak sacramental havoc, because it would mean that every Mass and wedding and baptism conducted by a gay priest (his ordination invalid) was not licit in the eyes of the church. Not to mention what it would say about the untold numbers of saints and popes in church history, as well as any bishops and cardinals currently in the hierarchy who are gay.

By the fall, Rome was moving to put these hard-line views into practice. In early September, Pope John Paul II told a visiting group of Brazilian bishops not to ordain as priests men who "have obvious signs of affective deviations," a phrase that was widely viewed as referring to homosexuals. Later that month, in a trial balloon of sorts, a U.S. priest who works at the Vatican's powerful Congregation for Bishops wrote an article in *America* magazine in which he trotted out a whole series of stereotypes that presented a catch-22 for homosexuals who want to be priests.

The Vatican official, Father Andrew Baker, wrote that men with what he called "S.S.A."—same-sex attraction—should not be ordained because gay men are already prone to "substance abuse, sexual addiction and depression," and one more affliction (i.e., homosexuality) would be too much to bear. He also said that homosexuals fall prey to "duplicitous or pretentious behaviors" and said that such "personal defects" not only make them inherently unsuitable as candidates for the priesthood, but can leach into the souls of other seminarians. Baker went on to argue that homosexuals have more difficulty controlling their sexual impulses, and that even if a homosexual could live chastely he would be likely to disagree with the church teaching that homosexuality is "intrinsically disordered." Baker also contended that gay cliques and the "effeminate affective manners" of gay men would have a negative impact on the priesthood and thwart other young men trying to develop a proper understanding of "manhood."

Baker concluded by arguing that homosexuals should be disqualified from the priesthood because the priesthood involves no sacrifice for them. His argument went like this: since the church teaches that homosexual behavior is a "moral depravity," gays must be chaste anyway, whether priests or laymen; and since homosexuals would not marry a woman in any case, the vow of celibacy would be no big deal. Thus, said Baker, "To avoid doing something (heterosexual acts) that one does not have an inclination to do is not a sacrifice."

Moreover, Baker argued that without the possibility of a "spousal" relationship, a gay man cannot then take on "the spousal character of Christ's relationship with his bride, the church. Through the celibate life, the priest redirects his sexual attraction to the opposite sex toward another 'body,' the church, which is a 'bride' in a complementary spousal relationship. He exercises a spiritual fatherhood and lives a supernatural spousal relationship as a sign to the church of Christ's love for her. Someone afflicted with S.S.A. cannot redirect his inclination toward a complementary 'other' in a spousal relationship, because homosexuality has disordered his sexual attraction toward the opposite sex. It then becomes difficult to be genuinely a sign of Christ's spousal love for the church."

A month after Baker's treatise appeared, the Vatican began circulating a draft proposal among curial departments outlining a plan to bar homosexuals from the priesthood. Rome has some allies in the U.S. hierarchy. At the height of the scandal, the incoming head of the American bishops' Committee on Priestly Formation, which oversees standards at all forty-seven of the nation's seminaries, promised that new criteria would seek to eliminate homosexuals from consideration by requiring candidates to accept several guidelines. Among them:

> "He must be willing to give internal consent to the church's teaching ... that a homosexual inclination is objectively disordered since every homosexual act is intrinsically disordered."

> "He cannot espouse a 'gay' identity, by which is meant allowing himself to define his personality, outlook or self-understanding by virtue of a same-sex attraction."

> "He must be prepared to admit that the sacrifice rendered by a celibate commitment is the renouncing of wife and children for the sake of the kingdom and he must be ready to make that a personal and substantial, not merely symbolic, gift of self."

The fate and effectiveness of the new push seems uncertain, in large part because of quiet lobbying by American bishops who know that if such a policy is successful, not only will it sow discord and confusion among priests, but it could cause the overnight collapse of the American priesthood, since so many priests today are homosexuals.

At this point, determining exactly how many of America's 47,000 priests are gay remains a matter of conjecture, with the estimates ranging anywhere from 20 percent to nearly 50 percent. Donald Cozzens puts the number at 30 to 50 percent, while A. W. Richard Sipe, a well-known writer on the sexuality of priests (and a former Benedictine who left the priesthood to marry), puts it at 20 percent, half of whom he says are sexually active. A *Los Angeles Times* survey of more than 1,850 priests conducted in 2002 revealed that a total of 15 percent of priests identified themselves as homosexual, with 9 percent saying they were gay and 6 percent describing themselves as "more on the homosexual side." Another 5 percent placed themselves "completely in the middle" between homosexuality and heterosexuality. (These rates contrast with research identifying 3 to 8 percent of the larger population as gay or lesbian.)

Given the natural human tendency, conscious and unconscious, to deny socially (or theologically) unacceptable behaviors, the figures from such surveys are probably low. In any case, it is clear that given the growing shortage of priests and the diminishing vocations, any wholesale purging of gay priests or a policy barring homosexuals from seminaries would result in a massive restructuring of the daily life of American Catholicism.

Exactly *why* there are so many homosexual priests is another issue. Is the Catholic priesthood an inherently "gay profession," or is the presence of large numbers of gay priests a contemporary spike that can be chalked up to an unusual confluence of factors?

In the public's mind, the priesthood has always been sexually suspect. Well before the scandal of sexual abuse of minors there was plenty of fodder for such stories in everything from the sexual excesses of the Borgia popes to the casual intimacies of parish priests with their suspected concubines.

But the priest as homosexual has always been the favorite bit of gossip for village wags. When one's sexuality is a mystery, people tend to fill in the spaces with the most salacious and scandalous images. For Western culture, that would be homosexuality. A Gallup poll released in August 2002 is telling in this regard. The pollsters asked Americans what percentage of the population they thought was gay or lesbian. The answers were 21 and 22 percent, respectively, as opposed to a true figure of 3 to 8 percent. All those homosexuals have to hide somewhere, the thinking goes, and the priesthood seems as logical a closet as any.

The history and dynamic of the male celibate priesthood in the Catholic Church also helps to explain the popular assumptions about the homosexuality of the clergy.

From monks whipping each other into sexual asceticism, to the modern Catholic churchman, swishing about in shot-silk robes and fussing over the details of the theater of liturgy, priests have always projected a sexual complexity and ambiguity that have prompted equal parts denigration and fascination. "We priests are sneered at and always shall be— the accusation is such an easy one—as deeply envious, hypocritical haters of virility," the country priest laments in Bernanos's 1937 novel, *The Diary of a Country Priest.*

The questions began with the original priest, Jesus, a man who never married and who spent his adult life with a close band of male disciples, though always as a mystically solitary figure. "Because Jesus is single he can be more available to us," says Amy-Jill Levine, a New Testament scholar at Vanderbilt University. "He can be a friend, he can be a lover, he can be a parent, he can be a child. It is a wonderfully eroticized, as well as a malleable, role." Jesus, Levine notes, has always been a sexually androgynous figure whose later representations in the arts (which are the only representations we have of him) tend to present a Jesus who "looks more like Mommy than Daddy." The discomfort over dealing with Jesus as a human being, for fear of compromising his divine nature, adds to the distancing from his sexuality even as the church exalts his gender as the normative one for leadership. "We want him to be masculine but we don't want to talk about what makes him masculine," said Mark Jordan, a professor of religion who has drawn on his experience as a gay Catholic seminarian in a number of books on homosexuality in the church, including *The Silence of Sodom.*

The outrage that greets the periodic attempts to fill in the blanks proves how sensitive the topic is, and how much Catholics would rather ignore the subject, at least publicly. When Terence McNally's 1998 play, *Corpus Christi,* opened on Broadway, his recreation of Jesus as a gay man who has sex with his disciples and is martyred for his orientation prompted immediate outrage and even bomb threats. McNally's artistic intent was lost amid the din of condemnation. Not that it mattered. As one reviewer rightly noted, the play was so bad that the evening's dramatic highlight was the thrill of walking through a metal detector at the theater door. McNally's art was also overtaken by events: the image of Matthew Shepard, who was beaten and left to die on a fence on a freezing night in Wyoming that year because he was gay, conveyed the same message, but far more powerfully.

Sexual suspicion also envelops Jesus' apostles, and their heirs in the priesthood, like a cloud. Jesus invited the men around him to become "eunuchs for the kingdom of heaven," but in my experience parishioners do not see their priest as a sexual neuter. On the contrary, while I was covering religion for newspapers, congregants angry over some issue or another would regularly call me demanding that I write an exposé of their pastor. Not only was he rude to them, they would say, but, by the way, he was also sleeping with the parish secretary. The next caller would claim that the same priest was gay. And another would pass along the rumor—fact, they would swear—that he was actually fondling altar boys.

Or girls. It mattered not. And of course, Father X had also plundered the parish till to finance exotic vacations with his various lovers.

Not having sex is assumed to be an impossible goal, so in the popular imagination the priest is a sexual omnivore. Chastity in the modern world must be exhausting.

At certain times in history the very doctrines that Jesus preached (when they weren't being inverted to justify chest-thumping military conquests) have been viewed as a weak-willed philosophy that breeds supine men who are just this side of the feminized homosexual. Submitting to authority and volunteering for martyrdom rather than fighting back, and hanging on a cross in an embarrassingly exposed way rather than dying with one's boots on, has been indicted as wimpy (not to mention unseemly). The eroticism of Saint Sebastian, whose arrow-pierced male body has been a gay icon for centuries, was used as evidence to support the views of both critics and gay apologists. It came as a shock but no surprise that the name of a Web site run by a Maine priest was called "saintsebastian." Father John Harris was suspended from ministry in 2002 when Portland bishop Joseph J. Gerry found out about Harris's enterprise, which included sexually explicit material available to the fifty or so other priests and brothers with access to the site.

In the nineteenth century Friedrich Nietzsche grew so disgusted with what he saw as the emasculation of Western civilization by the Christian religion that he spent himself trying to upend the exaltation of the idea of suffering-as-triumph. Nietzsche's philosophical freebooters in the German National Socialist Party were even more upset with the inimical effects of the Catholic priesthood, which they considered the epitome of sissification. "Within four years," Heinrich Himmler declared in February 1937, "we will have proven that the Church, on the level of both its highest leadership and of its priests, constitutes in its greatest part, a men's erotic association which has terrorized humanity for more than 1,800 years and which has shown itself sadistic and perverse." At a Nazi rally later that year, Joseph Goebbels whipped the crowd into a lynching frenzy, declaring, "Priests systematically perverted youth, and this is not a question of only a few regrettable and isolated incidents, but of a general moral decadence that would never be able to be measured in the history of humanity." The rampant homoeroticism of the Nazi leaders themselves was not public knowledge until much later.

With the splintering of Christendom in the Protestant Reformation, sexual innuendo about priests became the stuff of dogma as Protestantism rejected a celibate clergy and set marriage as the norm for pastors who were to be more like their flock than a separate, privileged clerical class. Thus rumors about Catholic prelates became another weapon in the wars of religion. One of the more imaginative examples of this propaganda is the endurance of the so-called Legend of Pope Joan, which posits that a woman who passed herself off as a learned cardinal was elected pope in either the ninth or the eleventh century (depending on the version). Joan's cover was blown when her procession halted one day while heading to the Lateran Palace in Rome and she suddenly gave birth to a child by the side of the road. According to legend, the people of Rome tied Her Holiness's feet together and dragged her behind a horse while stoning her, until she died (a reaction that doesn't bode well for the popular acceptance of women's ordination).

The Pope Joan myth first surfaced in the thirteenth century, and up through the eighteenth century it was a standard item in anti-papist literature, which also included the inventive rumor that for years after Joan's reign the papal throne had had a hole in the seat so that church officials could reach up and assure themselves that it was a Holy Father, not Mother, seated there. In fact, a fifteenth-century prefect of the Vatican library concluded that such thrones did exist, but were simply to allow a prelate to answer the call of nature in the midst of lengthy ceremonies. (That is always a problem, given that the church is as much a geriarchy as a hierarchy. But advances in medical equipment have made life much easier and more dignified for the old men who occupy the Throne of St. Peter and preside at interminable liturgies that send much younger folk running for the bathrooms.)

Legends aside, the image of clerics as waspish crones persisted in the popular imagination, especially among Protestants. During one of his early visits to Rome, Henry James derisively referred to the aged Pope Pius IX as "that old woman." At the time James wrote those words (his disdain for the pope would mellow over time, especially as the "old woman" was subjected to the indignities of the new Italian lay state), American Protestantism was launching a campaign to rescue Christianity from feyness. Importing a British model of "Muscular Christianity" to promote manly Christians, Protestants pushed a new culture of masculinity through organizations such as the YMCA and various scouting and camping groups. Those organizations have been supplanted today by popular revivals of the men's movement, especially the Promise Keepers rallies, which seek to develop "men of integrity" who will fulfill their manly duty to be head of the house.

Catholic clerics, on the other hand, are depicted in contemporary culture as sashaying up the nave as the prelates did in Fellini's famous ecclesiastical fashion show, or else as tortured, closeted gays like the suffering young cleric in the 1994 movie *Priest.* Bing Crosby is dead in more ways than one. At best, priests today can hope to be depicted hilariously by Nathan Lane as in the 1995 movie *Jeffrey;* at worst, as the villainous archbishop in the 1996 film *Primal Fear.*

Scott Appleby, the Notre Dame historian, recounts how in 1993 his ten-year-old son participated in career day at his school by dressing as a priest. (The other option he had entertained was shortstop.) His son returned home crestfallen. "Kids had made fun of him, asking him, 'Are you queer?'" Appleby said. "Now if I had dressed up as a priest for career day in 1966, my friends might have thought I was special—in a good sense."

Even before the abuse scandal, the perception of priests as sexual deviants hurt faithful clergymen.

"Priests today stand awash in a floodlight of suspicion in the eyes of contemporary American culture," Cozzens wrote in 2000. "Neither macho playboy nor successful careerist, they go about their work without wife and children, without a home of their own, without the cultural symbols that define achievement. In the eyes of many, their manliness drifts about in a sea of ambiguity."

The scandal of 2002 brought all those questions into the open, and in the rush to judgment the hurried verdict was that all priests are gay. While that is clearly not the case, the scandal did force the church to begin openly discussing how much these perceptions conformed to reality, why so many gay men might be priests, whether this was bad for the church, and whether it could be changed.

The simplest explanation for the steep and apparently sudden rise in the proportion of homosexuals in the American priesthood is the fact that in the past thirty years some 25,000 heterosexuals have left the priesthood to marry. While a number of gay men have also left, that rate is far lower. Conservative critics would argue that there is a snowball effect to these defections; they say that the "lavender Mafia" running the priesthood intimidates straight men from entering or remaining in the seminary, thereby maintaining a gay chokehold on the presbyterate.

Others contend that the revelations of the sexual abuse scandal only drew the curtain back on what has existed for centuries, since celibates began living in cloistered, all-male (and all-female) environments.

Already in the fourth century, for example, St. Basil of Caesarea, the architect of Eastern monasticism, set out tough penalties for clerics caught making sexual advances on other men, including a public whipping, a six-month imprisonment, and a diet of water and barley bread. In the eleventh century St. Peter Damian penned his famous *Book of Gomorrah,* which decried "the befouling cancer of sodomy" afflicting the priesthood and demanded that Pope Leo IX wipe it out. According to the late Yale historian John Boswell, those warnings were for naught. The priesthood and religious life, Boswell argued in his classic work *Christianity, Social Tolerance, and Homosexuality,* always provided a haven for men and women seeking to avoid the societal expectations of marriage and parenthood, and hence were especially attractive to gays and lesbians who would have no better sanctuary; in the religious life they could live among like-minded men and women.

The passion that a monastery's enforced mix of chastity and sexual confusion can stir is evocatively portrayed in Remy Rougeau's 2001 novel of the cloistered life, *All We Know of Heaven.* Rougeau is himself a Benedictine living in a community in the upper Midwest, where he sets his tale of Paul Seneschal, a young novice from Quebec. Seneschal enters a strict-order Cistercian monastery, takes the name of Brother Antoine, and tries to adapt to life with forty other monks who live by vows of poverty, chastity, obedience, and silence in a day ordered by the rhythms of regular prayer and manual labor. The novel portrays all of the virtues and foibles of men at prayer, and its frank honesty is evident in a chapter in which Brother Antoine develops a crush on another monk, a Scotsman named Brother Martin. Rougeau graphically recounts the fantasies and dreams and sleepless nights, the sweat-soaked, parched-throat moments of Antoine's days in silence around the beloved Martin, as his homoerotic passion builds to a boil. At one point Antoine even cuts his genitals in an effort to still the desire. Brother Martin finally leaves the abbey, and Antoine confesses his desires—never acted upon—to the abbot. "Yes," the abbot responds. "Each of us has his burden to bear. Listen, Brother, it's getting late. You'd best get to bed."

The drama dissipates as quickly as that, with no echoes in the rest of the novel. That, too, seems to mimic real life in priesthood, as gay priests often shove their homosexuality into a clerical closet. Rougeau never explicitly states which he thinks comes first, the homosexuality or the desire caused by sexual deprivation in a hothouse male environment. The commonly accepted idea that human sexual orientation is found on a spectrum, rather than in fixed categories, provides few answers.

Experts believe, however, that gay priests are born, not made. The priesthood draws gay men, rather than turning straight men into homosexuals.

One longstanding explanation for this is that the drama of the liturgy and the theatricality of the liturgical costumes exert a particular attraction for gay men to join the priesthood. "Mass was the ballet of my youth," a former Jesuit, John Shekleton, wrote in a 1996 essay in *Commonweal*, explaining why he was attracted to the priesthood from the time he was an altar boy. "As the cassock fell back down to your ankles, a young boy knew that he had stepped into another world, a slightly feminine world, a world where your walking and turning were the peaceful glide of a sacred corpus. . . . Within these sacred robes, an altar boy's body became a stage prop. Even a young, shapeless youth could feel in his flesh that his movement was grand and dramatic. The bows, the genuflections, the well-timed turns, the subservient presentation and movement of holy objects during the liturgy, all these were part of a great sacred drama."

From *The Picture of Dorian Gray* to *Brideshead Revisited*, writes Mark Jordan, the Catholic Mass has been the favorite stage for "liturgy queens," the denigration that Jordan reclaims as a badge of honor. "The liturgy creates its own divas, on both sides of the communion rail. It is a show that makes for ardent gay fans," he writes. "Liturgy Queens need not be members of the clergy, but they are typically found in the vicinity of the altar—or at least in the choir loft."

In fact, research has shown that gay men are significantly more likely to be active in religious organizations than are heterosexual men, which would suggest that many of them would naturally pursue the further step of ordination. In April 2002, Darren E. Sherkat, a sociology professor at Southern Illinois University, published an article speculating that the attraction for homosexuals may be due in part to psychological and theological factors: "Gay men may avoid the risk of eternal punishment by gravitating towards religious consumption—much like heterosexual women do." By contrast, he said, lesbians appear more like heterosexual men in their greater diffidence to religious activity. Unlike gay men and straight women, lesbians and straight men tend to be more comfortable with their odds in the afterlife. Sherkat offers several other possibilities for the churchgoing disparity, including the idea that gay men may find greater identification and solace in a male-oriented religion where salvation is attained through devotion to a male god—namely, Jesus. (Hence the irreverent quip among gay clergy: "Was Jesus divine—or simply gorgeous?")

Whatever the reasons behind the presence of homosexuals in the priesthood, the reality is that they are here today, and they are going to be here in the future, just as they have been since the days of the apostles. Scholars have long noted the "queer steam" that pulses through Saint Paul's self-flagellating writings on sexuality, to cite one example. The real question about gay priests is, as Seinfeld might have put it, "Is there anything wrong with that?"

"I've done everything I can to serve the church faithfully," said Father Ralph Parthie, a Franciscan priest from New Orleans who spoke out in defense of gays in the church after the 2002 scandal. "Why would people now say there is something wrong with me because I'm gay?"

The problem is not homosexuality, per se—although some orthodox Catholics and church leaders would dispute that—but the kind of homosexuals that are becoming priests and the effect that the burgeoning number of gay priests is having on the priesthood.

First, the growing gay subculture in the priesthood, which may soon border on the dominant culture, is threatening the internal cohesion of a priesthood that is already facing serious divisions over myriad other issues.

At a press conference in Rome during the summit between U.S.

church leaders and Vatican officials, several conservative Catholic writers pressed leading American churchmen to take a stand on weeding out gays from a priesthood that they said was rife with incontinent homosexuals. In a response that startled observers in its frankness, Bishop Wilton Gregory, the president of the National Conference of Catholic Bishops, conceded that keeping a balance between gays and straights in the priesthood "is an ongoing struggle" for the church.

"I'd like to admit that one of the difficulties we face in seminary life and in recruiting is made obvious when there does exist, within any given seminary, a homosexual atmosphere or dynamic that makes heterosexual young men think twice before entering into a seminary for fear of being identified with that orientation or, as you say, that they would be harassed," Gregory told his questioners. "It is most importantly a struggle to make sure the Catholic priesthood is not dominated by homosexual men. Not only that it is not dominated by homosexual men, but that candidates that we receive are healthy in every possible way—psychologically, emotionally, spiritually, intellectually."

Marianne Duddy, executive director of Dignity/USA, a national organization for gay Catholics, said she was "shocked and horrified" by Gregory's comments. But Catholics, including many priests, admitted that Gregory had raised a valid point. The old seminary quip, "In bed by nine, in your own bed by ten," was no longer a joke. In the twenty years leading up to the scandal, the tensions caused by a growing homosexual subculture in the priesthood had become a festering crisis.

"Seminary personnel face considerable challenges dealing with the tensions that develop when gay and straight men live in community," Cozzens wrote in April 2002 in the *Boston Globe*. "Circles of influence and social comfort zones tend to divide presbyterates, with notable exceptions, into straight and gay networks. Suspicions arise that appointments to prestigious offices and other promotions are somehow influenced by these networks. Whether well grounded or not, when such suspicions surface, sexual orientation becomes the fuel feeding clerical politics and gossip.

"Heterosexual priests, moreover, remark among themselves that celibacy is, in effect, optional for gay priests," he continued. "Only the integrity of the gay priest, who is free to travel and vacation with another man, sustains his life of celibacy. Celibacy, the straight priest understands, is impossible to enforce for the priest who is gay. Of course, when celibacy has to be enforced, whether for straight or gay clergy, it has lost its ecclesial meaning and power."

Right-wingers such as Michael S. Rose, a conservative polemicist whose 2002 book on homosexuals in the priesthood sparked sharp debate, jumped on such admissions to argue that there has been a "deliberate infiltration of Catholic seminaries by . . . a clique of homosexual dilettantes." The title of Rose's book, *Goodbye, Good Men: How Liberals Brought Corruption into the Catholic Church*, pretty well sums up where he wants to take his unscientific collection of about 150 anecdotes from heterosexual priests who describe all manner of oppression and harassment in allegedly gay-run seminaries. (Rose's other claim to fame is his book *Ugly as Sin*, in which he attributes the decline in Mass-going to the modern architecture of newer churches. It is hard to dispute his aesthetic sensibility, but the logic is a leap.)

Rose was rightly criticized for his methodology, his exaggerated tailoring of stories to suit his thesis, and the fact that he did not check with the heads of the seminaries he criticized. Nor did he include viewpoints that might have undercut his vision of a vast left-wing—and gay—conspiracy. But the tales he recounted rang true for many Catholic leaders. Even liberal, openly gay Catholics such as Mark Jordan agreed that the network of gay priests "isn't pale lavender; it's hot pink."

Those impressions were bolstered in August 2002 with the release of a survey, taken the previous year, showing that more than half of American priests perceived a "homosexual subculture" in their diocese or religious institute. The researchers defined *subculture* as a "definite group of persons which has its own preferential friendships, social gatherings, and vocabulary." The research found that 19 percent of priests said such a subculture "clearly" existed and 36 percent said it "probably" did. "It was extremely corrosive," one unnamed thirty-seven-year-old priest told the researchers in one of several follow-up interviews. Said another priest: "It created a certain kind of atmosphere and a certain kind of irreverence; that for me was a problem."

More ominously, there are indications that the subculture is growing, and the divisions within the priesthood widening. Forty-five percent of the priests surveyed in the twenty-five to thirty-five age group said that gay cliques clearly existed, compared to only 8 percent of those over fifty-six and 3 percent of those over sixty-six. "Our conclusion, based on the data and on our focus groups, is that homosexual subcultures increased in visibility, and probably also in numbers, in recent decades," said Jacqueline Wenger, who coauthored the study of 1,200 priests on behalf of the National Federation of Priest Councils.

The very fact that priests are so sharply split in their perceptions of their own brotherhood is also troubling. "What happens in a community when one-third of the members are gay, know they're gay and know all the others who are gay, while the other two-thirds don't know anybody who is gay?" Father Donald Wolf, a past president of the National Federation of Priest Councils, has said. "It's got to be extremely destabilizing."

The growing presence of gay priests also raises the issue of diversity, odd as that may sound. Catholics are forever justifying their absence from church or the confessional by complaining that a guy who isn't married and has no children and an "easy" life would have no conception of their daily circumstances and thus could have nothing useful to say to them. "So why go to a priest?" they say. That logic fails on any number of points. Those same people would think nothing of seeking advice from a therapist whose family background, sexual orientation, or personal experience was a complete mystery to them. Such thinking also presumes that any person can fully know the vicissitudes of another's experiences, even if their lives appear as mirror images. What if there were a married priesthood? Would priests with wives and children know what it is to be a single mother or a childless woman approaching midlife? Or a gay man, or a minority person in a white-bread world, or a migrant worker? A good pastor knows how to meet people where they are, as the phrase has it—to simply be with them, to enter into their suffering as best he can, and above all to refer them to the proper professional to deal with their particular problem, be it domestic abuse, alcoholism, clinical depression, or anything else outside the pastor's spiritual purview.

There is, in fact, a good argument to be made that as a distinct minority with a history of rejection, especially within the church, gay men might have a greater experience of suffering and a deeper reservoir of empathy for their flock. The overarching issue is that while religion should be a sanctuary and a balm to life's wounds, faith is not psychoanalysis, and the church's ministers, especially in the sacramental system of Catholicism, exist to open pathways to worship and holiness and the assurances of salvation. Mental health advice is a bonus that most of them do quite well, but expecting every priest to also solve every problem for hundreds of parishioners is a reductive, consumerist view of religion.

Still, diversity within the priesthood, especially given its single, male, and overwhelmingly white makeup, can only help both the priesthood and the church. A predominantly gay priesthood would work to narrow, rather than broaden, the horizons of the presbyterate.

The second part of the challenge raised by the growing percentage of homosexuals in the priesthood goes to the dark heart of the current scandal—namely, that too many of the gay men entering the priesthood are not psychologically healthy. They have not come to terms with their sexual orientation, and that too often leads to harmful, inappropriate, and criminal behavior. For these homosexuals, the priesthood becomes either a comfortable refuge where they can settle into easy relationships with like-minded men, or a shooting gallery full of vulnerable teenagers on whom they can prey. Either way, these priests are in a closet of hypocrisy, publicly professing one thing while privately doing otherwise.

"We were only taught about sexuality in the abstract," a gay priest who was ordained in the 1970s told me. "I wasn't taught anything about my own sexuality. That's something I had to come to work out on my own, many years later, like a lot of priests do."

That priest successfully came to terms with his orientation, and he is now a popular, effective pastor and a model of celibacy. But many more do not cope, as the year of scandal showed. The dysfunction is not only in the chronic abuse of teenage boys. Since 2000, news reports and the church itself (increasingly, though grudgingly) have begun to reveal the high rate of HIV infection and AIDS deaths among the priesthood. That rate is estimated at about 1 percent of the priesthood, which is about twice the rate of HIV infection among the general adult population. (The secretiveness that characterizes the disease in the wider culture is even greater within the church and thus makes conclusive numbers elusive; they could be much higher.) If the AIDS cases are restricted to the population of homosexual priests—say, one-third of the priesthood—the rate goes up significantly. And while that rate is still lower than it is for many sexually active gay cohorts, it clearly points to a level of sexual activity that is not only a violation of a priest's vows but also an indication of un-healthy sexual attitudes and practices. "With all the stress lately in the Catholic Church, I just wanted to have sex," a Baltimore priest, Steven Girard, told police in April 2000 when he was accused of filing a false carjacking report to cover up a night spent with a male prostitute.

Perhaps the most destructive type of homosexual priest is the one who sees the priesthood as a means for repressing his orientation altogether—a stratagem that backfires with spectacularly harmful results.

These men are especially susceptible to the witches' brew of forces inherent in contemporary priestly life—the loneliness of celibacy, the sexual abstinence of chastity, and the guilt over their homosexual yearnings (a guilt that is intensified by their sacred role as the defender of church teachings that see homosexuality as "intrinsically disordered"). Orthodox-minded priests are fleeing their own desires as much as they are embracing a priestly vocation, and the mental switchback often manifests itself in attacks against other homosexuals—their own alter egos.

The spiritual writer Henri Nouwen, whose struggles with his own orientation eventually led him to develop the great pastoral style that made him so popular, recalled dealing harshly with his gay students when he taught at Harvard, telling them that homosexuality was an evil state of being. According to Nouwen's biographer Michael Ford (who also wrote the Mychal Judge biography), Nouwen remained largely closeted and resisted pressures to "come out" as a gay man. "This took an enormous emotional, spiritual and physical toll on his life and may have contributed to his early death," Ford says.

Despite the heavy price, Nouwen by all accounts managed to cope with his sexual orientation and live a chaste life. But other gay priests who try to subvert the reality of their sexuality can inflict far more damage on others than they do to themselves. Unable to deal with themselves or others on an adult level, they seek out vulnerable youths, and in the pressure-cooker of their own tortured psyches, they develop all manner of bizarre rationalizations for their behaviors. They argue that their molestations are a form of ministration, for example, or that they are helping to "educate" the young person, or that their sexual encounters are not sex because procreation is impossible—and thus their promise of celibacy is intact. "Doctrinal orthodoxy is not a firewall against child sexual abuse," says Father Stephen J. Rossetti, president of St. Luke Institute in Maryland, which treats priests and religious with psychological problems, including those with sexual disorders.

Even the Jesuit journal *Civiltá Cattolica*, which has a Vatican imprimatur, has recognized that priests of the most upstanding bearing can commit the worst depredations. "Very often, pedophiles have a double personality," the magazine warns. "On the one hand they may have a very rigid moral attitude, which often casts doubt on the truth of accusations against them. On the other hand, they are capable of extreme violence and cruelty, without bearing any feelings of guilt."

The fact that the number of gay men in the priesthood is rising even as new priests declare themselves to be more traditional, in the vein of their role model John Paul II, points to a fatal contradiction in the argument of conservatives who want to "solve" the problem by banishing homosexuals from the priesthood, or by reasserting a lockstep orthodoxy. And one can never forget that the bishops who covered for the abusive priests were also John Paul appointees who ostensibly reflected his views. The problem for people on the Catholic right is that they are very much on the hook for the abuse scandal, and they don't offer much in terms of a solution.

So far, the favorite strategy of the Catholic right for dealing with the issue is the simplistic idea of banning homosexuals from the priesthood. Aside from issues of fairness and the great contributions of gay men to the church, the impracticability of such an idea is obvious; many seminaries currently ask candidates about their sexual orientation with the goal of keeping homosexuals out, and yet homosexuals still manage to become priests. More intrusive inquiries would only drive gay men further into the closet of repression and deception, making the priesthood even more of an incubator for unhealthy homosexual activity. The idea of barring gays leads conservatives into an additional bind, because that practice would require a greater reliance on psychological testing, which they have frequently criticized as an imprecise tool for evaluating seminary applicants.

In the wake of the scandal, the American bishops acquiesced to the Vatican demand that Rome conduct a "new and serious" apostolic visitation—essentially a bunk inspection by the church's High Command—of U.S. seminaries to get them morally shipshape and to ensure the "criteria of suitability" of their candidates. But a similar visitation by Rome, from 1982 to 1986, was supposed to do the same thing. The final verdict of that earlier inspection declared American seminaries "generally satisfactory," an assessment that was reiterated in 1990. Obviously, the heavy-handed white-glove treatment is not very effective.

Also dubious is the tack adopted by Father James Mason, the vocations director of the Diocese of Sioux Falls, South Dakota. A young priest who was ordained in 2001, Mason recalls encountering another newly ordained priest who was wearing a gold anklet and matching earring. That led him to write an essay on the need to foster greater masculinity among priests, a thesis he made public in 2002 in response to the scandal. Mason's argument is that more "manly" priests could more effectively "share Christ," and they would also attract similarly oriented tough guys who are now turned off by the priesthood. "The fact of the matter is, they are not used to, and are uncomfortable living in, an environment that is often effeminate," Mason told *Our Sunday Visitor*.

South Dakota is not the only source for such thinking. In 1997, the Vatican's Congregation for Divine Worship sent a letter to the world's bishops, proposing some guidelines for the selection of candidates for priestly ordination. Among the required characteristics were "a clearly masculine sexual identity." Under that definition, the Village People could become seminarians.

Any effective resolution by means of a sweeping policy will be complicated by the fact that the Catholic Church itself is of several minds about homosexuality.

In 1986 the Vatican's guardian of doctrinal orthodoxy, Cardinal Joseph Ratzinger, issued a document on "The Pastoral Care of Homosexual Persons." That document defined homosexuality as having "a strong tendency toward an intrinsic moral evil." The 1997 re-edition of the Catholic Catechism sharpened the definition, declaring that not only are homosexual acts "intrinsically disordered," but a homosexual *orientation*, in and of itself, is an "objective disorder."

That pejorative language contrasts with the church's teaching, also in the catechism, that the homosexual "must be accepted with respect, compassion and sensitivity." The American bishops have been even more diligent in stressing the pastoral, rather than the clinical, aspects of church teaching on homosexuality. In 1983 the Washington State Catholic Conference said the church should avoid even the appearance of homophobia, which it described as a worse evil than homosexual acts. In 1997 the United States Conference of Catholic Bishops issued a moving statement called "Always Our Children," which urged parents, and the church, to accept homosexuals for who they are and not to use the church's teaching against them. "Generally, homosexual orientation is experienced as a given, not as something freely chosen," the bishops wrote. "By itself, therefore, a homosexual orientation cannot be considered sinful, for morality presumes the freedom to choose."

The document also encourages parish priests to welcome homosexuals into their churches, to help establish or promote support groups for parents of gay children, and to let people know from the pulpit and elsewhere that they are willing to talk about homosexual issues. When they lead chaste lives, the bishops said, homosexuals should be given leadership opportunities in the church. "All in all, it is essential to recall one basic truth. God loves every person as a unique individual. Sexual identity helps to define the unique person we are. . . . God does not love someone any less simply because he or she is homosexual." In the Lexington, Kentucky, Cathedral of Christ the King in October 2002, Father Paul Prabell blessed two men as he would any other couple and baptized their quadruplets, three boys and a girl who were born with the aid of a surrogate mother. Prabell said he was not endorsing homosexuality but exercising his pastoral duty on behalf of the children and the men. "This is what Christ would do," said Michael Meehan, the quadruplets' biological father. The babies "are God's children. That's how the church should view it."

Most bishops have also adopted that approach in ordaining gay men to the priesthood, as long as they agree to be chaste (just as any priest must). But the scandal brought to light sharp and unusually public differences among the bishops over that approach. Philadelphia Cardinal Anthony Bevilacqua, for example, noted that he has barred—or tried to bar—gay men from his seminary since 1988, because homosexuality is an "aberration, a moral evil." Other cardinals, including Bernard Law of Boston, have publicly said they see nothing wrong with ordaining a chaste gay man to the priesthood. And New Hampshire bishop John McCormack, a conservative churchman whose actions while he served as an aide to Law drew withering criticism, did not back off his contention that it was the maturity of the candidate, rather than his orientation, that mattered. "I think pedophilia is one issue," McCormack said in November. "I think men who abused post-pubescent boys is another issue. And I think living one's life with integrity, be you heterosexual or homosexual, is another issue."

Outside the United States the differences were equally stark. Mexican Cardinal Juan Sandoval Iníguez declared that men "with homosexual tendencies have always been prohibited from entering the priesthood," while the bishops of Switzerland asserted that homosexuals can carry out church ministries as long as they lead celibate lives.

This kind of open confusion is unusual in the Catholic hierarchy, which likes to be on the same page, at least publicly, and it does not bode well for the main goal of the bishops, which should be to cultivate emotionally and psychologically healthy priests, be they straight or gay. Lay Catholics seem to have made up their mind; surveys show that they have little objection to a gay pastor and are in fact more accepting of homosexuals than the laity of most other denominations.

The truth is that homosexuals are no more likely to abuse minors than are heterosexuals. Consequently, a "straight" priesthood saddled with a high number of sexually dysfunctional heterosexual men would yield a high number of female teenage victims rather than male victims. Of course, the most effective solution is also off-limits, at least for now—that is, to ordain women, since men account for 90 percent of child molesters.

Gay men have always been a vital part of the priesthood, and of the church, and they will continue to be so, no matter what policy the Vatican may adopt. As the Jesuit author Father James Martin has put it, "Blaming gay priests for the current scandals is like blaming all accountants for Enron." Imagine the church without gay priests and you have to imagine 9/11 without Mychal Judge, or spiritual writing without Henri Nouwen. Catholicism would be vastly poorer by their absence.

Much can be done to ensure that seminaries and the priesthood draw men who have successfully come to terms with their sexuality, whatever their orientation. Problems of psychosexual development clearly exist, and the vocations shortage has made some bishops even more willing to accept questionable candidates. Banning gay priests would only make that crisis into an overnight disaster for the church. And again, trying to suppress evidence of homosexuality among priests would only lead to more scandalous actions.

Revising the church's teachings on sexuality or celibacy may be part of the answer, but it is not central to the question of sexual abuse or homosexual priests. A cleric of any stripe holds a sexually charged role, and that role is too often exploited, be it by pastors who are married or celibate, straight or gay. Whatever the level of dysfunction in the Catholic priesthood, and despite the trail of destruction left by so many Catholic priests, it must be remembered that priests are no more likely to molest than other segments of the population.

The defining aspect of the scandal—the truly *scandalous* part of it— is that the bishops and religious leaders charged with overseeing their priests willfully ignored or actively covered up for abusive priests, and that they consistently put the interests of their criminal brethren ahead of those of innocent victims. What characterizes the Catholic sexual abuse scandal is that men such as John Geoghan could claim hundreds of victims over three decades. In other denominations and organizations, such criminals would have been found out or ratted out long before they exacted such a devastating toll.

The main culprit in the scandal, then, is this so-called clerical culture that has come to infect the church—the notion that the priesthood is an insular club of spiritually superior divines whose guiding principle is to protect their own under the cover of protecting the faith. "Clericalism is the pernicious ideology—destructive for both people and priests—that the ordained one should enjoy preference and deference, even in the eyes of God," as Boston College's Thomas Groome puts it.

Revamping this clerical culture is the crucial first step toward the coming reform of the priesthood.

Nine

CLERICALISM

THE ORIGINAL SIN

As remarkable as it seemed at the time, by Thanksgiving 2002, after an *annus horribilis* that would have brought down any other leader of any other organization, Cardinal Bernard Law appeared to be in the clear.

In story after story, newspapers were heralding his "reemergence" as a player in the public life of the church, and the prognostications were confirmed when the U.S. hierarchy gathered in Washington, D.C., in November to pass a final sexual abuse policy that would (or so they hoped) mark the beginning of the end of the crisis. In Washington, Law was not hermetically sealed off as he had been in Rome in April or in Dallas in June. After the bishops were introduced to the National Law Review Board that had given the hierarchy, and Law in particular, so much grief, Law hurried up to the podium, almost obsequious in his manner, to thank the panel's leader, the outspoken Frank Keating. Law told him to keep up the good work. "We all have to be part of the solution," Keating responded warmly, giving the cardinal an unexpected glimpse of a future role. The next day, Law drafted and publicly presented the bishops' policy statement on Iraq, the kind of foreign policy wonkery he was known for, and good at. After the debate and passage of the Iraq statement—which urged President Bush to put the brakes on the rush to war—Law even showed up with four bishops for a post-vote briefing open to the media.

Yet for twenty minutes, as reporters launched questions about every aspect of the bishops' deliberations, not a single query went to the cardinal of Boston. Bernard Law stared ahead blankly as his fellow bishops, men who were hardly household names to Catholics, took the spotlight. When the briefing was over, Law got up to leave. A couple of reporters made a feint in his direction but seemed to decide it wasn't worth the effort. As I stood watching, I wasn't even sure what any of us would ask him. He had made his apologies, he had said all he was going to say, and the Vatican had made it clear he wasn't going anywhere. They all had their story and they were sticking to it. Law's aides made ready to clear a path through the reporter pack, just as they had been accustomed to doing for nearly a year. But there was no need. Cardinal Law walked on, nothing in his way.

Yet almost as soon as Law returned to Boston, a new storm broke, and incredibly, it was as if the intervening months, the negotiations and the tentative steps toward healing, had never happened.

On December 3, two days after the first Sunday of Advent in 2002, and following a series of questionable legal maneuvers by Law's attorneys that left Superior Court judge Constance Sweeney seething with anger, the Boston archdiocese was forced to release the first batch of some eleven thousand pages of internal church documents on eighty-three priests accused of sexual misconduct. Much information from the two thousand pages was redacted, and it was only a foretaste of what would be made public in the next few weeks. But the initial revelations were more than enough to cast a pall over a season in which Catholics would normally be preparing for Christmas and the celebration of the Savior's birth.

The Long Lent, as Richard John Neuhaus called it, was about to get an Advent extension, and the church's Ground Zero was once again the Boston cathedral.

From one dispassionate memo to another, the documents showed that for decades church officials had covered up a host of abuses by priests that included the rape of boys, the sexual molestation of girls preparing to become nuns, and drug use by priests with parish youths who were then sexually abused by the pastor. During it all, the archdiocese had routinely ignored parishioners' complaints and put a priority on minimizing the church's financial exposure. As late as 1999, the documents showed,

Cardinal Law had assigned a military chaplain who admitted to beating his housekeeper, molesting a boy, and leading a "double life" with a woman and her teenage son to the archdiocese's "emergency response team" of priests who fill in for vacationing clerics.

Another file showed that in 1993 Law learned that one of his most troubled priests had been in bed with his longtime girlfriend when she died of a drug overdose in 1969, and that the priest, Father James D. Foley, had delayed calling for an ambulance, a factor that may have contributed to the woman's death. According to the files, Foley had begun a relationship with the woman shortly after he was ordained in 1960. They had two children together, but the woman was emotionally troubled and underwent a lobotomy not long before she died. Law never told authorities any of this when he found out in 1993, nor did he reveal the facts in 2002, *after* he claimed he had given the authorities all relevant information about sexual misconduct, with his solemn assurances that no problem priests remained in ministry. In an absurd postscript, the archdiocese said a week later that it had released Foley's file by mistake; the archdiocese had meant to release the file of a Father James J. Foley, who was accused of sexual molestation, and instead gave authorities the file of James D. Foley, whose sins then came to light, along with the complicity of the archdiocese in keeping them quiet.

On the bitterly cold December morning that the files were released, Foley was parochial vicar at a Salem parish. As reporters gathered outside the rectory, he initially tried to deny the reports. "This is absolutely whole cloth," he swore. But he eventually confessed, and he also admitted that he had fathered at least one other child by a second woman.

That was not to be the end of this new round of revelations, however. Once again, the litany of episodes was chilling, and at times it flatly contradicted the assertions by Law and his top aides that the abuse was not widespread, that they had not known abusers might strike repeatedly, and that they had cleared up all the problems years before.

In one case, a priest from Youngstown, Ohio, Father Robert Burns, was sent in 1981 to a counseling program for pedophiles in Massachusetts after Ohio church officials determined that he had sexually abused boys. Shortly thereafter, Burns applied for a temporary post in the Boston archdiocese. James W. Malone, then bishop of the Youngstown diocese, warned the Boston archdiocese not to assign him to church work where he might have contact with young boys. In reply, Father Gilbert S. Phinn, director of personnel for the Boston archdiocese, promised that Burns's placement would be handled with "sensitivity and concern." But Burns was placed in two parishes where he regularly came into contact with minors, and the parishes were not notified of his record.

Over the next nine years Burns sodomized and sexually abused several boys. He was finally removed from his post by church leaders, who urged him to once again undergo counseling. He was eventually charged with a crime in New Hampshire, where he pleaded guilty in 1996 to sexually molesting two boys under the age of thirteen. He was sentenced to two consecutive four- to eight-year terms and was formally stripped of his clerical status three years later by order of the Vatican.

In yet another case in the newly disclosed files, Boston church leaders had been warned as early as 1981 that a parish priest, Father Richard Buntel, was an alcoholic and drug addict who was distributing drugs to young people at his parish. As late as 1994, an internal memo recorded, Buntel showed pornography magazines to young visitors in his rectory bedroom, which stank of marijuana. The memo reported that Buntel had oral sex with males ages fifteen to twenty-one, who saw bags of cocaine and piles of money in his room. The priest was never reported to the civil authorities.

As terrible as these crimes were, however, once again it was the reaction—or lack of one—by church leaders, from the cardinal on down, that appalled Catholics and plunged Boston back into crisis. Time and again, Law and his aides had covered for miscreant priests, automatically forgiving them their trespasses with nary a word about penance, and ignoring the people whose lives had been destroyed by the abusive clerics.

For example, when Law finally removed Father Burns from ministry in 1991, he was extremely solicitous of that cleric's well-being as well: "Life is never just one moment or one event and it would be unrealistic to have too narrow a focus. It would have been better were things to have ended differently, but such was not the case," Law wrote to Burns. "Nevertheless I still feel that it is important to express my gratitude to you for the care you have given to the people of the Archdiocese of Boston. . . . I am certain that during this time you have been a generous instrument of the Lord's love in the lives of most people you have served." The language would be parodic were it not so appalling.

In a similar vein, Law's top aide, Bishop John B. McCormack, whom Law later got promoted to the head of the Manchester, New Hampshire, diocese, recounted in the files how he was trying to quash any payment to the family of one of the boys Burns had raped. "I didn't think compensation would be helpful to their son," McCormack wrote. "It is not what he needs." McCormack also plotted to keep church papers from plaintiffs' lawyers and to throw reporters off the trail. At one point Law's aides drafted a misleading press release that sought to minimize Burns's ties to Boston. The entire preoccupation was with preventing "scandal," with nary a word of concern or compensation for the abused children.

While Boston's infamy stands out, as it did throughout the scandal, similar revelations came to light across the country, in diocese after diocese, regardless of whether the bishop was considered "liberal" or "conservative."

In deposition after deposition, church leaders recounted their episodes of moral blindness in terms so matter-of-fact that it chills the soul. Under questioning from lawyers who themselves seemed shocked by the disregard for children, ranking church officials spoke, in language that had the forensic tone of a medical examiner dissecting a stranger's corpse, of how they had repeatedly covered up for abusive priests.

In a case in Louisville, Kentucky, the former chancellor of the archdiocese, Father John W. Hanrahan, was questioned about several priests who had been accused of various incidents of molestation during Hanrahan's tenure as the chief administrator. He said that, when a parent had once complained to him that a priest had taken advantage of his son, Hanrahan had told the parent, "I think you ought to approach that priest and talk to him about it." Hanrahan did not investigate the complaint or even record it, and he never asked the accused priest about it; in fact, during Hanrahan's sixteen-year tenure as chancellor, no priest was ever punished for misconduct—even those who admitted molesting children.

"Didn't you feel a sense of responsibility to the children, to protect the children of the church from what might be a potentially abusive priest?" asked a lawyer representing most of the 185 plaintiffs who were suing the Louisville archdiocese over abuse allegations.

"No, I didn't at the time," Hanrahan replied.

Hanrahan's sense of compunction did not seem to grow much more acute with the passage of time: he also told the lawyer that he still did not believe parents needed to be notified if the bishop assigned their parish a priest with a record of child abuse. "I think they can adequately protect them without knowing it," Hanrahan said.

In Illinois, under questioning in a 1995 deposition that came to light in 2002, Joliet Bishop Joseph Imesch was asked about his decision to invite a priest into the diocese even though the man had been convicted and sentenced to six months in prison for sexually abusing an altar boy at a Michigan parish. Imesch had worked at the same Michigan parish and had known the priest before he himself became Joliet's bishop. When the priest, the Father Gary Berthiaume, arrived in Illinois, Imesch assigned him to a busy parish with lots of children.

"If you had a child," the lawyer recalled asking Imesch, "wouldn't you be concerned that the priest they were saying Mass with had been convicted of sexually molesting children?" "I don't have any children," Imesch replied.

In the Detroit archdiocese in the 1960s, the rumors that the priest-principal at Bishop Foley High School was abusing boys grew so insistent that church officials finally took action—but not against the principal, Father Robert Haener. Instead, several priests came in, pulled some thirty boys out of class, and read them the riot act. "They scared the hell out of me, to be honest," one of the students, Ray Cunningham, said in 2002 to the *Detroit Free Press* after Haener was finally removed by Cardinal Adam Maida for child abuse, thirty years after the incidents. "They told us what we were doing was spreading rumors about Father Haener and that was a mortal sin and could lead to eternal damnation."

How did things reach such a point? How could pastors who were often so empathetic to the downtrodden and marginalized, so outspoken and prophetic on issues of human rights, so courageous in demanding social justice at home, be so callous in putting the interests of their fellow priests over those of innocent children?

The answer is found in a corruption of the idea of "clericalism," the reflexive notion that clerics are a privileged fraternity whose sacred status guarantees them eternal protection from the reproaches of the world, even when they do wrong. This caste mentality is not unknown in other, especially male, cohorts. Look no further than the "blue wall of silence" among police, or the sometimes pathological camaraderie of elite military units. Moreover, the clerical culture is in many ways no different from the corporate culture, in which executives see themselves and their interests as identical to those of the institution. It is a trap that the rest of the church's members, and the rest of society, inadvertently help to set by equating the men in Roman collars with "the church." Thus the Catholic sexual abuse scandal stems in large part from the same self-interest that regularly leads to the downfall of otherwise successful business titans and politicians. It is no coincidence that the worst abuses revealed by the scandal were committed by the most "corporate" and least pastoral of leaders—namely, Bernard Law and his aides.

But the Catholic priesthood, and its extension in the episcopacy, is also a unique institution whose members are not majority-rule demagogues or bottom-line execs. Their very mission is to put the needs of the people they serve above all else, while at the same time maintaining a healthy and necessary unity among themselves, for their good and for the good of all the church. In fact, that is the remarkably altruistic dynamic that characterizes the daily life of the church, and has for most of its history.

More important, the temptation of self-protection among the clerical ranks is more insidious and, because of the priest's exalted role in the Catholic superstructure, more dangerous than in other "corporate" organizations. Graphic evidence of the sin of clericalism was splashed across the newspapers in 2002, and made understanding and transforming that mentality the single most urgent priority for the coming Catholic Church.

One obvious source of the clericalist mentality is unique to the past generation—namely, the defensiveness caused by a shrinking priesthood left to fight for its survival amid a culture that is increasingly hostile to the cleric's reason for being.

These simultaneous trends acted like a pincer movement that prompted a circle-the-wagons reaction among priests and bishops, especially during John Paul II's restorationist papacy. In a hostile environment, church leaders reasoned, priests must be protected more than ever, "for the good of the church" and to comply with the traditional Catholic exhortation that church leaders must not "give scandal." Failing to preserve the flock from a loss of faith would be a greater sin than any sexual abuse, because of the eternal consequences of unbelief. To see priests as criminals would, the reasoning went, be too great a shock to the body of believers.

"While clericalism is a complex phenomenon, at its heart resides the notion that the clerical vocation and way of life are the norm for all other states of life and vocations in the Church," wrote Russell Shaw, a Catholic journalist and a former spokesman for the bishops conference. "The more you look and act like a priest, the better Catholic you are—that's the idea."

Priests and bishops were the paradigm of piety, and thus they were bulletproof, or at least had to appear to be (as in the case of Caesar's wife or, in more contemporary terms, an ostensibly virginal Miss America contestant).

Moreover, if the shrinking priesthood was increasingly dysfunctional, as appears to be the case, then the stage was set for a downward spiral of deception and denial—more cases of abuse followed by greater efforts to cover them up followed by more abuse. Soon the bishops were in too deep, and too few clerics had the courage to admit that they were protecting themselves rather than the faithful. Seen from this point of view, clericalism is actually dehumanizing, because it shields a man with no real regard for him as a person, but only for his exalted station in the Catholic firmament. More galling, of course, is that the self-protective reflex of the clerical culture winds up leaving the flock's most vulnerable members completely defenseless.

Still, these are all largely sociological explanations. More relevant to the church's crisis is a peculiar source of clericalism that is inherent in and unique to the Catholic system, for good and, when misunderstood and misapplied, for evil—namely, the unequaled sacred role of the priest. This role has two interconnected aspects: first, the relationship between the priest and his bishop, his "father in Christ"; and second, the rapport among the priests themselves. Both of these relationships are powerful, and in many respects they are indispensable to a healthy priesthood. Yet they can also be exploited to devastating effect. In the current crisis, the most immediate questions surround the first relationship—the powerful alliance between the priest and his bishop.

The priest-bishop bond is nurtured during the long years of the ordinand's education, or "formation," under the prelate's tutelage, and it is sealed during the ordination Mass, a solemn celebration that invokes all of the sacramental power and tradition of the Catholic Church. During the liturgy, each candidate for ordination kneels before the bishop—who is the only one who can ordain a priest, and only then with the explicit permission of Rome—and folds his hands, head bowed. The bishop covers the priest's hands in his own, and administers the oath of fealty: "Do you promise respect and obedience to me and my successors?" the bishops asks. "I do," the new priest responds, in a deliberate recreation of the medieval pledge of a vassal to his lord. Then, at the Litany of Saints, the newly ordained priest prostrates himself before the altar in a sign of submission, before rising to his knees to once again face the bishop, who then lays his hands on the priest's head. As the official Catholic Catechism (no. 1567) puts it: "The promise of obedience they [the priests] make to the bishop at the moment of ordination and the kiss of peace from him at the end of the ordination liturgy mean that the bishop considers them his co-workers, his sons, his brothers and his friends, and that they in return owe him love and obedience."

The service is profoundly moving, and every priest I have ever known recalls the moment with great emotion, decades after the event, as a spouse remembers a marriage or a parent the birth of a child. That is no coincidence. With his ordination the priest in a sense leaves behind the traditional family life, in keeping with Jesus' call to those who wanted to follow him most closely. The church is the priest's bride, his fellow priests his siblings, the flock his children, and the bishop his father. "I loved to act as feeling myself in my Bishop's sight, as if it were the sight of God," Cardinal John Henry Newman wrote in his *Apologia*. Ordination is transforming. A priest becomes a new man, "indelibly" marked by the sacrament. Or, as one midwestern bishop used to say to each newly ordained priest: "Welcome to the club!"

In short, once you're in, you're in for life (or you were supposed to be, until the bishops passed their new disciplinary policy); and membership entails a bond of loyalty that extends both ways. Cardinal John O'Connor of New York used to clear his calendar every Tuesday so that any priest could stop in and chat with him about any problem, even without an appointment. Cardinal John Krol in Philadelphia had a standing order that any priest could make an appointment with him for any reason on twenty-four hours notice, no explanation needed. "It is my conviction that a bishop's primary responsibility is for the pastoral care of the priests," New

Orleans archbishop Alfred C. Hughes, a onetime aide to Law in Boston, told the assembled presbyterate of his archdiocese. He was speaking at the height of the scandal, when everyone was wondering why the bishops had not shown greater concern for sexually abused children. His words have been echoed by any number of bishops, none more forcefully than Pope John Paul II. "The spiritual care of priests is a primary obligation of every diocesan bishop," John Paul told 117 newly appointed bishops from thirty-three countries during a September 2002 audience at his summer villa outside Rome. When a priest places his hands in the hands of his bishop and pledges his "filial devotion and obedience" at ordination, the pontiff said, the bishop "becomes responsible for the fate of those hands."

Yet for many prelates it turned out to be a short step from that pledge of "supernatural charity," as the Vatican II document on the priesthood, *Christus Dominus,* put it, to covering up for ghastly misconduct.

In retrospect, one should have seen it coming. In his 1989 book on the hierarchy, *Archbishop: Inside the Power Structure of the American Catholic Church,* Father Thomas Reese quoted a diocesan personnel director who described his archbishop as being like a stern father, gruff but unfailingly loyal:

"He is very formal, demanding, insists on 100 percent obedience. But if a man is in trouble in any way, any kind of trouble, trouble with the law, drinking or drugs, women, boys, anything—he is the most kindly, understanding, helpful man you would ever hope to have on your side. . . . If he can help you come to terms with whatever the problem is and you come back to active ministry, then the whole thing is off the record like it never happened. There is no grudge held, no 'Well, we can't trust him anymore.' He is very fair."

Reese went on to add: "If the priest approaches the archbishop before there is a public scandal, usually all can be forgiven and dealt with if the priest is willing. Here the bishop is not an employer, but a father or the representative of the forgiving Christ. If the priest reforms (and sometimes even if he does not, as long as it does not become public), he can continue in his ministry."

This clericalism-masquerading-as-charity became so ingrained to clerics that it even became a defense of sorts, at least in their view. "When I arrived in Boston in 1984, I assumed that priests in place had been appropriately appointed," Cardinal Law wrote in a May 2002 letter to

Boston Catholics as he sought to explain his long efforts to shield Paul Shanley, the abusive priest who openly advocated man-boy love. "It did not enter into my mind to second-guess my predecessors, and it simply was not in the culture of the day to function otherwise."

Much of that culture remains. As Russell Shaw—no liberal—wrote, "Clericalism in the Catholic Church is something like the pattern in the wallpaper: it's been there so long you don't see it anymore."

Breaking down the walls between the ordained class and the rest of the church is a vital first step toward ending the isolation that helps breed a clericalist mentality, but it will not be easy.

In a long memorandum to the bishops' Committee on Sexual Abuse, which had solicited opinions prior to the hierarchy's meeting in Dallas, the well-known orthodox theologian Germain Grisez gave the bishops a devastating diagnosis of just how far off course they had strayed. "The degeneration of priestly fraternity into self-serving clerical solidarity and the prevalence of managerial concerns over authentic pastoral charity are systemic evils," Grisez wrote in a withering critique, claiming that this warped vision "blinded bishops to the victims." "Of course, they [the victims] were visible, but they were tiny, nebulous, and marginal. Clerical sexual offenders, by contrast, were big, solid, and near the center of the bishops' field of vision."

When the bishops gathered a few days later, however, many of them continued to cite their holy bond with their priests as an argument against including a mandatory reporting clause in their policy. "For us, as bishops, to simply hand over allegations, we are not carrying out our sacred responsibilities to our priests," said Bishop Raymond Burke of La Crosse, Wisconsin. Bishop Thomas Doran of Rockford, Illinois, agreed: "When we do that we rat out our priests, and I am not favor of doing that."

While those arguments did not carry the day, the metaphor of priests as a clan unto themselves remains the defining mark of the clerical world. "The priesthood is a 'fraternity,' after all, and bishops are supposed to be 'fathers in Christ,'" Father Bruce Williams, an American theologian teaching in Rome, wrote in an essay on the eve of the Dallas meeting. "How many people now raging at the bishops would be immune from the impulse to try to shield their own sons accused of comparable offenses? How eager would they be to deliver their children to the tender mercies of prosecutors, as bishops are now expected to do with accused priests?"

But priests are not, in fact, the bishops' sons, nor are priests defense-less children, and some critics see the enshrinement of the filial metaphor into a *de facto* dogma as a perilous development for the priesthood, one with profound psychological roots and enormous ramifications for the Catholic Church. As Thomas Reese put it, "The diocese is like a family business—Uncle Charlie may be incompetent but you can't fire Uncle Charlie and you can't fire a priest. . . . Somewhere along the line some of them forgot that parents and their kids are also part of the family."

The leading analyst in this regard is Father Donald Cozzens, who frames the unhealthy priest-bishop relationship as a new take on the Oedipal archetype—a take that he calls the "presbyteral Oedipal com-plex." In Cozzens's reading, which is both detailed and controversial, the new Oedipal triangle has the church as mother, the bishop as father, and the priest in the middle as son—one who upon ordination suddenly finds himself with hundreds of siblings in his brother-priests.

"This maternal Church, while supportive and pointing to his dignity as a priest, is also demanding and controlling. His sexuality is restrained, his dress is determined, his residence assigned," Cozzens writes. "The defining decisions most men make as they claim their personal ground as men are denied. At the same time, the ecclesial mother in partnership with his father-bishop provides identity, status, and security. Add to this the rich and meaningful life of pastoral leadership and service and you have the makings of a well-established Oedipal conflict."

Left unaddressed, that conflict can result in damaging behaviors, or at the very least an unreflective conformity that, as Cozzens says, requires "staggering" courage for the priest to overcome.

"From every side he is cajoled to simply stop thinking and buy, un-critically, into the system. Should he succumb to this temptation he is likely to be rewarded. His own inner anxiety appears to recede and his ec-clesiastical superiors take note of his docility and deference. Often ad-vancement in a career track is remarkably swift. . . . Finally he surrenders to the artificiality of the clerical world."

Thus the more a priest conforms, the more likely he is to become a bishop—a "son" to the Holy Father—and the pressure to go along to get along becomes that much more intense, and the courage needed to break free that much greater.

In Cozzens's view, this environment too often raises a boy, not a man—the *puer aeternus* who finds a comfortable niche in the church without ever having to brave the rite of passage to adulthood. It is often said, "No mother ever lost a son who became a priest." That acknowledges the special role that the unattached priest can maintain in the life of his mother, and vice versa; her death is often the greatest crisis the adult priest will endure. The mother of a priest has a son who is special; he can maintain an unsullied, unburdened tie to her. (It should be noted, however, that recent surveys show that Catholic parents are now actively discouraging their sons from becoming priests—a sea change in Catholic culture, and another worrisome sign for vocations.) This intense mother-son rapport echoes the story of Jesus, which is irreverently, but artfully, summed up in the riff that lists the reasons why Jesus must have been Jewish: "He went into his father's business, he lived at home until he was thirty, he thought his mother was a virgin, and his mother thought he was God."

Jesus surely overcame any Oedipal complex he may have had. Many of his priests, however, do not. They are "eternal youths" living a never-ending adolescence. That immaturity is harmful on any number of levels, but in terms of sexual behavior it often translates into casual relationships for gay priests and "Don Juanism" for straight priests. Evidence of the latter behavior has been all but subsumed in the larger crisis over child abuse and homosexuality, but it reflects some of the same dysfunctions revealed in that crisis.

For the Don Juan priest, the temptations are everywhere, as they are for most any clergyman. The cleric has always been accorded an elevated status in society, an influential figure whose "otherworldliness" gives him an inherent allure to many women. That spiritual cachet is especially strong for the "unattainable" celibate of the Catholic priesthood. "God gets the best, we get the rest," as the Catholic schoolgirls used to sigh at the arrival of a hunky new priest (usually nicknamed "Father What-a-Waste"). Such flattery is a powerful elixir for any male ego, and is an especial peril for the immature priest whose job provides a steady interaction with a variety of women, many of whom come to him vulnerable and looking for the kind of attention he is trained to provide. "Clergymen have better manners and are better educated; besides, they have a quality that others seldom have—they listen," a Polish priest once said, by way of explaining why female parishioners display an embarrassing interest in priests.

For the mature priest, friendship with a woman can be invaluable. For the Peter Pan priest, it is a disaster that hurts both parties.

In 1993, at the height of an earlier round of sexual abuse revelations, Archbishop Robert Sanchez of Santa Fe, New Mexico, who was a top official of the national Catholic hierarchy at the time, was forced to resign after admitting to a string of affairs conducted over eighteen years. In 2002, at the height of the latest scandal, an auxiliary bishop in New York, Bishop James F. McCarthy, was forced to resign after he admitted to "several" affairs with women. McCarthy was one of the best known and most popular priests in the archdiocese, and he had served for twelve years as the personal aide to Cardinal O'Connor. Sexual freelancing is a peril for clergy in every denomination, and always will be. But under the current circumstances, the Catholic Church has to consider the factors that may make its clergy especially suspect.

"We need to ask if the clerical system itself may be setting the table for misconduct," Cozzens writes. "In other words, do we have a system that spiritually and emotionally immature individuals find inviting?"

That reassessment will also have to include the other aspect of clericalism, which is the fraternal bond among priests that is as strong, or often stronger, than their filial attachment to the bishop. As much as they are sons, Catholic priests are comrades with their fellow priests in the adventure of sanctity. This band of brothers is united by a shared, sacred commitment to live as few others would, all for the greater glory of God. "The fewer the men the greater the share of honour," as Henry V put it to his outnumbered troops at Agincourt. Priests are lonely sentinels of holiness in a secularized world, and that in itself is a powerful motive for watching each other's back. But their bond goes beyond the foxhole camaraderie of the soldier or the woofing solidarity of the frat brother. Priests are bound to each other through strong affective relationships that are remarkable, and fascinating, to outsiders—especially men who may envy the easy way that priests can express their affection for one another. To be sure, priests are as captious and competitive as any bunch of siblings. It's been that way since the beginning, when the apostles were always jockeying for position near Jesus, seeking his favor over the others. Yet even priests who don't like each other stand by each other. "It's as if they share the same ecclesial genes—the same tribal blood running through their veins," writes Cozzens.

I think that the experience of the priesthood has endowed Catholic priests with a certain genius for friendship, honed no doubt by their solitary state, but also by their vocation and the formation of their priestly identity through years of seminary training and life in the trenches of parish work. Lay people should consider themselves fortunate when that friendship is extended to them. But as rich as that gift is, it is only a reflection of the deeper camaraderie within the priesthood.

That is why the sexual abuse scandal has been so shattering to so many good priests—an experience easily as traumatic for them as it was for the laity. "Paul Shanley and John Geoghan, we know, are aberrations. But they are our aberrations," said Father Robert W. Bullock, pastor of Our Lady of Sorrows Parish in Sharon, Massachusetts, and head of the Boston Priests Forum, which he organized just before the scandal broke.

When I met Bullock it was mid-summer 2002, in the midst of the crisis, and in Boston, at the epicenter of the scandal. The pain of the scandal showed on Bullock's craggy features, yet his honesty in describing the agonizing quandary of today's priests was moving, and showed why his is a voice that is listened to by all sides.

As Bob Bullock described it, when he entered the seminary in the 1950s it was the Golden Age of vocations, and he felt immediately that he had found a permanent home and a new family. "The problem I had was going in, not staying in," Bullock recalled. "All the tensions and inner turmoil were in the last year of college. But once I got in, I loved it. It [the seminary] was packed with people, it was vibrant. In many ways it was alive although the atmosphere was very restrictive. But I felt that we were all involved in something noble, that we were doing something noble, and that we had been chosen by God for inexplicable reasons to be servants of God's people.

"So when we talk about a brotherhood that we have, I felt that and I still feel that. We are brothers. We have been through something together and we shared common ideas and common goals."

One of those brothers was three years behind Bullock, yet Bullock looked up to him as "the most gifted, studious, charismatic and pious seminarian I have ever met." He was Paul Shanley, a man who would never break a rule as a seminarian, but who as a priest became the most notorious pedophile after Geoghan. Three days before I saw Bullock, he had gone to visit Shanley in jail. There Bullock found a seventy-year-old man who had lost all of his famous confidence and charm, whose hands were shaking and lips quivering, and who complained for an hour that all the charges against him were false. Shanley had prepared notes so as to remember what to tell Bullock. The first said, "No one's visiting me."

It was a self-pitying display by an awful abuser, but after it all, Bullock said, "I felt still, he's a brother. He's a priest. There's an identification with him."

Two days later Bullock convened a meeting of the Priests Forum to hear from Arthur Austin, one of Shanley's victims. "In terms that were graphic, almost physical, anguished, he spoke about his story, about six years of abuse by Paul Shanley—six years in which he was seduced, violated, criminalized in the most graphic and terrible ways," Bullock recalled.

"So there are the terms, for me, of the dilemma we have. On the one hand there is that sense of connectedness with one of ours, and then the unbearable nature of the crimes that have been committed.

"That must drive us to the deepest sort of investigation of what it is about us, what led us not to be able to protect our parishioners. We didn't protect the children. They were our brothers who did these things. We heard the rumors. We heard the suspicions. Only two or three of us spoke up, at great risk to themselves," Bullock said. With pain in his voice and on his face, he asked, almost of himself: "What is it that has made us, the Boston presbyterate, to be so supine, so inert, so passive, so unwilling to react, to take risks, and to speak out?"

It was not just Boston, of course; it was dioceses all around the country. While priests did not cover for priests the way bishops did, there were enough examples of outright aiding and abetting of molesters to raise suspicions that the fraternity had become co-conspirators in much of the abuse.

In Connecticut, for example, it was revealed that at least two priests had for years been in touch with a former priest of the diocese, Laurence F. X. Brett, who for a decade had been in hiding in the Caribbean, in the Virgin Islands, to escape prosecution on charges that he had molested more than two dozen youths in Connecticut, New Mexico, California, and Maryland. At any time the two priests could have helped bring Brett to justice. When the reports surfaced in 2002, Bridgeport's new bishop,

William Lori, disciplined the men and sentenced them to several months of isolation and penance. When they emerged, they publicly apologized to their parishioners and tried to explain:

"I ask you to understand that I knew Laurence Brett and reached out to him as a friend," said Father Gerald Devore. "I did so without understanding the harm and pain it might cause." Father David Howell told his church that the assigned period of prayer and reflection had been helpful. "What I did or failed to do arose out of mistaken sense of fidelity to a person who had at one time been a brother priest."

But little could be done about Brett, who fled authorities again when the stories became public.

For priests, part of the shock of the scandal was discovering how little they knew of each other's lives, for good and for ill. Sexual abusers, especially pedophiles, are notoriously deceptive, and priests were often as stunned as everyone else at the hidden misconduct of the criminal few, and alarmed at the suspicion it sowed among their ranks. "When we get together today, the first thing someone always asks is, 'Has anyone else gotten into trouble?'" said one priest I know.

The priesthood remains a "club" in principle, but in reality the fraternity's ranks have thinned alarmingly, and that has altered the dynamic. Priests today are scattered in isolated rectories, overworked, and allowed little time to renew their bonds or recharge their spiritual batteries in any meaningful way. "The social network supporting a celibate male priesthood has disintegrated," says Frank K. Flinn, an expert on the priesthood at Washington University in St. Louis. "Parishes no longer have three, maybe four priests living under one roof. What we find is a disconnected association of priestly loners who get lost in the swirl of modernity."

In Bob Bullock's ordination class in 1956 there were seventy men who became priests. In 2002, the Archdiocese of Boston ordained five men. "Something is happening to us, among us," Bullock said.

The change is evident in surveys that show how much the cohesiveness of the priesthood has deteriorated. Surveys conducted in recent years show that about a third of priests, when asked about their views on religious and moral matters, describe themselves as liberal, another third as conservative, and another third as moderate. Moreover, the splits were clearly along generational lines, with the younger priests embracing old ways and the older priests left as the aging guardians of the ideals of the

Vatican II era. This does not bode well for the priesthood, whose growing internal conflicts threaten to mirror the tensions afflicting the wider church.

The dynamic between bishops and priests is also changing, but that is primarily due to changes forced on the clergy as a result of the scandal.

When the American bishops finally passed a policy on clergy sexual misconduct, American priests felt that they had been sold out. Their bishops, their father-figures, had taken them to the woodshed without asking the priests themselves for their side of the story. The hierarchy had, in galling fashion, dumped the scandal on their heads without a single bishop resigning or even being called on to resign by any of the other nearly three hundred bishops. Even before 2002, polls showed that a majority of priests expressed little confidence in the leadership of the bishop, and just a quarter of them said that their bishop gave them strong support for their own ministry.

With the events of 2002, the priest's worldview grew darker. "The bishop is not your friend," as one New York pastor told me. New York priests already had reason to be dour. Cardinal Edward Egan, who succeeded the late John O'Connor, had alienated priests at his previous posting in Bridgeport, Connecticut, when he testified in a sexual abuse trial that he had no responsibility for wayward clerics because he considered pastors "independent contractors." That corporate, rather than familial, mindset infuriated the presbyterate. Many bishops recognized, and were concerned about, the gulf that had opened. "I could see a bishop calling to see a priest, and he says, 'Well, I'm bringing my lawyer with me.' I mean, is that what we want?" asked Bishop Joseph Sullivan, an auxiliary in Brooklyn who opposed the zero-tolerance provisions on pastoral grounds.

In October, the *National Catholic Reporter* reprinted a letter from a Los Angeles priest to a priest in another state that summed up the prevailing view of priests toward their bishops: "The holier-than-thou, judgmental pose they [the bishops] have taken is the most sickening aspect of this whole sordid affair, and if they are so anxious to cast out everyone who may be a potential financial liability to them (and only an idiot would fail to see that this is the true motive), perhaps they should consider resigning themselves," the priest, who remained anonymous, wrote. "The fact that we now have a feeble pope, and that everyone over there seems to be taking advantage of that situation, does not help in the least. So, we are caught between two fires, really, and neither is very inviting. Thank heavens God is so much bigger than all of that. I am not optimistic, but for priests these days realism is synonymous with pessimism." Unfortunately, that pessimism has too often translated into a deeper clericalism.

In the wake of the scandal, priests in many dioceses banded together to protest their vilification. New York priests formed a group called Voice of the Ordained, which was a pointed takeoff on the lay organization Voice of the Faithful. This was the first time in decades that priests had shown some public assertiveness, yet it was largely on behalf of their own interests, to protect themselves, rather than on behalf of the victims. When Voice of the Ordained met, over an Irish bar in Manhattan, one canon lawyer advised the 150 or so priests and former priests not to admit any wrongdoing to their bishop. "A priest should say nothing," said Msgr. William A. Varvaro. "It's that old question of the father-son relationship that's been destroyed."

In Boston, there was significant internal opposition to the Priests Forum that Bullock helped to organize. The group grew out of a dinner among three priests in the summer of 2001—a meal among friends at which they tried to come to grips with their everyday concerns, such as loneliness and burnout. By the end of 2001, the forum had fifty members, despite Law's warning that any priest who joined would face a rocky career. The number was still just 10 percent of the 550 active priests in the archdiocese, the nation's fourth-largest presbyterate, but it was enough to draw attacks from tradition-minded priests, who labeled it divisive and needlessly political. "The church is like a family," said Father Joseph Hennessey, who called on the forum to disband. "Families settle things . . . face to face. The church is not Ward 16 politics. The church is not a union hall."

Rather than knee-jerk self-protection, however, what is needed is a healthy clericalism, a united and vocal priesthood whose members will confront their bishops and, if need be, their own members. "I think we're overly docile," said Frank McNulty, the New Jersey priest who spoke his mind to Pope John Paul II in Miami in 1987. "We need the courage to say what we think." McNulty lamented the passing of the priest senates that sprang up in dioceses in the ferment after Vatican II. "Priest senates were very powerful. They were almost totally elected. Very often the bishop didn't control the meetings," McNulty said. "That was a place where you could show courage and speak up and work for change."

But the senates went by the wayside. Bishops gradually reasserted their control and won the authority to replace them with presbyteral councils, whose members are generally appointed by the bishop. The loss is felt acutely now, when a countervailing voice is needed more than ever. "There was more dialogue and honesty and openness right along through the ranks in those years," McNulty said. "Bishops didn't like giving up that power. At one of our committee meetings—I'll never forget the moment—we were in a committee with the archbishop, and one of our guys says to him, 'The trouble with this whole thing, Archbishop, is you think this is your church. But it's not. It's ours.'"

This is difficult terrain for priests to negotiate. The sacred pact between the bishop and the priest means that the bishop has a canonical responsibility to look after a priest. The priesthood is a comforting sinecure in that sense. But the deal cuts the other way, too. A priest who displeases the bishop can be exiled to a pastoral gulag. The promise of obedience taken at ordination means that priests go where the bishop tells them. In the clerical world, retribution for breaking the code is all too commonplace, and knowledge of that fact contributes to the hear-see-speak-no-evil culture that helped to foster the abuses. "I will tell you, I fear retaliation," said Father Patrick Rohen, a Toledo priest quoted in the *Washington Post*. Rohen and another priest had called on their bishop, James R. Hoffman, to step down when it was revealed that Hoffman had taken no action against several abusive priests. "But somebody's got to speak out on this," Rohen said. "The whole problem is the world of secrecy and shame."

This is no time for lonely rebels fighting lost causes, however. As the theologian Hans Küng has written, "One parish priest does not count in the diocese, five are given attention, 50 are invincible." Küng was writing in 1979, but the events of December 2002 showed that he got the math almost exactly right.

On Monday, December 9, after two weeks of renewed upheaval caused by the new round of documents incriminating Cardinal Law and his minions, fifty-eight Boston-area priests signed an unprecedented petition calling on Law to resign. The three-paragraph letter was hand-delivered to Law's residence. The cardinal was in Rome for discussions with Vatican officials and the pope at the time but he got the message. Four days later he resigned.

"There is some form of clericalism in all denominations, but it's epidemic in Catholicism, that tendency toward being secretive and privileged and entitled," Bob Bullock told reporters when the letter was delivered. "And it's that clericalism of the priesthood that contributed enormously to this crisis. We need a radical change. We all have collective responsibility for creating the environment where this took place, and we have to examine that.

"There should be more openness, more mutual accountability, and more candor between priests and their bishop," he said. "Cardinal Law did not listen to what we thought and what we experienced."

And Law paid the price for his insensibility. It was the first time in the history of the Catholic Church in America that a bishop—not to mention a cardinal who was the most senior and powerful churchman in the country—had been forced to resign under public pressure. Other bishops had resigned for engaging in sexual misdeeds themselves, but no bishop had ever been forced to step down because his underlings thought he wasn't doing his job. "Priests by their very calling and their relationship to the bishop are docile," Father Robert Wister, a church historian at Seton Hall University, said. "For them to call for Law's ouster is unprecedented. It is a sea change in the behavior of the American Catholic priesthood."

Many still resist that change, and clericalism will die hard, if it dies at all. Months after Law's resignation, the tandem of conservative Catholic intellectuals, George Weigel and Father Richard John Neuhaus, published separate columns that maligned "the Boston fifty-eight," as they came to be known, casting suspicions on their own moral character (Weigel) and claiming that priestly dissent was the root cause of the Catholic crisis (Neuhaus). "Whoever succeeds Law as archbishop should, it has been suggested, keep that list of fifty-eight handy, for they represent the subculture of infidelity that is the source of priestly miscreance in doctrine and life," Neuhaus wrote in his journal, *First Things*. "Officials in Rome could see that the signatories included priests who had never truly accepted Cardinal Law's authority," Weigel wrote in a column published by the archdiocese's own weekly, *The Pilot*. "Roman authorities could also

see that priests whose ministerial paths had not been without major pot-
holes (to put it gently) were among the signatories."

The salvos reopened the wounds within the Boston priesthood, as
some priests praised the Weigel-Neuhaus sentiment and others stood by
their decision to speak out against Law. "It feels to me like one of those
pivotal moments in the history of the church, like the Edict of Constantine, the Orthodox-Catholic split, the Protestant Reformation, or the
Second Vatican Council," Father Emile R. Boutin, Jr., who signed the petition, told the *Boston Globe.*

It was pivotal because, after a year of fierce outrage and protests and
lawsuits and depositions and a national scandal that left the country's
largest denomination in a state of clinical depression, it was only the actions, hesitant and anguished as they were, of a few dozen priests that
brought down the chief perpetrator of the crisis. "When you lose your
priests, you lose your diocese," one bishop told me.

That dynamic is telling. It speaks to the positive role priests can play
in revamping the culture of Catholicism. But it also underscores the need
to rethink the position of the priest in Catholicism. Investing too much
blind power and responsibility in the priesthood can lead to terrible
abuses, as the scandal showed. A careful reimagining of the Catholic
priesthood would benefit not only the laity, but priests themselves.

This is as delicate an issue as there is in the church today. The perils
are many. Dilute the sacramental role of the priest too much, and the edifice of Catholicism loses one of its fundamental pillars. A reactionary reflex that tries to put the priest back on an unassailable pedestal would be
just as bad, further skewing the structure of the church. And an antago-
nistic process that pits priests against bishops and against the laity would
only hasten the worrisome trend of building higher walls among the various estates of the Catholic community.

Still, the coming change is inevitable. Well before the scandal, though
unbeknownst to much of the outside world, the debate over the changing
identity of the priesthood was already underway. The scandal accelerated
the process by revealing the myriad problems and dysfunctions in the
priesthood. But the scandal also served to obscure so much that is good
and unique about the Catholic priesthood.

There is both opportunity and danger in the discussion over the priesthood, but the debate cannot be put off. Apart from the scandal, too many other forces are exerting themselves on priests today, as the church experiences a moment of flux the likes of which has not occurred for centuries. The better our understanding of the meaning of the priesthood and the ways that it is changing, the better the chances of emerging from this dark night of the soul with a renewed Catholic Church.

Ten

THE CHANGING FACE
OF THE PRIESTHOOD

"You are a priest forever" is the formula of ordination that is as old as the hills and as integral to the nature of the priesthood, and hence the character of Catholicism, as anything in the contemporary church. The priesthood is supposed to be the unchanging axis around which Catholic life revolves, and priests are permanently, ontologically marked as the *alter Christus,* the dispenser of absolution, the presider at weddings and funerals, the irreplaceable gateway to sanctity for the practicing Catholic.

"Through the ordained ministry, especially that of bishops and priests, the presence of Christ as head of the Church is made visible in the midst of the community of believers," the Catholic Catechism states. "By ordination one is enabled to act as a representative of Christ, Head of the Church, in his triple office of priest, prophet, and king." With that trifecta behind him, the priest's identity and role was unquestioned through centuries, and he became a fixed presence in the Catholic cosmos. In years past, it was the rare Catholic who did *not* wear a medal with an engraved alert to anyone who should find him or her in danger of death: "I am a Catholic. Please call a priest." Priests usher you into this world at baptism, and on to the next one with last rites.

And yet, in this period of enormous change in Catholicism, nothing else is as open to question as the role of the priest, and nothing is more unsettling to Catholicism's self-understanding.

For priests themselves, the debate is not new. But the sexual abuse scandal intensified and publicized the scrutiny, to an unprecedented and unsettling degree, and made the resolution of the debate a matter of the greatest urgency. "This crisis has pointed a dagger at the priesthood, and there is nothing more important to the sacramental life of the church," says Father Richard McBrien of Notre Dame. "When the priesthood is under a shadow, it calls into question the church's ability to provide that sacramental life." Little wonder that the effort to recast the priest's role and identity is the most volatile flashpoint in modern-day Catholicism.

What is it about the Catholic priest that makes him so vital to the life of the church?

Simply put, it is the short, straight line that the Catholic Church draws between the priest and his spiritual forebear, Jesus Christ. The priesthood's foundational event and mission statement, as it were, is recreated daily in the Mass, through the reenactment of Jesus' words at the Last Supper and the institution of the Eucharist, which in turn is the sacramental linchpin of Catholicism:

> *On the night he was betrayed,*
> *he took the bread and gave you thanks and praise.*
> *He broke the bread, gave it to his disciples, and said:*
> *Take this, all of you, and eat it:*
> *This is my body which will be given up for you.*
> *When supper was ended, he took the cup.*
> *Again he gave you thanks and praise,*
> *gave the cup to his disciples, and said:*
> *Take this, all of you, and drink from it:*
> *This is the cup of my blood,*
> *the blood of the new and everlasting covenant.*
> *It will be shed for you and for all*
> *so that sins may be forgiven.*
> *Do this in memory of me.*

It is the priest and only the priest, filling the role of Jesus, who can say these words and give them the power to effect the miracle of the Eucharist, the distinctive sacrament of the Catholic Church. The church teaches that the Last Supper marked the foundation of the Christian priesthood itself. Thus at the same time that Jesus gave his followers the divine formula for the consecration of the bread and wine into his body and blood, he also set up a corps of hierarchs to provide the sacrament. In Catholic theology, these two elements are inextricably bound up in each other. No priesthood, no Eucharist. No Eucharist, no Catholics.

"The priest is the re-presentation of Jesus Christ to His people. The priest is the continuance of Jesus on earth to carry out Christ's role as head of the Church and shepherd of the flock," Philadelphia's Cardinal Anthony Bevilacqua said in a homily in 2003. "In more functional terms, the priest is the visible presence on earth of Christ teaching, Christ preaching, Christ listening, Christ healing, Christ feeding, Christ consoling, Christ weeping, Christ blessing, Christ leading, Christ searching, Christ forgiving, Christ laughing, Christ embracing, Christ loving and, as we are pitifully aware today, Christ suffering, Christ bleeding, Christ dying."

That is a mighty lineage.

Today, such an emphasis on sacramental power, invested in a single person by divine fiat, seems barely comprehensible. Again, modernity is not the priest's friend. By contrast, the ancient world of Jesus' time took it for granted that any religion worth its salt would have a professional priesthood to carry out its most sacred functions, to tend the holy flame of faith. Naturally, these priests would also be the best and the brightest that society had to offer. Considering the stakes, why offer the gods any less? Pagan faiths always had their high priests (and priestesses) and oracles to guard the sacred mysteries. India's religious traditions developed especially elaborate caste systems in Vedism, Buddhism, Hinduism, and, most recognizably, Brahminism.

But Judaism at the time of Jesus, himself an observant Jew, also followed a similar pattern. As a faith centered around the Temple, focused on the Holy of Holies where God was said to reside, Judaism had a highly developed priestly structure (led by the *Kohanim*, the root of the contemporary surname Cohen and its many variations) to celebrate the ancient, carefully prescribed rituals. The Jewish priesthood was dynastic, tracing its roots to Aaron, the first high priest, and his progeny, a system established by Moses to protect the Israelites from straying after the apostasy of the Golden Calf in the desert. The high priest (always a man) was anointed like a king, and the rest of the *Kohanim* were subject to special laws designed to keep them separate from and undefiled by the rest of the people. They wore elaborate, bejeweled vestments, and the Priestly Code required them to have no physical deformity and to be of irreproachable moral character. A *Kohan* could not marry a convert, touch a corpse, or even touch anyone who came in contact with the dead. Separate gates to the Temple were set aside for the *Kohanim*. Only they could enter the innermost sanctuary, and they had to do so barefoot, so that they would come into direct contact with the floor on which the Ark of the Covenant resided.

In A.D. 70, that entire hierarchical structure disappeared in the ruins of the sanctuary itself when the Romans sacked the Second Temple, the apocalyptic event some believe Jesus may have been prophesying with his dire warnings to repent. Hardly a stone of the great shrine was left standing. The Jewish nation was scattered and its sacramental traditions effectively ended, held in abeyance until the coming of the Messiah and the restoration of the Temple. From that point, Rabbinic Judaism became the norm, the means for preserving and transmitting the faith down through generations of Jews who now lived in communities scattered in hostile lands.

Emerging from the tumult of the first century, the fledgling Christian religion took the opposite tack, maintaining and even elevating the institution of the priesthood at the same time that Judaism was diminishing the priestly role. This new Christian priesthood was dynastic only in the spiritual sense (although there is some evidence that James, the brother of Jesus and the first bishop of Jerusalem, achieved his rank because of his family ties to the Savior), but it was just as tribal. Christian priests were one with the Christ whose sacrifice they recreated each day. This eucharistic action was considered as true and real as any Temple ritual, and the ordination of priests who could perform the eucharistic miracle was life-changing and permanent. Ordination conferred a grace that could not be undone; it changed a man's very being, and it cemented his identity with Jesus. *"Tu es sacerdos in aeternum!* This challenging call echoes in our hearts making us conscious of how our own life is indissolubly united with his. Forever!" John Paul reassured the world's five hundred thousand priests with these words in his letter for Holy Thursday, issued at the height of the scandal.

The exalted role of the priest was cemented as Christianity's center shifted from Asia Minor to Rome, where the church took on the aspects of the Roman system of worship, which was more closely entwined with the functions of the state than that of any other ancient culture. (It has been said that Christianity was born in the Middle East as a religion, went to Greece and became a philosophy, migrated to Rome and became a legal system, spread through Europe and became a culture, and finally headed to America, where it became Big Business.) In the Roman civilization where Christianity first flourished, the pagan priesthood was largely a privilege of the ruling classes; the emperor himself was the high priest, the *pontifex maximus* (a title later borrowed by the Roman pontiff when Caesar was no longer around to complain about the usurpation).

Soon the model and means of Christian practice were set in place. The Germanic barbarians of the northern reaches and the Druids of the Celtic Isles could worship in their sacred groves, calling forth the various spirits of the earth in primitive rituals. But Christian priests were inheritors and integrators of the elaborate Jewish and Roman religious systems, and the serendipity of that merger is evident in the remarkable cohesion and endurance of the Catholic Church.

Despite this powerful legacy of sacrament and organization, however, the priesthood of the first millennium of Christendom took time to become the socially distinct class we have come to associate with modern Catholicism. At first there were no seminaries to train would-be clerics, and a man who wanted to become a priest had only to present himself to the bishop three days before ordination to take an oral exam. If the candidate was at least twenty-four years old, had no bodily defects, was not illegitimate or of servile birth, and had a grasp of the faith and could communicate it, he was ordained. "The local priest was often hardly indistinguishable from his parishioners, even though in theory and theology there was supposed to be a sharp separation," writes Father Thomas Bokenkotter in his history of the Catholic Church. To be sure, priests were often literate, as opposed to the vast majority of their congregants. But they could also be found working the fields side by side with their flock.

That changed as the Middle Ages progressed and reformer pontiffs revamped the priesthood into "a disciplined army moving completely in step under the Pope, set off from all profane occupations, with their special uniform, the long cassock (a relic of the Roman toga), and ruling over an obedient and receptive laity composed of kings, lords and peasants alike," as Bokenkotter writes.

The distinction grew over the ensuing centuries, to the point that "the people were gradually excluded from all participation, and the Mass became exclusively the priest's business, with the people reduced to the role of spectators," Bokenkotter continues. "In the medieval Mass the priest no longer wore his ordinary street clothes, as he once did, but glided into the sanctuary draped in a heavily embroidered chasuble and began to whisper the prayers in a language no longer understood by the people. They stood at a distance separated from him by a heavy railing, which emphasized the sacredness of the sanctuary. No longer were they allowed to bring up their ordinary bread for consecration; the priest consecrated unleavened bread already prepared in coinlike form. Nor were they allowed to take the wafer in their hands, standing as they once did; now they had to kneel and receive it on the tongue, while the chalice was withheld from them." (Only since Vatican II have lay people been allowed to drink from the cup, the blood of Jesus. But the traditions of centuries die hard, even among the most liberal-minded Catholics, and still, relatively few take the wine.)

It was also around this time that celibacy became universal church law for the West, further setting the priesthood apart as a separate, higher caste.

The eruption of the Protestant Reformation only underscored the uniqueness of the Catholic priest's role because Protestants unceremoniously dumped the idea of holy orders and thus set the stage for the sharp contrast in Christianity that we see today. Although the conception of ministry varies from one denomination to another, the general Protestant view embraces the theology of a "universal" priesthood over an adjunct, "specialized" priesthood. In practice the Protestant understanding means that a "minister" can be drawn from the ranks of the faithful, and can return there, and he can be married and have a family, like everyone else. The Protestant goal was to reclaim a supposed pristine, pre-clerical polity of primitive Christianity.

Rome's reaction to the Protestant tide also wound up exalting the Catholic notion of the priesthood, because in its zeal to differentiate Catholicism—the one, true church—from the Protestant "heresy," Rome sanctified every tradition that Protestantism rejected. That went doubly for the priesthood, as the Counter-Reformation-era Council of Trent made clear: "If any one shall say that in the New Testament there is no visible and external priesthood nor any power of consecrating and offering the Body and Blood of the Lord, as well as of remitting and retaining sins, but merely the office and bare ministry of preaching the Gospel, let him be anathema." As *The Catholic Encyclopedia* puts it, "The priesthood forms so indispensable a foundation of Christianity that its removal would entail the destruction of the whole edifice. A Christianity without a priesthood cannot be the Church of Christ."

The onslaught of modernity, often borne on the wings of anti-clericalism, further cemented Catholicism's hyper-clericalist view, and the United States, with its combination of a Protestant hegemony, an Enlightenment ethos, and a doctrine of individualism, became, in Rome's eyes (and often in reality), the enemy of everything the Catholic priesthood stood for.

"There will soon be no more priests. Their work is done. A new order shall arise, and they shall be the priests of man, and every man shall be his own priest," wrote Walt Whitman in his preface to *Leaves of Grass* (1855), his matchless hymns to the sacredness of the individual. Beautiful words, but not a very Catholic sentiment. Other declarations of spiritual independence took less lyrical forms. For example, *The Awful Disclosures of Maria Monk* was a nineteenth-century recounting of a poor young woman who was dragooned into a Montreal convent where, like the rest of the nuns, she was forced to have sex with priests who entered through a secret tunnel. (So much for literary subtlety.) The babies born of these secret liaisons were baptized and then killed and dumped in a lime pit in the basement. Poor Maria fled this hell hole after seven years and published her diaries, which were a bestseller in America and remained in print into the twentieth century, despite the fact that Monk's story was as much a hoax as *The Protocols of the Elders of Zion*. Maria Monk never actually lived in a convent—she was apparently a prostitute—and the story was concocted by nativist Protestant ministers who sought to stir up anti-Catholic sentiment.

It worked, because the nineteenth century was a fertile time to sell such hoaxes. Even the irenic Ralph Waldo Emerson took to complaining of "Romish priests, who sympathize, of course, with despotism." Priests were the symbols of everything wrong about Catholicism. They were considered agents of a foreign government and corrupters of youth, an attitude that persisted with alarming doggedness well into the twentieth century. Paul Blanshard's 1949 book, *American Freedom and Catholic Power,* effectively retailed all the previous canards about Catholicism and its priests, and became a widely praised bestseller. More recently, the 2000 debacle over the selection of a Catholic priest as chaplain of the House of Representatives also betrayed biases that seemed to reverberate from another era. The reflexive Catholic reaction, from the earliest phase of this anti-Catholic sentiment, was to build up the priest's pedestal even higher. "By World War I the Catholic pastor was the lord of his neighborhood with lifelong tenure," Msgr. George A. Kelly, founder of the Fellowship of Catholic Scholars, has written.

Within the church, the pastor remained in his lofty post, unchallenged, until the Second Vatican Council and Catholicism's Velvet Revolution.

Then, in a flash, the once static Catholic world was turned upside down—or twisted around. And the priest was the unwitting axis around which that change revolved. With the promulgation of the revamped liturgy in 1968, the Catholic pastor woke up one day and suddenly found himself facing a congregation that was expecting pearls of wisdom to drop from his lips in the kind of homilies he had never been trained to give. "You have no idea what a shock that was," said a friend of mine who had been ordained only a few years when the revolution came. "We had no idea what to do. Guys were completely discombobulated. It took us years to adjust." In fact, the adjustment is still underway. Vatican II was a wonderful and liberating experience in so many ways. But it was problematic for the priesthood, in part because although the Council Fathers had a lot to say about the role of the bishop (which they greatly enhanced) and the role of the laity (which they greatly enhanced in theory), they said little about the men who were on the front lines of the lived faith: the priests.

In the period of upheaval and uncertainty that followed the liturgical reforms of Vatican II—changes that paralleled an extraordinary tumult in society—priests had few guideposts. The result was an identity crisis in the priesthood that had no precedent. The crisis was debated with quiet desperation in seminaries and rectories and chanceries, while Rome generally tried to quash any hint of a problem.

In his 1989 book on the power structure of the church, Thomas Reese quoted several priests—anonymously—who were livid over a statement by John Paul that the identity crisis of the priest was over. "I feel really bitter about those kinds of statements coming out of Rome," one priest told Reese. "I have felt so much of the personal pain of really good men who have tried so hard to do a good job, and I see what they are going through. And then to hear that there is no crisis, that is really bad." Said another: "What the pope said is just absurd. I am stunned by that remark, because it is just so ignorant. Diocesan priests, we have no idea what our charism is. How we fit in. The morale is abysmal. Bishops are denying it, or they are paralyzed by it. You have someone like the pope saying that it is all over. That is idiotic. Just idiotic. He is just poorly informed."

When the teetering icon of Bing Crosby's *Going My Way* priest finally tumbled and shattered in 2002, there was no way to avoid the tough questions any longer. To many church leaders, and priests themselves, that may not be such a bad thing. At least now the issues are out in the open. "Remember the first step in rebounding from a crisis or a trauma is to look reality squarely in the face," Tucson bishop Gerald F. Kicanas told a national gathering of diocesan vocation directors in Boston in September 2002. He compared the crisis today with periods in the Middle Ages and the sixteenth century "when the church seemed decayed, decadent, a failed vision." He added, "A reforming spirit gradually pervaded the church in those troubled times. The church rebounded. A new holiness came over the church. Her ministers turned back to the Lord." But Kicanas also warned his listeners that the renewal of the priesthood will not come quickly or easily.

Indeed, the process is likely to be fraught with difficulties, given the centuries-long development of the priest's role and identity in Catholicism. Yet given the depth of the scandal and its impact on the priesthood, the reforms cannot be postponed.

The issues at stake are manifold: Is the Catholic priest a plaster saint or just another one of the faithful, with all the foibles of his flock? Is he there to lead by serving or to serve by leading? Is his work a job or a vocation? Can the Catholic priesthood as it has been constituted for more than a millennium survive? And if it is changing irrevocably, what will replace it? What will the priest of the new millennium look like?

In the end the solution will boil down to how Catholics come to understand two basic yet competing truths about the nature of the priesthood:

One stresses the priest's unique theological role. The other focuses on his workaday position as a leader of the flock, a manager of sorts, yet a Christian like everyone else. This faultline neatly cleaves church thinking between those who want to emphasize the first, or "cultic," model and those who want to emphasize the latter, or "servant," model of priesthood. Again, priests themselves are caught in the middle, usually between bishops who want them to be guardians of orthodoxy and lay people who want them to be regular Joes, only better. The burden of reconciling these competing roles is often too much to bear.

The answer to the dilemma does not lie fully with one camp or the other. Continuing the trend of past centuries and exalting the priest still further, placing him higher on a pedestal and beyond the reach of ordinary mortals, would only play into the very problems that fed the sexual abuse scandal—a closeted, clerical culture that could not admit the humanity of its members and therefore covered up for them at every turn.

On the other hand, turning the priest into Everyman would vitiate the historical understanding of the priesthood at a time when the priest's sacred role and countercultural voice are needed more than ever. Deconstructing the priest's role would be tantamount to admitting that the fantastical prejudices about Catholic clerics were right and were at the root of the scandal, neither of which is true. Such a move would be a disastrous blow to the church at a perilous moment.

What is needed is a way to rehumanize the priesthood without desacralizing it, a reimagining of both aspects of the priestly function: the daily role, and the theology that is at the very foundation of the priesthood.

The chief problem with the current theological understanding of the priesthood, a problem that was so disturbingly exposed by the sexual abuse scandal, is the degree to which many priests and church leaders—and the lay faithful—have allowed the sacred view of the priest's role to obscure or replace his status as one of the baptized, as another sinner in need of redemption. The tendency to lionize the pastor is certainly not unique to Catholicism. In every denomination, from the most liberal to the most conservative, clergymen (and -women) are revered figures who too often conflate their role with their own interests, with disastrous results.

But the instinct to grant the minister protected status endures most visibly in the Catholic Church, whose priests, with their promises of celibacy and obedience (and poverty, for religious order priests), and their sacred power to loose and bind in cooperation with the Almighty, are virtually the lone avatars of the ancient priestly caste in the modern world, especially in America. Their role has been a great grace and a principal source of Catholicism's enduring identity and unity. But as the scandal showed, the understanding of that role has at times come to be interpreted so mechanistically that it obscured the humanity of the priest and fostered the abuse of innocents.

The theological seeds of the current problem were sown in the early church during its initial struggles to define the role and nature of the priest and his relation to the sacraments. This struggle burst forth in the bitterly disputed fourth-century heresy (one among many in that wooly era of the faith) that was known as Donatism, essentially a school of thought that grew out of an argument over who should be considered a Christian in good standing.

At the time, the church was undergoing frequent persecutions, and some church leaders argued that Christians who denied their faith rather than submitting to martyrdom, or who in other ways publicly sinned, must either be banished from communion or be required to resubmit to the sacraments—namely, baptism and penance. This debate extended to the priest and the efficacy of the sacraments he administered. Would baptism or the Eucharist be invalid if administered by a sinful cleric? Fortunately, the Puritans of the day did not prevail, and the arguments of Church Fathers such as St. Augustine won out. They noted, after all, that St. Peter, the first pope in Catholic tradition, was himself a flawed vessel who denied Jesus three times on the night he was betrayed. Grace was always available, the sages decided. And as for the sacraments, they were to be considered the work of Christ through the Holy Spirit; the priest was expected to be holy, but if sin stained his soul—indeed, even if he were a heretic—the sacraments he administered for the good of the flock would still be valid.

"Christ's gift is not thereby profaned by a sinful priest," wrote Augustine. "What flows through him keeps its purity, and what passes through him remains clear and reaches the fertile earth. . . . The spiritual power of the sacrament is indeed comparable to light: those to be enlightened receive it in its purity, and if it should pass through defiled beings, it is not itself defiled." The act itself was holy, *ex opere operato*—that is, regardless of the actor.

That view has persisted, even at times of the greatest clergy scandals the church has known. In the thirteenth century, as he sought to rebuild a church that had fallen into ruin, the humble Francis of Assisi was asked by a brother monk, "What would you do if you knew that the priest celebrating Mass had three concubines on the side?" Francis replied, "When it came time for Holy Communion, I would go to receive the sacred Body of my Lord from the priest's anointed hands."

The Protestant Reformation again marked a decisive break with this view. Disgusted by the abuses of priests who claimed holy powers even as they lived immoral lives, Protestants deemphasized the sacramental structure of Catholicism, and along with it the sacramental role of the pastor. Baptism and Holy Communion were, with some variations, the only sacraments. It was now the Word more than the Deed that mattered, and to speak the word and convict people's hearts required a minister who was an unsullied channel for those communications. The Calvinist theology of the inherent corruptness of human nature put an added burden on the Protestant minister, as the woeful adulterer Arthur Dimmesdale lamented to his scarlet-lettered paramour during their fateful encounter in the forest:

"As concerns the good which I may appear to do, I have no faith in it," Hawthorne's Puritan tells Hester Prynne (whom he blames for his corrupted state). "It must needs be a delusion. What can a ruined soul, like mine, effect towards the redemption of other souls?—or a polluted soul, towards their purification?"

Catholic priests, while often as holy as saints, did not have to suffer such angst. They simply had to *appear* to be above reproach. If they were in a state of sin, that was incidental to their job. "To be a good pastor you have to be a good liar," Msgr. Richard Antall, a missionary in El Salvador and columnist for *Our Sunday Visitor,* recalls his priest-mentor telling him years ago. "You see, the whole reason you are the pastor is to help people to be holy. So you have to pretend to be a saint. And that is the biggest lie you'd ever want to see. But they have to believe that holiness is possible."

There was a great truth in that pragmatism, yet the underlying deception in it—the temptation to view priests as "sacramental machines," as one archbishop has put it—also meant that Catholic clerics faced a different sort of burden, one that emphasized the purity of appearances as much as the condition of their soul.

This extended even to a priest's physical condition, with Jesus as the model and mold to which priests were to conform. (Obviously, church leaders had an idealized vision of Jesus, who recent research has demonstrated may have resembled an undernourished, swarthy New York cabbie more than hunky actors who have played him, such as Jeffrey Hunter or Willem Dafoe.) The result was that for years, especially when seminary candidates were plentiful, would-be priests were rejected because they were too tall or too short or too fat; some were even rejected because they suffered from what was labeled "extreme ugliness." Stuttering, of course, was an automatic 4-F. Likewise, any "deformity" that would make a priest "an object of horror and derision," as *The Catholic Encyclopedia* puts it, was considered an impediment to ordination under the canon law requiring the "physical integrity" of a priest.

Even lesser irregularities could thwart a vocation. For example, a man could not be a priest if he lacked sight in his "canonical eye"—the left eye—because that is the eye closest to the missal that the priest would read from while presiding at the altar. A priest could not have an artificial limb, and he had to have the "canonical fingers" intact—the opposable thumb and index finger by which he would hold the Host and bless the faithful. Today's priest shortage and a more munificent view of physical imperfections often lead bishops to provide dispensations for men who would in the past have been automatically rejected. But progress is slow.

Take the example of Father Michael Joly, a priest of the Diocese of Paterson in New Jersey. Apart from being a popular pastor, Joly waterskis, hikes, and is an accomplished musician. But when I met Joly it was 1994 and he was about to become the first blind man to be ordained a priest in the United States, a tougher challenge than anything else he had faced. At the time Joly was working on a Braille lectionary—also the first of its kind. Joly was not one to dwell on his disability and its attendant challenges, however. Instead, he used his blindness as an aide to his pastoral ministry, a way of connecting with people. The success of that approach was evident even in the way he dispensed the communion wafer, by brushing his hand against the communicant's open palm. "When I do that I can tell by feel if they are little children's hands or old men's hands.

I can tell when someone works at manual labor, I can tell when it is a woman's hands, and when someone has washed a lot of dishes, or even if they have been working at a computer."

One can only welcome the gradual openness to disabled priests, and marvel that it has taken the church so long to hail their example. The delay is particularly ironic given that John Paul himself, once the vigorous Outward Bound pope who left weary journalists behind as he embarked on jet-setting pilgrimages, is nearly confined to a wheelchair by a degenerative neurological disorder. Rather than see his infirmity as a cause for pity, however, many rightly see the pope as a poignant symbol of hope and encouragement, an example of coping with infirmity through Christian faith. Should his vocation be denied because of his physical limitations? Or is he, like a disabled person, perhaps closer to the Christ of the Cross because of his weakness?

In Rome's eyes, the most important physical template for the priest, of course, is maleness, and on that score Rome shows no signs of easing its rules. Quite the contrary. Jesus was a man, as were the apostles, and gender remains the Vatican's historical trump card in its firm opposition to ordaining women. So great was the concern over ensuring that the priesthood is physically configured in Jesus' image that seminarians used to undergo a testicular exam before ordination to guarantee that they are "physically intact as a male." That, of course, led to numerous jokes.

In one hoary tale, the genital-checker encounters a seminarian who has just one testicle. *"Habeo unam,"* reports the unnerved priest.

"Ecclesia supplet," his superior assures him. ("The Church will provide.")

The checker finds that the next candidate has the regulation two testicles. *"Habeo duas."*

"Hoc sufficit," the superior responds with satisfaction. ("That is enough.")

The final candidate comes up and the checker is stunned to find three testicles. *"Habeo tres!"* he announces.

The superior is delighted. *"Gloria in Excelsis Deo!"*

While emphasizing the priest's resemblance to Jesus, both superficially and sacramentally, was an effective strategy for a church trying to maintain the holiness of the sacraments, the perils of conflating the man with his Christ-like powers was graphically demonstrated by the scandal. For sexual predators, this over-identification was a perverse gift. A former

Illinois priest, Bill Cloutier, who was himself abused by a priest when he was a child (a not uncommon history among abusers), said that the experience may have actually led him to the priesthood, where he could commit the same acts. "It was kind of like, I would have the power he had. There was a power he very much exuded," Cloutier said. "I wanted that power."

Once a man like Cloutier has that power, the Catholic mindset that invests the priest with a Christ-like role can all too easily lead to terrible exploitation. "I was trying to get them to love Christ even more intimately and even more closely," a Boston priest, Father Robert Meffan, said when confronted with charges that he sexually abused girls whom he was spiritually counseling. Meffan encouraged the girls to be "brides of Christ" and told them he was like "the second coming of Christ," according to the archdiocese's files.

As Mary Gail Frawley-O'Dea, a leading expert on the sexual abuse of children, told the bishops at their Dallas meeting, "Make no mistake about it. The sexual violation of a child or adolescent by a priest *is* incest. It is a sexual and relational transgression perpetrated by *the* father of the child's extended family; a man in whom the child is taught from birth to trust above everyone else in his life, to trust second only to God." Frawley-O'Dea's graphic précis on the horrific impact of sexual abuse was another eye-opening moment during that meeting, as she took the bishops on a guided tour of a psyche shattered in a way no one but a Catholic priest could do.

"It is from this epicenter of betrayed trust that the mind-splitting impact of sexual abuse ripples outward. The victim of early sexual violation simply cannot reconcile the respected figure who may help him with his homework, teach him how to throw a curve ball, or take him to the local hockey game with the sexually overstimulated and overstimulating man presenting an erect penis to suck. It is simply too much and the resulting fracture of the victim's mind and experience often leads to a debilitating post-traumatic stress disorder that affects every domain of the victim's functioning and lasts for years and years after the abuse has stopped."

As Dan Shea, a lawyer and Catholic who became a crusader on behalf of clergy abuse victims, said, "When you are violated by a priest you are being violated by God. It's worse than a Baptist minister abusing you because he's not claiming to be like God." It was no coincidence that as part of their zero-tolerance policy against abusers the bishops stipulated that a suspended priest may not use the title "Father" while he is awaiting the formal process of defrocking known as laicizing.

Even for the good priests who make up the vast majority of the priesthood, the focus on their sacramental power, their separation from the rest of the baptized, their "specialness," can have difficult personal consequences. For some it can lead, often unconsciously, to arrogance in interpersonal relations, a quality that researchers have found to be the single most corrosive element in parish dynamics. For others, the constant comparison to Christ as God, rather than Jesus as man, sets an impossible standard that leaves them coming up short every day. "We have to get over this thing about Jesus being perfect," one priest, no rebel, told me with a roll of the eyes. "After all, what do we know about him except for three years?" Priests feel the burden of their special role to the point that they are often afraid to seek help for concerns that, if treated quickly, might be kept from growing into the problems that the scandal unearthed.

"Many priests . . . shrink from getting help or seeking therapy because they fear being labeled or even giving scandal," John Quinn, the retired archbishop of San Francisco, has written. Quinn knows whereof he speaks. In 1987 Quinn shocked the archdiocese—and the hierarchy—by taking a five-month "sabbatical" at a Hartford, Connecticut, psychiatric hospital to learn how to deal with stress and what he told friends was "an increasing and prolonged depression." At the time Quinn was a rising star—an "ecclesiastical superman," he was called—who played a key role in planning a papal visit to the United States in 1987 and in trying to ease heightened tensions between Rome and the American church. Those duties, coupled with the death of his mother, left him "a classic burnout case." But because he was a priest and a bishop, he felt trapped. "You feel this tremendous responsibility," he told an interviewer on his return. "These issues coming at you are very important ones. But you come to understand that you're only a servant of the Lord—not the Lord."

Quinn found time for leisure, he moved in with a small community of fellow priests and bishops, and he got a dog (though that relationship didn't work out). "I no longer feel that I have to deal with everything that comes along," Quinn said. "I know my own limitations now, which brings a lot of composure and serenity in the face of all the overwhelming problems that are always coming at me. I know now that I can't be perfect. Nobody can."

Quinn's experience should have been a moment of insight and inspiration for clerics. Instead, Quinn was subject to unfair whispers from Catholics who felt he was betraying his office and clearly did not have the "right stuff" to be a bishop, and in his writing a decade later he acknowledged the ongoing challenge—and danger—that such high expectations pose for a cleric. "If people know that I am getting therapy, they will think I have some terrible problem of a scandalous nature," Quinn wrote, voicing the priest's fear. "Some priests are afraid of being blackballed if they get the therapy they need. As a consequence their problems quietly but insistently grow until there is a catastrophe."

The theological misunderstanding that has led to this dangerous pass can be addressed relatively simply by reemphasizing the primacy of the sacrament of baptism over that of ordination. As the Jesuit Karl Rahner put it, "First I am a man; then I am a Christian; only then am I a priest." This thinking in no way undermines the theology of the priesthood or its centrality in Catholicism's historic understanding of itself. But it does begin to recalibrate the role of the priest, to restore a healthy balance in the Catholic community between the cleric and the laity.

Along with a reordering of the hierarchy of sacraments, Catholics from bottom to top must also start taking a more humanistic view of priests as fellow members of the Body of Christ. Emphasizing the humanness of priests was very trendy in the post–Vatican II years, as many pastors dispensed with their clerics (the black suit and collar) and tried to blend in. The reaction against that egalitarian trend, which admittedly had its downside, went too far the other way, as the Vatican tried to get priests to wear clerics everywhere and to reconstruct the façade of the 1950s-era pastor. That didn't work, either. As Jacques Maritain, the influential philosopher of Vatican II, put it in his final book, "The Person of the Church is indefectibly holy; Her personnel is not." The mission of the priests sets them apart, he wrote, "but with regard to their personal conduct and the wounds of nature, they are just like other men. They are members of the Church just like everyone else, all exposed to falling more or less gravely into error and sin."

Recasting the place of the priest in Catholic life is not brain surgery, and it does not require a revolution in Catholic theology. Indeed, if the

current crisis was born out of a distortion of the theology of the priesthood, the change back to a healthier understanding of the priesthood will
come in the trenches of daily parish life, not in the seminaries. Church life
is ultimately relational, and in the Catholic Church in the wake of the
scandal, the chief relationship that needs tending is that between priests
and laity. The first step in this process is for Catholics to see priests as the
human beings they are, and for priests to accept that view of themselves.
This will come about not by reducing the priest's sacramental role, but
by increasing his collaboration with the laity in running the parish.

While the solution is simple, it won't be easy. At every turn, the system of
Catholic governance and the Catholic culture have reinforced the iconic
image of the priest to the point that the life of the priest, and by extension
the parish fiefdom he runs, is cloaked in mystery. Parishioners too often
do not know their pastor as a person, and priests too often do not let
themselves be known. From the inside, of course, priests have always realized that they were never the lesser gods that Catholics made them out
to be. As would-be priests are often told in seminary, "Half the priests are
ordained to make up for the failures of the other half."

But to most of their congregants, the daily life of the Catholic priest,
like the priest's sexuality, is masked by ambiguity. A parish priest usually
does not have his own home but lives in some unseen and therefore mysterious room somewhere in the complex of church buildings. (Is it a
boudoir or a cell? In my experience, it is typically like any small apartment,
only neater.) Everyone addresses him as "Father," but he has no evident
family. He is an apostle of Jesus, who preached that the Kingdom of God
was at hand, and that those who would follow him most closely should re-
nounce the traditional ties of brothers and sisters and parents and family.
That was easier when the prospect of apocalypse was imminent. To live
out Jesus' command across the centuries, as priests do, taking everyone as
your brother and sister, is much tougher. The church itself tried to foster
this separation of its clerics from their biological families. In fact, canon
law used to hold that priests and nuns and brothers who took vows of
poverty and joined religious orders were "dead" for civil legal purposes,
which meant that the priest's order, rather than his blood relatives, was
considered the prime beneficiary of any postmortem financial legacy.

While the church has relaxed those rules to a degree, uncertainty about the status of a priest's family ties remained, legally as well as culturally. In 2001, fifteen years after Father Lawrence Jenco was freed from eighteen months as a hostage in Lebanon, and five years after he died of cancer, a federal judge finally ruled that Jenco's extended family, like the nuclear family members of several other hostages, was eligible for hundreds of millions of dollars in damages from Iran, which was held liable for backing the kidnappers. The crux of the case was whether Jenco's nieces and nephews were, in the words of one lawyer, "his alter-ego children."

In reality, priests, of course, do have family relationships—brothers, sisters, nephews, and nieces—yet when such relatives show up at Mass, parishioners often find their presence disorienting, like students who run into a teacher at the store, outside the context where they expect (and want) them to remain. One of the qualities that made Pope John Paul II electable was his lack of entangling family ties. Karol Wojtyla's mother died when he was eight years old, and his beloved older brother, Edmond, a doctor, died three years later, after contracting scarlet fever from a patient. A sister he never knew died in infancy. His father, a retired soldier, died in 1941, when Wojtyla was twenty-one. For years, until her death, his only blood relation was a maternal cousin. With no beery brothers or adulterous sisters to embarrass him, Wojtyla was a safe pick as pope. But upon his election, John Paul, like many other priests who find themselves thrust into a strange new assignment, gathered an ersatz family to him, and a generation of sons and daughter of aides and friends grew up around the pontifical household with the man they call "Uncle Karol." To everyone else he is "Holy Father."

Such facts don't often make the news, and that's unfortunate for both the pope and his church.

Perhaps because I came to Catholicism as an adult, and from a Protestant environment that views priests as even bigger ciphers than Catholics do, the shock of recognition that priests had affective lives always stuck with me. I clearly recall the first time I went to interview a priest in his rectory. His Labrador retriever padded in after him and curled up at his feet. That a priest would have a pet seemed strange at first blush, and yet was perfectly sensible on a moment's reflection.

The exact nature of the priest's "job" is also a source of much mystery and rumor. A vocations campaign once tried to spark interest in the priesthood by asking, "And what does the priest do the other six days of the week?" Most Catholics would probably scratch their heads. Unfortunately, too many would assume that he is a slacker with a gig that God would envy: work on the seventh day and relax the rest of the week. Others would take the opposite tack and figure that the priest is an empty vessel waiting for the Spirit to pour in on him, and thus he spends his day praying or doing "priestly" things.

Father Robert Kress, a semi-retired priest who writes about pastoral life, chalks these views up to the "monasticizing" of the church that began with the medieval reforms, which in turn led to the misperception that every professed religious is a monk who flees the world. Priests have to be paragons of holiness, and holiness demands as little participation in worldly affairs as possible, the thinking goes. Kress argues that this misunderstanding does not allow for the fact that priests are as much managers as consecrators. They get the roof fixed (when they can scrape the money together), they make sure the bathrooms have enough toilet paper, and they pray the office daily.

The widespread misperception of priests as monks is most evident in the common confusion between the two principal types of priests—the secular and the religious priest. A religious priest is a man who is ordained as a member of an order, such as the Franciscans or Dominicans. He lives in community and takes vows of poverty, chastity, and obedience. Diocesan priests, also called secular priests, are ordained for a specific geographical diocese. They do not take the three vows of poverty, chastity, and obedience, but "promise" to be celibate, to respect and obey their diocesan bishop, and to live a simple lifestyle. Secular priests generally serve in parishes, and they are the priests that lay people usually come in contact with.

While the lives of parish pastors are quite different from those of contemplative priests who live in community, and are much closer to those of their lay parishioners, the average Catholic tends to view a parish priest as a kind of monk, and to hold him to the same standard of religious observance (even as they demand that he put an air-conditioning system in the church, and cheap). Many priests would be happy if all they did was recite prayers and preside at Mass. As Msgr. Philip J. Murnion of the National Pastoral Life Center has noted, "Pastors find their greatest satisfaction in their sacramental ministry and their greatest challenges in organizational demands—administration, personnel management, finances. They suffer from the killer b's: buildings, budgets, boilers, bulletins and bingo—and one bishop admitted he could be another 'b.'" Still another "b" might be "burnout," an affliction common to clergy of all denominations, but one that congregants are usually unaware of.

Increasingly, there is a push by priests to have their workaday lives be recognized as comparable to those of their lay constituents. A study by the National Federation of Priests' Councils showed that 65 percent of priests feel they need to achieve greater status as competent professionals in the eyes of the Catholic community. These priests rated themselves as equal to doctors, lawyers, or educators in depth of knowledge, skill, and responsibility. Priests are also pushing for a lower retirement age (currently seventy, in general) and better pay. At an average of $22,568 in annual income, a Catholic priest's salary is one-third that of his Protestant counterparts. (Neither figure includes housing benefits and car allowances, nor the fact that Protestant clergy may have children to support.) Most priests would also like the option of living in their own apartment rather than "over the store," as most do now; they feel like shopkeepers rather than well-educated professionals.

It is not that priests want to become lay people. Rather, they just want to bridge the social reversal caused by the tremendous changes in post–World War II America. In the United States today, the Catholic clergy is facing a congregation that is better educated (Catholics attend college at a higher rate than Protestants), better off, more self-assured, and much more demanding than ever before. This friction goes beyond neuralgic liturgical questions about the role of lay people at the altar. Now it's personal.

As the historian Eugene McCarraher put it in a provocative 1997 essay in *Commonweal* titled "Starbucks Catholicism," since World War II "Catholics of the professional and managerial classes have been in the vanguard of the American aggiornamento and they now set the tone for much of the Catholic church in the United States. Their participation in the national culture of expertise, consumption, and therapeutic spirituality marks the triumph of a new American Catholic religious culture: a Starbucks Catholicism embodied in a Church Mellow."

In this new soft-focus church culture, McCarraher argued, the priest is envisioned as the "clerical sidekick," while "the 'layman'—organization

man, technopolitan knight of faith, and darling of two successive generations of Catholic intellectuals—emerged from suburban sidewalks with his
cross, his briefcase, and his ball-point pen that parted the clerical waters."

If McCarraher was a bit "breezy" in his characterization, as he conceded, he surely hit on some sensitive truths that will complicate the
future clergy-lay relationship, especially as lay reform movements prolif-
erate in the wake of the sexual abuse scandal.

The danger for the laity, and the threat for priests, is that now that
the laity have become like the priests, at least educationally and econom-
ically, they will expect the priests to become like them. But it doesn't
work that way, and the newly triumphant laity must gain a greater understanding of how completely their middle-class ethos has swept Catholic life, and how jarring it can be to the priest who represents the sign of
contradiction to that ethos. "I go to parties all the time, people are always
inviting me over, taking me out," one priest told me. "Everyone tells me
jokes, acts like I'm one of the gang. But I'm not. The problem is we are all
mimics. We want to be what we see. And soon we [priests] want what
they have. But we can't have it.

"Everyone wants to think I'm their best friend," he said. "We can
have deep friendships. But not with everyone."

Catholics think that priests envy them because lay people can have
sex and buy nice cars without guilt. But the envy may have more to do
with the self-assurance of a newly regnant laity. Priests were once lords of
the manor and are now trying to redefine their role when they step out
from behind the altar and leave behind the sacramental job that is their
chief distinction. In the old days, the priest occupied a place of honor not
only because of his revered sacramental position but also because he was
likely to be looking out for the welfare of his people. The labor priest of
On the Waterfront had a clear purpose, and his heroic activism was in visible defense of the interests of his flock. That was how it had been for
American Catholics for centuries. Faith and observance were taken for
granted. Putting bread on the table and voters in the booths was where
the priest could really shine.

In the context of the contemporary United States, the worker-priest
who labors with his people in the fields makes no sense. Today that priest
would need an MBA, and he'd look silly to boot. It's hard to be heroic
when you're not staring down the powerful on behalf of your people. But

that's how things stand. The laity are better off than the priest, and often as well educated. Catholics have broken out of their ghetto socially, but they are now focused internally, on their sense of inner well-being, as much as on the corporate good. We demand that priests know *our* lives, while we know little of *theirs*.

Catholics are, in short, more American than ever, and that can leave the Catholic priest, whose role has always been out of step with American culture, at sea. Beliefs that once went unquestioned must now be explained at every turn. The priest is left with his religious role as his chief identifier, but at a time when organized religion is becoming less important than ever and in a culture where religion's role is therapeutic, it's tough for a priest to gauge how "well" he is doing.

Another challenge to the reimagining of the priesthood comes not from the laity, but from within the priesthood itself, which is sharply divided over priests' identity and future course.

Within the clerical world, and especially in the United States, Catholic priests are split between the "cultic" versus the "servant" models of leadership, between those who would restore the older vision of the all-powerful pastor and those who see the priest as more integrated into the Christian community. The divide breaks down cleanly along generational lines, with younger clergy tending to be far more conservative than their older counterparts.

"You had a whole generation of priests who grew up in Vatican II who were trying to change the church, renew the church," Frank McNulty told me in explaining the gulf. "Then you had another whole crowd of young priests who came into the system who looked upon that crowd as social workers—too loose, too liberal, giving too much to lay people, maybe wanting more of that clerical culture back, the clothing and such.

"The generation I knew best willingly stepped down from the pedestal—willingly, because we realized that the true sacrament was baptism and not holy orders."

In a study released in 2002 at a symposium titled "Priestly Identity in a Time of Crisis," Catholic University of America sociologist Dean Hoge graphically illustrated the divide and warned of the tensions it is creating among priests and between clergy and lay people. In his study, Hoge found that 30 percent of priests fifty-six to sixty-five saw the notion of a priest as "a man set apart" as a barrier to Christian community, double the rate of priests twenty-five to thirty-five. Similarly, one-third of younger priests said they would welcome optional celibacy, as opposed to 70 percent of older priests who were open to a married priesthood. Some 62 percent of priests over fifty-five said they should have a say in choosing their bishop, while just 22 percent—a drop of forty points—of younger priests agreed with that view.

Moreover, 86 percent of older priests said they would like to see the church empower lay people in ministry, in contrast to just over half of younger priests who wanted lay people to have an expanded role. Catholic priests today are almost evenly divided between those who believe that the laity need to understand the priest's unique status and give priests greater respect, and those who disagree with that view. "The servant-leadership model of the priesthood, espoused by many priests after Vatican II, has gone out of favor, and the priests ordained in the 1960s and 1970s are not the wave of the future," Hoge said. "If there are tensions in the future, they will probably be between the more educated, older lay ministers and the younger priests." Given that lay ministry is growing by nearly 80 percent a decade, and that there are more lay ministers than priests in parishes today, that does not bode well.

"A newly ordained [priest] today faces a divided church and a divided parish," Father Stephen Rossetti, one of the nation's top experts on the psychological problems of the priesthood, said in September 2002. "It will be easy for a new priest, and very tempting, to align himself with one group or the other. . . . But his vocation is to be a shepherd, a pastor of souls, to all regardless of their theological or cultural makeup, orientation or age. He is to be a 'man of communion.'"

More ominously, Rossetti noted that many abusers who were unmasked by the sex scandal "have been our most stridently orthodox of priests," and he warned that "doctrinal orthodoxy is not a firewall against child sexual abuse."

The divide can certainly be seen as a victory for the conservative policies of John Paul, and the younger generation of priests he has inspired will have powerful allies in Rome.

In September 2002, as lay reform groups in the United States were stepping up pressure on the Vatican to dump Cardinal Law and to assert their own voices, John Paul warned in a speech against a "tendency toward the growing clericalization of the lay faithful. He said that "grave abuses" can result when the role of the priest and the consultative voice of the laity are blurred.

A month later the Vatican issued a new "instruction" on the parish priest—a document that spent forty pages delineating those roles and reminding the faithful that the priest is to be in charge by dint of his ordination and his traditional role as "a father to the community and to each one of its members." Introducing the document, Cardinal Darío Castrillón Hoyos, the prefect of the Congregation for the Clergy, told a news conference that "a priest does not simply 'work' as a priest." He also warned strongly against the twin dangers of the clericalization of the laity and the secularization of the clergy.

If a strongly "cultic" model of the priesthood triumphs in this debate, it will be a tragedy for the church. In the wake of the clergy abuse scandal, the world has seen that while icons are powerful, they are also brittle and can shatter with destructive results. A return to the exclusively cultic model would signal a fearful, if understandable, defensiveness on the part of the clergy. A more "human" priesthood, on the other hand, would signal a more confident, forward-looking church. A positive, optimistic approach would certainly benefit priests (especially in this time of crisis and alienation), and lay people as well. "We have to show people more of our humanness," said McNulty. "If ever we needed it, we really have to become experts at compassion, as people who will just be there for them, to get them through their tough moments, to preach homilies that relate to their lives, and show them God's love."

Above all, a broadening of the concept of priesthood, a true embrace of the concept of "the priesthood of all believers," would not necessarily dilute the historical role of the priest as much as it would broaden the concept of holiness to include lay people more fully. The focal point would be the Eucharist, what Father Bob Bullock called "the summit and source" of Catholic life. "We have changed the language and we face the people, but the largest reform that must be taking place is conceptual," he said. "That concept is, We are all celebrants. Our whole space is sacred." The gulf between lay life and Catholic life has grown in the past generation. Just as a more human priesthood would help bridge the gap, so, too, would a holier laity.

While the "cultic leadership" camp might seem to be dominant at the moment, there is a final factor that will have a greater impact on the reimagining of the role of the Catholic cleric than any ecclesiastical development in the past millennium. That is the inexorable return of a married priesthood.

Eleven

MARRIED PASTORS, CELIBATE PRIESTS

As pastor of the largest Catholic parish in the Diocese of Fort Worth, Father John Gremmels knows that he has a lot to be thankful for. The booming Church of St. Elizabeth Ann Seton in Keller, Texas, which bills itself as "Vatican West," has a vibrant religious life fueled by 17,000 congregants who Gremmels says are "just magnificent." But the job also brings enormous responsibilities and concerns, just as it does for thousands of other harried Catholic priests. In Gremmels's case, however, he must juggle not only his duties as pastor to the parish, but also his role as husband to his wife, Tracy, and father to their three children. "You can never get it all done," Gremmels told me. "With 17,000 people the demands are wild. Plus the children and my wonderful wife. You always feel inadequate. There are a lot of benefits that come with celibacy."

In fact, even though Gremmels is a fan of traditional priestly celibacy, he is also on the leading edge of the next great wave of change as the Catholic Church begins to ordain married men.

Like most of the estimated 150 to 200 married Catholic priests in the United States, Gremmels is a former Episcopal priest who was allowed to bring his vocation into the Roman Catholic Church, along with his wife and children, when he converted in 1988 under a special "pastoral provision" granted by Pope John Paul II. There are also a smaller (though growing) number of Lutheran ministers and other Protestant pastors who have become Catholic priests and fathers in both the familial and ecclesial sense.

Yes, married priests are a reality in the Catholic Church today, a *de facto* change in church discipline that augurs a wider acceptance of optional celibacy. Although these priests are still a fraction of the total Catholic presbyterate, their very existence gives them a visibility out of proportion to their numbers. For example, Gremmels is one of five married priests in the Fort Worth diocese; next door, the Diocese of Dallas has six. More important, the rationale for their presence is inexorable—a logic that grows out of the turmoil of the current scandal, the preexisting vocations shortage, and the Catholic Church's own history of a married priesthood, which is increasingly being cited as church leaders prepare the faithful for a major new shift in pastoral life.

While a celibate priesthood, like so many other traditions in Catholicism, is depicted as having existed since the church's foundation, a quick perusal of the New Testament and a few history books shows that that was clearly not the case, and not even the staunchest defenders of celibacy would try to argue the point. The Second Vatican Council's Decree on the Ministry and Life of Priests recognized that celibacy is "not demanded by the very nature of the priesthood, as is evident from the practice of the primitive Church," and Pope John Paul II himself has acknowledged that as well.

St. Peter, the first pope, was married, as were many of the apostles; St. Paul refers to Peter's mother-in-law at one point, and in his first Letter to the Corinthians he argues that Christ's emissaries "have the right to be accompanied by a wife, as the other apostles and the brothers of the Lord and Cephas [Peter]." Some sources argue that as many as thirty-nine popes were married during the first 1,200 years of Christianity. Between the years 400 and 1000, six popes were the sons of popes and nine were the sons of bishops.

In First Timothy, Paul's checklist for a good church leader shows no concern about a clerical spouse; indeed, Paul commends the practice: "A bishop must be irreproachable, married only once, temperate, self-controlled, decent, hospitable, able to teach, not a drunkard, not aggressive, but gentle, not contentious, not a lover of money. He must manage his own household well, keeping his children under control with perfect dignity; for if a man does not know how to manage his own household, how can he take care of the church of God?"

Protestant apologists and advocates of a married clergy often cite these verses as backing their claims and say that the biblical citations should put a definitive end to the historical underpinning of a celibate priesthood. But that view is simplistic and fails to take into account either the authority of early church tradition or the larger picture presented in the New Testament. Just as the New Testament writers—and Jesus himself in the Gospels—do not mandate celibacy for church leaders or anyone else, neither do they require that church leaders marry. In fact, the overall message of the Christian canon is that while marriage is fine, chastity is the faster avenue to holiness.

"The unmarried man is anxious about the affairs of the Lord, how to please the Lord; but the married man is anxious about worldly affairs, how to please his wife, and his interests are divided," Paul writes to the Corinthians. "I say this for your own benefit, not to lay any restraint upon you, but to promote good order and to secure your undivided devotion to the Lord. . . . He who marries his betrothed does well; and he who refrains from marriage will do better."

The most powerful argument for celibacy, of course, is that Jesus, the model for the perfect Christian life and for priests in particular, was himself unmarried and chaste, and he seems to advocate that model for his closest followers. As Jesus says in the Gospel of Matthew: "For there are eunuchs who have been so from birth, and there are eunuchs who have been made eunuchs by men, and there are eunuchs who have made themselves eunuchs for the sake of the kingdom of heaven. He who is able to receive this, let him receive it." If the celibacy Jesus lived and exalted is indeed a bizarre and unhealthy practice, then Christian critics of celibacy have some serious rethinking to do.

Moreover, the idea that sexual continence is next to holiness was not by any stretch a Christian invention. Throughout history, cultures everywhere have equated chastity with purity, and because purity is universally considered the goal and sometimes the means to spiritual perfection, it makes sense that spiritual superiority would be linked to those who practice sexual continence. Indeed, centuries before Jesus came along, the Buddha lamented the "pit of burning cinders" that was sexual lust, and he led millions of devotees to believe that celibacy, especially as practiced by

Buddhist monks and nuns, was an integral part of the renunciation and asceticism necessary to achieving a higher plane of existence. Likewise, sexual repression is a powerful part of Hinduism. Shiva is the destroyer of the world (along with Brahma the Creator and Vishnu the Preserver), but his attributes also have the positive sense of renouncing old habits. Hence, he is celibate, the god of the yogis, and the paradigm of self-control and essential goodness.

Pagan religions, for all of their orgiastic shenanigans in the empyrean, also had traditions of celibacy, though mainly for their mortal followers, who duly followed those dictates. In extreme cases, such as the cult of Cybele, novices were physically emasculated so that as priests they could better work to purify the world.

In the Roman Empire of Jesus' day, six Vestal Virgins were drafted to maintain sexual purity by proxy. As in other religious systems, the perks of their role compensated for their sacrifice. The prospective virgins had to be physically unblemished young girls drawn from the ranks of the patrician class, and as they grew to adulthood, trained within their insular system, they assumed a status of power and privilege unheard of for other Romans, especially women. For maintaining their virginity (and tending the city's sacred fire, which, if it went out, portended terrible misfortune), the Vestals were entrusted with the greatest secrets and accorded the greatest rights. They had the power to pardon any criminal, and anyone who jostled them in the streets could be put to death.

As with all celibates, however, the price of purity was steep. If a Vestal fell from grace, she was sentenced to die. Because she was considered holy she could not be killed directly, however, but was dressed in a shroud, carried through the streets like a corpse, and then sealed in an underground vault with a bit of food and drink. She soon either starved or suffocated. Her offending lover, with no divine protection, was simply beaten to death.

The Judaism that Jesus grew up in also had traditions equating sexual purity and holiness. Drawing on the strictures of the Book of Leviticus, priests who served in the Temple were enjoined from sexual activity for at least a day before ministering the rites, and they were required to use a ritual bath, or *mikvah*, before they entered the Temple, to ensure their pure state. Even after the destruction of the Temple and the scattering of Jews, the rabbis emphasized the connection between sexual purity and the greater holiness of the priesthood:

"Heedfulness leads to cleanliness, cleanliness leads to cultic clean-ness, cultic cleanness leads to abstinence, abstinence leads to holiness, ho-liness leads to modesty, modesty leads to the fear of sin, the fear of sin leads to piety, piety leads to the Holy Spirit, the Holy Spirit leads to the resurrection of the dead, and the resurrection of the dead comes through Elijah, blessed be his memory," it says in the Mishnah, the oral tradition that developed in the second century A.D.

First-century Jewish offshoots such as the desert Essenes, who were believed to have authored the Dead Sea Scrolls, also valued chastity and as-ceticism, as did Jesus' spiritual mentor, the proto-hermit John the Baptist.

As Christianity developed into a religion distinct from Judaism, it once again elaborated on some of the aspects inherited from its spiritual forebear. For many reasons—the virginity of Jesus, the notion of suffering and sacrifice underlying his message, the Stoical philosophy that under-girded early Christian thinking—sexual abstinence was one of these at-tributes.

So strong was the early Christian adherence to chastity that the disci-pline was often extended to lay people, who were to refrain from sexual intercourse before taking communion and for the whole forty-day period of Lent. For a while, abstinence by married couples was extended to in-clude three forty-day periods throughout the year. Sex while a women was menstruating or pregnant was also considered sinful. Naturally, this focus on the evils of sex led to all manner of repression and dysfunction, and women suffered most of the consequences. Since men, with their raging sexual desires, were running the church, which frowned on such impulses, someone had to take the fall, and women were the natural tar-get. The vagina, Tertullian wrote, was "the Gateway to the Devil," and Christian virgins who died rather than surrender their virtue were auto-matically considered saints. (The growing cult of the Virgin Mary was the apotheosis of the chastity-equals-holiness school.) "For chastity has made even angels," St. Ambrose wrote. "He who has preserved it is an angel; he who has lost it a devil."

Some early Church Fathers were as tough on themselves as on any-one else. St. Augustine loathed his frequent erections, and Origen, upon reading Jesus' words about being a eunuch for God, castrated himself at age eighteen. He was sharply criticized for it later, but that did not stop Christian ascetics throughout the centuries from copying him. Hugh of

Lincoln, an eleventh-century Carthusian monk and bishop who was eventually canonized, claimed that he was relieved of sexual desire when an incubus came down from heaven and castrated him in his sleep.

In general, the growing focus on celibacy centered on the priesthood. At first, priests were required to abstain from sexual relations the day before celebrating the sacred mysteries, as in the Jewish tradition. But as the need and demand for the sacraments became greater, along with the emphasis on the Eucharist, priests began celebrating Mass daily, leaving them in a state of almost perpetual chastity. This was a hard discipline to keep, as St. Paul had predicted, and as early as the third century local bishops and synods were struggling to force their ordained ministers to either live away from their spouse or live chastely with her. (Divorce, of course, was not possible, as that would have entailed breaking one sacrament to aid another.)

In the year 305 a gathering of bishops in Spain at the Council of Elvira passed the first legislative decree mandating rules about sexual relations for priests: "It has seemed good absolutely to forbid the bishops, the priests, and the deacons, i.e., all the clerics in the service of the ministry, to have relations with their wives and procreate children; should anyone do so, let him be excluded from the honor of the clergy."

Still, the message was that you could be a married priest; you just couldn't have sex.

In 385, Pope Siricius I issued the first papal edict mandating this practice universally, a decision that was confirmed by the Council of Carthage five years later. The Council of Toledo in 633 ruled that a priest needed a bishop's permission to marry. At about that same time, at the Council of Trullo in 692, the Eastern churches, which we know today as Orthodox Christianity, moved the other way and legislated that priests and deacons could marry, but not bishops. With the Great Schism of 1054 between Rome and Constantinople, the divide between East and West was cemented. Today, Orthodox churches allow priests to marry (as long as they do so before ordination); monastic communities, from which bishops and patriarchs are drawn, remain the province of celibates.

The Latin-rite church of Rome, on the other hand, increasingly emphasized the virtues of monasticism; and the growing abuses of the clergy during the Middle Ages—including the transmission of church property to a priest's heirs—led to a clampdown that prohibited any priest from having a wife and sought to end the common practice of priestly concubinage. Pope, Gregory VII, himself a monk, was the driving force behind making celibacy church law. A council that Gregory convened in 1074 ruled that priests who paid money for their ordination should be barred, and went on, "Nor shall clergymen who are married say Mass or serve the altar in any way." The First Lateran Council in 1123 formally prohibited wives from living with priests, and the Second Lateran Council in 1139 definitively voided marriages entered into after a priest was ordained.

Church law for the next millennium was set: now celibacy was equated with chastity for priests. Not only did a priest have to remain sexually pure, but he could not marry. This was a sharp break with Christianity's Jewish forebears, and in fact with most cultural models. Periodic abstinence is a fairly common religious practice; mandated lifelong abstinence is unusual.

The Counter-Reformation Council of Trent further enshrined priestly celibacy in the sixteenth century, and much later, in the 1960s, the Second Vatican Council's Decree on Priestly Formation exalted "the greater excellence of virginity consecrated to Christ," as opposed to the lives of married lay people. In 1967, in his encyclical on priestly celibacy, *Sacerdotalis Caelibatus,* Pope Paul VI called celibacy a "brilliant jewel" of the church whose value was greater than ever. Lauding the "virile asceticism" of celibacy, Paul said, "The true, profound reason for dedicated celibacy is . . . the choice of a closer and more complete relationship with the mystery of Christ and the Church."

Yet even as Pope Paul was reiterating this centuries-old tradition, profound changes were sweeping the Catholic priesthood—changes that would begin to alter the centuries of church teaching and culture and make way for the landmark shift to a married priesthood that will be a hallmark of the future Catholic Church.

The principal change that began transforming the church in Pope Paul's era was the steep decline in new vocations and the mass exodus of some 25,000 priests, most of them to marry. Despite the Second Vatican Council's praise of priestly celibacy, Catholics had the sense that the church was changing, and that "antiquated" traditions such as the celibate priesthood would soon be replaced. Many priests who left to marry expected to be welcomed back into a new church, together with their wives; potential priests were reluctant to take a vow that might be changed imminently. Moreover, during the 1960s and 1970s authority structures and institutions of every kind were under siege, and they were losing their power to draw and hold acolytes.

The change to optional celibacy did not materialize as expected. But the trend toward relaxing the rules on celibacy continued, even after the conservative rebound that took off with the election of Pope John Paul II in 1978.

Historians may eventually regard 1980 as the turning point for optional celibacy. That is when Pope John Paul II responded to the Episcopal Church's decision to ordain women by offering a special dispensation, or "pastoral provision," to married Episcopal priests who disagreed with women's ordination and wanted to migrate from Canterbury to Rome. (The Episcopal Church is the United States branch of the Anglican Communion.) The trickle turned into a flood in 1994 when the Church of England itself opened holy orders to women. By 2003 the number of married Catholic priests in Britain alone numbered in the hundreds, a figure that is far more than a quirk of history, or canon law. Just as notable, but largely unheralded at the time, was the ordination on January 24, 2003, of Alan Stephen Hopes, an Anglican priest who converted in 1992, as an auxiliary bishop to Westminister's Cardinal Cormac Murphy-O'Connor, Britain's senior Catholic churchman. Hopes thus became the first Anglican priest to convert and become a Catholic bishop, and while he is not married, his elevation is another remarkable breakthrough that raises the possibility that there could one day soon be a married Catholic bishop.

For the Vatican, welcoming married Episcopal/Anglican priests was not that much of a leap. Although the Catholic Church rejected Anglican ordinations as invalid, Rome always considered Anglicanism close to the Catholic Church in form and substance, since it was not created through the theological transformation of the Protestant Reformation but broke off almost whole from Rome after Henry VIII's marital and political disputes with the pope in the sixteenth century.

Still, integrating the hundreds of Anglican/Episcopal priests who have made the switch since 1980 into daily parish life was another matter altogether. Most of them had wives (and children), and their arrival was an eye-opener. "I understand the looks. How often do you see a priest checking into a hotel with his wife?" said Father Thad Rudd, a former Episcopal priest who pastors a church in Georgia.

The sight was especially jarring in the United States, where the strictures of priestly celibacy have been guarded more closely than elsewhere. In 1929, for example, at the behest of the American hierarchy, the Vatican issued a decree that specifically barred married Eastern-rite Catholic priests from American parishes. Eastern-rite Catholics are a small segment of the larger Roman Catholic Church, based largely in the Middle East and Eastern Europe, and their practices closely resemble Eastern Orthodox traditions, including allowing married priests. Because of the vagaries of history and geography, some of these Eastern-rite Christians remained under the jurisdiction of Rome rather than Constantinople after the Great Schism of 1054. As a result, the Roman church has always had a remnant of married clergy.

The 1929 banning of those Eastern-rite Catholic clergy culminated decades of hostility by the American bishops toward married Eastern-rite priests, one of the more shameful and damaging episodes in U.S. Catholic history, and one that carries an important lesson for today: when the U.S. bishops tried to force the Eastern clergy, who were arriving in the United States in the late nineteenth century along with other Eastern Europeans, to adopt the Latin discipline on celibacy, the clergy instead left the Catholic Church for the more hospitable Orthodox Church, and they took hundreds of thousands of Eastern-rite Catholics with them. Today, married Eastern-rite Catholic priests number about five thousand worldwide—Catholic priests in good standing—but because they are married they cannot serve in the United States. With the arrival of married priests from the Episcopal Church after 1980, the logic of that ban began to wear thin, along with the patience of Eastern-rite Catholics, whose bishops in the United States have begun making noises about defying the Vatican ban and admitting married men to their seminaries.

Many Latin-rite Catholics also see a disturbing inconsistency in the fact that the Catholic Church will ordain a married Protestant man as a priest, but not a married Catholic. Moreover, the Vatican's solicitous overtures to married Protestant pastors only underscores Rome's unbending exclusion of thousands of Catholic priests who left the active ministry to marry. In allowing Protestants to join the priesthood along with their wives, John Paul was essentially saying that one sacrament cannot cancel out another, so both the marriage and the ordination are considered valid, as long as the marriage predated the ordination. But the thousands of Catholic clerics who did marry remain priests, sacramentally speaking, and growing numbers of Catholics—and priests—believe they deserve a role in the sacramental life of Catholicism.

It is also notable that John Paul's reincarnation of the married presbyterate is more liberal than the original version because he reversed the ancient church's demand that a married man who became a priest abstain from future sexual relations with his wife. The new generation of married convert-priests must only agree to what is called "secondary celibacy," which means they agree not to remarry should their spouse die. Otherwise, he is allowed to have a full conjugal relationship with his present wife, which means that for the first time in a millennia, Catholic priests can have a bride other than the Church, in every sense of the word.

Unsurprisingly, the Vatican does not like to broadcast any of this information. In a pledge they sign at ordination, convert-priests are specifically enjoined from giving "undue publicity" to their status, and it is often difficult to convince married Catholic priests to talk on the record. (The church officials responsible for shepherding convert pastors to the Catholic priesthood also declined to respond to any requests for information, and even the U.S. bishops conference can only estimate the number of married priests in the American presbyterate.) Also, Rome specifies that married priests not be entrusted with "the ordinary cure of souls"—that is, they cannot be the pastor of a parish, and can only assist a celibate pastor. But it is estimated that about 30 percent of married priests are given a dispensation to become the pastor of a parish, an exemption rate that effectively vitiates the rule.

In short, the decision by John Paul to allow married convert-priests grew out of a desire to keep the Catholic priesthood exclusively male, but it is leading to a revolution in clerical life by effectively reestablishing the principle of a married priesthood in Catholicism. And the principle proponents of this revolution are the world's bishops, who have grown tired of having to ordain men of dubious quality while they watch good priests burn out from overwork. These bishops are not about to let the opportunity pass, and after years of quiet lobbying, as church politesse requires, they are becoming increasingly vocal in pushing Rome to find other ways to ease the ban on married priests.

At a 1998 Vatican meeting that gathered together the bishops of Asia and Oceania, for example, the prelates repeatedly asked John Paul and the Roman Curia to relax the rules on clerical celibacy. Speaking on behalf of the Indonesian hierarchy, Carmelite Bishop Francis Hadisumarta noted that the Indonesian bishops had been asking the Vatican for thirty years for permission to ordain married men, but that now the situation was critical. Because of a shortage of celibate priests, he said, the majority of Indonesian Catholics "live by the Word, rather than by Word and sacrament. We are becoming 'Protestant' by default," he said. "Cannot such pastoral concerns be worked out and decided upon by the local episcopal conference?"

Bishops in Latin America, where the priest shortage has reached truly critical proportions, know that concubinage among their clergy is rampant, and many of these bishops are desperate for more priests who can serve their people and battle the inroads being made by aggressive Protestant proselytizers.

In Africa, as well—the continent of most explosive growth for the Catholic Church, where members now surpass one hundred million— the problems associated with clerical celibacy are debilitating. Apart from the need for priests to minister to this huge flock, the idea of a celibate priesthood is totally foreign to the African mindset. As the influential African Cardinal Polycarp Pengo of Tanzania told a Vatican conference on celibacy in 1993, mandating an unmarried priesthood "presents seemingly insurmountable problems for the inculturation of the Christian faith." As Pengo explained: "Failure to procreate continues to be one of the greatest misfortunes in society that can befall an African man or woman." He said that the pressure to incorporate a celibate priesthood into the African context is leading to "strange solutions" as well as scandals in which priests sire children and then steal church funds to support them. As one missionary sister has said, "Celibacy in the African context means a priest does not get married, but does not mean he does not have children."

Cardinal Pengo was apparently understating the extent of the problem. In March 2001 the *National Catholic Reporter* broke the news that the Vatican had for years known about widespread sexual abuse of women in Africa, especially nuns, by priests who used them for sex because they feared getting AIDS from women who were not virgins. The stories, recounted in memos to Vatican officials during the mid-1990s, were shocking.

"The superior of a religious community in one country was contacted by priests who asked her to make the nuns available for sexual services," Sister Maura O'Donohue, of the Medical Missionaries of Mary, wrote in one report to Rome. "On the superior's refusal, the priests said they would otherwise have to go to the village to look for women, exposing themselves to the risk of AIDS." Young female candidates for religious life were sometimes obliged to have sex with a priest to obtain certificates to proceed with their vocation, and nuns who became pregnant were forced to leave their congregation while the priests responsible were simply sent away for a two-week retreat. In one community, twenty-nine nuns were reported to have become pregnant by priests. When the nuns' superior complained, her archbishop simply removed her.

"Examples were also given of situations where priests were bringing sisters (and other young women) to Catholic health institutions for abortion," Sister O'Donohue wrote, recalling her February 18, 1995, briefing with Cardinal Eduardo Martinez, prefect of the Vatican Congregation for Religious Life. "I gave one example of a priest who had brought a sister for an abortion. She died during the procedure and the priest officiated at the Requiem Mass. The response was of stunned silence."

Father Robert J. Vitillo, who was at the time executive director of the United States Bishops Campaign for Human Development, wrote in March 1994: "I myself have heard the tragic stories of religious women who were forced to have sex with the local priest or with a spiritual counselor who insisted that this activity was 'good' for the both of them. Frequently, attempts to raise these issues with local and international church authorities have met with deaf ears."

When the reports surfaced in 2001, Vatican spokesman Joaquin Navarro-Valls issued a statement saying that the problem was confined to "a limited geographical area" and was being addressed. He said, "A few negative situations cannot make one forget the often heroic faith of the great majority of monks, nuns and priests." A year later, in August 2002, the Vatican released a plan that did not explicitly mention the abuses but called for closer oversight of the training of nuns and for efforts to ensure the autonomy of their orders.

The scandal in Africa drew relatively little notice when it became public, and by the time Rome released its "solution" to the African problem in 2002, the scandal of clergy abuse of children in the United States had overwhelmed any other church news.

The prominence of the American over the African scandal may reflect the scant concern that Western media have for news in developing nations, and perhaps it says something about a lingering belief that this sort of thing goes on between priests and nuns all the time anyway. Whatever the reason, to a degree that the African story did not, the U.S. crisis—and the groundswell for married priests that accompanied it—exposed the latent prejudice and misguided notion that celibacy somehow causes sexual abusiveness. If priests were to become like us, lay people implied, all would be fine. This "Let them eat cake" response ignored reality and was rightfully offensive to many priests. Still, the issue of celibacy was front and center, and the willingness of so many senior churchmen to keep it out there indicated that the Catholic Church was ready to tackle the question head-on in a way it hadn't for nearly a thousand years.

"I have no problems with celibacy withering away," Scottish Archbishop Keith O'Brien said in April 2002. "There is no great theological argument against celibacy ending, nor any theological problem with it ending." The reaction to O'Brien's statement was just as telling. A year earlier he would have been hammered. Instead, his remarks were welcomed. "If people of his caliber are saying that this needs to be discussed, then it does need to be discussed," said a spokesman for the Bishops Conference of England and Wales.

At the same time, on the other side of the globe, the bishop in charge of the Australian church's response to the sexual abuse crisis, Auxiliary Bishop Pat Power of Canberra, said that the celibacy requirement was outdated and needed to be revisited. "Many good potential candidates for the priesthood are deterred by the fact that they must also accept celibacy as part of a 'package deal.' There are, too, many good men who have left active ministry, married and are now debarred from exercising a priestly ministry," Power wrote. "All this is happening at a time when more and more is being demanded of remaining priests in terms of providing pastoral care and a sacramental ministry to their people."

At a meeting of the Canadian bishops in November 2002, prelates representing the vast northernmost dioceses of Canada told their fellow churchmen that they were in desperate need of priests and that the only way to rectify the situation was to ordain married men, especially from the indigenous communities. The Canadian bishops had made a request for married clergy a decade earlier in a meeting with the pope, and in 1997 they had followed that up with another request. The situation continued to worsen, however. In some Catholic communities in the sparsely populated north, Mass and other sacraments are now celebrated only two or three times a year. The Diocese of Mackenzie–Fort Smith is geographically the largest Catholic diocese in the world, yet only seven priests serve its forty parishes and missions totaling 20 thousand people. "It's not easy there," said Bishop Vincent Cadieux of Moosonee. "The priests are isolated. They live with people who have a very different culture than theirs and also the lifestyles are very different."

Apparently it is not much easier for priests in other areas of the country. In December 2002 a retired Quebec bishop, fifty-two-year-old Raymond Dumais, announced that he was preparing to marry and that celibacy was one of the reasons for his departure from the episcopacy. Again, the response from Catholic officialdom was hardly censorious. "It's time that we woke up to a new culture within the church," Father Guy Lagace, president of the archdiocesan forum of the Archdiocese of Rimouski, told the Quebec newspaper *Le Soleil.* "Celibacy should not become a barrier to men interested in becoming priests. Raymond Dumais is not the only person to be living this situation."

Also during the year of scandal, senior American churchmen began publicly broaching the idea of changing the rules on priestly celibacy in a way they never had before. While they extolled the virtues of celibacy, bishops and several cardinals said straight out that since the Catholic Church had always had married priests in its ranks in the Eastern-rite Catholic churches, the principle and precedents existed for allowing married priests generally. Standing on the leafy grounds of North American College, the main U.S. seminary in Rome, his back to the great cupola of St. Peter's Basilica, Los Angeles cardinal Roger Mahony told me in April 2002 that relaxing the celibacy rules should be on the table.

"We've had a married clergy since day one, since St. Peter," Mahony said. "We've always had a married clergy. The question is whether it's something that needs to be revisited and expanded. Having that discussion, there's certainly nothing wrong with that." Mahony was speaking even after his efforts to bring up the celibacy issue at the top-level Vatican summit on the scandal had been quashed because, he explained, "we don't want to confuse the issues"—meaning sexual abuse and celibacy. But he clearly indicated that the celibacy matter would not go away. "I'm for discussion of anything within the church. The Holy Spirit is there, and wherever the Holy Spirit leads us, let's have a discussion."

Other bishops and several cardinals expressed similar views, and privately they were even more explicit about wanting to have married clergy, as long as that practice would not mean excluding or marginalizing celibates.

Such openness was not limited to so-called liberals, either. A March 2002 editorial in Cardinal Law's weekly newspaper, *The Pilot,* raised the question, "Should celibacy continue to be a normative condition for the diocesan priesthood in the Western (Latin) Church?" Merely bruiting the issue at a time of such intense scrutiny guaranteed that the editorial would receive enormous coverage, and the next week *The Pilot* backed off any notion that it had reached a conclusion on the matter. But the question, coming from such an authoritative source, was telling. Likewise, in a 2002 interview with the *Westchester Journal,* Father Benedict Groeschel, a Franciscan who heads the Office of Spiritual Development of the Archdiocese of New York, said that the priest shortage and the scandal had made previously unthinkable ideas serious options. "If we get stuck, we may have to think about ordaining permanent deacons, many of whom are married men, to the priesthood. We could get to that point. It might not be far down the road," said Groeschel, a hero to tradition-minded Catholics whose words carry great weight in church circles. (Left unsaid in that acknowledgment was the possibility that women may be deacons one day, and thus could be "next in line" for the priesthood.)

The conservative Groeschel is not alone among the priesthood. A 2001 survey by Duke University Divinity School, "Pulpit and Pew," found that 72 percent of Catholic priests in the United States agree that the church should continue to welcome married Episcopal priests, and 52 percent believe that priests who have resigned to marry should be invited to reapply for permission to function once again as priests in good standing. Another 56 percent believe that celibacy should be a matter of personal choice. "We all thought that there would be some resentment by celibate priests, but by and large that is not true," said Dean Hoge, who conducted the study.

Hoge also estimated that simply introducing optional celibacy to the priesthood would quadruple vocations immediately. Combine that influx with the impact of thousands of married priests, who have already been trained and seasoned, returning to ministry if the Vatican allowed them back, and overnight the vocations crisis would be over.

Support for married priests is even stronger among lay Catholics. Polls show that more than 70 percent of parishioners consistently support the idea of ordaining married men, and nearly eight in ten lay people think that priests who left to marry should be welcomed back. The support is constant across generational and ideological lines. Archliberal Phil Donahue and archconservative Mel Gibson, for example, rarely agree on anything, but they do on ending celibacy. "Ministers and rabbis get to be married," Gibson said in a 2002 interview. "So do Greek Orthodox priests and Episcopalian priests. So why not Catholic priests? It might bring into the church a higher caliber of men. I'm all for it."

Amy Welborn, a heralded Catholic writer known for her orthodox views of the faith, is herself married to a laicized priest. In an essay in *Commonweal,* Welborn voiced her "rage" at the way bishops pledged to financially support pedophile priests no matter what, even as they took away her husband's pension and any means of support after he left the priesthood to marry. Her husband would make an excellent priest, she said, as she battled her feelings of cynicism toward her church and marveled at "the puzzle of such pointless waste."

Once again, the church is not a democracy, so poll numbers have only so much weight. But the priest shortage strikes at the heart of Catholic life—namely, the availability of the Eucharist—and that may well be the issue that finally forces the Vatican's hand.

"We are a sacramental church. We must celebrate the Eucharist or we will die," Father Norman Rotert, former vicar-general of the Kansas City–St. Joseph diocese and a priest for forty-two years, said in a speech to the Catholic Press Association. "I see no possibility of salvaging the priesthood as we know it today. We must talk about the issue if we are to find a creative solution. Non-ordained lay pastors, closing parishes, twinning parishes are all temporary, stopgap measures."

That was in 1995. The arguments have only intensified since then.

John Gremmels of Fort Worth, who like most married convert-priests is strongly conservative ("I always support what John Paul does," he says), told me that he backs mandatory celibacy in general. But he said that a critical priest shortage could change his mind, and he noted that just a few weeks before we spoke, the bishop had announced that some parishes would have to do without a priest, and without the Eucharist on Sunday. "If you are talking about taking Mass away from the people, then that would change my mind. If it meant denying people those sacraments, then I would have to flip-flop."

Conservatives across the board share that view, not to mention liberals and moderates who for years have been sounding the alarm. The celibacy requirement for priests is an obstruction "in the way of our fulfilling the law of God," the late Minnesota bishop Raymond Lucker wrote in a 1998 pastoral letter. "I bring up this issue because of my concern for the church, because of my love for the church, and because I believe that the Eucharist and the celebration of the sacraments are at the heart of what we are as a church."

A married priesthood was coming before the crisis; now it is inevitable. We have to be careful about forecasts, of course, especially where the Catholic Church is concerned. In the early 1960s, the Jesuit theologian and Vatican II expert John Courtney Murray predicted that the Vatican would soon accept a married clergy. Then in 1967 Pope Paul VI issued his encyclical hailing celibacy as a "brilliant jewel." But most church insiders expect that the next ten to fifteen years will see a definitive change.

The question then becomes, What will be the impact of a married priesthood? And what of the celibate priesthood? Will it disappear? Should it? And most urgently (given the current crisis), does celibacy contribute to sexual dysfunction and abuse?

First off, celibacy per se does *not* lead to sexual abuse, and certainly not the sexual abuse of young children. As we have seen, those are problems of sexual pathology and psychological immaturity. An influx of married men with psychosexual problems would result in similar abuses.

There are legitimate questions, however, about how celibacy is taught in the seminaries today, and whether the church is forcing chastity on men who, in Jesus' words, are not able to receive such a discipline.

Chronic loneliness has become a corrosive factor in the priesthood, exacerbated by the decline in the number of priests and the concomitant fraying of the bonds of priestly community. Dean Hoge's 2001 study of priestly life found that about half of all priests who leave do so for a woman (20 to 30 percent), for another man (5 to 15 percent), or because they feel "lonely and unappreciated" (20 to 30 percent). And it is estimated that about half of the priests who remain violate their vow of celibacy at some point, a rate confirmed to me by any number of priests. In other words, priests violate their promise of celibacy at about the same rate that their parishioners violate their marriage vows. Hoge said that the responses in his study were "suffused with talk about celibacy, loneliness, desire for intimacy and homosexuality—more so than we expected."

The priests who stick it out often try to cope by taking the "Lone Ranger" approach to ministry, a romantic notion born perhaps out of a mistaken notion of glorified suffering, and one that eventually loses its appeal and becomes a burden with destructive results for parish life and the pastor himself. In one indicator of the problem, a 1995 study showed that nearly 11 percent of U.S. religious priests and brothers (that is, those in religious orders) were alcoholics, almost double the rate measured in a 1982 study.

Father James J. Gill, a Jesuit and psychiatrist who trains clergy educators at the Christian Institute for the Study of Human Sexuality, has argued that despite the scandal and its pathologies, Catholic leaders have been too slow to revamp seminary education to better help men adjust to a sexless life. "Countless men have told me that they had had serious questions about their sexuality since adolescence but were reluctant to bring these issues to the faculty preparing them for ministry. Most feared that if they described their sexual problem, they would be told they didn't belong in the seminary or priesthood," Gill wrote in a 2002 op-ed piece. "Just as frequently, they have told me there was no one knowledgeable enough about human sexuality on the seminary staff to understand them and guide them toward a resolution of their difficulty. It was only after ordination and a prolonged, stressful and often lonely life as a priest that they slipped into the behavior so damaging to their young victims and their own lives as well."

Statistics show that one in seven priests now leaves the priesthood within five years, a significant increase over past years and an indication that seminary training is inadequate.

Better preparation and screening may help offset some of the problems facing today's celibates, but by reducing the number of vocations it could also worsen the priest shortage that underlies so many of the difficulties priests face. It is a vicious cycle.

Another point to keep in mind is that the advent of married priests would not suddenly morph the Catholic Church into a liberal utopia. The vast majority of married priests who have entered the Catholic Church from other denominations did so because they were upset by the liberal bent of their home church. They are primarily Episcopalians who disagree with women's ordination and the acceptance of active homosexuals in the clergy. Most of the married convert-priests I polled believe that celibacy for the priesthood should be maintained, except in particular cases like their own.

Married priests will also bring their own set of challenges. Chief among the adjustments will be the financial accommodations parishes will have to make. As it stands now, married Catholic priests struggle to make ends meet on a priest's meager salary and often have to work a second job to pay the bills. They should be compensated justly, and the Canon Law Society of America has determined that in fact canon law mandates appropriate financial support for married priests. I frankly do not see this as the obstacle that some others do. Today there are more Catholics than ever supporting fewer priests than ever, and the amount of money involved to adequately provide for a priest and his family would be relatively small. Moreover, parishioners are always willing to spend more on their own church if they feel the church is responsive to them.

Today's married priests are also harried priests, just as overworked as their celibate colleagues, and perhaps more so. That poses emotional as well as financial dangers for their family lives. "It's a major source of guilt," Father Robert McElwee of Frontenac, Kansas, told the Associated Press in a 2001 story. McElwee, who jokingly calls himself a "bigamist" because of his dual loyalties, recalled rushing out to perform last rites after his youngest son was born. "There are days when I know I'm short-changing my family," he said. His wife, Ginger, also said that "as a wife or a child, you can't compete," and their son Jordan is not a supporter of a married priesthood. "I'd never recommend it."

A married priesthood would also not ensure a scandal-free church. Married priests would eventually mean divorced priests or, as history has shown, straying priests. Protestant clergy have been the object of adulation by their women congregants every bit as much as the alluring Catholic celibate, and from the Arthur Dimmesdale of fiction to the pre-eminent nineteenth-century preacher Henry Ward Beecher (brother of Harriet Beecher Stowe of *Uncle Tom's Cabin* fame) to the modern televangelist Jim Bakker and his ilk, Protestant clergymen have had trouble resisting such temptations. In keeping with the enduring spirit of the Genesis account of the Fall, of course, the blame has typically fallen on the Temptress. This plotline was a staple of nineteenth- and twentieth-century Protestant romance fiction. In novels such as *A Circuit Rider's Wife* (1910), a Methodist minister's wife bemoaned the women—"the real rotters of honor and destroyers of salvation"—who "make a religion of sneaking up on the blind male side of good men without a thought of the consequences."

If contemporary society is a bit wiser about just who is to blame in such relationships, the incidence of clergy adultery has apparently not changed much. For example, in a 1983 survey, 12 percent of Protestant clergy admitted to sexual intercourse with a parishioner. The researcher, Richard Blackmon, believes that number to be an underestimate, given the understandable reluctance of pastors to admit to a fault so grievous. Blackmon also found that 38 percent admitted to other "sexualized contact" with a parishioner. In separate denominational surveys a decade later, 48 percent of United Church of Christ female ministers and 77 percent of United Methodist female ministers reported having been sexually harassed in church.

There is also a common supposition—a kind of lay snobbery, if you will—that married men would somehow be "nicer" and more pastoral than celibate priests. "A man without a wife to puncture his pomposity, without children to challenge his authority, in relations carefully structured to make him continuously eminent, easily becomes convinced of his superior wisdom," Garry Wills has written. Writers, who are by nature convinced of their own superior wisdom, should know better. Married pastors of all stripes can be the most overweening lords of the manor, as condescending as the most patronizing, pre-conciliar Catholic priest. In fact, many female Protestant clergy have told me that they prefer working with Catholic priests over married male colleagues of their own denomination, because priests are more likely to view them as an equal rather than as the pastor's wife, whose main job is still seen by many as serving tea and shaking hands.

Another expectation is that married priests can better relate to a parishioner's problems, because a spiritual "Father" who is also a biological father will know what it is like to have a child with strep at 3 A.M. That may be true to a degree. Father Raniero Cantalamessa, the preacher to the pontifical household, gave a series of Advent talks on celibacy to Pope John Paul and his aides in 2002, in which he urged the church to see both celibacy and marriage as vocations. He stressed in particular that celibate priests—who he said sometimes have an exalted view of their own sacrifices—should get to know married couples and their families so that they have a realistic understanding of their problems and will thus be better able to minister to them. But there can also be a one-sided presumption in the idea that married men would be better pastors. "I don't think being married makes me a better priest," said Father Thad Rudd. "Married people often say they're more comfortable with me, but I have no better empathy with them, despite what they think. Some people think I can magically bend the rules."

What a married priesthood will certainly do is to alleviate the critical priest shortage, which is by itself ample justification for facilitating the change. And there would be many other benefits, many of them just as urgent.

For one thing, introducing married priests into the ossified world of diocesan life figures to loosen the bonds of clericalism, which is a central cause of the present crisis. When married Catholic priests encounter resistance, it is far more likely to come from the chancery than from the folks in the pews, who almost universally welcome them. "When the pope approved my petition to become a priest—even though I was married and had three kids—no church wanted anything to do with me," said Rudd. "The monsignor, officials in the chancery office—they didn't want an oddity like a married priest thrown into their rigidly controlled world. A bishop told me the church frowned upon married priests because the scandal factor was too high. . . . At one parish the pastor wouldn't allow me to say Mass on Sunday. I wondered if I'd chosen the right path."

With a married priesthood a commonplace reality, bishops would be forced to take into account the feelings of a pastor's family before transferring him hither and yon. Rather than undermining the church, such "diffuse" loyalties might actually ease the reflexive, martial quality that the celibate priest's promise of obedience often fosters.

Some scholars, such as Peter McDonough, who coauthored a controversial study about the Jesuits called "Passionate Uncertainty," argue that celibacy by its nature is actually the critical enabler of its insidious counterpart, clericalism. "Because a vow of chastity is the necessary condition for clerical leadership, sexuality and ecclesiastical power are hard to disentangle," McDonough wrote. "The credibility of the authority structure wanes largely as the credibility of the sexual teaching declines, and so does 'the point' of the celibate priesthood."

In his final book, *Goodbye Father: The Celibate Male Priesthood and the Future of the Catholic Church,* the late Richard A. Schoenherr, who for years documented the tremendous changes in the priesthood, wrote that "male exclusivity and celibate exclusivity reinforce one another. Letting go of celibate exclusivity would expose male exclusivity for what it is: a historically developed form of gender dominance." Schoenherr was optimistic that a married priesthood would happen fairly quickly, and in two or three generations would lead to the ordination of women and perhaps to a rethinking of Catholic teachings on sexuality.

That timeline may be wishful thinking. The most important immediate effect of a married priesthood would be psychological. Welcoming such an important adaptation, despite centuries of church teachings and prejudices against it, would be a powerful reminder that the Catholic Church does change, and is changing. It would be a sign of hope that church leaders are willing, and humble enough, to put the spiritual needs of the flock—which is the canonical Golden Rule and the priest's very reason for being—above their loyalty to the "merely ecclesial law of celibacy."

Vital to this changeover, however, is that it take place under an orderly, logical, and pastoral process that will preserve the core celibate priesthood while introducing married priests into the mix in a constructive way. This will require planning and an open discussion of the issues in order to better prepare the lay faithful as well as the present corps of priests.

Among the likely scenarios for the future Catholic Church is a "mixed" priesthood, akin to the current Orthodox system, in which most celibates live as monks in religious orders, where they can find the support of like-minded brothers, while married priests serve as "secular" pastors in parishes. There would also be much crossover, however (as there should be), with monk-priests working in parishes. Such an evolution does carry the danger of encouraging a two-tiered caste system, as in the Orthodox churches, which privileges celibates with leadership positions over and above married priests. While the system seems to function fairly smoothly in the Orthodox world, it remains to be seen how Latin-rite Catholicism would adjust to such an enormous change. (The potential ecumenical benefits of a married Catholic priesthood should also not be underestimated.)

Another possible reform is the introduction of limited terms of celibate service—what Andrew Greeley has called a "Priest Corps," akin to the Peace Corps. As Greeley notes, a century ago the average priest's career lasted twelve years; today, because of increased life expectancy, the average priest will probably serve for fifty years. "If someone burns out after a couple of terms or can no longer stand teenage noise or wants to start a family of his own, let him go forth in dignity and gratitude," Greeley says. "Why assume that the priesthood in this age of long life expectancy must be a lifetime vocation?"

This option would be novel for today's church, but like so much else in Catholicism, it has a historical precedent of sorts: in the Beguine and Beghard communities in the late Middle Ages, large cloisters of non-vowed women and men who lived like monastics were free to leave and wed. The Beguines and Beghards eventually crossed swords with the popes and were suppressed. But renewing that idea today could foster religious life throughout the church and might serve to reinvigorate dying religious orders by allowing men and women to live prescribed periods of abstinence. Plainly the answer to the question of celibacy is not "either/or" but "both/and"—what *National Catholic Reporter* columnist Kris Berggren calls both the "wild" (celibate) and the "domesticated" (married) priesthood.

With the transition toward optional celibacy already underway, and given the great stresses the scandal has placed on the celibate priesthood, it is vital that the Vatican engage the issue constructively rather than hope it will go away. Dodging the celibacy debate will only complicate the renewal of the church.

Also, a systematic process of transition would actually better protect and value the celibate priesthood and ensure its continuity. For the

Catholic Church, the acceptance of a married priesthood should never mean the elimination of priestly celibacy, nor should the church ever discount the irreplaceable contribution of celibacy. Even if we dump the cultural baggage about the spiritual superiority of the sexually chaste, the role of celibate Catholic priests is integral to the Christian witness. This goes beyond the pragmatic arguments that a celibate priest can be more available to people, or is able to do more work and take greater risks. While there are merits to the arguments, there is also the danger of reducing celibacy to a "practical" matter rather than the spiritual discipline that is at the core of celibacy.

Sure, celibacy is hard—"being empty for God," as it is called, in imitation of Christ on the Cross. But so are marriage and parenting and a lot of other disciplines. And the Christian life was never meant to be a cakewalk. The value of suffering is perhaps the most countercultural and misunderstood aspect of Christianity today. Suffering is at the heart of celibacy, just as it was at the heart of Jesus' sacrifice, because suffering is part of life, much as we want to deny it. But a central Christian teaching is that suffering can be redemptive, and if a properly lived celibacy—a "white" martyrdom of wordly renunciation, as opposed to the early church's "red" martyrdom of peril and death—goes by the wayside, a vital part of this Christian witness disappears as well.

That witness is arguably more important today than ever before. Despite the impulse to immediate gratification, the desire and admiration for asceticism still echo in the culture. The celibate Jedi knights of the *Star Wars* saga are much admired by today's youth, and the most popular hero during the summer of the sex scandal was Peter Parker, alias Spiderman, who chose a swinging life of service over love. "With great power comes great responsibility," as he told the tempting Mary Jane (Kirsten Dunst). Priests loved that movie. Putting flesh on the bones of celluloid ephemera is a great vocation.

Also lost in the prurient focus on sexual activity and clergy is the obvious fact that celibacy is about more than sex. It is also about a life of intense, regular prayer, a life of poverty and of self-giving and all those other things that vowed religious can do, and that we continue to hold in high esteem. When a priest (or a nun such as Mother Teresa or a brother such as St. Francis of Assisi) forswears riches, we call him a saint. When he renounces sex, we think him weird.

Indeed, if the heart of the Gospel message has survived and remained at all palatable to a Western civilization in thrall to the Darwinian system of economic self-interest, it is due in no small part to the celibate Catholic priesthood. Priests today are sentinels of asceticism amid a culture of acquisitiveness and consumer sexuality. They somehow manage to mediate, as much by their very existence as by their sermons, the radical call of Christianity and the antithetical demands of contemporary life. Priests choose to live on this frontier, drawn from one side of the border or another, both men and icons, standing apart from and yet remaining part of the larger community. "A monk is valuable in the market-place if he preserves a nostalgia for the desert," the late English Cardinal Basil Hume, a Benedictine, once wrote.

The coming changes in the priesthood, and in the Catholic Church as a whole, will entail formidable stresses at a time when the priesthood is undergoing its greatest trial. In the final analysis, the nuts and bolts of those changes (and the responsibility for shepherding them from drafting table to reality) will rest with the hierarchy.

But no other segment of the church lost as much credibility during the year of scandal as the Catholic bishops, and just how effectively the hierarchy can manage the imminent changes is a question that looms almost as large as the power the bishops have to affect that future.

Part Three

THE HIERARCHY

An institute run with such knavish imbecility that if it were not the work of God it would not last a fortnight.
—Hilaire Belloc on the Catholic Church

Twelve

THE BISHOPS AND
THE FALL OF ROME

Washington, D.C., nearly five months to the day after the debacle in Dallas, and the American hierarchy was gathered again, in yet another hotel ballroom, lined up at rows of draped tables with pitchers of ice water, an international press corps still watching their every move. Much appeared the same as it had months earlier, but in reality everything had changed.

This time there were no abuse victims standing before the hierarchy recounting how predator priests had seduced them as children. There were no experts detailing the lifelong psychological damage of such abuse. Above all, there were no lay people telling the bishops where they had gone wrong, how the prelates themselves had fostered the sexual abuse by abusing their authority, and how they could go about repairing the harm.

None of those Catholic voices was present at the November meeting in the shadow of the U.S. Capitol.

But all of the bishops were. During the year of scandal four bishops had resigned, all before the Dallas meeting, and only because they had been directly implicated in sexual abuse or misconduct. No bishop who had covered up for the abusers, who had enabled abusive priests to continue molesting children, who had used legal and pastoral stratagems to intimidate and deceive victims and their anguished families, had faced even the threat of censure from his colleagues. In fact, the emerging storyline on Boston's Cardinal Bernard Law that November concerned his nascent rehabilitation; he had survived the worst, the thinking went, and he figured to stay in power until a graceful retirement. (This was a month before another surprise round of revelations would finally topple Law and exile him to a convent in Maryland.)

That Law had been able to stick it out this long was thanks in large part to the silence of his brother bishops, who didn't much like Law but felt that they had to protect him publicly. One of the few hints of internal discord came the day the Dallas meeting ended, when Illinois bishop Joseph Imesch suggested in an interview with Boston's WBZ-TV that Law should step down. Imesch was saying what everyone knew: that the bishops were angry with Law, and that some had expressed their anger in closed-door sessions. But it was telling that Imesch quickly backed off his statement when pressed: "In conversation among the bishops, it was more than one that felt he [Law] should resign, but no one said that publicly but Joe Imesch," Imesch told the Associated Press a few days after Dallas. "It was probably not good judgment on my part to say that. . . . I regret having said what I said."

Imesch's further clarification was no more reassuring. He explained that he had thought the cardinal might resign simply because "it would be very difficult for someone to minister in that kind of a climate." Law should quit, he was saying—but not because he had done anything wrong.

After Dallas, the bishops began circling the wagons. They felt that they had tried hard in Texas, that they had at least made a good-faith effort to implement a tough new policy and restore their tattered reputation; but their efforts had been dismissed. The bishops had been stunned by the criticism they took on the floor of their own meeting that June, and blindsided by the outrage over their zero-tolerance charter. Priests had ripped them for selling out the clergy, while lay people had scored them because no bishops had been punished for their role in the scandal. Finally, the Vatican itself took a shot at the prostrate hierarchy, telling them in October that the Dallas policy was too strict and would have to be reworked in accordance with the Vatican's dictates.

By November, the bishops were looking for a victim of their own, and it was telling that they were training their sights not so much on Cardinal Law, but on Bishop Wilton Gregory, the president of the conference and the bishop many of his colleagues now believed responsible for making matters worse for them. Just a year earlier Gregory had been elected to his job in this same Capitol Hill hotel, basking in the glow of universal praise. Fifty-three when elected, he was young by episcopal standards, and more important, his demeanor was youthful. He was African-American, no small feat for a hierarchy (and a church) dominated by white-haired Europeans, and born a Baptist, he was the first convert ever to head the conference. For much of his first year in office he had been seen as the perfect spokesman for a sclerotic hierarchy.

When the scandal hit, Gregory had proved his agility by skillfully navigating the currents slamming the conference, and he had showed a deft pastoral touch by orchestrating a Dallas meeting that exposed the bishops to their own sins. But to the bishops' mind, the summer strategy had backfired, and by the fall, they were not about to cut Wilton Gregory any slack.

"The sharks are circling," one longtime bishop told me as the prelates gathered for their opening session on the morning of November 11, 2002. "There's blood in the water." The bishops were especially angry over Gregory's appointment of Oklahoma governor Frank Keating to head the lay review board, a move Gregory engineered largely on his own. From the moment Keating was introduced to the media at a briefing after the Dallas meeting, he had been a scourge to the hierarchy. At that press conference Keating had compared some bishops to mere criminals and had said he would push for them to resign. Despite Keating's efforts to become more politic in his pronouncements, he hadn't let up, and the bishops were not about to let Gregory forget his maneuver.

As another senior prelate told me at the Washington confab: "In Rome they have a saying: You can throw the chestnuts in the fire, but you have to pick them out without burning your fingers."

A few minutes later, Bishop Gregory let his brethren know he had received the message loud and clear. In a strongly worded speech that was as remarkable for its defiant tone as his Dallas speech had been for its penitence, Gregory drew a line around his fellow bishops and alerted the world, and the rest of the church, that the hierarchy was not going to roll over any longer:

"As bishops, we should have no illusions about the intent of some people who have shown more than a casual interest in the discord we have experienced within the church this year. There are those outside the church who are hostile to the very principles and teachings that the church espouses, and have chosen this moment to advance the acceptance of practices and ways of life that the church cannot and will never condone," Gregory said, waving a virtual enemies list without naming names. "Sadly, even among the baptized, there are those at extremes within the church who have chosen to exploit the vulnerability of the bishops in this moment to advance their own agendas. One cannot fail to hear in the distance—and sometimes very nearby—the call of the false prophet, 'Let us strike the shepherd and scatter the flock.' We bishops need to recognize this call and to name it clearly for what it is."

(Two days later, when pressed on the *Newshour with Jim Lehrer* to name the groups he believed were exploiting the crisis for their own ends, Gregory named three: supporters of abortion rights, same-sex couples, and backers of the ordination of women.)

The bishops loudly applauded Gregory's challenge and his affirmation of their role as "presiding in place of God over the flock whose shepherd they are." Gregory also underscored the bishops' traditional mandate to exercise their threefold office "as *teachers of doctrine, priests of sacred worship,* and *officers of good order.*" The italics were his, and the emphasis was unmistakable: the bishops were back in charge.

Gregory then went on to try to mend fences with priests, the bishops' most important constituency outside of Rome, and one that had been bitterly alienated by the Dallas meeting and the ensuing efforts to crack down on abusive clergy:

"Priests today too often are being unfairly judged by the misdeeds of other priests, men often long departed from ministry or even deceased. One can hardly talk of the priesthood today without mentioning that some priests and bishops have seriously failed to live up to our vocation. Whenever I am listening to or reading a story about the good work of priests, I have gotten into the habit of anticipating the 'but . . . ,' which will lead into some terrible tale of malfeasance.

"Well, this morning there is no 'but.' We need to pay more than lip service to the truth that the overwhelming majority of priests are faithful servants of the Lord," Gregory said. "*God bless our priests! They have surely blessed us!*" Again, the italics were his, and each line got rousing applause. Gregory's brief reference to the "opportunities for the laity to assist us" and his nod to Keating's lay review board were met with silence.

Gregory also signaled his determination to move the bishops on to other issues and not to let the scandal paralyze the hierarchy or dominate its agenda. He listed the scandal last among the four major concerns for the bishops, after the threat of war, a weakened economy, and the "scandal of poverty and disease." He also worked in guaranteed applause lines, such as his condemnation of *Roe v. Wade.*

In the days that followed, Gregory stuck to his new blueprint, guiding the bishops past a divisive debate over the revamped (but still confusing) sexual abuse policy and keeping them on message. In the end, the revised "norms," as the canonical language was known, passed 249 to 2, with four abstentions.

Then, as if to show that things were back to normal, the bishops spent several sessions immersed in the comfortable minutiae of liturgical matters and engaged in impenetrable discussions on fund-raising guidelines and the "alienation" of church property, all of which left the press corps blessedly (for the bishops) narcotized. In one surreal moment, the bishops awoke to the realization that they should say something about Iraq. That meant they had to turn to Cardinal Law, who as head of their international policy committee would draft a statement. Thus the principal villain of the sexual abuse scandal stood up on the meeting's final day to warn against a rush to war, asking that he be heeded as the moral voice of the nation's largest church.

The reactions to the November meeting were hardly surprising. Most Catholics didn't like Washington any more than they had liked Dallas. "The Bishops on the River Kwai," author Eugene Kennedy called the hierarchy, comparing the prelates to Alec Guinness's British officer, so transfixed by the structure he was building that he grew blind to its real purpose. Conservatives such as Richard John Neuhaus gave a qualified two cheers. "At last they are no longer jumping through media hoops and giving the impression of scurrying about like scared executives in search of a public relations fix," Neuhaus wrote. "After a year of frequent floundering, of embarrassed pandering, and of pathetic excuse-making, Gregory's message was that the bishops are prepared to reassume their office, recommit themselves to their tasks, and speak again in the distinctive language of the Church. At last."

But even Neuhaus, like most everyone else, was dismayed that no bishops had been called on the carpet for their actions. Accountability had been promised, and expected. Nearly nine in ten Catholics thought that prelates who had covered for abusive priests should resign, and on the eve of the Washington meeting Chicago cardinal Francis George had told reporters that "there have to be sanctions for a bishop who has been negligent, the same as there are sanctions for a priest." At the same time Detroit's Cardinal Adam Maida had called for a kind of "Warren Commission" to review the bishops' conduct.

By the time they got to Washington, however, the bishops had lost any enthusiasm for disciplinary measures, and they were asked only to approve a pledge that they would commit each other to "fraternal support, fraternal challenge, and fraternal correction," which they did by a vote of 231 to 5. "Pretty limp," as Neuhaus put it.

The cost of this solidarity was high. Where the bishops saw virtue in not ratting out a brother, the public saw a conspiracy of silence and self-protection. The hierarchy's unified front succeeded only in reinforcing the image that they were all equally guilty—that they were all like Cardinal Law, only they hadn't been found out yet. As happens in any scandal, the entire institution was judged by its worst offender. Law (and his associates, who were arguably more culpable than he was) had lowered the bar, and all of the bishops, many of whom were blameless or had done nothing on the scale of what had happened in Boston, voluntarily squeezed under.

At the Washington meeting, all of the dysfunctions that plague the U.S. hierarchy—and contributed to the scandal—were on display: extreme deference to Rome, supreme concern for their own standing and ambition, and a fixation on internal political divisions that was matched by an equal determination to cover rifts with a veneer of unanimity. Some of these dysfunctions stem from the all-powerful role of the bishop as it has come to be understood in Catholic theology. But much of it is directly traceable to the ecclesiastical politics of the past twenty-five years, starting with the pontificate of John Paul II. A consensus is growing, at all levels of the church (including the hierarchy itself), that these dysfunctions must be addressed.

Fortunately, politics yield to concrete action in a way that theology does not. What one policy created, a new policy can undo, and the bishops are the ones to do it.

While every constituency of the Catholic Church has a part in resolving the current crisis, the bishops bear the greatest responsibility for acting quickly and decisively. The scandal occurred on their watch and because of their sins of commission or omission. Furthermore, the American bishops, due to their hard-line approach to orthodoxy and their role as chief expositors of the faith, present themselves to Catholics and non-Catholics alike as "normative" Catholics. Catholic bishops are "good" Catholics, according to this perception, and the Catholic hierarchy *is* the Catholic Church. That is not actually the case in theory, however, and when it becomes so evidently untrue in reality as well, as it did during the scandal, the entire church suffers guilt by association. The bishops embarrassed all Catholics.

Finally, the burden of amendment is on the hierarchy because just as the abuse of their authority fostered the crisis, that same authority, unmatched in the ranks of the clergy or laity, can also revitalize the church as nothing else can. Like it or not, bishops are the constituency that is least subject to outside pressure, and that status is not going to change anytime soon. Yet that also means that bishops can effect immediate changes, and thus they, more than any other group in the church, hold the keys to resolving the crisis in Catholicism.

From the rough beginnings of Catholic history in America, the church has always been blessed by bishops with remarkable character and outsized egos. Yet even as those bishops, like all newcomers to a scene, worked diligently to prove to Rome that they were better churchmen than the Old World prelates, they were also proud of their accomplishments in the United States and often used their influence (backed by the weight of money) to keep their people from getting trampled by a Roman rush to judgment.

In the 1780s Bishop John Carroll spoke his mind to Rome, and in the 1960s New York's legendary Cardinal Francis Spellman (archbishop from 1939–1967)—hardly a pope-defying liberal—knew how to get his point across. Father Philip Murnion recalled how the man who ran the "Powerhouse," as Spellman's chancery was known, would defend seminarians from Vatican critiques, give jobs to radicals such as the late Ivan Illich, and send innovative thinkers such as the Jesuit John Courtney Murray to the Second Vatican Council. "Creativity and solidarity were not enemies," Murnion said of that era.

One thing Rome was not keen on, however, was the idea of any nation's bishops banding together in some sort of league that could pose a collective challenge to Vatican authority. The traditional view saw the bishop as the lord of his own realm (the diocese), appointed by the Roman pontiff and answerable only to Rome. To the Vatican, only the entire College of Bishops—that is, the worldwide episcopacy—was a legitimate deliberative body, and Rome cast a suspicious eye on national groups that might undermine Rome's primacy in any way. There was a long history of such threats.

Starting in the fifteenth century, for example, a religious movement in France known as Gallicanism strove for independence from Rome on matters of governance. Gallicanism flared again around the time of the French Revolution, as many thought a national Catholic Church free of Rome would be more in keeping with the revolutionary spirit. As that spirit got out of hand and turned on its own, anyone associated with Catholicism became a target. Gallicanism died on the gallows, along with so much else. After barely surviving the ensuing Napoleonic era in the early 1800s, the popes wanted to hear nothing more about national independence.

Later in the nineteenth century, however, local hierarchies found it necessary to respond to the enormous changes overtaking society—namely, the ongoing waves of popular, often anti-clerical revolutions, and the convulsive process of industrialization. Rome could see the value in having strong national representation, since the bishops were largely presenting Rome's own views, which were at odds with most of the "modern" changes. So bishops of various countries began establishing ad hoc national structures, although they always sought to ease Vatican fears by restricting the actions of these provisional bodies to statements on political, social, economic, and cultural issues rather than the internal church matters that were Rome's province.

In the United States the nationalizing process started in 1919 with the establishment of the National Catholic Welfare Council, or NCWC (soon to become *Conference* in deference to Vatican concerns that *Council* smacked of an ecclesial body). The process moved ahead despite the objections of churchmen such as Boston's Cardinal William O'Connell, who declared that the church was already "divinely organized" and at most needed "an annual meeting to discuss a few leading questions and pass on them."

The collective identity of the American bishops coalesced over the years, a natural evolution that was formally recognized when the Vatican allowed the establishment of the National Conference of Catholic Bishops of the United States (NCCB) on November 14, 1966. (Simultaneously the bishops created the United States Catholic Conference, which was to deal with public-policy issues, while the NCCB concerned itself mainly with internal church matters. In 2000 the bishops replaced the dual structure with a single entity, the U.S. Conference of Catholic Bishops, or USCCB.) The NCCB of 1966 had much more status and authority than the earlier NCWC. The Second Vatican Council, once again, was the turning point. In the Council's decree on bishops, *Christus Dominus,* and in several other documents, the Church Fathers essentially mandated the establishment of national bishops conferences while carefully proscribing their legislative and juridical functions so as not to threaten the autonomy of an individual bishop or the most important bishop, the bishop of Rome. As with so many of the initiatives of the Council, it was the diocesan bishops with pastoral experience who pushed for the national conferences over the opposition of Rome-based curial prelates.

The key innovation of these new conferences was their directive to deal with church matters as well as public-policy issues. That was necessary because the Council produced so many changes in liturgy and governance that even Rome knew it could not micromanage the transition and translations in each country and culture. The local bishops would be responsible for the first draft of reform.

In the heady aftermath of Vatican II, the Americans needed little encouragement to run with their newfound liberty, and soon the NCCB was a flourishing bureaucracy with a top-notch staff that helped the bishops prepare an increasing number of important statements on both public policy and church matters. Throughout the 1970s and 1980s, the Catholic bishops became arguably the most prophetic and powerful voice on the American religious scene. Through a lengthy and consultative process, the hierarchy produced a range of pastoral letters (the most authoritative statements bishops can make) that courageously presented church teachings on a range of controversial topics. Most notable were their 1983 statement on nuclear weapons (issued at the height of President Reagan's nuclear buildup) and a 1986 letter on economics that called to account many aspects of American society. Only nine bishops voted against the final drafts of each.

Then came the backlash.

It started with the 1983 Code of Canon Law, which was going through its first updating since 1917. Following John Paul II's election in 1978, new drafts of the revised code progressively reduced the role and authority of the bishops conferences. The final version, published in 1983, "so restricts the authority of bishops and conferences that it often looks as if they receive what little authority they have from the Holy See," as Thomas Reese wrote in *Inside the Vatican*.

Then in 1985 the Vatican announced that Cardinal Joseph Ratzinger, the pope's doctrinal overseer, would lead a further reexamination of the role of the bishops conferences. Few doubted that the end result would undermine the authority of the bishops. In 1964, as a priest and an expert on church doctrine at the Second Vatican Council, Ratzinger had been a stout defender of the role of national conferences, saying claims that they lack a "theological basis" were "one-sided and unhistorical." Now, twenty years later, Ratzinger had switched sides.

"We must not forget that the episcopal conferences have no theological basis," Ratzinger said in a widely noted 1985 interview. The Catholic Church, he said, "is based on an episcopal structure and not on a kind of federation of national churches. The national level is not an ecclesial dimension."

A first draft in 1988 took that thinking further and specifically barred any collective authority by the conference, fearing that a nation's bishops "would claim an undue autonomy from the Apostolic See and would thus end up by setting themselves against it and its doctrinal and disciplinary directives." Ten years later the final draft, released in the form of a papal letter, *Apostolos Suos,* ensured that bishops conferences would operate in practice as the pope wanted them to do in principle. In the 1998 letter, John Paul stated that conference documents on church teachings (a broad and vague category) must be approved unanimously. If they receive anything less than unanimous support, they must be submitted to Rome for a final okay. Thus one negative vote out of nearly three hundred could botch an initiative.

This effectively muted the bishops' collective voice and confirmed their role in church affairs as advisory, at best.

At the same time the Vatican was restraining the national conference, it also began micromanaging American church business to remind the

Americans just who was in charge. The Vatican demanded greater input into U.S. pastoral letters and succeeded in drastically altering or even quashing some of the bishops' efforts. In 1990 the Vatican issued *Ex Corde Ecclesia* ("From the Heart of the Church"), a document aimed at preserving and strengthening the Catholic identity of Catholic colleges and universities. The document was intended for all countries, but it was clearly aimed at the United States, where 230 Catholic colleges and universities enroll more than 600,000 students, and where the Vatican suspected that Catholic identity was being watered down through unchecked secularization. The Vatican's prescription was to enforce Catholic identity through a number of measures, including bishop-approved mandates (or what some called "loyalty oaths") that university leaders and theology professors would have to sign to remain employed. The American bishops tried to compromise, cajole, and finesse their way out of the unpopular measures, but got nowhere with Rome. In 1999 they were forced to capitulate.

Even eminent American churchmen such as Cardinal Law could not stop the Roman steamroller. It was Law who, at a 1985 Vatican synod of bishops, suggested that the Vatican update the Catholic Catechism—the definitive compendium of Catholic teachings. The proposal brought Law kudos from Rome and resulted in the new version a decade later. Yet Law's own first draft of the English version of the catechism was rejected by the Curia because of its "inclusive" language. His efforts to defend the work were ignored and he was forced to do a rewrite.

No issue was too small for the Vatican to pronounce on, from altar girls to terms for parish priests to the role of retired bishops in the conference.

Liturgy was a frequent source of tension between the U.S. bishops conference and the Vatican. In 1994, for example, the Vatican withdrew the permission it had granted in 1991 for a Psalter that the American church had authorized for use at Mass. Rome also reversed the bishops' decision to use the New Revised Standard Version of the Bible in liturgies. Both resulted in long delays in updating church services. Despite the bishops' efforts to accommodate the Vatican's demands, several similar embarrassing rejections followed. It didn't seem to matter how much the bishops protested; indeed, they often didn't know what was happening, and thus could not raise objections effectively. For example, following the 1995 rejection of a lectionary translation that the American church had already approved, the Vatican crafted "secret norms" for translations, and Rome waited until two weeks before the bishops' annual meeting in 1997 to present the complex new standards to the bishops for their approval.

In March 2002 the American bishops made a routine request to Rome to continue allowing lay ministers to stick with Mass customs that they had been using for almost thirty years. The Vatican responded by denying the request and further restricting the role of lay ministers, specifying that they could no longer distribute wine into chalices or touch anything on the altar until it was handed to them by a priest. This micromanaging is "illustrative of a growing authoritarianism in the church," Father Edward Foley, a Franciscan professor of liturgy at Chicago's Catholic Theological Union wrote in an *America* article titled "The Abuse of Power." The authoritarian approach in liturgy, he argued, is directly related to the attitudes that fostered the sexual abuse scandal.

The crackdown on the U.S. bishops conference must also be seen in the context of the wider battle between the Vatican and American culture, a replay of the long-running drama that has always afflicted U.S.-Rome relations, and one that came to play a role in the current crisis. For Rome, reining in the American church is crucial because America is considered the pacesetter in terms of moral relativism and the host of other ills that Rome sees afflicting modern life. The Vatican's strategy, especially under Pope John Paul, has been to take out the lead dog so that the rest fall in line.

This pressure started coming to bear in the 1980s with Vatican complaints about what it said were America's dissident theologians and easygoing bishops. As usual, sexuality was the prime arena of debate, and the Roman Curia quickly picked out two men who would be used as examples: Catholic University of America theologian Charles Curran and Seattle archbishop Raymond Hunthausen.

Hunthausen had drawn Rome's fire for a number of actions, including his decision in 1982 to withhold half of his income taxes to protest the Reagan nuclear buildup. But it was Hunthausen's perceived laxness on sexual matters that really riled the Vatican, especially his outreach to homosexuals. His use of general absolution for the faithful, rather than insisting on individual confession, was also upsetting to Rome. In September 1986 Pope John Paul took the extraordinary step of stripping Hunthausen of authority in five areas of his ministry and reassigning it to an auxiliary bishop, Donald Wuerl, who would serve with Hunthausen in what turned out to be a disastrous forced alliance. The Vatican's peremptory action touched off a storm of protest and months of turmoil in the American church. Finally, after protracted negotiations between Rome and the U.S. bishops, Wuerl—who was vilified at the time but has since gone on to become a highly regarded bishop in Pittsburgh—was replaced by another assistant bishop, who actually had more power to overrule Hunthausen, and eventually succeeded him.

In August 1986, a month before Hunthausen was disciplined, theologian Charles Curran was notified that Rome had stripped him of his right to teach as a Catholic theologian. While the Hunthausen controversy raised concerns about the governance of the church, the Curran case prompted fears about the future of the intellectual life of American Catholicism. Curran had been pushing the envelope on Catholic teachings on sexuality, but the Vatican's hard-line stance led to a confrontation meant to show theologians that no dissent would be brooked. After months of wrangling within the church and in U.S. courts (Curran tried to sue to retain his post), Curran left CUA. But his case and the Hunthausen affair got Rome's message through: bishops and theologians would have to toe the Vatican line.

It is noteworthy that at the same time the Vatican was cracking down on those considered lax on doctrine, it was promoting bishops—namely Cardinal Law and his progeny—who were protecting clergy abusers. The other message from the 1980s was that if a bishop granted general absolution, he would be disciplined; if he kept a lid on pedophile priests, nothing would happen.

Throughout the 1980s the Vatican kept up the pressure on the Americans. Rome was especially upset when the NCCB rejected the Vatican's initial 1988 draft on the legitimacy of bishops conferences and when the Americans raised concerns over issues such as the selection of bishops. In March 1989 John Paul brought the confrontation to a head. He called all thirty-four active U.S. cardinals and archbishops (twenty-one of whom he had appointed) to Rome to explain themselves, and to hear what Rome thought.

Arriving in Rome, the late St. Louis archbishop John May, then head of the NCCB, opened the summit with an honest effort to explain the challenges the bishops faced in America: "Authoritarianism is suspect in any area of learning or culture," May told the pope and a bank of curial officials. "To assert that there is a church teaching with authority binding for eternity is truly a sign of contradiction to many Americans who consider the divine right of bishops as outmoded as the divine right of kings."

The Vatican wasn't buying that line. In his response to May, Cardinal Ratzinger told the American bishops that they were "guardians of an authoritarian tradition" and they had to be firm and not overly tolerant: "For pastoral activity consists in placing man at the point of decision, confronting him with the authority of truth," Ratzinger said. "There is, to put it bluntly, a right to act immorally but morality itself has no rights." This was a fateful echo of the papal dictum "Error has no rights," which for centuries was a weapon to curb individual liberties.

The result of the Vatican's pressure, combined with the steady increase in the appointment of bishops loyal to John Paul, was a divided conference that was more politicized internally while more quiescent externally. By 1990 John Paul had appointed more than 130 of the conference's approximately 285 voting bishops, which Vatican officials considered the "tipping point" that would inevitably bring the conference in line with Rome's thinking.

The political calculus proved true, but it came at the price of the fraternity and collegiality of the American hierarchy—and of a united American Catholic voice.

There were early indications of a fatal split when John Paul favorites such as New York's Cardinal John O'Connor took his fellow American bishops to task in front of Vatican officials at the 1989 summit. Many American prelates, he said, have lost "confidence, first in themselves as persons, then in their magisterial authority, perhaps in the face of some hard-hitting theologians, perhaps out of fear of the press." Speaking to the pope, O'Connor added, "At times the bishop convinces himself that peace is the highest good."

John O'Connor was never guilty of such public reticence, of course, nor was his friend Bernard Law. Law frequently derided the authority of the bishops conference and often opposed its motions—such as the NCCB's protest over Reagan aid to the Contras—in deference to Roman wishes. Law's criticisms earned him few friends in the conference. In 1986, he lost eight NCCB election bids. But he was favored by the one bishop who mattered, John Paul, who increasingly relied on a "kitchen cabinet" of cardinals, whom he considered—in a novel theological interpretation that irritated other churchmen—to be a special class of bishops.

The first major public breakdown in collegiality among the Americans came in 1992, when, after nearly a decade of consultation that drew on testimony from 75,000 women, the bishops were forced to abandon their efforts to write a major pastoral letter on women in the church. Initial drafts of the letter had been overwhelmingly positive, with most welcoming the strong condemnation of sexism. The Vatican worried about the letter's orthodoxy, however, and the Holy See forced the bishops to tone down the language against sexism and to focus on the bans on contraception and on women's ordination.

In a November 1992 vote, a divided, exasperated conference split deeply and failed to pass the letter—the first time that had happened in the history of the NCCB. At the same meeting, faced with a round of clergy abuse reports, the bishops unanimously called for prompt action when priests are accused of sexual abuse. Tellingly, however, they were unable to adopt stringent, binding measures on abusive priests, settling for "guidelines" that would prove tragically insufficient. That 1992 meeting was also the last time until 2002 that leaders of the NCCB met with abuse victims.

The failure of the women's pastoral letter signaled the end of major initiatives by the bishops. There have been no significant pastoral letters or innovative statements to capture the public's imagination since then. Just a steady stream of fairly predictable pronouncements on public-policy issues. This represents a historic change.

For a few years after the women's pastoral fiasco, some bishops fought a rearguard action to reinvigorate and unify the conference.

In June 1995 a dozen bishops (with the silent support of an estimated forty others) published a remarkable statement that diagnosed the ills afflicting the American hierarchy. The dense twelve-page statement detailed all manner of dysfunctions. The list included fearful bishops waiting "like children" for the Holy Father's judgment; a "fundamental and serious problem of distrust among bishops"; a penchant for "political maneuvering"; and the problem of a few, favored bishops having direct access to Rome at the expense of the larger conference. The letter concluded by decrying a "lack of openness and honesty" within the conference on a host of substantive issues. Chief among them, they wrote in a Cassandra-like warning, was the unaddressed issue "of pedophilia among priests."

The letter did little to change the situation.

A year later, in 1996, several months before his death, Chicago cardinal Joseph Bernardin, alarmed by the enduring divisions in the church and the increasingly "mean-spirited" quality to the conflicts they were producing, presided over the launch of a more formal initiative to heal the breaches, called the Catholic Common Ground Project. Recognizing that "the Catholic Church in the United States has entered a time of peril," the Common Ground mission statement was optimistic about the chances of bringing Catholics together in renewal, but was nonetheless clear about the depth of the precipice yawning before the church:

"Will the Catholic Church in the United States enter the new millennium as a Church of promise, augmented by the faith of rising generations and able to be a leavening force in our culture? Or will it become a Church on the defensive, torn by dissension and weakened in its core structures? The outcome, we believe, depends on whether American Catholicism can confront an array of challenges with honesty and imagination, and whether the Church can reverse the polarization that inhibits discussion and cripples leadership.

"A mood of suspicion and acrimony hangs over many of those most active in the Church's life; at moments, it even seems to have infiltrated the ranks of the bishops. . . . Many of its leaders, both clerical and lay, feel under siege and increasingly polarized. Many of its faithful, particularly its young people, feel disenfranchised, confused about their beliefs and increasingly adrift. Many of its institutions feel uncertain of their identity and increasingly fearful about their future.

"The near future of American Church life is at risk," it said.

The statement called for a wide-ranging dialogue on the role of women, on the sexual teachings of the church, and on the nature of collegiality and relations between the U.S. church and Rome, and above all it stressed that Catholics should recognize that "no single group or viewpoint in the Church has a complete monopoly on the truth. . . . Solutions to the Church's problems will almost inevitably emerge from a variety of sources."

Bernardin's statement concluded with the hope that the common ground statement had avoided saying anything that might "add to the finger-pointing and demoralization."

But that, of course, is just what happened, and Bernardin's own colleagues among the cardinals were the biggest critics.

"We cannot achieve church unity by accommodating those who dissent from church teaching, whether on the left or the right," said Washington cardinal James Hickey. Cardinal Law, a longtime Bernardin foe, said, "Dissent from revealed truth or the authoritative teaching of the church cannot be 'dialogued' away." Cardinal Adam J. Maida of Detroit said that the proposal would sow "confusion" among the faithful. Philadelphia cardinal Anthony Bevilacqua disagreed with everything about the idea, even its name, Catholic Common Ground Project: "It is not ecclesial terminology. It is an ordinary, everyday term, open to uncontrolled interpretation, including even the meaning that 'Catholic common ground' signifies 'lowest common denominator.'"

Just as the priesthood has its divisions between those who would emphasize a "servant" style of leadership versus the "cultic" model of the stern and remote God-the-father-figure, so, too, is the American hierarchy split.

Terminally ill with pancreatic cancer, Bernardin labored mightily to overcome the divisions, and when he died almost three months to the day after launching Common Ground, he was acclaimed for his holiness and his honesty in facing up to both his mortality and the crisis in Catholicism. But Bernardin's legacy fell on hard times, and as the events of 2002 revealed, Common Ground had not made much headway. Ideologues appointed by Rome (often after a stretch of indoctrination in the Curia) continued to sow discord. Men such as Bishop Fabian Bruskewitz of Lincoln, Nebraska, who left Dallas deriding his own colleagues as "this hapless bunch of bishops," did damage out of proportion to their real influence. "You can't have real collegiality unless we're friends, and we can't be friends unless we trust each other. And there's not much trust," said then San Francisco archbishop John Quinn.

With such dissension within their ranks, the bishops felt forced to look to Rome for direction. "Their constituency is the constituency of one—the pope," Notre Dame's Richard McBrien told me. "The people do not come first. The bishops feel it is their job to represent Rome to the people rather than representing their people to Rome."

Given that limited audience, ambition among bishops often turned into a craven careerism that further undermined collegiality. That is not the judgment of church lefties alone. In 1999 Cardinal Bernardin Gantin, a distinguished African prelate who had recently retired as head of the Vatican's Congregation for Bishops (the department that determines episcopal assignments), blasted the "arrivism and careerism" rampant among bishops. Gantin said he had been shocked during his sixteen-year tenure in Rome at how many bishops asked for a "promotion" to a more prestigious diocese. Gantin was so disturbed by the pattern that he proposed changing canon law to return to the ancient church practice by which a bishop would remain for life in the diocese where he was first made a bishop. "The bishop cannot say, 'I will be here for two or three years and then I will be promoted,'" Gantin said.

Several other high-ranking officials echoed Gantin's concern. Cardinal Ratzinger, who headed a diocese in Bavaria before being called to Rome by John Paul in 1982, repented for his own failing in leaving his home diocese. "The view of the bishop-diocese relation as matrimony, implying fidelity, is still valid. Sadly I myself have not remained faithful in this regard," he told the Italian magazine *30 Giorni*. "In the church, above all, there should be no sense of careerism. To be a bishop should not be considered a career with a number of steps, moving from one seat to another, but a very humble service."

Of course, such critiques might carry more weight if they did not come from two men who facilitated the problem for years by moving favored bishops to increasingly prestigious dioceses.

A correlative to the careerism of the John Paul era was an even more dangerous phenomenon, an obsession with conformity that in turn breeds secrecy. Because the pope places such an emphasis on preaching orthodoxy, bishops who hope to advance up the clerical ladder must look tough in public and in private must quash anything that would hint that their diocese is less than traditional. In April 2002, Cardinal Law admitted that he had fallen into the secrecy trap and conceded that it was a mistake "inspired by a desire to protect the privacy of the victim, to avoid scandal to the faithful, and to preserve the reputation of the priest." He said, "We now realize both within the church and in society at large that secrecy often inhibits healing and places others at risk."

Secrecy has a storied history in the church and won't be easily banished. "Let not the world see us quarreling like children, giving material for angry contention between those who may become our respective supporters or adversaries," the contentious St. Jerome wrote in the fourth century to the equally stubborn St. Augustine. This concern for what the Romans call *la bella figura* became enshrined in canon law and the catechism: "The person who gives scandal becomes his neighbor's tempter." The precept draws on Jesus' warning to anyone who leads innocents into sin: "It would be better for him to have a great millstone around his neck and to be drowned in the depth of the sea." But bishops came to take that as meaning that they should shield the faithful's eyes from any churchly wrongdoing, a dubious virtue that deteriorated into a self-protective vice, especially when it came to molester-priests.

Even as the heightened competition for the appearance of orthodoxy and sanctity divided the bishops, it also drove a wedge among the hierarchy, the clergy, and the laity. "The great ones make their authority felt over them. But it shall not be so among you," Jesus warned the first apostles. Yet the Vatican's insistence that the bishops crack down on perceived moral laxity led the bishops to become regular scolds; as they focused on picayune matters at the expense of pressing issues (such as clergy abuse), they became known for their hectoring as much as for their pastoring.

One priest told the *Boston Herald* of how Cardinal Law called him on the carpet for attending the wedding of a Catholic friend whose previous marriage had not been annulled. The priest did not officiate or offer a blessing to the couple, but only read a poem. Still, Law told the priest that his presence had been a scandal, and he put a letter to that effect in the man's personnel file. "I remember him using that word: *scandal*," the priest said. Father Thad Rudd, the married priest from Georgia, recalled that when his wife was battling cancer, he never heard a word from his bishop. "But if I say something wrong from the altar and someone complains, I'll get a call the next day."

The Vatican instructed the bishops that Catholics were not to even discuss women's ordination, and it made abortion the single-issue litmus-test for the "good" Catholic. While most Catholics are uneasy about abortion, the contemporary political equation in America leaves Catholic voters trapped between an abortion-rights Democratic Party whose so-cial policies are more in line with Catholic teaching and a Republican Party whose pronouncements against abortion and for personal morality are more in keeping with the bishops' language. The bishops rightly crit-icize both parties, but they do not leave lay Catholics much room to live in the world and live up to their pastors' demands.

The consequence has been a tragic repetition of the birth-control de-bacle—a bind that forced Catholics to exit from the teaching and go their own way. That strategy feels like the only option for many Catholics, not only on birth control and abortion rights, but on the other crucial issues that the bishops address, from the death penalty to social justice. Given the hierarchy's history of hard-line sermonizing at the laity while tolerat-ing all manner of misconduct within the clerical world, the bishops are lucky that Catholics cut them as much slack as they did when the scandal broke.

The bishops rightly worried that the scandal could accelerate a "creeping congregationalism" in American Catholicism, but in order to avoid that fate they also have to prove that they are in fact necessary to church life. For centuries bishops placed themselves at the center of reli-gious practice, and now that they are the central villains, they risk being displaced from that position altogether. If Catholics were to decide that the hierarchy doesn't matter, it would be yet more collateral damage from the scandal. A loss of the sense of hierarchy would eliminate a vital link between American Catholics and the wider church, and it would di-minish still more the bishops' indispensible prophetic voice.

The bishops have the duty to speak hard truths to the world, and they have the privileged position to do so, free of electoral cycles or term limits. But to regain their audience the bishops must better negotiate the difficult path between love and belief, between mercy and admonish-ment, and they must prove themselves worthy of the message they preach. The trust of their people is a necessary precondition for episcopal leadership, every bit as much as their sacred ordination.

Thirteen

THE BISHOPS AND THE KEYS TO THE CRISIS

T he story is told of a cabbie and a bishop who are killed in a car crash, and both ascend to heaven. But the bishop gets a cubbyhole apartment while the taxi driver gets a mansion. Naturally, the bishop complains to St. Peter, but the apostle isn't having any of it. "Here in heaven we reward results," he said. "When you were doing your job, teaching and preaching, what were the people doing?" The bishop conceded that, yes, many (perhaps most) of the people were nodding off. "Exactly," Peter said. "But when the cabbie was driving, everyone was awake, paying attention, and praying hard."

The question today is, Can anything shake members of the Catholic hierarchy out of their ingrained ways, or are we seeing in the crisis the destiny of the bishops' collective character?

No one expects the bishops conference to turn into a communion of saints overnight. Catholics have always complained about the worldliness of their bishops, about their temptation to ambition; and even bishops recognize their own failings. When informed that Napoleon vowed to destroy the Roman Catholic Church, Cardinal Ercole Consalvi, papal statesman *nonpareil,* replied: "He will never succeed. We have not managed to do it ourselves!"

Yet bishops are by nature in a tough spot, especially in today's world, where the reservoir of respect for churchmen was running dry well before the scandal. In the Age of Miracles, in the generation of the first apostles, it was far easier to wield authority. Those men could perform wonders, and many of them had supped with the Christ. Today's hierarchy is many generations removed from that time and that culture, and now have the stench of scandal about them, rather than the odor of sanctity.

Moreover, today's bishops are expected to be prayerful pastors and theologians while also running a multi-million-dollar nonprofit corporation—the diocese—that comprises schools, colleges, hospitals, and social services, all financed by donations from a flock that is the stingiest in the country. They have fewer priests, nuns, and brothers at their disposal than ever before, and thus they now must pay lay people living wages and deal with their labor unions. Bishops are the public face of the church who must lobby politicians one day and excoriate them the next, yet they can no longer count on a Catholic voting bloc. They are a hierarchy in a culture that is more anti-institutional than ever, yet more than ever is demanded of them. They have to confirm your kids, smile for the photo afterward, and then keep the Vatican happy by telling remarried people they can't take communion, women they can't be priests, and lay people they can't get too close to the altar. "I can no longer command, I have to persuade," Cardinal Bernardin said upon taking office as archbishop of Chicago.

More than ever, today's bishops have to heed Jesus' advice to be "wise as serpents and innocent as doves."

Still, many bishops do manage to accomplish all of this, or at least make a good effort, without being derelict in their pastoral duties. The current problems are not endemic—not by any means.

The boiler-plate conservative solution to the present situation is as unconvincing as it is predictable. As summed up by the Weigel/Neuhaus camp, it essentially argues that the bishops have to reassert themselves, be more loyal to Rome rather than more independent, and fend off any intrusion by the laity rather than opening up to consultation and dialogue. "One of the reasons the church has gotten itself into this crisis has been a deficient notion of headship in the episcopate," George Weigel says. "Bishops are not ordained to be discussion group moderators. They are ordained to be the head of a local church." Father Richard John Neuhaus's remedy is a riff on the old real-estate line: "Fidelity, fidelity, fidelity"—which basically means cracking down harder on anyone perceived as "liberal."

The controversial Jesuit conservative, Father Joseph Fessio, has his own three-ingredient recipe: appoint only bishops who will make opposition to women's ordination, contraception, and homosexuals their main platform. Everything else will follow, he says. Author H. W. Crocker advocates the "Magnum Force" approach: "Today, the American Church would be well served if the Pope were to dispatch a 'Dirty' Cardinal Harry to ensure that every priest, every bishop, every cardinal, every seminarian and seminarian instructor upheld true Catholic teaching—with power to discharge those who don't."

What remains unclear from the conservative prescription is how a bigger dose of what got the church into the crisis—secrecy, authoritarianism, political footsie with Rome—is going to help.

Other avenues of reform, however, could significantly alter the dynamic of the bishops conference so that the church not only avoids a repeat of 2002, but moves forward with vigor and optimism.

First, bishops should begin to assert themselves collectively, as spokesmen for their American flock. That will likely have to start with bishops asserting themselves individually. "There's a lot in this system that I disagree with right now, but I don't want to end up like Archbishop Hunthausen—humiliated and immobilized for standing up for those justice issues that threaten the structures of ecclesial power," an unnamed bishop told the *National Catholic Reporter* in May 2002. That bishop's fears are understandable, but if you can't stand up now, then when? What greater cost could there be?

In his memorable speech to the bishops in Dallas, Notre Dame's Scott Appleby put the matter succinctly: "The current crisis has removed any doubt that the church in the United States must understand itself as a national body and act accordingly," he said. "This will not diminish but enhance fidelity to the local and universal church. There is no threat of a Gallican model, one that privileges national over Roman, that is, universal jurisdiction. But has it ever been clearer to us that what occurs in the church in Boston, New York, or Los Angeles can have immediate repercussions for the church in Iowa, Ohio, or Washington?

"Please pardon the question," he continued, homing in on the soft spot in the bishops' psyche, "but it is a natural one: Are you not trusted by the Vatican? It seems incredible to the interested outsider that on matters of faith and morals you would veer one millimeter from orthodoxy. . . . To the extent possible, then, I urge you to formulate the policies that make the most sense for this environment, without anticipating how the Vatican might respond. Let Rome be Rome; it will be, in any case."

Lest these sentiments be dismissed as the bias of a "liberal" layman, consider that the formidable English Cardinal Basil Hume advised the American church in 1999 to "stop looking over [their] shoulders at Rome." (Hume had been invited to address the bishops at their retreat but sent a videotape of his remarks instead, because he knew he was being over-taken by cancer. He died a few days before the bishops heard his frank comments.) After Rome's April 2002 emergency summit on the scandal, Belgian Cardinal Godfried Danneels also marveled that the Americans had run headlong to the Vatican rather than dealing with the problem on their own. "I believe panic played a large role," Danneels said. Elsewhere around the world, bishops conferences act on their own in many spheres, successfully thwarting undue Roman interference. Yes, the American church looms larger in the Vatican's field of vision, and Rome will meticu-lously review anything the Americans do. But the American bishops also have a heft—financial, cultural, and ecclesiastical—that they could begin to wield on behalf of themselves and their flock.

Episcopal collegiality would also be enhanced if the bishops simply got to know each other better. Over the years, conference meetings have become weighed down with bureaucratic dross that drains the bishops' energy and saps their spirit. Much of the committee work is forced on them by the unprecedented flow of directives and paper from Rome. Even with their twice-yearly meetings, the bishops barely get to know one another. The bishops who attend are often known to each other only by reputation—a reputation molded by the media or, more likely, by angry church interest groups, which are almost always conservative groups that have Rome's ear. That results in a conference run by a few powerful insiders and prominent committees.

To address this problem, the U.S. bishops began holding periodic closed-door retreats in 1982, in order to facilitate better communication and promote the "affective bonds" that are so important to their collec-tive identity. But the last one was in Arizona in 1999, and it is unclear when the next such retreat will be. (The main presentation during the Tucson retreat was a talk by Stephen Covey, author of *Seven Habits of Highly Successful Managers*. Apparently not everyone was listening.)

The eroding sense of episcopal fraternity is also undermined by the rapid turnover rate among the bishops; John Paul has been appointing bishops who are older and may spend only a few years in a diocese before retiring. The average age of bishops went from fifty-nine in 1978, the year John Paul was elected, to nearly sixty-seven in 1999. As many as thirty-five active bishops (or more than 10 percent of the membership) were eligible to retire in 2003. In addition, despite the wishes of Cardinals Gantin and Ratzinger to keep bishops *in situ,* the Vatican is increasingly shipping bishops from one end of the country to another, with little or no consultation. That is hard on any bishop who is suddenly transplanted, but it is also hard on the other bishops in the area, who suddenly have a powerful stranger in their midst.

During the year of scandal, some groups proposed convening a plenary council for the United States, a rare, far-reaching convocation with ecclesiastical authority that would bring together all of the American bishops, along with clergy and laity for months of discussions about the future course of American Catholicism. The last plenary council for the United States was in 1884, so a new council would be momentous. But it would also have the potential to be a grand failure. The meeting would raise great expectations of change—expectations that would fade to disappointment if the bishops themselves were not in a better frame of mind, or not of a *single* mind at all. The first proposal for a plenary council, signed in July 2002 by eight bishops, emphasized stricter sexual morality for the laity and clergy in order to overcome the scandals in the church, hardly an inspiring or insightful agenda. "A Plenary Council like the one the eight bishops propose would make the Catholic Church a laughingstock. Again," added Andrew Greeley. "It would indeed be sadly comic if bishops tried to use the sex abuse crisis to muscle laity into giving up birth control." Greeley suggested that the bishops listen, a worthwhile suggestion.

Tomorrow's bishops must also rethink their own personal and pastoral styles in light of the current crisis. "The last shall be first and the first last," Jesus said. The power of that inversion theology has gotten lost somewhere in the superstructure of the church. That was more evident than ever after the trauma of the scandal, as some bishops began hedging on their promises of humility and transparency in dealing with victims.

In Boston, Cardinal Law's interim successor, Bishop Richard Lennon, initially showed the power of what Andrew Greeley has called "authority as charm" when he was thrust into the line of fire just before Christmas 2002. His simple change in tone altered the entire atmosphere overnight. Lennon not only pledged to reach a quick and fair settlement with the victims, but he also signaled an accommodation with the lay group Voice of the Faithful (VOTF) and greeted protesters outside the Cathedral of the Holy Cross after his first Mass. At that service he was more conversational and animated than the formal Law, mugging with kids and hugging parishioners and most of all confessing his own nervousness and his desire that they help him at a difficult time. "What I am for you terrifies me, what I am with you consoles me," Lennon said. He got a standing ovation and raves from a flock hungry for a hopeful sign.

A month later Lennon demonstrated the flipside of that dynamic. In January, after the diocese had offered to pay for therapy for abuse victims, Lennon's lawyers suddenly demanded that the therapists the church had sponsored testify in court on behalf of the archdiocese. Victims felt betrayed, abused all over again. Catholics everywhere felt outraged. "He came in with a great deal of goodwill from all of the parties because of the difficulties he faced," said VOTF president James Post. "Unfortunately he has continued to draw down on that goodwill bank account, and he has put nothing back in." All Lennon's initial good work was for naught.

Likewise, Los Angeles cardinal Roger Mahony, considered the lone liberal among the American cardinals, angered Catholics by backing away from his earlier pledge of candor and arguing in court that the archdiocese could keep its records on abusive priests secret. His claim of First Amendment protection was a tack that other prelates would try with little success, either with judges or with the court of public opinion. "I'm very concerned about what this suggests to other dioceses and the Catholic lay community at large," Frank Keating said of Mahony's legal strategy. "Transparency, the clear light of day, a fresh breeze, open windows—that's the policy of the board and the bishops," he told the *Boston Globe*. "It's just so sad that the front pages are still filled with stories of avoidance and denial and coverup."

Mahony picked a particularly bad time to start playing legal hardball.

He was already under fire for spending $190 million on a new cathedral. (Known as the "Taj Mahony," Our Lady of the Angels was intentionally built a foot longer than St. Patrick's Cathedral in New York City.) Then a week after dedicating the cathedral, on September 2, Mahony announced drastic cutbacks in archdiocesan services because of a $4.3 million short-fall (a gap that soon grew exponentially). The cuts were a surprise even to church insiders, and a month later Mahony's five top executives resigned in unison. Mahony's fall from grace was not cushioned by his earlier hiring of a prominent, pricey public-relations firm best known for representing Enron and Orange County during its 1995 fiscal debacle.

The tough-guy approach was repeated in dioceses across the country, and there was little anyone could do. "The bishops are spending more time with their lawyers than with their consciences," a Massachusetts priest, Father James J. Scahill, said from his Springfield pulpit in February 2003. Parishioners congratulated Scahill for the remarks, but he later said that his comments came at a high emotional cost, as fellow priests often shunned him. "In some real way, we're the last of the landed gentry. They give us beautiful houses to live in, housekeepers to clean. Who else has that?"

The bishop on Long Island, William Murphy, for one. Having arrived at the Diocese of Rockville Centre in 2001 after years as one of Cardinal Law's top aides, Murphy already trailed a good deal of baggage. But he made things worse by proceeding to displace six Dominican sisters from their convent so that he could spend $800,000 transforming their quarters into a 5,000-square-foot palatial apartment for himself and "visiting dignitaries" who would stay in the "cardinal's suite." Murphy's new digs featured a fireplace with a solid oak mantel, a marble bathroom off the bishop's bedroom, and a kitchen with top-of-the-line appliances, including a double Sub-Zero refrigerator and a wine cabinet with dual temperature controls for red and white wines. The dining room ceiling was lowered so that a new chandelier could be installed, and "Mansion Murphy"—*Newsday* columnist Jimmy Breslin's nickname for the bishop—spent $120,000 (of the diocese's money) on three Oriental rugs and a new dining room table.

Reports of Murphy's renovations surfaced in October 2002, in the midst of the national anger over the scandal, and bitterness over this salt-in-the-wound move was not assuaged by Murphy's equally controversial hiring of the prominent Manhattan public-relations firm Howard Rubenstein Associates, which represented troubled celebs such as Leona Helmsley. To make matters worse, just days after the renovation story broke, the diocese's Catholic Charities program announced that it was ending a $1.1 million home-care program for five hundred indigent and mentally ill people. The program's $140,000 deficit, its director noted acidly, was about the same as what Murphy had spent on Oriental rugs and kitchen appliances.

Perhaps leery of the publicity over Murphy's debacle (though insiders say the fury of his priests was the real reason), Philadelphia's outgoing Cardinal Anthony Bevilacqua delayed longstanding plans to take nearly $400,000 in donations and build a 4,800-square-foot retirement home for himself at a time when parish schools were closing. Asked what Jesus would do in such a situation, Bevilacqua said: "He'd think about it."

Breaking out of the monarchical mentality of privilege will not be easy, given that bishops were for centuries treated like royalty, wearing a king's purple and having their rings kissed by genuflecting supplicants. "The episcopate is monarchical. By the Will of Christ, the supreme authority in a diocese does not belong to a college of priests or of bishops, but it resides in the single personality of the chief," says *The Catholic Encyclopedia*. Indeed, during the Middle Ages and the Renaissance, bishops were often aristocrats and princes who wielded great influence in secular affairs, and while few bishops have royal bloodlines any longer, they like the remaining trappings. In the 1950s, after Rome began doing away with the more flamboyant liturgical vestments, a group of Roman cardinals petitioned John XXIII to restore the use of the *cappa magna,* a thirty-foot train of watered silk that was borne behind a cardinal. They insisted that its banishment in 1952 had reduced their dignity. In a typical gesture, John shrugged and agreed: *"Un po' di vanità fa bene alla Chiesa"*—"A bit of vanity is good for the Church."

In general, though, episcopal grandiosity continued to get downgraded, especially under the ascetic Paul VI, who to his credit started with the papal office itself. Paul did away with the coronation with a tiara, and John Paul I and John Paul II followed his example and were "installed" rather than crowned. At the end of the Second Vatican Council,

Paul VI descended the steps of the papal throne in St. Peter's Basilica and laid the tiara on the altar as a sign of humility. Paul also dispensed with the *sedia gestatoria,* the portable throne on which he was carried about by uniformed *sediari* on solemn occasions.

Under John Paul II, who likewise had little truck with needless pomp, the high art of church ceremony made something of a comeback, thanks to bishops who thought that John Paul's exaltation of their sacred role should be manifested in external ways. This suggests that the reflex to grandeur will be hard to repress. When Bishop Victor Alejandro Corral Mantilla of Ecuador stood up at the 2001 Synod of Bishops in Rome and proposed that prelates do away with the titles "Your Eminence" for cardinals and "Your Excellency" for bishops, the synod presider of the day, Cardinal Bernard Agré, who was apparently not paying attention, responded distractedly: "Thank you, Most Excellent Lord." "You're welcome, Eminence," an alert Corral shot back to laughter.

In the anti-monarchical United States, bishops have often preferred to communicate their unquestioned authority by demanding habitual deference rather than displaying sartorial grandeur. When a man becomes a bishop, it is said, he will never worry about having a roof over his head, he will never eat a bad meal, and no one will ever tell him the truth again. It's true, and it is an easy, and dangerous, seduction.

To their credit, many bishops have always lived simply. Bishop Kenneth Untener of Saginaw, Michigan, resides in different parishes throughout the year, so as to get to know their constituents better. The retired bishop of Sacramento, California, Francis Quinn, reportedly lived in a small apartment under the cathedral while he was head of the diocese, and in retirement he traveled in a motor home, ministering to the Pascua Yaqui Indians in Arizona.

There are signs that the scandal is spurring a rethinking by some bishops. The Diocese of Providence put the bishop's $4 million summer home on the block to help pay for a $14.25 million settlement with victims, and Chicago's Francis George explored selling his historic Gold Coast mansion, known as "the house with nineteen chimneys." George first broached the idea in a May 2002 ordination ceremony, wondering aloud, "How can I call on my priests to display humility in their lives if I'm living in a mansion like that?"

· · ·

The bishop's exalted status owes much to the birth of the episcopal office in a royal era. But as with so many church traditions, theology played a role, and that theology has changed and developed over the centuries.

Like priests, bishops trace their spiritual lineage back to the High Priest, Jesus Christ. But unlike priests, bishops are set apart by their special association with the original twelve apostles. Like the apostles, only bishops possess the "fullness" of the ministerial priesthood, while priests are ordained as their "co-workers" in the episcopal order. Priests "share" in the bishops' ministry and are "sons" to the bishops, who are "brothers" to each other and to the pope. (The pontiff always greets his fellow bishops as "venerable brothers" and priests as "beloved sons.") Thus when Catholics speak of "apostolic succession," they are speaking of the ostensibly unbroken line of bishops that started with the first bishop of Rome, Peter, and extends to all subsequent popes and fellow bishops.

But that lineage is not always easy to tease out from the New Testament. The original Greek word for bishop is *episkopos,* which means "overseer." That oversight role seems to have emerged largely after A.D. 65, when the church saw the need for a differentiated authority structure to keep its burgeoning flock on a single path. "Itinerant prophets and apostles had become a source of trouble and needed regulating," Richard McBrien writes in *Catholicism,* his compendium of church history and belief. "Eventually a monoepiscopal structure emerged in which each local church was governed by a bishop, and by the end of the second century a tripartite ministerial structure became the norm: bishop, presbyter, deacon."

(There are currently about 4,400 bishops in the worldwide College of Bishops. That is an increase of almost 20 percent since John Paul took office, and perhaps an indicator that the church is becoming top-heavy as well as heavy-handed. Some 2,600 of them are known as "ordinaries"— that is, they head a diocese. About 1,000 are retired, and the rest serve as auxiliary bishops to an ordinary, or in administrative functions, often at the Vatican or in the Holy See's diplomatic service.)

Exactly what a bishop was to do, however, or how his office fit in the armature of Christian theology, took centuries to figure out. His one unique function was always the power to ordain priests and deacons—a potent combination of administration and sacrament. And a bishop's power to ordain a new member into the college—with papal permission—guaranteed that apostolic succession would be a self-perpetuating institution. Other than that, however, Paul's early advertisement for a bishop in First Timothy didn't go into much detail: "A bishop must be irreproachable, married only once, temperate, self-controlled, decent, hospitable, able to teach, not a drunkard, not aggressive, but gentle, not contentious, not a lover of money."

For centuries a point of contention was the theology of the bishop's office, and whether a bishop's elevation from priest represented another sacrament. The Counter-Reformation Council of Trent largely decided that issue in the affirmative, and the Second Vatican Council in the 1960s definitively ruled on it: "This sacred Synod teaches that by episcopal consecration is conferred the fullness of the sacrament of orders." In other words, a bishop is a special kind of priest, a "mini-pope" who rules in his diocese as the pontiff rules in the universal church. "Whoever is listening to them [the bishops] is listening to Christ," as Vatican II put it. "In the beautiful expression of St. Ignatius of Antioch, the bishop is *typos tou Patros:* he is like the living image of God the Father," echoes the Catholic Catechism (1549).

The great protection afforded by this unique double-dip sacrament became painfully clear during the scandal. Even as scores of priests were forced to resign or were laicized, their bishops remained in office; and even those few bishops who stepped down retained the privileges of their position. In writing their abuse policy, the bishops took pains to clarify that it was the "lower clergy" who were subject to penalties, not the bishops, the "higher clergy." Cardinal Law frequently invoked the unique role of the bishop as he fought off demands for his resignation. "Archbishop is not a corporate executive," Law said at a Mass in February 2002. "He's not a politician. It's a role of pastor. It's a role of teacher. It's a role of a father. When there are problems in the family, you don't walk away."

That argument played well in Rome at the time, where John Paul's loyalists were trying to blunt any discussion that the pontiff, whose ailments grew almost debilitating during the year of crisis, should resign to make way for a younger, more energetic successor. "He thinks of himself as the father of a family. And you don't resign paternity," said George Weigel, the official papal biographer. Defending bishops from popular pressure was seen as tantamount to defending the theological underpinning of the hierarchical structure. "The Vatican was afraid of the domino effect," one high-ranking American churchman told me. In other words, if Law left under popular pressure, then any of them could be forced to go. And the bishops knew that if they stuck it out, the Vatican wouldn't push.

One of the more egregious examples of this intransigence emerged in early 2003, when it was revealed that Dallas bishop Charles Grahmann had cut a secret deal with prominent Catholics in August 1997 to resign his post. In 1997 a jury found the diocese guilty of conspiring to conceal abuses by Father Rudy Kos and leveled a stunning $120 million judgment on Grahmann, who was under attack but defiant to the end, and who showed no signs of leaving office. Shortly thereafter, a group of laymen who met secretly with Grahmann told him that they would publicly denounce him if he did not fulfill four conditions: 1) drop plans for an appeal; 2) fire his defense lawyer; 3) remove a pastor who had publicly blamed the victims; and 4) resign from his post of bishop.

Grahmann agreed to the first three but dug in his heels over quitting. Finally, after tense negotiations, he agreed to resign—but only after a few months, to save face. The Vatican appointed a coadjutor, Joseph Galante, who was expected to take over as bishop when the resignation took effect. But Grahmann reneged on the agreement, the promised few months turning into years.

When reports of the broken deal emerged in 2003, Grahmann defiantly indicated that he would stay on until his mandatory retirement age of seventy-five, in 2006. The tension that had existed from the start between Grahmann and Galante, who had stayed on as coadjutor, continued to grow. Galante was central to the U.S. bishops' efforts to discipline priests and was seen as one of the bishops conference's most credible, and affable, spokesmen. But he had no leverage as long as Grahmann remained the top bishop in Dallas. He found himself unable even to get Grahmann to remove a priest who was guilty of sexual misconduct—a violation of the very policy Galante had helped forge and Grahmann had signed on to.

So powerful is the bishop's role as a member of the College of Bishops that there is almost no way to force any bishop to resign if he does not go voluntarily or if he is not directly implicated in acts of moral turpitude.

In October 2001, Archbishop John Aloysius Ward, the most senior member of the Catholic Church in Wales, finally stepped down after blistering criticism over his mishandling of dozens of clerical abuse cases. Ward was being pushed to leave by all sides, but the seventy-two-year-old churchman was obstinate, resisting even entreaties from the papal nuncio (the Vatican's ambassador to Wales) to step down. Pope John Paul eventually invoked the strongest measure available to him, Canon 401:2. But even that canon says that a bishop can merely be "earnestly requested" to resign. Thus Ward was able to depict his resignation as a retirement for health reasons.

Other bishops outside the United States have resigned voluntarily in response to criticism that they did not do enough to act against abusive priests. Irish Bishop Brendan Comiskey of Fern, for example, considered the most popular bishop in Ireland, resigned in April 2002 after acknowledging that he had failed to do enough to prevent a priest, Sean Fortune, from molesting boys. But the Vatican conspicuously avoided pushing any American bishops to do likewise, fearing that such pressure would only encourage the "creeping democratization" of the American church, and thus encourage others to take the populist route. Cardinal Law's resignation was stunning and unprecedented, but it was also voluntary. No one in the Vatican wanted Law to stay, but neither did they want him to be pushed out. He would have made it to a face-saving retirement had not the final batch of documents left him (and Rome) no choice.

Still, his resignation was a political and pastoral decision, not a disciplinary one. Law resigned; he was not fired or demoted. Furthermore, all he gave up was his job as head of the archdiocese; he remained a cardinal, bishop, and priest in good standing. He was still a voting member of seven out of nine Vatican congregations in Rome (more posts than any other bishop), including the powerful Congregation of Bishops, which names bishops for the world's dioceses. Moreover, the man considered the Richard Nixon of the American Catholic Church, the central figure in the worst crisis of the church in the United States, retained the right to enter a conclave to elect the next pope. (That privilege will continue until he reaches the age of eighty, in 2011.)

Likewise, Austrian cardinal Hans Herman Groer held the same voting power until he turned eighty in 1999, despite his 1995 resignation for sexual misconduct with boys—a resignation that John Paul accepted only with bitterness, saying that Christ had also faced "unjust accusations."

After Groer's resignation the pope rewarded him by making him head of a Benedictine monastery. Three years later further abuse allegations against Groer emerged, and when the bishops of Austria told the pope that they were "morally certain" the charges were true, Groer resigned. He died in March 2003.

Unlike priests, who can be laicized and stripped of the right to wear clerical garb or be addressed as "Father," misbehaving bishops are never subjected to any such "degradation," as it is known. Once a bishop, always a bishop; and that divine status will always represent an insidious threat to the bishop's ego. As Bishop Nestor Ngoy Katahwa of the Congo told his fellow prelates at a 2001 Vatican meeting on the episcopal office in the modern world: "With our title of 'princes of the church,' we are led to cultivating the search for human honors and privileges, while the king, in reference to whom we are princes, finds his glorification on the cross. . . . We are more at ease with the powerful and the rich than with the poor and the oppressed. And the fact that we maintain sole legislative, executive and judicial powers is a temptation for us to act like dictators, more so inasmuch as our mandate has no limitations."

In the wake of the sexual abuse scandal and the crisis it revealed, the debate over the theology of the bishop—his sacred status and its relationship to his role as a pastor—may well be renewed. But that discussion is likely to go on for years among theologians and ideologues, and it is unlikely to gain much traction with even the most liberal of popes. For the foreseeable future, then, bishops are going to be the principle teachers and sanctifiers in the Catholic Church.

With change moving slowly in the arena of episcopal theology, the church should look to reform that focuses on the third duty in the bishop's brief—the power to govern. Therein lies the greatest promise for constructive hierarchical change. Reform in this area would largely avoid neuralgic issues of the sacramental role of the bishop—issues that could have unsettling reverberations all the way to the Apostolic Palace. And the simple act of opening up the mundane workings of the diocese would have enormous, immediate benefits in diminishing cynicism, encouraging participation, inspiring communion, and avoiding scandal—all of which is what secrecy was ostensibly supposed to do.

A program of nuts-and-bolts changes should concentrate on three interrelated areas of governance: transparency in diocesan affairs, oversight of clergy abuse policies, and (most problematic of all) the selection of bishops.

Opening up a diocese's books and day-to-day operations to greater scrutiny and participation by the laity (and clergy, who are also often in the dark) is not a radical innovation. "I have made it a rule, ever since the beginning of my episcopate, to make no decision merely on the strength of my own personal opinion without consulting you [priests and deacons], without the approbation of the people." Those were the words of St. Cyprian, who was bishop of Carthage back in A.D. 248. Today's bishops have many more mundane executive duties than Cyprian. But because modern-day bishops have succumbed to the natural tendency to link everything they do to their sacred episcopal identity, ordinary processes such as the release of annual audits, the assignment of clergy, and, in the wake of the scandal, an honest accounting of the scope and cost of the abuses have become veritable sacraments, accessible only to the ordained. In daily reality, and in theology, such processes could easily be opened to the kind of scrutiny that might have averted the worst abuses of the scandal.

Whether transparency will become the trend of the future is unclear. If the divisions within the bishops conference are any guide, it could go either way. At least temporarily, the shock waves from the scandal seemed to have pushed back the bishops' encroaching obsession with secrecy, and there are hopeful signs that some members of the hierarchy want to be more open on administrative matters.

"The church is supposed to be a family and you can't have a family if only half the people know what you're doing," Washington's Cardinal McCarrick said. "The sunshine should come in." McCarrick said that church leaders "will have to be . . . more open in our financial dealings, more open in our personnel practices, more open in how we train our seminarians. . . . I think people are going to look [more closely] now, and they have a right to." The general secretary of the bishops conference, Msgr. William Fay, told a meeting of diocesan lawyers that he is "personally convinced that this moment will not pass from view until every stone that is hiding some secret has been overturned to let the daylight shine on that spot. Such a thing is happening now, and the more it is resisted, the longer and more painful it will be. This is not a day to hide from the truth, but to embrace it."

Bishops who took that advice and ceded ground immediately gained in stature, at least with the people in the pews. Baltimore cardinal William H. Keeler, for example, a consummate man of the church, stunned his fellow bishops (and his own archdiocese) in September 2002 by sending a letter to all 180,000 Catholic households in his jurisdiction detailing exactly how many priests had been accused of molesting minors and how much it had cost them. Keeler's tally included forty-one diocesan and forty-two religious order priests or priests from other dioceses, and he said that none was still in ministry. The cardinal also said that twenty-six of the accused had died before their victims came forward. The archdiocese, the letter said, had paid out $4.1 million to eight victims over the previous twenty years, almost all of it covered by insurance. Keeler also posted the list of accused priests on the archdiocese's Web site so that any other potential victims might see their names and come forward. Keeler wrote that clergy abuse of a child was "the spiritual equivalent of murder" and asked "forgiveness for my mistakes."

But Keeler also took heat from many of his fellow bishops, and in a speech several months before Keeler's actions, Dallas bishop Joseph Galante foresaw, with characteristic frankness, the difficulties in store for bishops who would choose to break the mold: "The question of secrecy has killed us, and some still see that as a principle to be upheld."

Galante's superior in Dallas, the intransigent Bishop Grahmann, was one of those. But there were others. On Long Island, Bishop Murphy, who as noted earlier had spent an estimated $800,000 on pricey renovations a few months earlier, in February 2003 released an annual diocesan audit that provided no information on either the renovations or the cost of the clergy abuse scandal. Catholics were once again outraged, especially since the district attorney had three weeks earlier released a scathing grand jury report that accused the diocese of conducting a "sham" sexual abuse policy for decades. "Victims were deceived; priests who were civil attorneys portrayed themselves as interested in the concerns of victims and pretended to be acting for their benefit while they acted only to protect the diocese," the report said. "Abusive priests were transferred from parish to parish and between dioceses. Abusive priests were protected under the guise of confidentiality, their histories mired in secrecy."

The grand jury report also showed that since 1990 the diocese had raised funds from parish collections for a special "uninsured perils fund," which was to cover payments for claims relating to sexual abuse, asbestos exposure, and trampoline accidents. In fact, the fund paid out $1.7 million on abuse claims and nothing for asbestos or trampoline mishaps, and the fund still had $11 million sitting in its accounts even as the diocese was cutting back on social services.

When the district attorney has to tell the Catholic faithful how the bishop is spending their money, something is seriously out of whack.

In Boston, where *glasnost* should have become doctrine, archdiocesan officials announced that they had no plans to make a full financial disclosure. Bishop Lennon also refused to accept $35,000 from Voice of the Faithful for the archdiocese's social services, because VOTF was trying to designate where the money would go and he saw that as infringing on his prerogatives as bishop. Law had said the same thing, but the week he resigned, Boston's Catholic Charities bucked his ban and accepted a $56,000 donation from VOTF. While Lennon saw himself as preserving the historic role of the bishop, his tactic backfired badly. Just before Easter 2003, the board of Boston's Catholic Charities voted almost unanimously to take VOTF's $35,000, even though Lennon had ordered the agency not to accept the money a week earlier. This was revolutionary, but in the same way Jesus was a revolutionary. "As a board we made thoughtful consideration of what the bishop had asked us to do, and compared that to another equally serious obligation we have, which is to meet the needs of poor people," said board chairman Neal F. Finnegan.

Just as tellingly, Lennon acquiesced to the move with barely a murmur.

Boston's dogged secrecy contrasted with the approach of Bishop Daniel P. Reilly in the neighboring Diocese of Worcester. Reilly told local Catholics that he felt it his duty to reassure the faithful about how their money was being spent and informed them that sexual abuse cases had cost the diocese $2.1 million over five decades.

Similar inconsistencies in diocesan policies dogged efforts to implement a comprehensive plan to ensure the bishops' compliance with their new policies on clerical abuse—a field of governance that the bishops would seem to have little justification for shielding from scrutiny.

At their October 2002 Washington meeting, the bishops adopted a policy of episcopal accountability whose only means of enforcement was "fraternal correction," with no mechanisms for reporting misconduct by a bishop (much less any penalties or even suggestions of penalties). San Diego bishop Robert Brom, author of the proposal, sold the reluctant hierarchy on the proposal only by assuring them that the policy would not give the bishops "authority over one another." With that guarantee, the "statement" passed by a vote of 231 to 5. Thus the bishops left the meeting without answering the age-old question of who would guard the guardians. "Swiss Guards aren't going to come and enforce these norms," Father Thomas Reese said, referring to the pontiff's largely ceremonial corps. "It is based on good will."

That became even clearer as the blue-ribbon National Review Board of prominent lay Catholics, appointed by the bishops themselves, started peering over the bishops' shoulders to see how they were doing. When the board visited New York in January 2003, Cardinal Edward Egan refused to meet with them, despite their mandate from Egan's own colleagues. The move was in keeping with Egan's personality. A canon lawyer who spent most of his ecclesiastical career in Rome, Egan never relished pastoral work and was dubbed "Alpine Ed" by Roman seminarians put off by his impersonal, often imperious manner. When Egan went to New York to succeed John O'Connor, he quickly alienated clergy by conducting "Roman dialogues"—meaning he talked and they listened—and constantly referring to wealthy friends, high-priced restaurants, and luxury hotels even as he was closing parishes and cutting the archdiocesan budget.

Egan was in similar form when the national lay board arrived. He refused to celebrate Mass for them, as other bishops had done, and he prohibited the group from attending a dinner for the Knights of Malta, a Catholic fraternal organization that was meeting in New York. He also forced Kathleen L. McChesney, a former high-ranking FBI agent that the board had named to the bishops' new Office for Child and Youth Protection, to postpone a speaking engagement at a Park Avenue parish. (A year earlier, Egan had also barred that parish, St. Ignatius Loyola, from enlarging the sanctuary to allow more room for parishioners to take part in services.) Egan won no friends with his snub of the review board. "We certainly mean no disrespect to him, but we have a job to do and we're going to do it, and we want and expect his full cooperation," Robert S. Bennett, a prominent lawyer and member of the board, told the *New York*

Times. "There's just no reason why he should not be working in a cooperative spirit with the board."

Although other bishops were more welcoming to the board than Egan, each of the nation's 194 dioceses still proceeded at its own pace in setting up local review boards to deal with clergy abuse. All of the dioceses were to create a board eventually, but there was no single template for the panels, and some were clearly constituted to have a lesser role than others. Even the most influential boards were only advisory, a situation that led to conflicts and some resignations when local bishops overruled the boards.

Perhaps the most important proposal to emerge from the year of scandal was the decision by the U.S. bishops conference, after resisting the idea for twenty years, to commission a reputable study of the frequency, causes, and costs of the abuse of minors by Catholic clergy. In March 2003 the national lay review board chose John Jay College of Criminal Justice of the City of New York, a non-Catholic institution that specializes in such studies, to undertake the project. However, the study relied on self-reporting by the bishops (though they were assured that the data would not be broken down by diocese, to spare them individual embarrassment)—potentially a fatal flaw.

Clearly if any headway is to be made in opening up diocesan administration to greater review and accountability, it will take heroic efforts by the laity and the priests, or a smidgen of good will by the individual bishop. The American hierarchy essentially emerged from the year of scandal like Microsoft after its antitrust case—conceding little and still holding an effective monopoly on oversight.

Apart from a mass conversion, the most promising structural means for letting some light into the closed world of the hierarchy is by changing the secretive process for selecting bishops. This reform is not as revolutionary as it sounds—indeed, the current episcopal selection process is a recent invention of policy, not theology—but it is also the most likely to face resistance from the current Vatican administration, which likes to claim that selecting bishops is a divine right of popes.

Certainly, the current system is redolent of ancient ways, a process so Byzantine that it is inscrutable even to church insiders. When a bishop dies or resigns, silence reigns for a few months, perhaps even a year, until one day there is suddenly an announcement from Rome declaring that the Holy Father in his wisdom has decided to appoint Father So-and-So as bishop. In reality, though, the means by which bishops are chosen should be neither mystery nor dogma.

In fact, throughout the first millennium of Christianity, bishops (and the pope himself) were generally elected by local laity and clergy who looked for candidates within their midst. "He who is to preside over all must be elected by all," said Pope Leo the Great (440–461). St. Ambrose was still a catechumen in 374 when he was elected bishop of Milan by popular acclaim. The crowd quickly realized that Ambrose ought to be baptized first and ordained a priest, which duly took place the next day. He was then made a bishop and went on to become one of the Doctors of the Church. Gradually, lay nobles and prominent clerics began reserving the nomination process to themselves, often feuding over whose right took precedence. Over time, a mixed system developed.

By the Council of Trent in the sixteenth century, three primary means existed for choosing bishops: nomination by the king, papal appointment, and election by the cathedral chapter (which was a group of leading priests in a diocese). The Council Fathers at Trent thought that the first two systems were fine but that the chapters could be sullied by politicking. So their principal change in the selection system was to reduce the number of chapters that could nominate bishops. Still, by the time Pope Leo XII died in 1829, 555 of the 646 Latin-rite dioceses under Rome (86 percent) had bishops appointed by the state, and 67 by cathedral chapters. Just 24 dioceses had their bishops appointed directly by the pope.

Only in the twentieth century was that formula reversed. By 1975, of the 2,000 residential sees, the Vatican directly chose bishops for about 1,800, while states appointed fewer than 200 bishops under the provisions of longstanding concordats. Cathedral chapters, principally in ancient European dioceses, retained the right of nomination in fewer than 20 dioceses. Interestingly, the American hierarchy flirted with a form of episcopal election by clergy early in its history. At the 1884 Plenary Council for the United States, the American prelates instituted a system by which some priests in each diocese would have the right to nominate candidates for bishop. In 1916 the Holy See erased that provision.

Under John Paul the papacy asserted even greater control of the process, often through extracanonical means.

The episcopal selection system as it has stood in the United States since 1972 leans heavily on the papal nuncio, always an archbishop. Ideally, when a diocese needs a bishop the nuncio collects names of potential candidates from other bishops in the area, and he can consult, under a pledge of strictest secrecy, with local clergy as well as "laity who are outstanding for their wisdom," as canon law puts it. After he collects a list of names, the nuncio sends out questionnaires to leading priests and bishops in the area inquiring about potential candidates' moral and spiritual qualifications. Candidates must be at least thirty-five years old and have been a priest for at least five years. The papal nuncio then places his top three picks on what is called a *terna*, indicating his own preference. Vatican departments vet the candidates for suitability, and the list then goes to the Congregation for Bishops, which meets every month to vote on each *terna*. The results are then presented to the pope, who can go along with the recommendation, make his own pick, or send the *terna* back with instructions to try again.

That is the ideal. In reality, the process has become impenetrable to all but a few powerful bishops in Rome and America who control the selections. During the decade before he was deposed, Cardinal Law was effectively the American church's kingmaker when it came to bishops. If you crossed Bernard Law, your career was over, and his legacy of appointments to the bishops conference will endure for years. There was little to stop this narrowing from happening. While canon law provides for consultation on candidates, it also stipulates that the papal nuncio will do so "if he judges it expedient." In recent years, it has not been deemed expedient, and this judgment has resulted in a skewed process that has often left even the American bishops themselves in the dark.

As Archbishop Quinn writes, "Even the modicum of consultation . . . has largely disappeared. Sometimes there has been no consultation whatever with the local clergy. Bishops of the region are usually consulted. But it is not uncommon that only selected bishops are consulted, not all the bishops of the province or region. An important factor is that, so far as I can determine, no one, not even the president of the episcopal conference, ever knows what names are on the list that the papal representative finally sends to Rome."

Rome insists that such secrecy is needed to avoid electioneering. But closing the process only produces a different kind of politics—the unedifying jockeying of the medieval court. "It is the ecclesiology of a monarchical, sovereign papacy above and apart from the episcopate," Quinn writes. This has resulted, he notes, in candidates whose foremost loyalty is to Rome and to a few powerful mentors. Advisers to John Paul describe his preferred candidates as men "with guts and pluck" who will toe the line in doctrine. Others see them as narrowly focused bishops whose primary qualifications are promoting orthodoxy and ruling with an iron hand—men like Law and his aides.

Even before John Paul was elected in 1978, the steady "papalizing" of the selection process was drawing complaints and proposals for reform.

In 1969, for instance, a young German theology professor at the University of Tübingen advanced a proposal, along with eleven colleagues, advocating eight-year term limits for bishops. The professor was Joseph Ratzinger, who has since changed his views considerably. Others continued the push, however, and there have been several viable models proposed, none of which, it is important to note, interferes in any way with the ultimate right of the Roman pontiff to have the final say.

In 1973 the Canon Law Society of America proposed a system whereby a ten-member diocesan committee composed of lay people and clergy would develop a list of candidates. Under the proposal, the bishop would also submit a list to the mixed committee, and after he and the group reconciled their lists, the slate would be sent to the head of the bishops conference and a committee of bishops who would have input. Rome would then choose from the final list. That proposal never had a chance, but efforts have continued to find what John Carroll, the first bishop of the United States, called an "ecclesiastical liberty which the temper of the age and of our people requires."

The clergy abuse scandal gave a powerful new impetus to the campaign to open up the process of selecting bishops. For example, a priest in the Diocese of Palm Beach, which in 1998 and 2002 lost two bishops in quick succession to charges of sexually abusing boys, proposed that the names of the three finalists for a bishop's job be posted, like marriage banns. That way any information on the candidate, good or bad, would be sure to get an airing.

Even George Weigel, in his post-scandal treatise, *The Courage to Be Catholic,* laments the secretiveness of the bishop-selecting process and says that it is "a serious mistake" not to involve lay people. "In assessing a priest's fitness for the office of bishop, lay people can see things clergy may miss. In any event, common sense suggests that a more broadly consultative process would produce a more balanced assessment of the needs of a diocese and the qualifications of particular candidates."

Weigel would also like to see younger priests put up for bishop. While the minimum age is thirty-five, in practice no one below fifty is normally considered, despite the fact that John Paul himself was made a bishop at thirty-eight. The goal of promoting younger men, Weigel says, is to bring into the hierarchy priests "formed in the image of John Paul II," presumably to sort out with stricter orthodoxy what their mentor could not. That element seems a bit self-serving. Still, Weigel is dead-on when he warns that "something is seriously broken in the process by which bishops are selected," and he adds, "The process must be fixed, quickly."

It can be, too—and without any great infringement on papal authority or some fantastical return to the popular elections of the fourth century. Merely following canon law as currently written would be a vast improvement, because it would broaden the preselection consultation process. Better still would be modest structural or legislative changes to formalize the consultation process and open it to clergy and lay people. At the very least, the nation's bishops themselves should have some formal say in the nominations to their own conference.

Of course, no proposal is likely to find favor with those who see consultation as the slippery slope toward an episcopal version of *American Idol*. In early 2003 a group of about 140 New York–area priests called Voice of the Ordained and asked that they be able to propose candidates for a successor to Brooklyn's Thomas V. Daily, who was retiring. Daily, who had been one of Law's auxiliaries in Boston (and was one of the more notorious offenders as far as covering up for clerical abusers was concerned), responded by barring Voice of the Ordained from church property.

Collaboratively inclined bishops do not fare much better. In April 2000, the Vatican rejected as "absolutely impossible" a proposal from Austria's hierarchy for a formal consultative process by which triennial assemblies of bishops, clergy, and laity would develop a list of names of potential bishops. Although the pope would retain the final say under the proposal, selecting from the list would be seen as "desirable."

The plan that Rome rejected was developed by Bishop Alois Kothgasser of Innsbruck, described as "a theological moderate with a stellar reputation as a pastor." Two years later, in November 2002, the cathedral chapter of the Salzburg archdiocese voted Kothgasser as their new archbishop. The Vatican quietly assented to their choice.

The momentum toward relaxing Rome's grip on every aspect of its "branch offices" is inexorable. That was true before the scandal, and it is even more so today.

The changes may come piecemeal, but they will start at the level of governance of the diocese, with more lay people (especially women) involved in daily decision-making, and with greater financial openness and accountability. This growing collaboration, one hopes, will be accompanied by a corresponding openness in the pastoral style of bishops. Being a good pastor is not that tough, as Leonard Feeney, of all people, knew well. Feeney was the Boston Jesuit who in the 1940s bitterly attacked the church's growing move toward ecumenism and was excommunicated for preaching that anyone not baptized a Catholic was condemned to perdition. But Feeney was also a popular poet and writer who said, "If you want your people to love you, no matter what your faults, be kind to their children, their brides and their dead."

That wisdom still holds, even in the midst of so much anger and agony, and the bishops might be surprised what a pleasant revolution that simple approach could bring.

Change can come surprisingly quickly in the hierarchy. The John Paul hard-liners, despite their visibility and influence, have never dominated the American church as much as their public record would indicate. Year in and year out, in secret ballots for NCCB offices, bishops of moderate temper and pastoral style—bishops such as Wilton Gregory of Belleville, Illinois, and Bishop William S. Skylstad of Spokane—are elected to conference offices over more polemical candidates favored by Rome. And with so many bishops set to retire, the changeover could come within a few years—the blink of an eye, in church terms.

Of course, nothing can bring change to the Catholic Church faster than the election of a new pope. With John Paul II so visibly infirm during the American crisis, and growing steadily weaker, the expectation of a change at the top of the Catholic pyramid was a major factor fueling the demands for reform during the scandal. Many Catholics were frustrated by the prospect of a clone of John Paul, a pontiff whose governing style, despite his undiminished personal appeal, was losing its charms even before the scandal. Some of them harbored sugar-plum illusions that the Holy Spirit would somehow conjure a liberal pope out of a College of Cardinals that bears John Paul's indelible impress.

That scenario is unlikely. But that does not mean change is not coming. An old Roman saying holds that a pope never succeeds himself, and that was never truer than after a year of crisis. The next papacy will follow a different path, and the change, of course, will not depend on the miraculous election of a dark-horse candidate or a sudden working of the Holy Spirit.

Fourteen

THE NEXT PAPACY AND THE NEW CHURCH

The old pope wasn't even dead yet, and already the leading lights of his own hierarchy were debating what the next papacy would look like.

It was October 2001, and the world's top Catholic churchmen were gathered at a month-long Vatican meeting to discuss the role of the bishop in the modern church. The nearly 250 cardinals, archbishops, and bishops sat behind closed doors in the stadium-seating of a modern Vatican audience chamber, with the frail pontiff front and center. The chamber actually resembled a university lecture hall, but John Paul II was in no condition to give many speeches. He was eighty-one and had just returned from an exhausting trip to Kazakhstan and Armenia. His hands trembled uncontrollably from symptoms of Parkinson's disease, and when he did speak his words were often slurred and indistinct. Many bishops suspected that the Holy Father was nodding off at points. "I don't think he understood a thing I said," one prelate, an English-speaker, told me after the synod.

As often happened, especially in his later years, the pontiff had delegated the operation of this meeting to his aides in the Roman Curia, the *bête noire* of bishops around the globe. The Curia intended that this particular synod (a *synod* being a periodic meeting of bishops that takes place every few years in Rome around a different theme—lay people, priests, religious life, etc.) should be a lesson in how bishops themselves should run their dioceses. The bishops had other ideas, however, and their assertiveness was a fascinating preview of the next conclave, the ultra-secret meeting of cardinals who will elect John Paul's successor upon his death.

Day after day, in session after session, bishops took advantage of their prescribed floor time, carefully doled out in eight-minute shares by the Curia to prevent such freelancing, to go off message. Repeatedly they told the pope and his Roman aides how destructive the Vatican's overweening ways had become to the necessary collegiality of the episcopate, and how a decentralized authority was the single most important issue facing the Roman Catholic Church today.

"The offices of the Holy See should be an expression of collegial unity, and not a universal decision-maker," said Bishop Joachim Phayao Manisap of Thailand.

"Communion involves mutual recognition and respect, confidence and trust, openness and reciprocal communication," said Archbishop Vernon Weisberger of Winnipeg, president of the Canadian Bishops Conference. "Today the Catholics of Canada think that official Catholic teaching comes from a centralized level of the church, and our responsibility as bishops is simply to apply it."

"The synod must heed the pope's call to rethink the Petrine ministry, so that the co-responsibility of bishops in governing the universal church increasingly becomes a deep sign of communion," said Colombian Bishop Rubén Salazar Gómez.

The bishops took the Vatican to task for everything from Rome's chokehold on the appointment of bishops to its meddling in liturgy. "Translations from a dead language"—namely, Latin—"belonging to a foreign dead culture"—that is, Rome—"though seen as a vehicle of orthodoxy, fail to respond satisfactorily to the character and style of living Indian and tribal languages," said Archbishop Henry D'Souza of Calcutta.

In another impassioned speech, the president of the bishops conference of Brazil, the world's largest Catholic country, with 137 million baptized faithful, called the Vatican's secretive process of appointing bishops "a source of constant suffering" and political maneuvering. "It is a dark process, full of surprises and disappointments, in which those who are most interested are those who influence the process the least," Bishop Jayme Henrique Chemello said. Chemello argued, as many others did, that embracing anew the ancient Catholic principle of "subsidiarity," by which decisions are left to a lower level if at all possible, "should produce a healthy and effective decentralization."

Eastern-rite Catholic bishops were especially pointed in their remarks. Coming from a tradition that is more closely associated with the autonomous Eastern Orthodox system, they chafed at constant Roman intervention and noted that such a top-down style would hurt, not help, the critical dialogue with Orthodox Christians. "The church of Rome is not a super-church, and the local churches are not vicariates of Rome," said Nerses Bedros XIX Tarmouni, Armenian patriarch of Lebanon. "An excessive centralization by Rome could suffocate the riches of the particular churches." Cardinal Varkey Vithayathil, archbishop of the Syro-Malabars in India, argued that all bishops, as successors to the apostles, share the status and authority that is currently vested only in the pope. And His Beatitude Gregoire III Laham, patriarch of Antioch, said that "with all due respect to the Petrine ministry, the Patriarchal ministry is equal to it. . . . Until this is taken into account in Roman ecclesiology, no progress will be made in ecumenical dialogue."

At least fifty of the bishops, representing every corner of the globe and more than one-fifth of the synod delegates, voiced their frustration at the centralization of authority in the hands of the pope and the Curia. They spoke openly of irritations that American bishops also experience but rarely give public vent to. Given that the churchmen were speaking in front of John Paul, the author of the policy of centralization and the man who held their fate in his hands, their numbers and their frankness were remarkable.

If this is how the bishops talk to Rome when the pope is alive, imagine what they will do when he is gone.

In that sense, the 2001 Synod of Bishops could be seen as a dress rehearsal for the conclave that will elect John Paul's successor. It was also a useful corrective to the prevailing view of the Catholic hierarchy as a slavish bunch of company men following to the letter every memo sent from the Rome headquarters of Vatican, Inc. In reality, the bishops are a diverse group who are already voicing their displeasure with Rome and essentially setting the agenda for the next conclave, and hence the next papacy.

More important, and again contrary to popular belief, the change being debated at the highest levels of the church does not necessarily depend on one camp's candidate winning the coming papal sweepstakes, or on a surprise choice emerging on the balcony of St. Peter's Basilia. Such handicapping is a favorite clerical parlor game, and a lot of fun. But the conclave remains a crapshoot. Some like to dream of a reincarnation of John XXIII, a perceived "liberal" who will miraculously free Catholicism from centuries of unnecessary strictures. (Blessed Pope John might not have welcomed such a mantle.) Others are resigned to more of the same—"the same" meaning John Paul's hard-line orthodoxy. They point to the fact that as of Easter 2003, John Paul had appointed all but five of the 112 cardinal-electors eligible to vote in a conclave in 2003, and he was planning to name more. That is the kind of power longevity confers.

But when the principal issue is collegiality versus centralization, labels of liberal or conservative, progressive or orthodox, become almost moot. All of the cardinals are "conservative" in the sense that none of them is about to upend Catholic tradition wholesale. That is not how things work in the Catholic Church. The omnipotence of a pope, like the supposed uniformity of the hierarchy, is another myth. Popes are forced by tradition to work within tradition. Thus every papal document bristles with reverential citations of a predecessor's writings (even if the new pope manages to reach conclusions with different shadings).

Yet that does not mean that the papacy, or the church, is immutable. That becomes obvious from a glance at papal history over the long term, or even the perspective of recent decades. One way change happens is when a pope simply allows bishops freer rein; he can thus foster reform without ever issuing a bull or an edict. If a bishop or a bishops conference has more freedom in celebrating Mass, or can be more aggressive in ordaining married priests, for example, the church changes, and then a backdated papal approval confirms the preexisting reality. Ironically, the inherent conservatism of the church works to preserve change when it occurs. Because the Vatican wants to project an image of rock-solid stability, and because the church is *semper reformanda,* yesterday's innovation quickly becomes today's tradition. Turning back the clock is almost impossible. In this process of constant change, dioceses are the laboratories of ecclesiology. But the latitude granted for experimentation waxes and wanes.

In any organization, the debate over centralization and decentralization is a pendulum that swings with almost metronomic predictability.

That is also true in the church. Yet this dynamic plays out differently in the Catholic Church. Catholicism is about holding the center. It is not an ebb and flow of winners and losers; it is not a succession of new administrations instituting one new platform after another. It is a polity of both/and, not either/or. "We need a strong pope as well as a strong episcopal college," Belgium's Cardinal Godfried Danneels told the 2001 synod even as he argued for greater autonomy. Change in the church usually comes through a change in style, a shift in balance and emphasis—in how the church conveys the same old things to a new generation.

Large-scale changes in Catholicism grow out of such minor adjustments. This has happened at various times in church history, and the last few decades have been such an era, even under John Paul. The Catholic Church holds the same firm beliefs that it did in the 1950s, but the church looks, acts, and sounds much different than it did before.

Take the pope himself. For decades the Roman pontiff was considered a "prisoner of the Vatican," a sullen refugee from a world turned upside down. Pope Gregory XVI (1831–1846), the last monk to be elected pope, banned railways in the Papal States. (Gregory also forbade the use of newfangled gaslights.) And even after 1929, when the Holy See made a grudging peace with the secular world, popes still did not venture far afield. Now consider that in the first twenty-five years of his papacy John Paul II made more than 100 trips abroad to some 130 countries, traveling nearly 750,000 miles (on modern jets, *pace* Pope Gregory), almost a round-trip to the moon and back again. He delivered more than 3,300 speeches and homilies during those trips and spent almost 12 percent of his pontificate outside Rome.

John Paul changed the church in profound ways. The next pope can share John Paul's zeal, his outlook, his beliefs and philosophy. But he may also be more willing to share authority with the wider episcopate and could change Catholicism still further, pushing the church—or allowing it to go—in different directions. He may be a "transitional" pope, an older man who is not quite as energetic as John Paul in traveling or in trying to export his personal brand of administration to every branch office. (John Paul was fifty-eight when elected—young, by papal standards—and in 2003 became the fourth-longest-serving pontiff.)

So how strong is the decentralization movement within the hierarchy? Will it prevail?

Nothing happens overnight in the church. John XXIII spoke of his decision to convene the Second Vatican Council as "a little holy madness," but in truth the idea had been brewing with bishops, theologians, Catholic intellectuals, and even John's predecessor, Pius XII, for decades. In a similar vein, Catholicism's twenty-first-century "revolution from above" has been years in the making. Even centuries.

The history of the Roman Catholic Church is often read as the history of the papacy, and for good reason.

Peter was the first bishop of Rome—the apostle to whom Jesus famously consigned the keys to the kingdom and the power to loose and bind (Matthew 16:18–19)—and subsequent Roman bishops did not hesitate to build on that power. The development was not surprising given the rough-and-tumble context of the early church, as emperors and princelings sought to assert their authority over the church, while heretics and schismatic tried to challenge the faith from within. A strong pope was necessary for a strong church. The great leap forward in papal claims to central authority came in the fifth century. Innocent I (401–417) is often considered the first pope in our modern understanding of the office, because he insisted that "the Roman custom" in liturgy and discipline should be the norm for the entire church. Leo the Great (440–461) built a "power papacy" on Innocent's legacy. Leo explicitly prefaced his writings with the statement that supreme authority had been vested in every bishop of Rome since Peter, and he declared that the pope was the earthly head of the heavenly church. Peter was the "Prince of the Apostles," he said, and he added to his own résumé the title "Primate of all Bishops." In 451 the Council of Chalcedon declared that "Peter has spoken through Leo," and neither Leo nor his successors was about to disagree.

At the same time, on the Eastern front of Christianity, Orthodox Christians were developing a different notion of hierarchical authority in which the patriarch of Constantinople was seen as the *primus inter pares,* the "first among equals," who governed with the patriarchs of the other autocephalous (or self-governing) national churches. (In the Anglican Communion the archbishop of Canterbury holds much the same power.) In Catholicism, on the other hand, the emphasis was placed on the *primus* of the bishop of Rome, and absolute papal primacy became the defining, distinctive characteristic of Catholic Christianity.

Naturally, the development of the papal claims took centuries, and it was highlighted by a number of dramatic controversies that fill entire volumes. Early in the church all bishops in the West were referred to by the title of "pope," from the Greek for "father," and it was only Gregory VII in 1075 who formally prohibited the title to anyone but the bishop of Rome. In his famous list, the *Dictatus Papae,* Gregory made a number of other claims: that the pope "may be judged by no one"; that "the Roman pontiff alone can with right be called universal"; that only the pope has the power to depose bishops *and* emperors; and, for good measure, that princes must kiss the feet of the pope and no one else. It was about that same time that the election of a pope was reserved to the College of Cardinals, rather than to the clergy, or even the laity, of Rome, who once nominated their bishop through acclamation.

Scandals and schisms punctuated the aftermath of this era—most notably, the Great Western Schism (1378–1417), in which as many as three popes vied for the Chair of Peter. The dispute was eventually resolved mainly through the force of the Holy Roman Emperor, Sigismund—one of the last times lay Catholics wielded much influence over the papacy—but the Roman power vacuum allowed the notion of "conciliarism" to flourish.

Conciliarism is the proposition that power in the church resides in the entire body of the faithful, and that the College of Bishops, advised by religious and lay people, can act with the same authority as the Roman pontiff. Once the Great Western Schism was over, however, and the popes were back in Rome in a settled succession, conciliarism's days were numbered. In 1460 Pius II condemned the "deadly poison" of conciliarism, and subsequent popes affirmed that judgment. The Reformation (caused in large part by the corruption of the popes) produced a counterreaction that further elevated the pope's status as the judicial, executive, and legislative branch all rolled into one. While the popes of the Counter-Reformation Council of Trent did not push the primacy issue for fear of alienating bishops, the emergent Protestant church engaged in its own bit of papal elevation by declaring, as Luther did in "An Institution of the Devil," that the pontiff was "the antichrist." That was more power than even Catholics had allowed the Holy Father.

In Catholicism, the process of consolidating authority continued as the papacy came to see the world, not without reason, as an increasingly hostile environment whose claims were in direct conflict with the interests of the Roman Catholic Church, or at least its head. After Napoleon's repeated humiliations, the popular revolutions of the nineteenth century, and the nationalist movements that left the pope stranded in his medieval fortress, the First Vatican Council of 1870 decided it had had enough: it declared the absolute primacy of the pope a sacred dogma.

As important as the papacy became over the centuries in theory, however, it is vital to recall that the pope was not the principal identifying characteristic of Catholicism until well into modern times.

"At the beginning of the last millennium—indeed, as late as Luther's posting of the Ninety-Five Theses—relatively few Christians knew that the papacy existed, and surely only a minuscule percentage believed it had anything to do with the way they lived their lives," the Jesuit historian John O'Malley wrote in a 2000 article. "If the papacy figured at all in the way they conceived of themselves, it figured peripherally. Even for bishops and princes it was at best a remote institution, a possible court of appeal if things got rough at home. At worst it was a political rival and an expropriator of financial resources."

Medieval catechisms, the principal teaching tool for the faith, did not mention the papacy, and the pope got only a passing nod in Aquinas's magisterial compendium of Catholic thought, *Summa Theologica*. But in O'Malley's apt neologism, the inexorable "papalization" of Catholicism during the second millennium eventually and radically changed that picture.

"To be a Catholic today[,] . . . as most Catholics and surely everybody else would say, is 'to believe in the pope.' Rare are the practicing Catholics anywhere in the world who do not know that John Paul II is the name of the current pontiff. More important, Catholics know that John Paul II 'runs the church.' That means, among other things, that he appoints their bishop. . . . The bishop in turn appoints their pastor," O'Malley says. "Catholics also know they are supposed to 'obey the pope's teaching,' not just on ethereal subjects of yesteryear like repudiating Marxism but on things as absolutely immediate to them as their sexual relations with their spouses. For many Catholics to say that 'the church forbids this or that' is the equivalent of saying that the pope forbids it."

The turning point, church historians would agree, came in 1870, when Garibaldi's troops entered Rome to proclaim it as the capital of the fledgling Italian state. Pope Pius IX, already unpopular with the Italians, locked himself behind the Vatican's ramparts. Other popes had been insulted in worse fashion, but thanks to the recent advent of modern communication tools (such as the telegraph), the world instantly knew of Pius's plight. The Holy Father was under siege, and a devout flock poured out their sympathy and prayers for a man whose name they might not even have known a month earlier.

Of equal significance, the papal imprisonment coincided with the solemn declaration by the First Vatican Council (which was interrupted by Garibaldi's siege and never formally concluded) of the dogma of papal infallibility, a sister dogma to the papal primacy that the Council also definitively established. Infallibility, which is the source of so much misunderstanding, simply avers that the church founded by Jesus Christ is protected from fundamental error by the Holy Spirit. In other words, the church, apart from her leaders, cannot err. This is essentially a "negative charism," as Richard McBrien points out, in that it does not guarantee that a specific teaching is *adequate,* only that it is *not wrong.*

The idea of the infallibility of the church goes back to the earliest years of Christian faith, but its identification with the papal office did not follow the same straight line as the teaching of the primacy of the pope, and the two came together in Catholic doctrine only at the First Vatican Council. Before that point, and ever since, the definition of papal infallibility has been a source of more dissension than consensus within Catholicism. Unlike papal primacy, there is no New Testament citation that can be used to undergird papal infallibility. The concept was a development of tradition and teaching. In fact, the first time the idea of infallibility was invoked through the papacy was during a controversy with the Franciscans in the fourteenth century.

During the Counter-Reformation and during subsequent threats to Rome, the idea gained currency. The declaration of Vatican I was in that sense a historical inevitability. Just as papal primacy developed as a means for the popes to assert their authority in church governance against secular rulers, papal infallibility was a means to assert the church's jurisdiction in the spiritual realm against an encroaching secularism. But it was one thing to support a pope's right to govern the church and another to declare a pope's seemingly unchallenged right to dictate beliefs. Even many of the Council Fathers at Vatican I were uneasy with it.

The Council vote in favor of papal infallibility was 533 to 2, but fifty-seven bishops left Rome the day before so that they would not have to vote against the motion. The infallibility definition was avidly opposed by such leading figures as Cardinal Newman, who considered the vote tantamount to turning "a theological opinion into a dogma." It was appalling to the devout English Catholic Lord Acton, whose famous dictum was made in reference to the papacy: "Power tends to corrupt and absolute power corrupts absolutely. There is no worse heresy than that the office sanctifies the holder of it." The Council did hem in the dogma with strict conditions: the pontiff must be speaking on a matter of faith or morals, not governance or discipline; he must be speaking formally as the earthly head of the church; and the dogma must be well established as infallible. "Infallibility, therefore, is not a personal prerogative of the pope," McBrien writes.

But subtlety was of little account in the tumult of 1870. Pius was infallible, he was the earthly head of the Catholic Church, he was under attack, and that is all Catholics (and anti-Catholics, who found endless fodder in Pius's pronouncements) cared about. "The cult of a papal personality began to take shape for the first time," O'Malley says. The mediamanic twentieth century intensified the focus on the pope, and the election of the mediagenic John Paul II, with his unprecedented travels, his charismatic personality, and his near-martyrdom in St. Peter's Square, sealed the alliance between papal theology and papal celebrity. Despite the efforts of the Second Vatican Council to balance out the triumphalism of Vatican I with a more collegial view of the hierarchy, John Paul's visibility accomplished what the affirmations of Pius IX could not: the church and the pope reigned in coequal majesty in the Catholic psyche.

For all of John Paul's unparalleled accomplishments, however, his popularity came with a hidden cost to the church: "This mystique, which has come to surround and engulf the Pope especially since the nineteenth century, creates a deep psychological barrier to speaking in critical terms about policies, declarations, or actions of the Pope," says retired San Francisco archbishop John R. Quinn, who has written movingly on the need to rethink the church's present balance of power. Bishops, in particular, he says, are reluctant "to say anything negative for fear of offending against the reverence due to the papal office."

For the Roman Curia, on the other hand, John Paul's popularity was a godsend. The Curia could now wield power that stemmed both from John Paul's celebrity and from the centuries of accumulated papal authority that his fame stood upon. Under John Paul, the Vatican brought new force to Augustine's proverb, *"Roma locuta est; causa finita est."* Translation: "Rome has spoken; the debate is over."

At points Rome's interfering ways would have been comical had they not been so harmful.

For instance, when the bishops of England and Wales reworked the language of their standard marriage ceremony, they sent the document to Rome for approval. It finally came back—four years later and marked up with four hundred objections. And Archbishop Quinn tells the story of how the Jesuit School of Theology in his own archdiocese wanted to award him an honorary degree, but could not do so until a troika of Vatican departments had certified Quinn's "suitability" for the award. "What does it mean that a Catholic bishop cannot even receive an honorary degree without assurance from three Vatican offices that he is a man of sound faith?" Quinn said.

Theologians came in for especially harsh scrutiny from the Congregation for the Doctrine of the Faith, the successor to the Holy office of the Inquisition, even if a theologian had been writing for years with his bishop's knowledge and consent—or had been dead for a decade, like the late Indian Jesuit Anthony de Mello. If offending writers were still living, the congregation's heresy detectives used secret proceedings to force them to rewrite their works or suppress them. "The inquisitional methods of the Congregation for the Doctrine of the Faith are out of date and do not respect human rights. They should be dismantled without delay," an editorial in the Jesuit weekly *America* declared after the distinguished theologian Jacques Dupuis was cleared of the suspicion of heresy in 2001 following a two-year trial.

The congregation in 1998 even began training its doctrinal crosshairs on popular books, perusing them for theological error more than thirty years after the notorious (and hapless) Index of Forbidden Books had been abolished. It wasn't an easy job. "When we dealt with a theologian who wrote books that were read by a few experts, it was much simpler to handle," a curial official told Catholic News Service. "The problem now is that we're dealing with the mass market—'do-it-yourself' spirituality, for example—and it's much harder to control."

In the late 1990s the Vatican also started releasing highly controversial documents, such as an equivocal statement on the church's role in the Holocaust and a paper declaring other Christian churches "gravely deficient" in their faith, without so much as a heads up to the diocesan bishops who were expert in these issues and who had to deal with the fallout. "We all suffer . . . from a distant bureaucracy that is increasingly deaf," said Cardinal Aloisio Lorscheider of Brazil. The Roman Curia buried bishops under an avalanche of directives unprecedented in papal history. "We must ask: Does paper bear fruit?" said Cardinal Joachim Meisner of Germany. Yet John Paul told all the prelates that they had to implement the documents for the sake of church unity.

In 1996 the progressive Brazilian Cardinal Paulo Evaristo Arns, whose authority had been undercut a few years earlier when the Vatican carved up his diocese, related a conversation he had with John Paul in which he told the pope that the Curia was running the church and that perhaps John Paul gave them "too free a rein." John Paul was unapologetic. "You are mistaken," the pope told the cardinal. "The Curia is the pope."

At times the pope openly took the bishops to task. In 1999, in an unusual public display of pique, John Paul told the bishops of Germany to comply with his order to stop providing counseling for women considering an abortion. Abortion in Germany is sharply restricted, but women can have a first-trimester abortion if they produce a certificate showing that they received counseling first. The Catholic Church operates many of the counseling centers, and the bishops say that five thousand of the twenty thousand women they advised opted not to have abortions. But because the rest used the certificate to legally procure an abortion, Rome was adamant that the church dissociate itself. After a protracted tug-of-war between the Germans and Rome, the pope finally had had enough. "I hope that this significant activity of the church in your country will soon be put back in order definitively according to my directive," he told them. Some bishops still refused the Vatican's wishes, and by 2001 talk of schism was in the air.

In February 2001, at a grand ceremony in St. Peter's Square marking the elevation of forty-four new cardinals, the largest batch ever, John Paul handed the four new cardinals, from Germany (as well as five other German cardinals in attendance) a letter that lamented the "weakness" in the German church. Among other things, the pope said that the bishops' stands on communion for remarried Catholics, on ecumenism, and on collaboration between priests and laity were too lax. The Germans were the only cardinals to receive such a letter, and it was a remarkable jab at a time of celebration for a church that is among the most influential in Catholicism.

Despite John Paul's Teflon popularity, the cumulative effect of the Vatican's imperious ways started to draw complaints from bishops and cardinals from across the hierarchical spectrum, and the tensions began erupting into public view.

"It hasn't quite come to blows, but views are put across very, very strongly," Scottish Archbishop Keith O'Brien told reporters after an especially frustrating session with curial officials during the Synod on Europe in 1999. The 1999 synod, like the 2001 meeting on bishops, was upsetting for visiting prelates who wanted to come to grips with urgent problems such as relaxing rules on celibacy or offering general absolution. "We are vicars of Christ in our own diocese. That's the teaching of the Second Vatican Council. But some of the bishops in Rome don't think that way."

O'Brien's lengthy interview was stunningly frank in its assessment of the anger with Rome, but he was no maverick. "Just asserting the authority of the church ever more strongly is not the answer," Father Timothy Radcliffe, representing the Dominican order, told the synod. "People will either resist or take no notice." Cardinal Carlo Maria Martini, since retired as archbishop of Milan, proposed a new council-like structure that would meet so that bishops could "discuss with freedom" issues of concern to the church. But curial officials carefully screened all proposals, and nothing remotely controversial made it into the final synod document.

Regular synods of bishops were established by the Second Vatican Council as a way to increase collegiality among the world's bishops and reduce the power of the Curia. But it hasn't turned out that way, and the month-long meetings, held every two or three years, are so scripted by curial officials that when jet-lagged bishops arrive in town they barely get their wits about them before the sessions are over. Bishops are not allowed to respond directly to each other's talks, and the "speeches" are not organized by topic. So the eight-minute talks never have any relation to the preceding or succeeding speeches, resulting in a mind-numbing jumble of subjects. The Vatican carefully edits speeches before releasing them to the media, and bishops are warned not to talk to reporters, though many do. After the bishops leave, the Curia redacts the proposals into a document that the pope issues about a year later. Sometimes the editing of documents starts even before the speeches have all been delivered. A summary report on the speeches at the Synod on Asia in 1998 was completed by the Curia on April 24 although the bishops did not finish their speeches until April 28.

The tensions fed by these repeated clashes were bound to produce something of greater consequence than a few bishops venting at news briefings; and indeed the Catholic Church, led by its most senior members, is currently engaged in the most far-reaching debate over papal primacy in centuries.

Ironically, the man who opened the door to the discussion was none other than John Paul II.

The pontiff's surprising invitation came in a 1995 encyclical on the subject of unity with other Christians. Called *Ut Unum Sint,* the encyclical's title came from Jesus' prayer that all his followers "may be one" in unity (John 17:21). John Paul made the ecumenical quest a hallmark of his papacy, but his insistence on the primacy of Catholicism resulted in a roller-coaster record of great advances in dialogue and bitter disappointments, the latter usually coming on the Protestant and Orthodox side.

The 1995 encyclical was a sharp break with that pattern, and for the first time in centuries a Roman pontiff was actually open to recasting his role, rather than just enlarging his dominion: "I am convinced that I have a particular responsibility . . . above all in acknowledging the ecumenical aspirations of the majority of the Christian Communities and in heeding the request made of me to find a way of exercising the primacy which, while in no way renouncing what is essential to its mission, is nonetheless open to a new situation."

As nuanced as the phrases may sound, this was revolutionary talk. John Paul cited the passage in the Acts of the Apostles that addresses the early church's debate over how to bring Gentiles into the fold of this new

Jewish sect (which was not yet known as Christianity). The apostles told the Gentiles that the goal of unity was so important that they would not require these converts to observe Jewish laws strictly, that they would "lay upon you no greater burden" than necessary. In his encyclical, John Paul pointedly used that same phrase, and vowed "patient and courageous efforts" to achieve that goal. He spoke in unusually personal terms—John Paul II, like his immediate predecessor, John Paul I, the pope who lasted just thirty-three days, often dropped the royal "we" and used the first person—about his "clear sense of my own human frailty."

"This is an immense task, which we cannot refuse and which I cannot carry out by myself. Could not the real but imperfect communion existing between us persuade Church leaders and their theologians to engage with me in a patient and fraternal dialogue on this subject, a dialogue in which, leaving useless controversies behind, we could listen to one another, keeping before us only the will of Christ for his Church . . . ?"

The crucial point about this new opening, however, was *not* the reaction from the wider Christian community, which welcomed the initiative. It was the reaction from within Catholicism—the flurry of speeches, books, debates, and conversations that the encyclical touched off at the highest levels of the church, an indication that Catholics themselves were more keen on reviewing the role of the pope than anyone else.

The first and most prominent pass at the issue came on June 29, 1996—the Feast of Saints Peter and Paul—in a lecture by Archbishop Quinn at the Jesuits' Campion House at Oxford University. Quinn was writing in the context of Christian unity, as John Paul had, but there was no mistaking his underlying message: the Catholic Church needs to examine itself before it can move forward on its own, not to mention ecumenically. Taking the pope's call as his starting point, Quinn laid out the tensions over authority as it was being exercised by Rome. He called for restructuring the Curia, greater collegiality, greater autonomy for bishops, and a better use of councils plus a revamped synod system, and he called for open dialogue on a number of hot-button issues. Quinn was careful not to take a position on any doctrinal matter, and he was diplomatic in asking for a "prudent" reexamination of papal primacy. (Quinn later expanded on his lecture in his 1999 book, *The Reform of the Papacy.*)

Given Quinn's prominence (he was president of the U.S. bishops conference from 1977 through 1980), the mere fact that he spoke openly about these topics caused an uproar. The year after his talk the Vatican rejected Quinn as a representative to the Synod for America, even though his fellow bishops had elected him. But others praised him publicly, and many more privately. The floodgate to debate was open, and it couldn't be shut.

In one of the most eye-opening exchanges, Cardinal Ratzinger crossed swords over the authority issue with his fellow German and theologian, Bishop Walter Kasper, who in a surprise move by the pope (John Paul's penchant for unpredictability feeds the constant sense of hope for change) was named a cardinal in February 2001. Over the course of several years in the late 1990s, Kasper and Ratzinger jousted openly about many of Kasper's positions. As a bishop, Kasper had encouraged divorced and remarried Catholics to return to the sacraments, which drew Ratzinger's fire, and after Kasper was named to head the Vatican's department for Christian unity, he blasted a document put out by Ratzinger claiming that other churches were inherently "defective" because they do not embody the "fullness of truth," like Catholicism. The document "offended" people, Kasper told a German newspaper. "And if my friends are offended, then so am I. It's an unfortunate affirmation—clumsy and ambiguous." Perhaps the easiest way to understand the two men's differences is by their monikers: Ratzinger is known by the loaded German term "the *Panzerkardinal*," while Kasper is named after a cartoon character: "Kasper the Friendly Cardinal."

Kasper's views gained a wider audience when his articles began to be translated into English in U.S. publications. In *America* magazine in April 2001, Kasper responded to what he considered a "highly questionable" critique by Ratzinger that "badly misrepresents and caricatures my position." In defending himself, Kasper declared that "the right balance between the universal church and the particular churches has been destroyed. This is not only my own perception; it is the experience and complaint of many bishops from all over the world." He spoke eloquently and forcefully about the dilemma of the bishop in the contemporary church, pulled between allegiance to Rome and to the faithful of his diocese. He spoke of Rome's "counterproductive" attempts to get bishops to enforce its directives "ruthlessly," and he noted that if a bishop is seen as not acting swiftly or vigorously, "he is quickly judged disobedient."

The bishop, he said, "seems to be caught in an impasse. Yet there is a solution: the bishop must be granted enough vital space to make responsible decisions in the matter of implementing universal laws." Kasper said that "to grant such responsible freedom does not mean opening the door to cheap compromises" and argued that church history itself is full of practical and theologically sound examples of a more effective collegiality and communion. Kasper and Ratzinger spoke of ecclesiastical Platonists versus Aristotelians and of the "ontological primacy" of the universal as opposed to the local churches. But the diplomatic language was gone. The debate was out in the open, and the next conclave was effectively underway.

The debate continued in leading Catholic periodicals, with heavy-hitting theologians such as Cardinal Avery Dulles and the Jesuit canonist Ladislas Orsy weighing in. Retired Austrian Cardinal Franz König, the *eminence grise* of the College of Cardinals (and the "grand elector" behind John Paul's 1978 election), argued strongly for decentralization, saying that "the curial authorities working in conjunction with the pope have appropriated the tasks of the episcopal college. It is they who now carry out almost all of them." Bishops are not "the pope's emissaries," König wrote in *The Tablet*. German Cardinal Karl Lehmann, who was promoted to cardinal in February 2001 along with Kasper, told an Italian daily that the Catholic Church needed a new churchwide council that would foster "greater collegiality." As it stood then, he said, the papacy was the "principal obstacle" to ecumenism. "It is time to think about the manner in which the Church should make future decisions on fundamental pastoral questions."

Clearly sensing the growing frustration, John Paul made another surprise move by convening a special meeting of the College of Cardinals to discuss collegiality and the ways in which the papacy "constitutes a difficulty" for Christians. That meeting took place in May 2001, followed by the Synod of Bishops in October. Still, the open debate showed no signs of slowing, and it was accelerated by the sexual abuse scandal and the harsh light that scandal cast on the way the Vatican and many bishops dealt with the crisis. "Sometimes it is right to be critical of authority and the way it is exercised," Cardinal Cormac Murphy-O'Connor of Westminster, Britain's top Catholic leader, said in an October 2002 lecture. "The Church should not be afraid to acknowledge mistakes in its exercise of authority and to remedy them. An obvious example is the way in which allegations of child abuse have been dealt with in the past."

The ferment also led to a number of proposals for how to go about effecting the desired changes. Liberal groups resurrected their longstanding ideas for reforms, which ranged from electing bishops to doing away with the Curia altogether, to the plan by the U.S.-based Association for the Rights of Catholics in the Church for the pope be elected to a single ten-year term by local councils from each nation.

More realistic proposals came from across the ideological spectrum. Noting that the mechanism for electing popes had changed many times over the centuries, Archbishop Quinn called for exploring ways to restructure the papal election process to include presidents of bishops conferences, with perhaps some clergy and lay consultation. He also called for greater consultation in the selection of bishops, a common thread among all reform proposals, as well as a greater and more authoritative role for the Synod of Bishops.

While Quinn would be considered on the moderate-progressive wing of the church, similar ideas came from more orthodox writers. Russell Shaw, in his 2000 book, *Papal Primacy in the Third Millennium*, defended papal primacy but still called for "prudent modification" in how primacy is exercised." "A fossilized papacy would be a calamity," wrote Shaw, a former spokesman for the National Conference of Catholic Bishops and an insightful, respectful writer on all things Catholic. He suggested that papal travels had unduly overshadowed local bishops, and he called for major changes to the synods. Shaw embraced the idea of the conservative moral theologian Germain Grisez that the synod should be a permanent, representative body that would advise the pope on a range of issues so as to exercise authority collegially.

Many bishops and Catholic intellectuals proposed a new take on the vanquished idea of conciliarism, in which a worldwide ecumenical council would be held at regular intervals, be they ten, twenty-five, or fifty years, rather than whenever the Holy Spirit moved the Roman pontiff. One common denominator was the need to reform the dreaded Roman Curia. That is nothing new. The Curia, like any civil service, is an easy scapegoat, and bishops have been complaining about the Holy See's bureaucracy since it developed in the late Middle Ages. In the twelfth century the abbot of Reichersberg, one of the most distinguished theologians of the day, wrote to the pope asking that the Curia "strive to shake off its Babylonian shame," while a fourteenth-century priest, Pedro de Aliaco, wondered why "Christ is so condemned in the Roman Curia, and gold is preferred?" To be sure, such a haphazard collection of agencies with overlapping jurisdictions modeled on Roman and Byzantine structures is always going to need some work.

But the Curia—or something like it—is indispensable. The Curia was also greatly internationalized in the last half of the twentieth century, to the point that Italians no longer predominate among its nearly 1,800 members. That was supposed to mend the Curia's ways, but it apparently it did not. That's because the problem is not predominantly about the personnel; the Roman Curia has always included men like Cardinal Kasper and some of the finest priests I know (as well as a few of the oddest characters I have ever met). The Vatican, and the church, would sacrifice much if it lost such men at headquarters. Surely, the Roman Curia could use more women, more lay people, more religious in its ranks. But the "problem" of the Curia is a problem of culture and management. The tone is set at the top, and only when that changes can anything else change.

That fact shadows all of the specific proposals currently in play. None will be effective unless there is a change in style and approach at the top. The Catholic Church is generally seen as a multinational corporation, but it is not that well organized, and thus it does not yield easily to programmatic solutions. That's a good thing, actually. The church was and is about communion more than systems or elections; it is relational before it is anything else, and that goes for pope and bishops. To that end, I think that the hierarchy should become *more* political, not *less*. I mean *political* in the sense of debating and hashing out issues, not of seeking electoral solutions to every problem. In a family, dialogue produces better solutions than majority rule. Unfortunately, the Vatican has sought to prevent debate by "doctrinizing" politics—reducing every issue, no matter how peripheral to the deposit of faith, to an issue touching on doctrine. Thus everything is out of bounds and a "creeping infallibilism" ensues. As Cardinal Angelo Sodano said in 1997, while he was secretary of state and the second-in-command at the Holy See: "If you love, you do not criticize."

In fact, Paul lit into Peter when he thought Peter was acting hypocritically. As Paul wrote in his Letter to the Galatians, "When Cephas

[Peter] came to Antioch, I opposed him to his face, because he stood self-condemned." Paul challenged the first pope, and carried the day.

Some concrete reforms are also needed and would surely be effective, and they would require no major changes in church teachings. Devolution from above leads to revolution from below.

Unfortunately, even the smallest suggestion tends to scare off conservatives, who view any programmatic change as akin to a Swiftian "modest proposal." That fear belies a "house of cards" mentality that in turn reveals how tenuous the conservative position is. If Jesus promised that the "gates of Hell will not prevail" against the church, then a few reforms can't hurt. The church is not that fragile. Neither is the papacy. It is important to remember that Catholics (and lots of non-Catholics) love the pope. They want a strong papacy. And not only is a strong papacy integral to the definition of Catholicism, it is also a vital voice in the modern world. The Orthodox or Anglican model has great virtues, but those denominations are also afflicted by national and ideological divisions that too often make it difficult for them to pronounce forthrightly and convincingly on pressing issues of the day. The papacy is a dangerous beast—and that is often its virtue. A pope can challenge and provoke; he can bring down the Iron Curtain and chide wealthy countries into forgiving the debts of developing nations. Those who have grown tired of John Paul II should ask themselves whether they would want to do away with the dream of another John XXIII.

The important thing is that the debate has been joined. The next papacy is in the works. The only question now is what will happen when the scarlet-clad cardinals file solemnly into the Sistine Chapel and lock the door behind them to elect a new pope.

It is a testament to the seductive omnipotence of the papacy that nothing stimulates the imagination as much as a conclave.

When the papacy was mired in one of its periods of corruption and worldliness in the thirteenth century, a reforming camp of monks and hermits started ginning up hopes for a "Papa Angelicus," an unworldly holy man who would become pope and miraculously pull the church from the pit of vice. When the founder of the Hermits of St. Damian was elected as Pope Celestine V in 1295, there was a feeling that the prayer had been answered. But Celestine was an eighty-five-year-old ascetic who had spent most of his life in a cave, and when it became clear that he couldn't manage the job, he was forced to resign and was imprisoned until he died at ninety. In the sixteenth century Nostradamus rekindled the fantasy by predicting (what *didn't* he predict?) the advent of an "Angelic Pastor" who would cleanse the church and pave the way for the Second Coming of Christ. The prophecies of Saint Malachy, attributed to a twelfth-century Irish reformer, foretold much the same thing, with the line of popes to come to an apocalyptic end with the election of a pope named . . . Peter. Turns out Malachy's "prophecies" were actually forgeries written centuries after Malachy lived (and about forty years after Nostradamus's predictions). Besides, according to Malachy's reckoning, Pius XII, the pope during World War II, would have been the *papa angelicus*.

Literary fiction is often a more reliable guide. The late Australian novelist Morris West wrote *The Shoes of the Fisherman* in 1963. In the novel, a Russian priest released from a Siberian prison camp goes to Rome and stuns the world (and himself) by being elected pope and preventing nuclear war. Ten years after Anthony Quinn starred in the film, a little-known Polish cardinal was elected the first non-Italian pope in 450 years and helped end the Cold War. (Morris's *Clowns of God* in 1981 is another entertaining conclave scenario, only somewhat more apocalyptic.)

Andrew Greeley's novel *White Smoke* (1997) also took a turn at the familiar plot, with the cardinals electing a liberal pope who is both a feminist *and* formerly married. Raymond Flynn, a former U.S. ambassador to the Vatican and Boston mayor, launched a career in fiction with *The Accidental Pope* (2000), in which a former priest and Cape Cod fisherman (get it?) named Bill Kelly is elected pontiff. All manner of fun ensues. Perhaps the biggest long shot occurs in the novel *Conclave* (2001), in which author Greg Tobin has a New Jersey cardinal elected. In one of my favorites, *Project Pope,* science fiction writer Clifford Simak envisions an outer space colony called Vatican-17, where a society of robots and humans toils for a thousand years to create a computer pope who will be really infallible.

True, nothing can change the Catholic Church (and often the world) like a new pope. So the dream endures, especially when Catholics are yearning for a reformer pope, as they are today.

But fantasies are not what the Catholic Church needs. For one thing, such great expectations inevitably lead to great disappointment, and they lead into the same "papalization" trap that has been feeding the dysfunction in the church for centuries.

Moreover, with more than a dozen—perhaps twenty—leading contenders among the *"papabile,"* any guesses as to who will be elected are just that—guesses. There are some fascinating choices, to be sure. Nigerian Cardinal Francis Arinze would be the first African pope and would give the papacy a dramatic new face. Cardinal Oscar Andres Rodriguez Maradiaga of Honduras is an engaging man who has said that the election of the first Latin American (not himself, he hastens to add, aware of the strict rules against "campaigning" for pope) would help heal the divide between the industrialized nations and the poverty-stricken developing world just as John Paul helped resolve the East-West conflict. Ukraine's Cardinal Lubomyr Husar is a down-to-earth Eastern European who eschews ecclesiastical finery and could provide an important link to the Orthodox world. He speaks excellent English, and does so in frank terms: "I am very much in favor of local synods and bishops conferences with the power to legislate for the local church. Who can legislate for the whole world? How can you come up with something realistic for everybody? It doesn't work that way," he told the *National Catholic Reporter's* John Allen. An Italian "restoration" after the Polish "experiment" is always a possibility, and given the Italian penchant for compromise, that could signal a greater flexibility in the governance of the worldwide church.

One thing that remains certain, especially in the wake of America's foreign policy under the Bush Administration, is that the next pope will not be an American. (That could prove a problem for Husar, who has dual citizenship, though he resides in his native Ukraine.) A pope who comes from the world's lone superpower and the wealthiest nation on the planet would be a tough sell to the other 900 million Catholics.

The diversity of the College of Cardinals today is also a major factor complicating any prognostications.

When the college was dominated by Italians, as it was for centuries, predictions were easier. The various camps and factions were more defined, and Vaticanologists, who were largely Italian, knew the cardinals and what they were thinking. That has changed dramatically, and quickly. It was only in 1939 that Pius XII ordained a Ugandan priest as the first native African bishop in the modern era. By 2003 there were ten African cardinals, almost one-tenth of the electors in a conclave, any of whom could become pope.

The Italian contingent, on the other hand, comprised more than half of the entire College of Cardinals (57 percent) in the 1939 conclave that elected Pius. In 2003 Italian cardinals accounted for 18 percent of the college, and their numbers were falling. Not counting the Italians, Western Europeans were less than 20 percent, and almost half of the college was from what would be considered developing nations. The Catholic Church is a worldwide movement, and for the first time the College of Cardinals reflects that universality. But such diversity also makes it difficult to tell how the politics will play out, because the cardinals are so dispersed around the globe that they do not know each other as well as they did when the Europeans ran the show. They have not been able to discuss openly who would succeed John Paul, and many of them will enter the Sistine Chapel looking to take the measure of their colleagues. With so many different faces and so many issues to deal with under the pressure of time—the cardinals don't like drawn-out conclaves of more than a few days—they will likely look for the kind of pope who will give the church room to breathe, and time to rest from the intensity of the John Paul papacy.

Any one of the cardinals may be able to accomplish that—an older candidate for a transitional papacy, perhaps, or a Western European who could try to restore the practice of faith in the birthplace of Christendom. A Third World pope would be a tribute to the church's "preferential option for the poor," while a pope from Asia, where Catholicism is a minority and the bishops have the gumption and naïveté to tell the Vatican where to get off, could be a powerful force for ecumenism as well as an attractive witness in Christianity's biggest untapped "market."

One thing that has remained true of the Catholic Church is that Rome must feel confident if the church is to move ahead. A defensive pope means a defensive church, secured behind ramparts and unable to converse with its people and the wider world. For the church to recover that sense of hopefulness, the church must make peace with itself, and that means making peace with the modern world. The British Benedictine and church historian Alberic Stacpoole has called John Paul II "a pope of the modern world, not the first modern pope." And in truth, for

all of John Paul's historic geopolitical accomplishments and his galvanizing charisma, he was often at odds with much of his own church, never
more so than as his papacy wound down. Questions over the voice of the
laity, the role of women, the future of the priesthood, and the authority
of his own bishops remained unresolved, while scandal darkened the sun-
set of his reign and left Catholics looking for a new, brighter era that
would see the church engaging these issues rather than suppressing
them. "A modern papacy needs to serve a modern church in a modern
world," Stacpoole says. "The papacy can be modern when the church is
at peace. Therefore, in any embattled time you are not going to get a
modern papacy."

The universal hope is that the next pope will reenergize the church's
ongoing dialogue with modernity and resist the temptation to wall himself in. The solution can be as simple as trusting his bishops, his priests,
and the laity to help find the way without constant papal direction. At
this point, the conclave could go either way. The next pope might support greater collegiality and decentralization, or he might try to assert his
authority more strongly. But the pendulum is swinging, and one day
soon a new pope will complete the unfinished business of the John Paul
papacy.

American Catholics will share in that task in a special way, because
the challenge of reconciling faith and modernity is also the unfinished
business of the American church. The fate of Roman Catholicism and the
future of the American church have never been so closely yoked. If an era
of greater autonomy is dawning in Catholicism, American Catholics will
be called on to act as steady guides to the uncharted new world. That is a
daunting challenge.

As Saint Teresa of Avila said, Be careful what you pray for.

CONCLUSION

MUTATIS MUTANDIS

An Irish-Catholic friend of mine who takes the idea of ethnic identity very seriously pleased his mother deeply by adopting the Gaelic version of his American name, and then promptly alienated her by converting to Judaism. Years later, in a gesture of reconciliation, my friend agreed to accompany his mother to Mass. Coming out of church afterward, she looked at her son expectantly, wondering if the liturgy might have triggered a latent Catholic reflex. He returned his mother's look by saying: "Okay, Mom. I'll tell you why I became Jewish if you tell me when you became Protestant."

The modern reformation of the Roman Catholic Church has been ongoing since the Second Vatican Council, *mutatis mutandis,* and the process is inexorable. But it has not been smooth. Its progress has been characterized by bitter disputes and false starts, raised expectations and dashed hopes. In the wake of the sexual abuse scandal, however, the church can no longer afford the luxury of endless debate among a divided laity, clergy, and hierarchy. Catholicism is at a crossroads. The church must find a unity of purpose and a common direction to move forward on her pilgrim way. There is no going backward, as a small but vocal minority would like to do. Likewise, there is no great leap forward that leaves centuries of tradition and millions of the faithful behind, as another camp would prefer. But neither is standing pat an option; a church that is paralyzed, frozen by fear, is a church that is slowly but surely dying.

In this process of reform, the first task before Catholics is to figure out what to preserve and what to jettison—what is essential and what is peripheral. This is not a time for ideologically driven fantasies of either the left or the right, visions of a sudden mass conversion to democracy, or bitter, wistful hopes for a super-pope who would enforce virtue and make all right and holy—in Latin, of course. Pursuing such dreams avoids the responsibility for realistic change that would fall within the bounds of Catholic tradition and the realm of the possible.

The second task, then, is how to effect change.

Father Thomas Reese has identified three levels of reform in the Catholic Church: structure, policy, and attitudes. All of them will come into play in shaping the coming Catholic Church. All three are interrelated and, in my ordering, flow from one to another.

Structural change seems to me to be the arena most amenable to the kind of reform that will be effective in addressing the immediate problems of clergy abuse and also visible enough to reassure the faithful that the future will be better than the past. Moreover, focusing on governance distances the reform process from circular arguments over doctrine and theology, the no-man's-land of church ideologues. Reforms of governance would focus on the laity and would help to restore their trust—the critical factor in resolving the crisis—by involving them more closely in the administration of the church.

Lay people were deeply embarrassed by their church during the scandal. They reacted either by growing defensive or, more often, by distancing themselves from Catholicism, if not formally, then enough to save face at cocktail parties. Mass attendance and donation levels are not adequate indicators of the damage wrought by the scandal. The revelations reinforced the tendency among Catholics, already widespread, to think of the church as something separate from themselves, an entity run (and run badly) by a few privileged clerics. Structural reforms that involve the laity concretely will reinforce the truth that they are the church spiritually, just as much as their priest, their bishop, their pope.

Lay-led diocesan review boards, broad-based parish councils, and lay consultation on personnel moves are easy first steps. A return to the trusteeism of the nineteenth century is impracticable and undesirable, but the spirit of that kind of engagement can be channeled into other, better structures.

In this plan of action, little else is as important as strengthening financial oversight mechanisms at both the diocesan and parish levels. While bishops moved relatively quickly to purge wayward priests, they did nothing to compel greater financial transparency. Such openness is a matter of justice: it is the laity's money, after all. And financial transparency is crucial to restoring faith and credibility in the institutional church. It is also critical if the church is to avert the next scandal, which is likely to be a scandal over money. Money in the Catholic Church is fungible in a way that it is in few other institutions, and while the abuse of minors forced sexual misconduct into the open, the misuse of church funds remains largely hidden from view, despite the fact that fiscal shenanigans are far more widespread than pedophilia.

Lay people are on guard now, and they are in no mood for excuses. If there is another scandal—or, just as bad, more institutional inaction to present concerns—the long-predicted exodus may finally happen. The danger to the Catholic Church is that Catholics will leave. The danger to Catholics is that they will have nowhere to go. They will become "unchurched," stranded by disillusionment with few viable alternatives in the American religious marketplace. Scott Appleby coined a new twist on the old "pay, pray, and obey" command, exhorting the American laity to "stay, pray, and inveigh." This should be the laity's motto for the coming decades.

At the level of the hierarchy, structural reform would also mean opening the selection process for bishops to wider consultation, incorporating lay people more prominently in pastoral and administrative matters, and allowing episcopal conferences to enact policies binding on all members. A priest who has resisted overtures to advance up the clerical ladder told me that he wonders why anyone would want to be a bishop today. In fact, it is a perfect time to take on that mantle. The bishop's role makes it easy to do a lot of good, and bishops still have more power than anyone else in the church to make things happen fast.

Effective structural change will mean a period of experimentation, and not all of the efforts will be successful or pretty. So be it. Nothing could be worse than what came to light during the year of scandal. Besides, there are plenty of effective models to choose from, in both dioceses and parishes. At St. Joseph's Church in Greenwich Village, for example the six hundred registered parishioners elect the twelve-member parish council, and the eight volunteer members of the finance council deliberate under the direction of a parish manager who is a retired CEO. The pastor, Father Aldo J. Tos, is happy to follow their advice. St. Joseph's is one of the most vibrant parishes in the city, with effective social-service programs and a thoughtful and challenging public lecture series that draws audiences from around the area.

Halfway across the country, in Eden Prairie, Minnesota, the church of Pax Christi has 12,500 registered members whose lay leadership has flourished in collaboration with their only priest, Father Tim Powers. Lay people preach at about one-quarter of the services each weekend, and when Powers announced in 2001 that he planned to retire in 2004, the church started a process of vetting potential candidates to replace him. Although the final decision remains in the hands of Archbishop Harry Flynn, the church selection committee plans to give Flynn their recommendation and expects that he will give it prominent consideration. Pax Christi is not a lowest-common-denominator democracy. The parish grew uneasy with its early system of "sound-bite elections" and eventually moved to a process of personal and collective discernment to find its eighty lay leaders, who are finally chosen by lot.

Any parish, and any diocese, can allow such innovations tomorrow. There is nothing revolutionary or heretical about any of these examples. Moreover, to focus on governance while leaving dogma and belief to the force of suasion and theological discussion is an inherently American solution to the dilemma of the American Catholic. Americans demand transparency, especially when it comes to their money, yet they remain worshipful of the deposit of faith left to them by the Founding Fathers. Americans debate everything, but bow before the received truths of the American Revolution and the traditions that have flowed from them. American Catholics are pretty much the same when it comes to their church, and there is no reason to fear that accountability and mystery will cancel each other out.

Structural change can also lead to dialogue about the second level of reform, namely, complex questions of *policy*. These are more controversial matters of church discipline and longstanding tradition, such as greater liturgical roles for lay people, especially for women, access to the sacraments for divorced and remarried Catholics, and optional celibacy for the priesthood. The implicit promise of more inclusive structures is that they will promote a constructive dialogue on contentious policy issues like these. The outcome of the specific debates is almost less important than the fact that the debates can take place at all. At this point, the Catholic Church is like a dysfuntional family at the dinner table, where everyone knows that problems exist but no one can say anything about them. Everyone is uncomfortable, and when things are that tense, a little dialogue can go a long way.

In these policy debates the clergy, of all the "estates" of the church, will face the biggest challenges, both internally and externally. In any church crisis, the "refiner's fire" always burns most fiercely on priests, even as it did in the prophet Malachi's day. Priests will face greater scrutiny from lay people and bishops alike, tougher screening, and uncomfortable questions about their sexuality and sexual pathology. All the while, they will continue to face problems of overwork, the demoralizing drop-off in vocations, and the growing likelihood that celibacy will become optional for the future priesthood. The loss of what for many priests was a comfortable cocoon will mean a wrenching journey to a new situation as the clerical culture that was to blame for the scandal is transformed. But the new priesthood must retain the great gifts of the old priesthood during the transition, and this will require—and deserve— the support of the laity.

What is too often overlooked in any discussion of the priestly crisis is the value and virtue displayed daily by the priesthood, and their love of their vocation. In a *Los Angeles Times* survey during 2002, conducted in the midst of the scandal, 70 percent of priests said they were "very satisfied" with their calling and 21 percent said they were "somewhat satisfied," a total of 91 percent. Dean Hoge's study, also released in 2002, found that 97 percent of priests said administering the sacraments and presiding over liturgies was their greatest source of satisfaction, followed closely by helping people in their daily lives. "People invite us into their lives and their hearts and secret struggles and pains and joys. . . . What a trust!" Frank McNulty said in May 2002 at a Mass for the fiftieth anniversary of his ordination. The waves of scandal were breaking as he celebrated Mass, but Frank McNulty had no regrets. "Theologians say part of our identity is being bearers of the mystery. That we help people catch fire . . .

the fire of God's great unconditional love for them. Lots of ways—pulpit, altar, sacraments . . . and by our very life."

Like McNulty, most priests are exemplars of holiness and mediators who bridge the chasm between the pew and the chancery, the modern and the classical worlds. They concretize the transcendent for us every day. A few—a very few—are criminal abusers. Catholics need to fight for the victims but also support priests as the church engages in an unprecedented debate over the priestly role, both sacramentally and within that burgeoning new tribe, the people of God.

The role of the papacy is facing a similar rethinking. If done with confidence and optimism, that reappraisal could serve to enhance rather than diminish the moral authority of the next pope—an authority that exhibits what Paul, in a Letter to the Corinthians, called "power made perfect in weakness." In an essay published a year before the sex scandal broke and the clamor for reform erupted, the church historian Paul J. Griffiths saw the problem of centralization coming: "Papal power lies in the judicious use of weakness. It grows not from the barrel of a gun but from the renunciation of coercion and its replacement with witness. That is how the papacy started: with a Galilean fisherman martyred by the imperial power of Rome. And as the 264th papacy approaches its end, it is to this that the papacy points again."

The pope's authority is not the issue as much as how that authority is exercised. Authority wielded improperly from the top of the ecclesiastical ladder was at the root of the sexual abuse scandal, and it will be at the heart of any resolution of the wider crisis. The pope not only appoints the bishops, he sets the pastoral tone of their ministry. The buck stops at his desk.

The third aspect of reform within the Catholic Church is a *change in attitudes*—the conversion of hearts that is the permanent, overriding mission of the church but is also the hardest reform to quantify or to plan. Yet that aspect of reform is the easiest to achieve. Such is the hunger for hope among Catholics today that the simplest gesture of openness and pastoral empathy will reap untold rewards. It takes only a word, and the word was how the Gospels began. Christianity is communication and communion, and Catholic Christianity today must use those tools to reconnect the estates of the church—lay, clerical, hierarchical—which are drifting perilously apart. Moral exhortation is not enough. Catholics can always *be* better. Now is the time to *do* better. The Holy Spirit animates the church, but the Holy Spirit doesn't move people like the pointer on a Ouija board. Catholics themselves have to act.

The backdrop to the entire crisis in American Catholicism is Catholicism's relationship to America. How future Catholics define themselves in America will go a long way toward answering the urgent question of how, or whether, ancient faith and postmodernism can coexist. In this regard, American Catholics face a dual challenge. They must accommodate to American society while confronting it as members of a universal church, especially on issues of culture, social justice, and international relations. And they must preserve their uniqueness as Catholics in the midst of a religious culture that, though vibrant, is profoundly different from theirs—fragmented, suspicious of authority, and at once leery of sacramentality and infatuated with the occult.

The temptation to homogenization is constant. Everyone in America is Protestant, G. K. Chesterton observed early in the last century; and early in the present century that observation is truer than ever. In her 2001 book, *The Transformation of American Religion,* Amanda Porterfield, a professor of religious studies at the University of Wyoming, argues persuasively that Protestant ideas have triumphed in American life, but at a cost to traditional Protestants themselves, who continue to decline in numbers while other religious traditions—from Buddhism to Judaism to Catholicism—backfill the cultural mold they have vacated.

For Catholics the trick will be conforming to the mold without losing their distinctive beliefs and ethos—without ending up like the "cut-flower civilization" that Elton Trueblood warned against in the previous century. "Beautiful as cut flowers may be, they die because they are severed from their sustaining roots," the Quaker theologian wrote. To move into the future while anchored in the past, the present generation of American Catholics must rediscover a common Catholic culture that can serve as a kind of *viaticum* for the coming journey. God, as is often noted, has no grandchildren. But the all-embracing Catholic life of rituals, of what the sociologist of religion Robert Bellah called "practices of commitment," was remarkably good at preserving what he called "communities of memory." Of late that memory has become clouded. One study found that half of young adult Catholics in their twenties and thirties have never even heard of the Second Vatican Council, the ecclesiastical revolution whose benefits they enjoy without knowing the source. "After this scandal, the American Catholic identity of the future, led by today's young Catholics, will be a deeper admixture of historically Catholic and Protestant understandings of the Church," predicted Tom Beaudoin.

A central Catholic understanding that must not be diluted in this process is the notion that one should embrace the whole as well as the part, an idea that is at odds with much of the Protestant ethos and contemporary American culture. "One of the biggest issues we face is that we have people who have their own particular concerns, whether it's on abortion, birth control, divorce and remarriage, civil rights or social justice," observed Father William P. Leahy, the Jesuit president of Boston College. Leahy spoke in October 2002 as he launched the "Church in the 21st Century Project," a multiyear project aimed at plumbing the crisis in Catholicism without leaving any issue, no matter how controversial, out of the discussions. "But the church has a much broader view," Leahy noted. "The challenge for the church is how do we have unity about basic beliefs and yet respect individual differences. . . . The Spirit hasn't deserted the church today. I think we can work through a lot of these issues."

Leahy's Boston College project is a constructive and encouraging initiative that ought to be replicated, a helpful antidote to the pessimism that can seem pervasive amid the crisis in Catholicism. The bleak outlook is understandable given that any accounting of contemporary Catholicism can read like a litany of frustrations, dysfunctions, besetting sins, and moral shortcomings. In a sense, that is the fate of the church, because she sets an impossible standard that her members, even at the highest levels—or *especially* at the highest levels—can never live up to but must always strive for. The Christian philosopher Romano Guardini (1885–1968) said that the church is the Cross on which Christ was crucified and so "one must live in a state of permanent dissatisfaction with the Church." So it has always been. The Catholic Church was divinely instituted but finds perpetual incarnation through the messiness of humanity and the quest for redemption.

"The joys and hopes, the grief and anguish of the people of our time, especially of those who are poor or afflicted, are the joys and hopes, the grief and anguish of the followers of Christ as well. Nothing that is genuinely human fails to find an echo in their hearts." So read the opening lines of *Gaudium et Spes* ("Joy and Hope"), the Second Vatican Council's landmark Pastoral Constitution on the Church in the Modern World.

Some Council Fathers wanted to flip the phrases so that "grief and anguish" prefaced "joy and hope." That was not the attitude of the Council, however, nor should it be the attitude of Catholics even in these turbulent times. It is a fundamental Christian belief that God can bring forth good from evil as long as there are people of good will to carry out the task. "If, in addition to all the terrible things we have learned, it was revealed tomorrow that the Pope had a harem, that all the cardinals had made money on Enron stock and were involved in Internet porn, then the situation of the Church today would be similar to the situation of the Church in the late twelfth century when Francis of Assisi first kissed a leper," the writer and theologian Msgr. Lorenzo Albacete wrote in the *New Republic*.

Maintaining a proper perspective without diminishing the extent of the crisis is part of the balancing act for today's Catholics. John Cavadini, chairman of the Notre Dame theology department, has noted that scandal is always public, whereas holiness is often hidden in the dailiness of life. That paradox has been true throughout history, and the dangers it poses to our outlook are always the same: "In reacting to a scandal," says Cavadini, "it is wise to remember that our own proclivity to overlook and downplay the goodness which would challenge us is itself a liability. For it is only by looking at that goodness, by acquiring the habit of noticing it, that we will find the inspiration and the courage to re-imagine a future for the church beyond the impasse that seems thrust upon us."

This is not to be a Pollyanna. It is, however, a reminder that Catholics are called on always to be hopeful, even if optimism is a bit too much to ask. "I'll define you a Christian people by the opposite," the Curé de Torcy told Bernanos's country priest. "The opposite of a Christian people is a people grown sad and old."

That should not be the definition of today's Catholic people. Just as the Catholic Church is facing a crisis of historic proportions, the future of the Catholic Church is more open than it has ever been. After two thousand years, the adventure of Catholicism is beginning anew.